THE ga

The Seven Magi

Volume 3

ILLUSTRATED BY

KAZUAKI YANAGISAWA

STORY BY

KAORU KURIMOTO

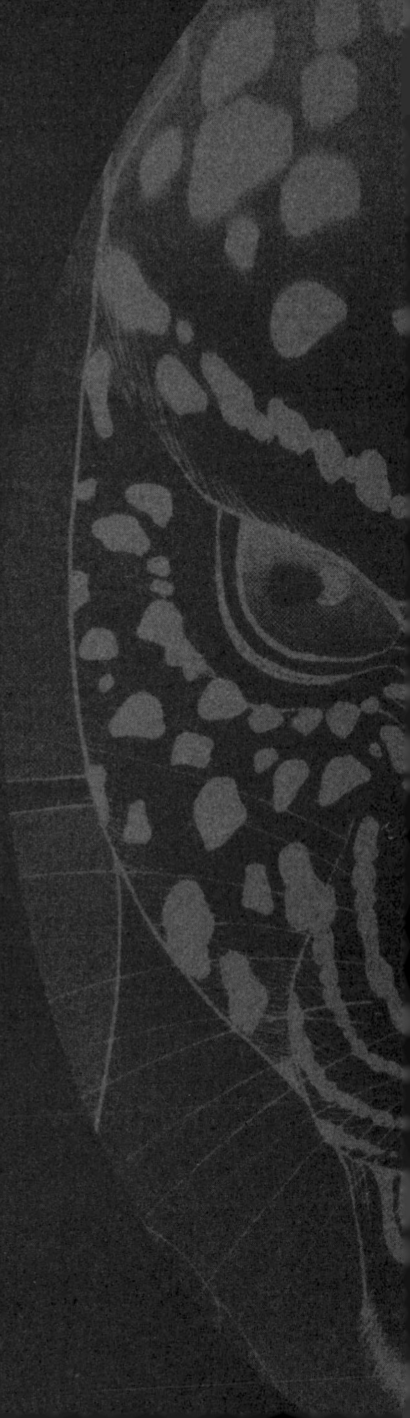

VERTICAL.

Translation—Ishmael Arthur
Production—Glen Isip

Copyright © 2008 by Kazuaki Yanagisawa and Kaoru Kurimoto
First published in Japan in 2003 by MEDIA FACTORY, Inc.
English translation rights reserved by Vertical, Inc.
Under the license from MEDIA FACTORY, Inc.

Published by Vertical, Inc., New York
Translation Copyright © 2008 by Vertical, Inc.

Originally published in Japanese as *Guin Saga: Shichinin no Madoushi*,
with a story adapted from the eponymous novel by Kaoru Kurimoto.

ISBN 978-1-934287-08-8

Manufactured in the United States of America

Vertical, Inc.
1185 Avenue of the Americas, 32nd floor
New York, NY 10036
www.vertical-inc.com

The Seven Magi

Volume 3

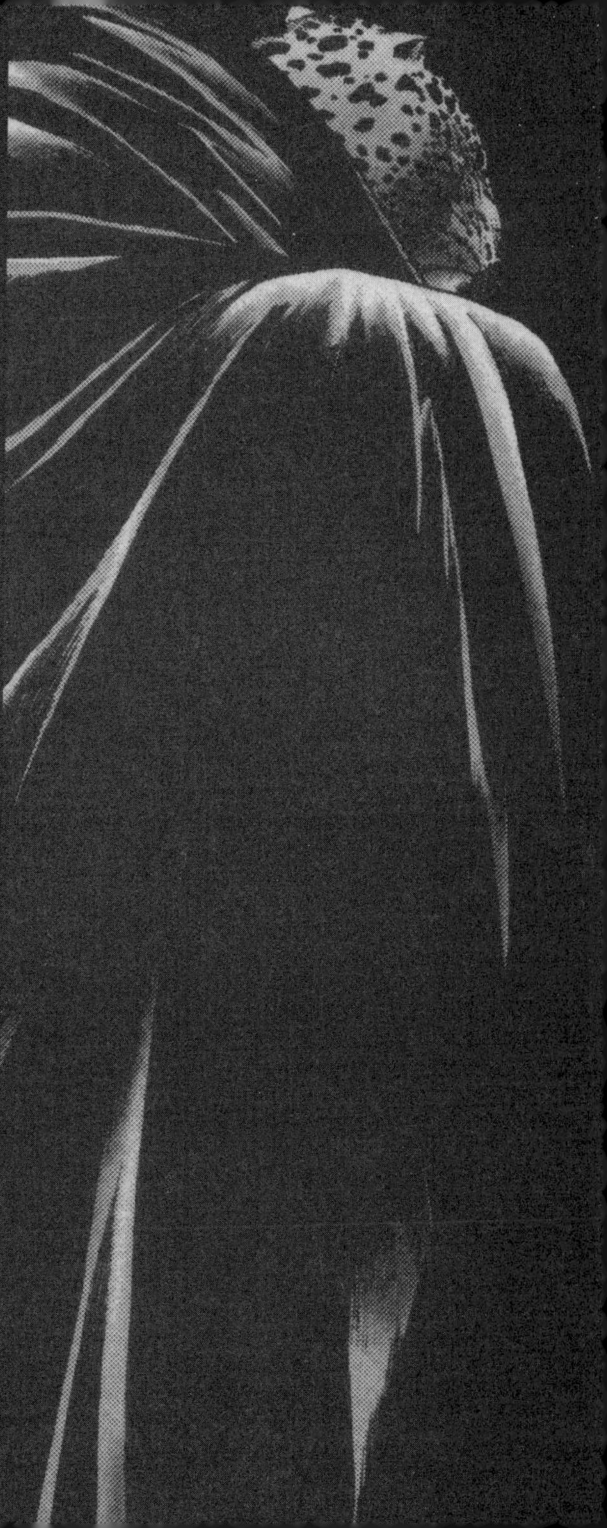

CONTENTS

CHAPTER 15

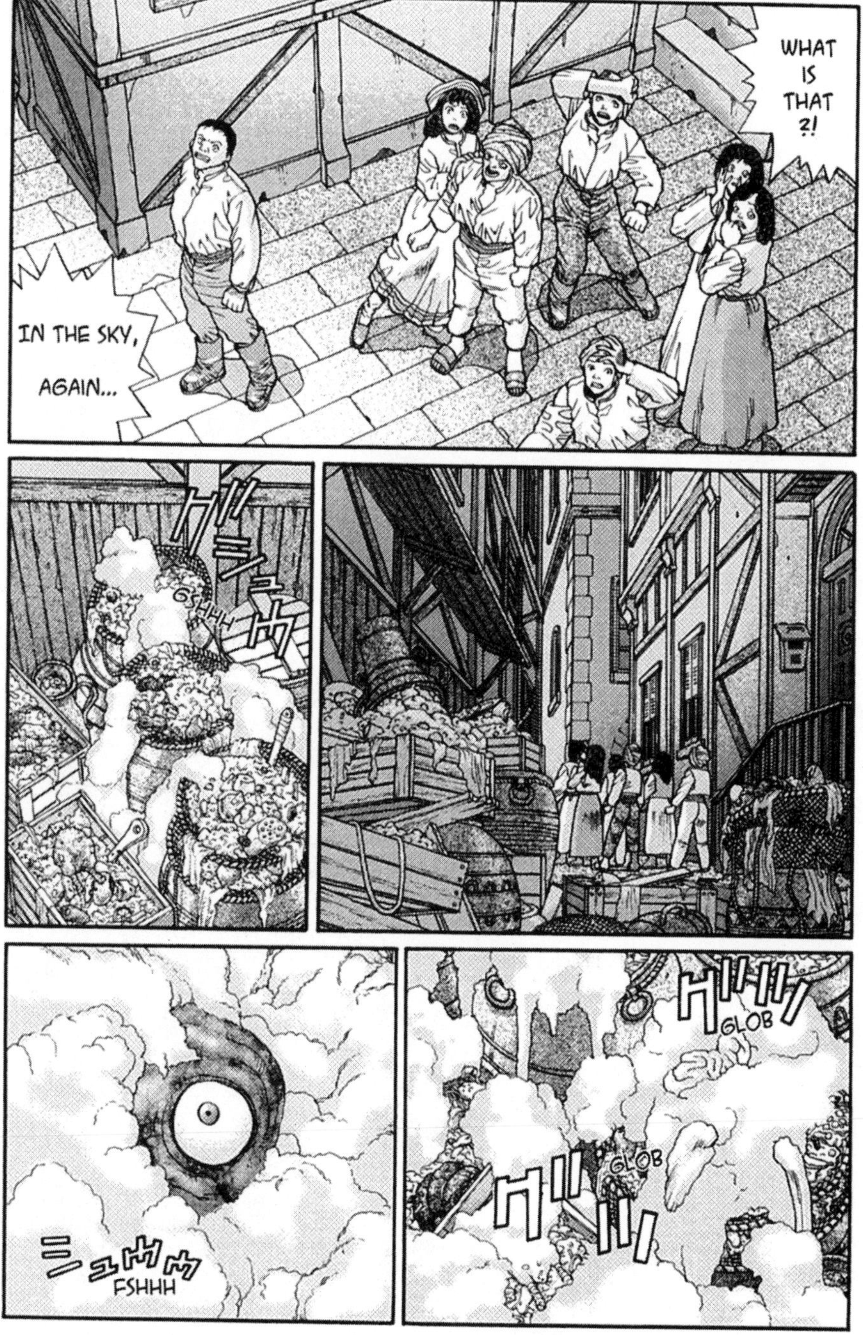
WHAT IS THAT ?!
IN THE SKY, AGAIN...
GSHHH
GLOB
GLOB
FSHHH

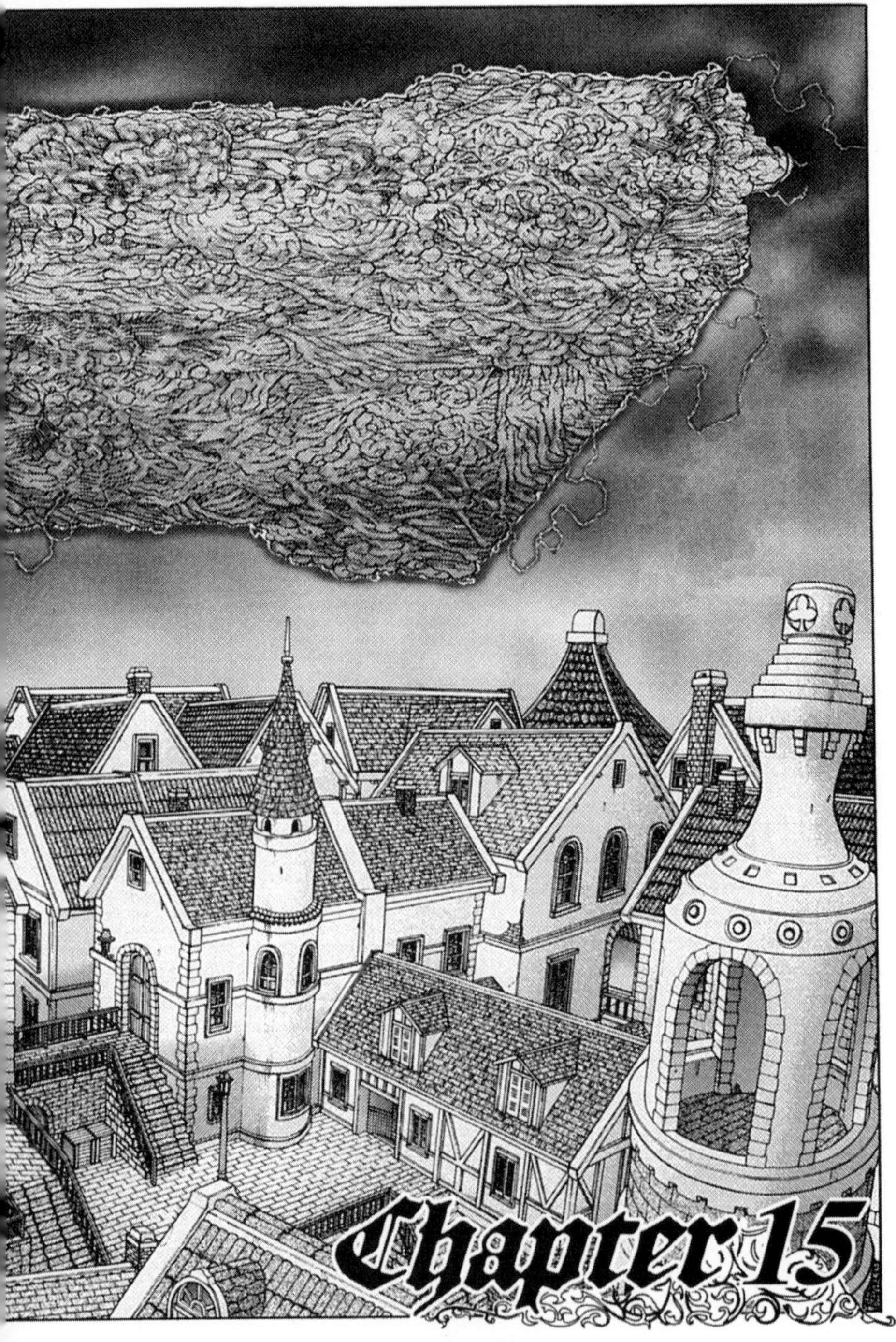
Chapter 15

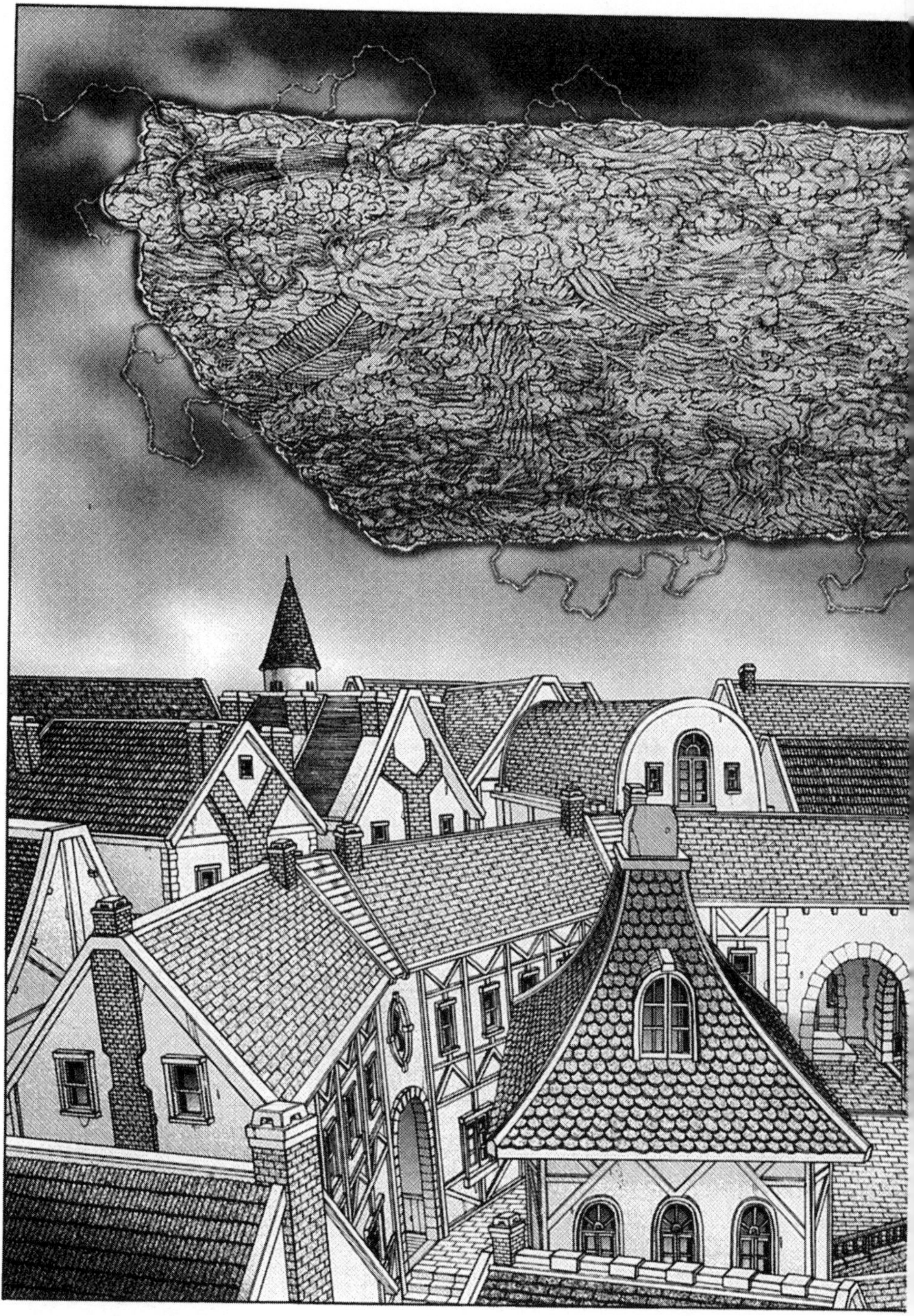

ゴゴゴ
BOOM
ゴゴ
BOOM

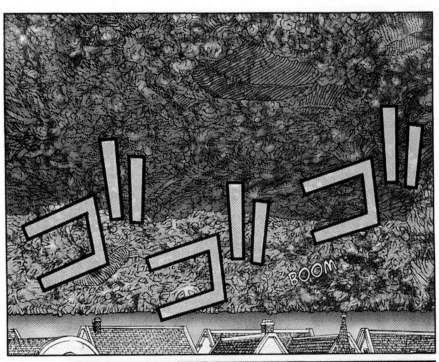

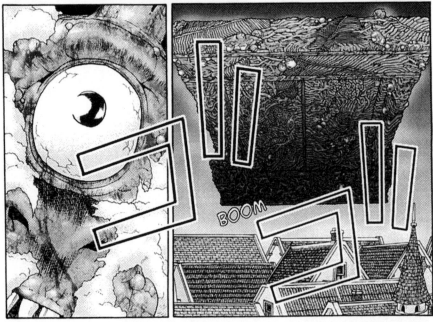

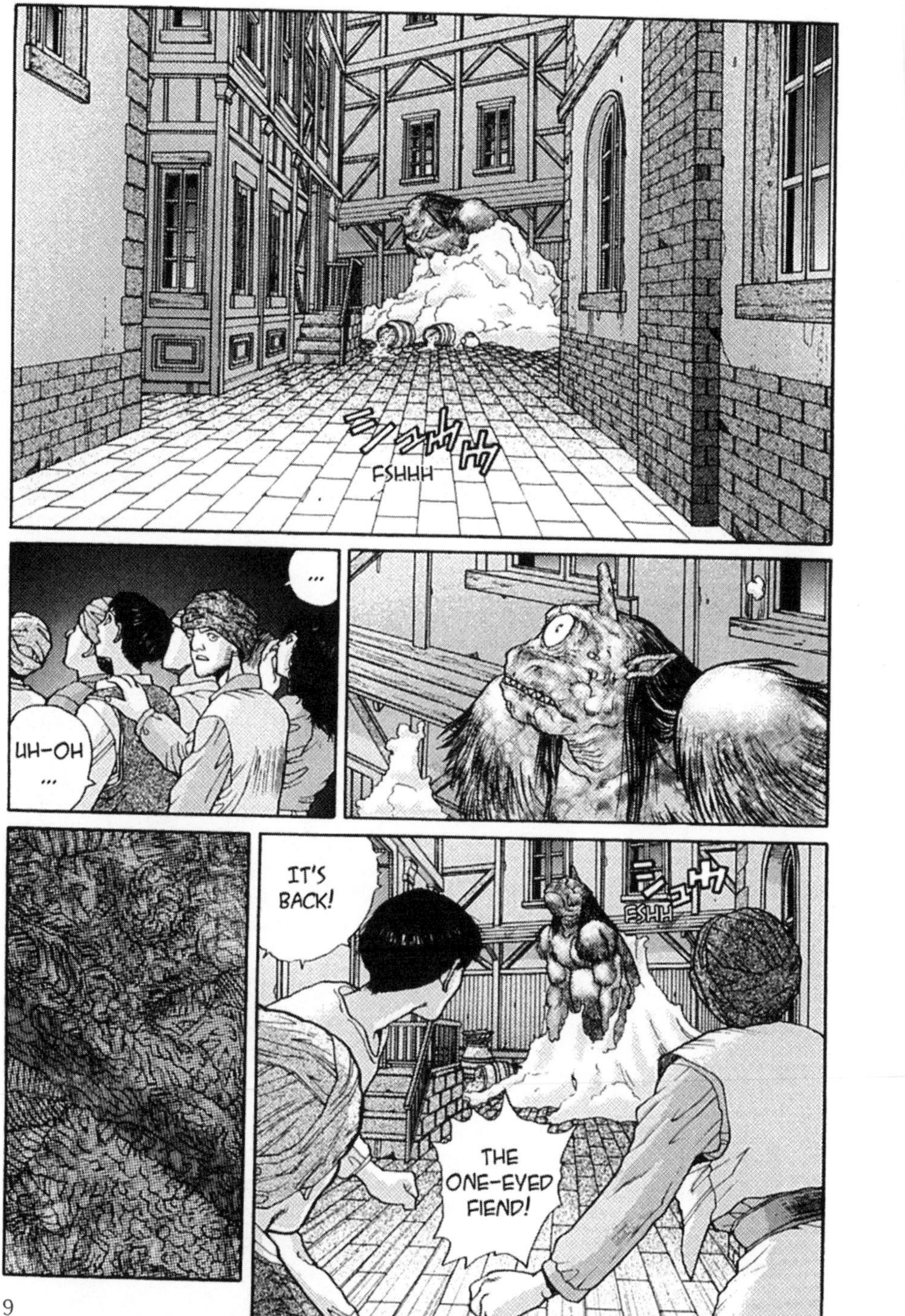
FSHHH
...
UH-OH ...
IT'S BACK!
FSHH
THE ONE-EYED FIEND!

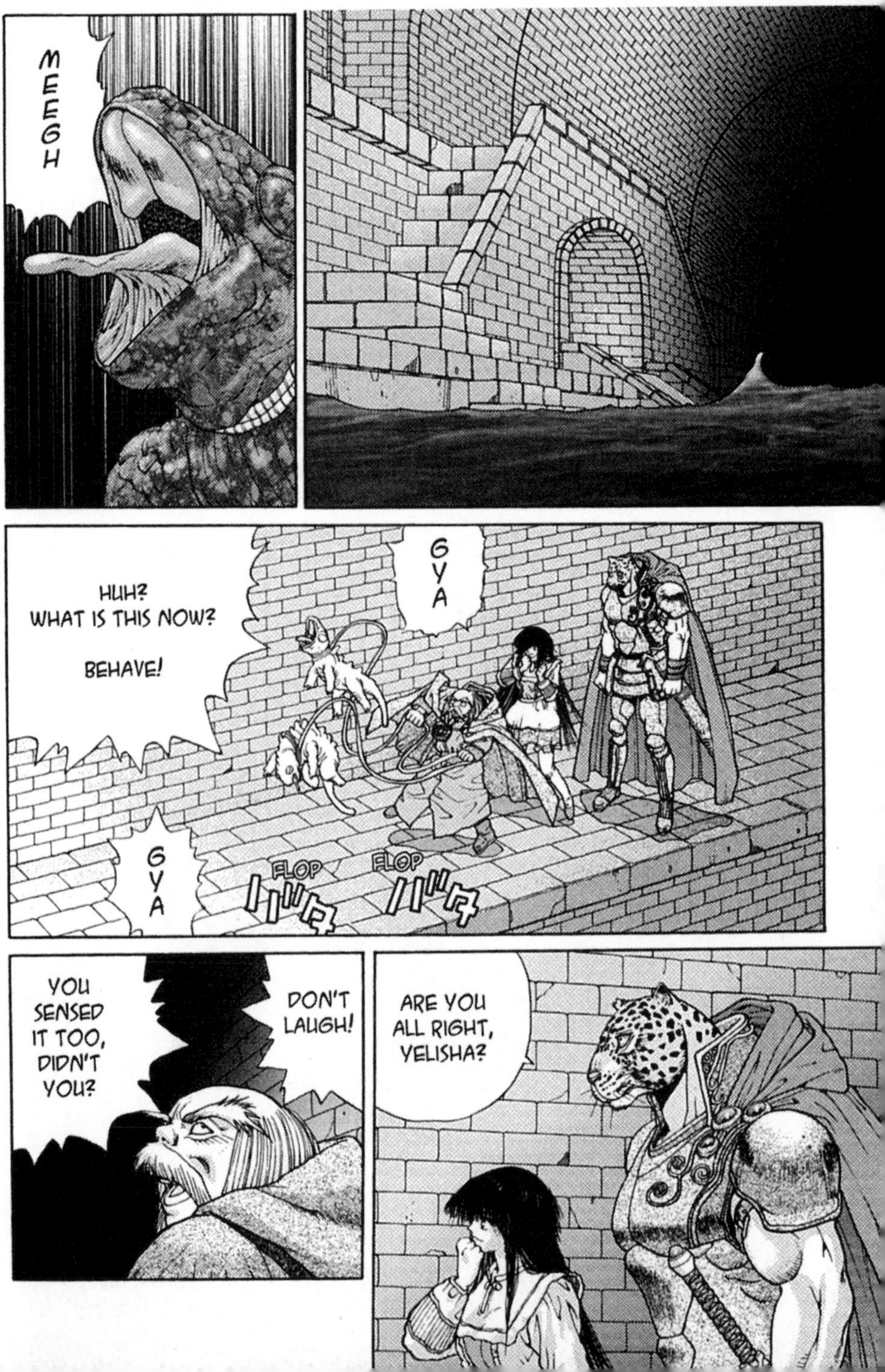

MEEGH
GYA
HUH? WHAT IS THIS NOW?
BEHAVE!
GYA
FLOP
FLOP
ARE YOU ALL RIGHT, YELISHA?
DON'T LAUGH!
YOU SENSED IT TOO, DIDN'T YOU?

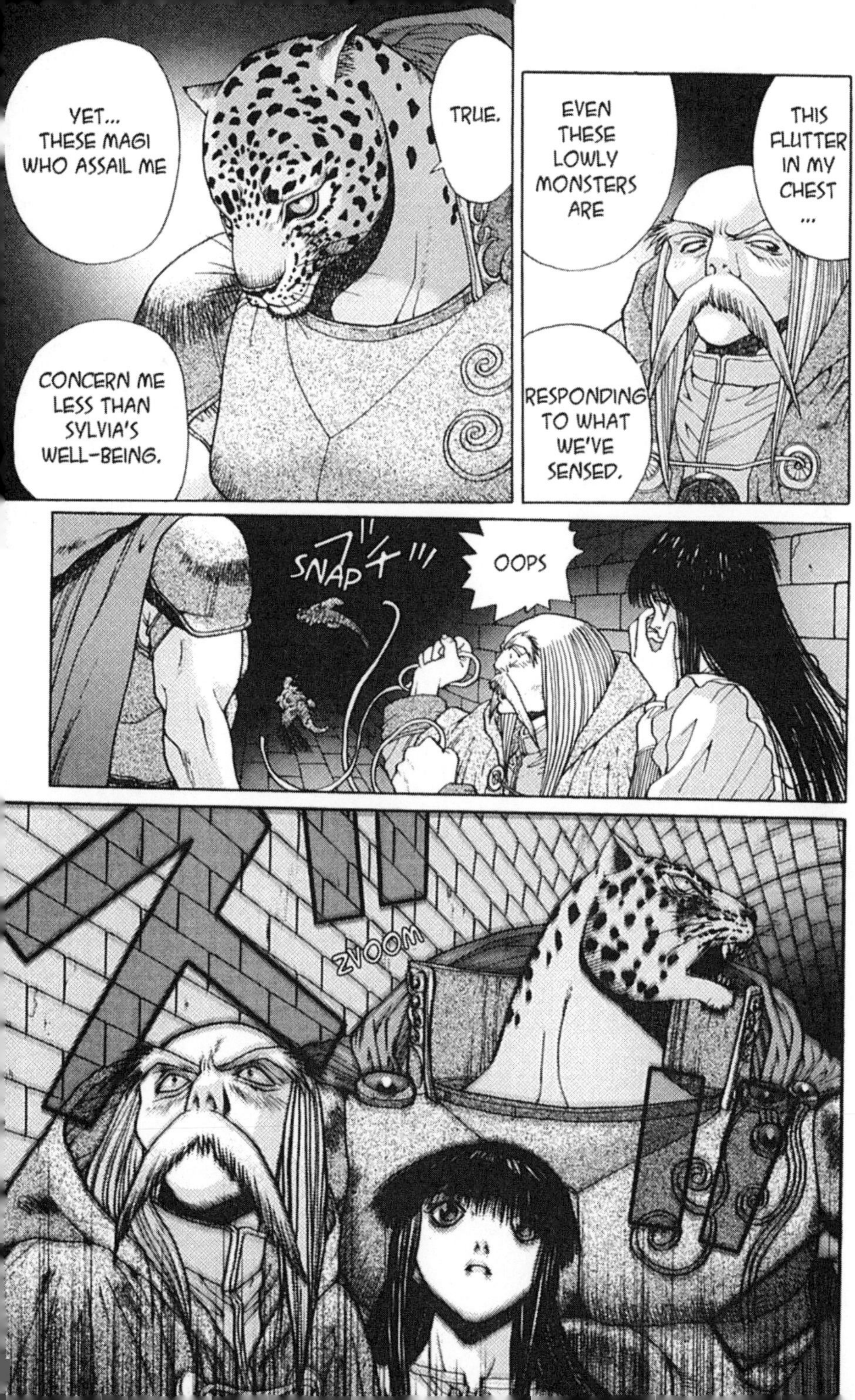
THIS FLUTTER IN MY CHEST ...
EVEN THESE LOWLY MONSTERS ARE
RESPONDING TO WHAT WE'VE SENSED.
TRUE.
YET... THESE MAGI WHO ASSAIL ME
CONCERN ME LESS THAN SYLVIA'S WELL-BEING.
OOPS
ブチッ
SNAP
ZVOOM

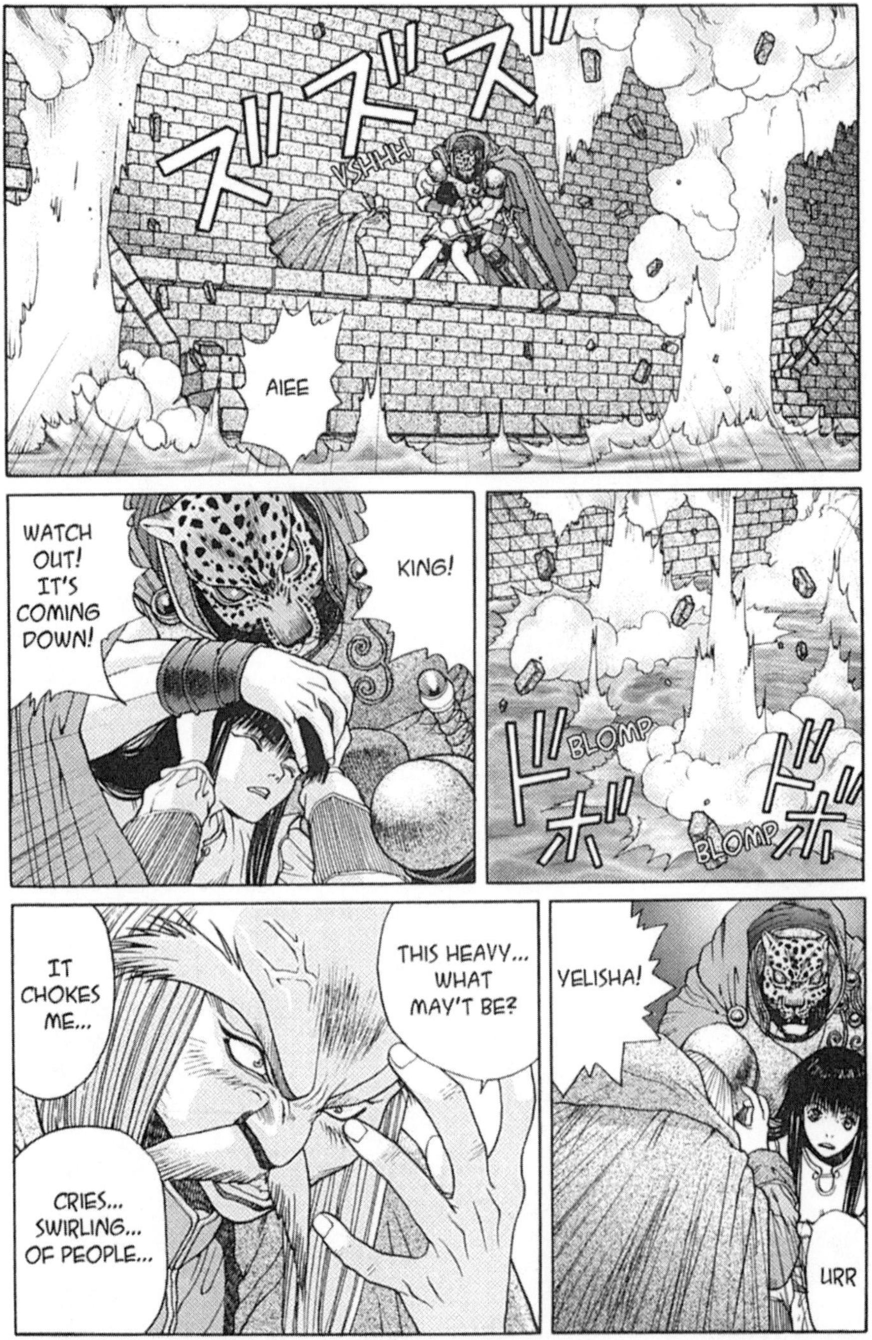
ズズズズ
VSHHH
AIEE
ドボ
BLOMP
ドボ
BLOMP
KING!
WATCH OUT! IT'S COMING DOWN!
YELISHA!
URR
THIS HEAVY... WHAT MAY'T BE?
IT CHOKES ME...
CRIES... SWIRLING... OF PEOPLE...

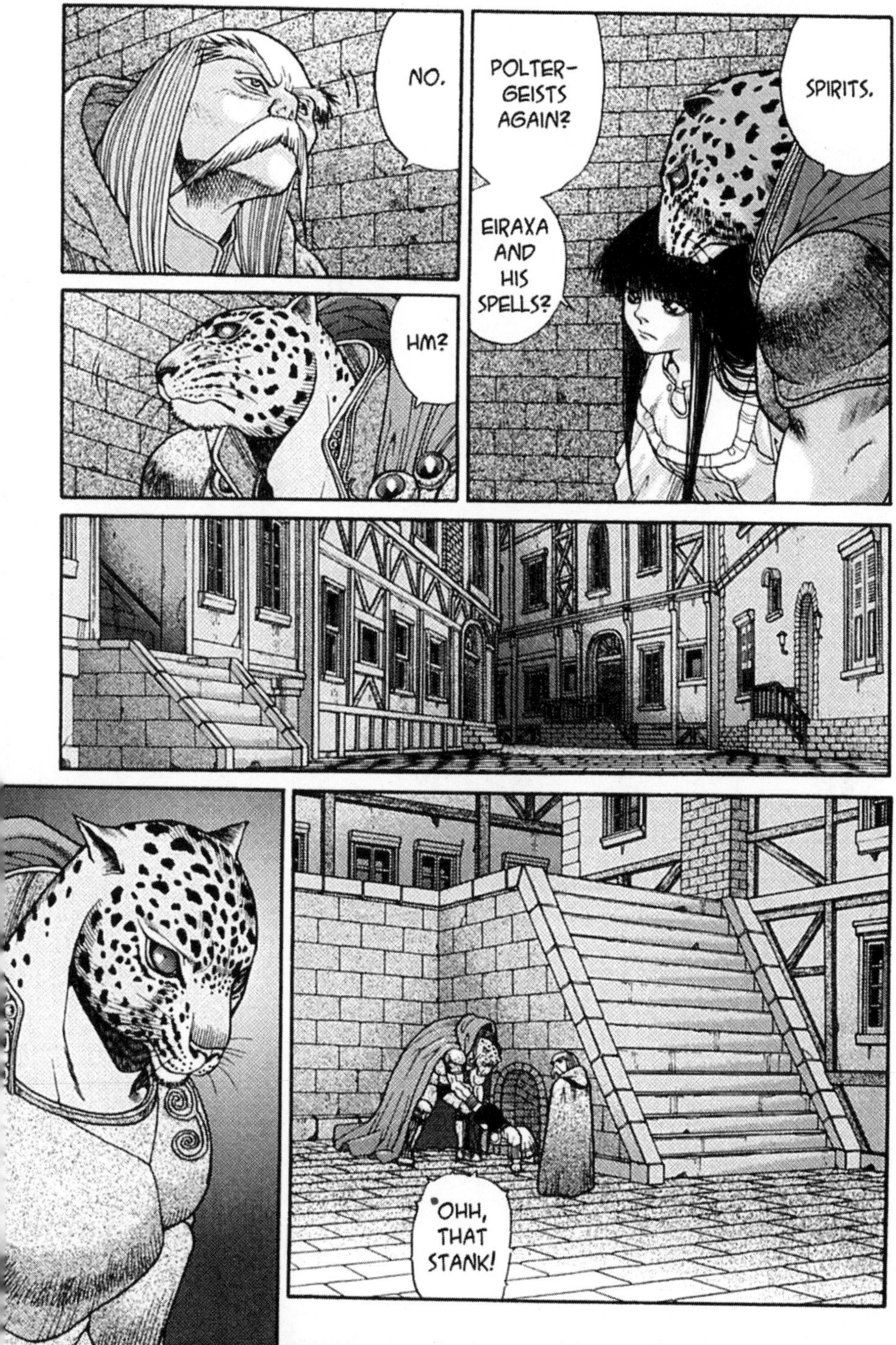
SPIRITS.
POLTER-GEISTS AGAIN?
EIRAXA AND HIS SPELLS?
NO.
HM?
OHH, THAT STANK!

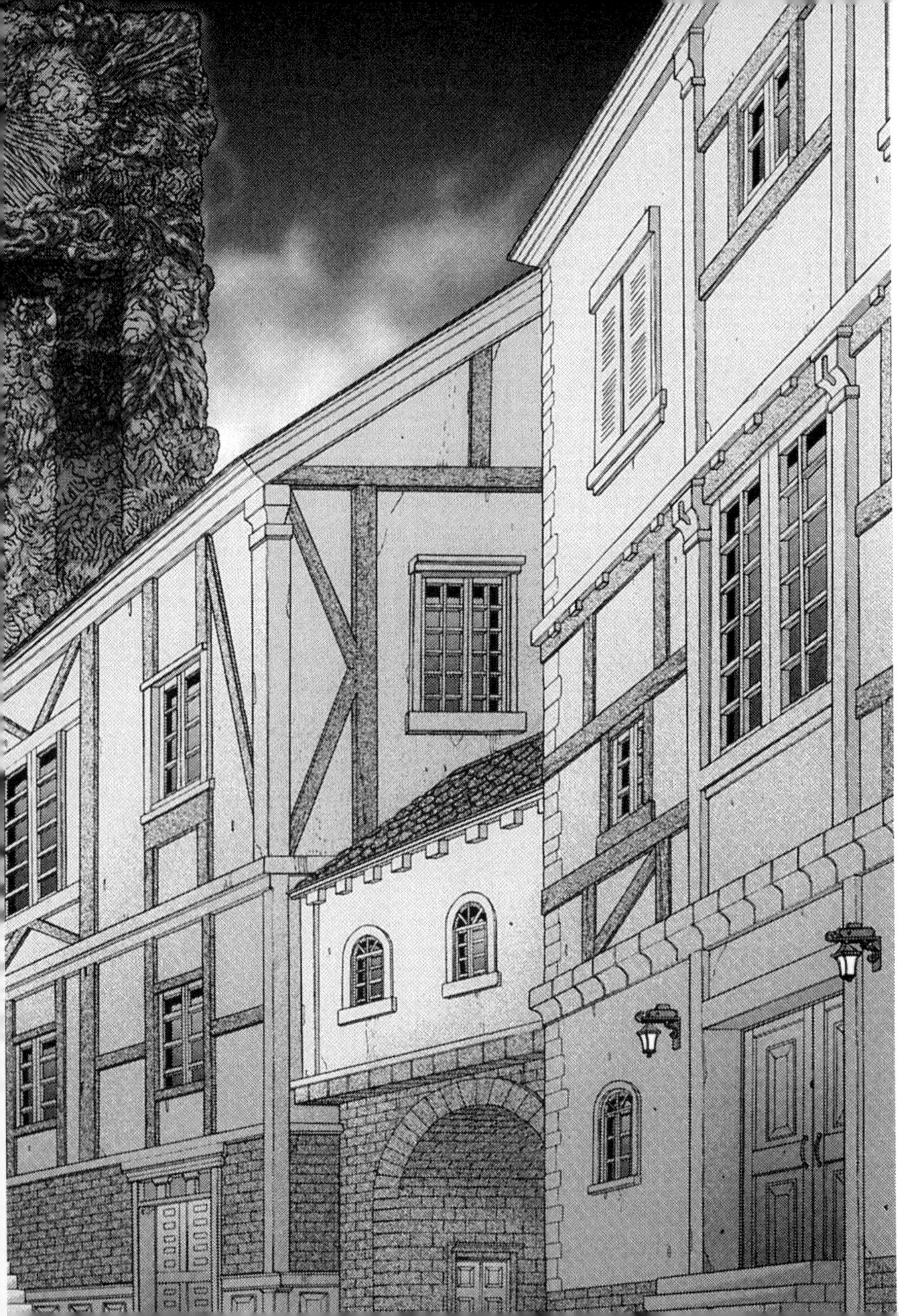

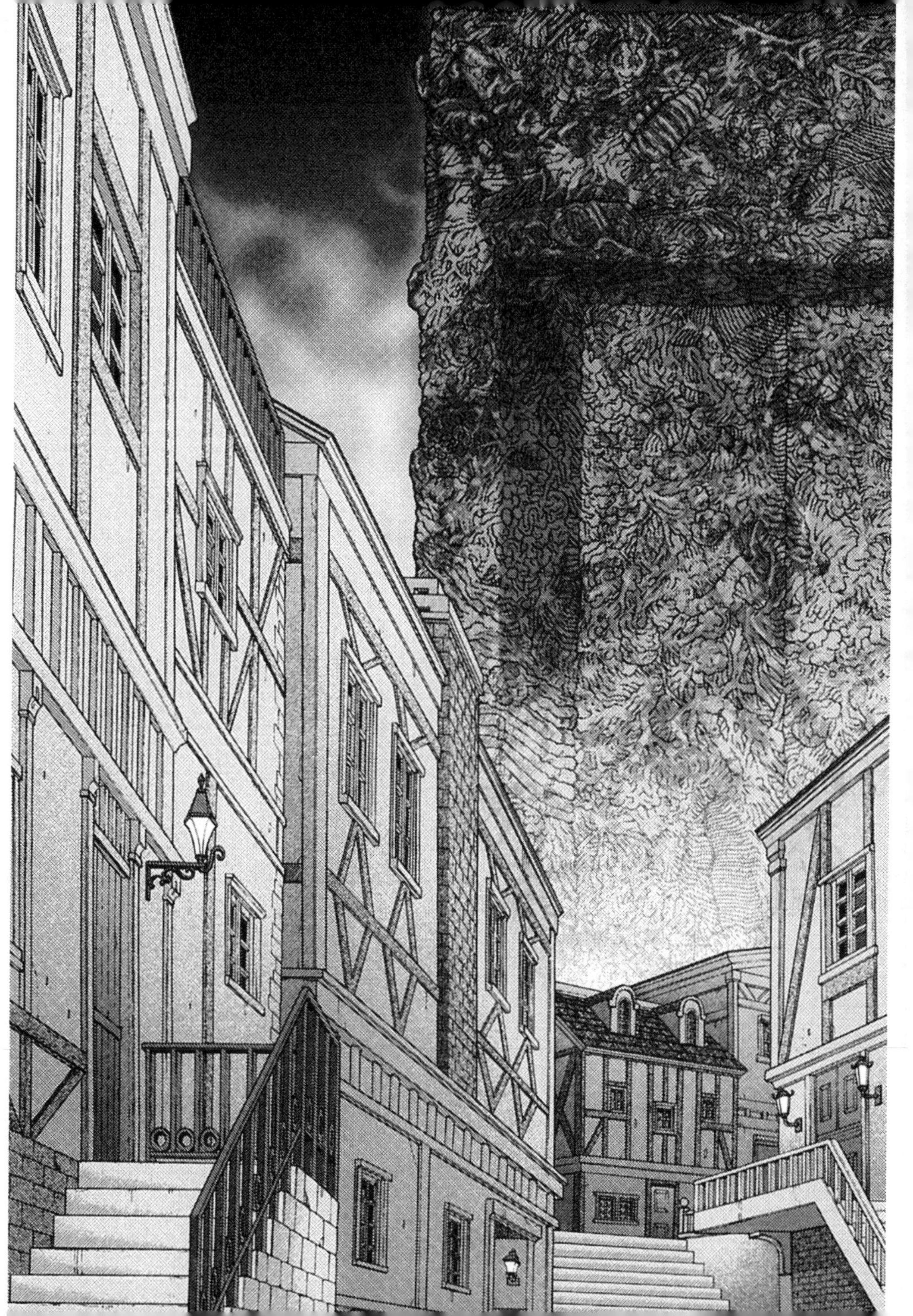

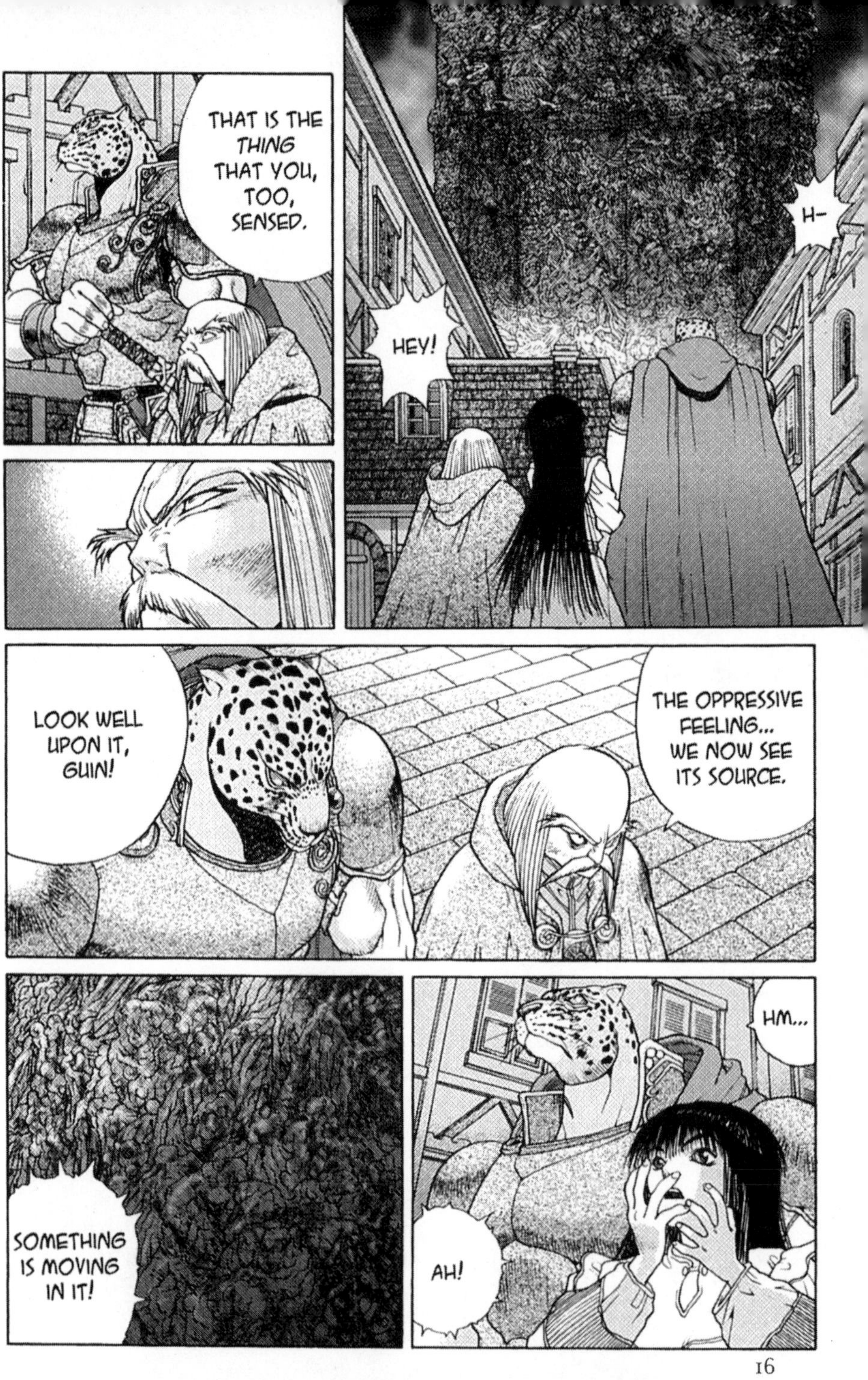
H-
HEY!
THAT IS THE *THING* THAT YOU, TOO, SENSED.
THE OPPRESSIVE FEELING... WE NOW SEE ITS SOURCE.
LOOK WELL UPON IT, GUIN!
HM...
AH!
SOMETHING IS MOVING IN IT!

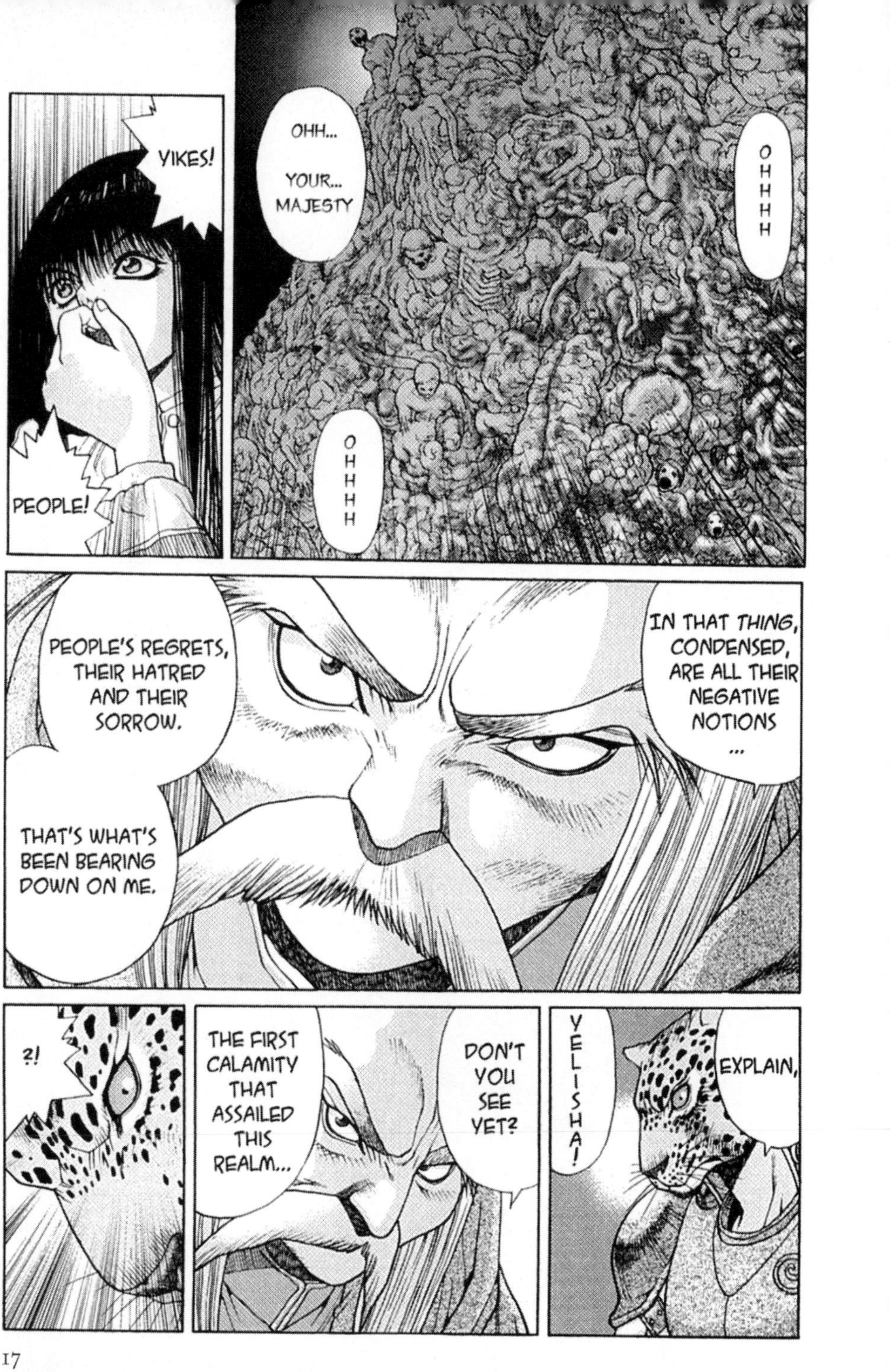
OHHHH
OHH... YOUR... MAJESTY
OHHHH
YIKES!
PEOPLE!
IN THAT *THING*, CONDENSED, ARE ALL THEIR NEGATIVE NOTIONS ...
PEOPLE'S REGRETS, THEIR HATRED AND THEIR SORROW.
THAT'S WHAT'S BEEN BEARING DOWN ON ME.
EXPLAIN,
YELISHA!
DON'T YOU SEE YET?
THE FIRST CALAMITY THAT ASSAILED THIS REALM...
?!

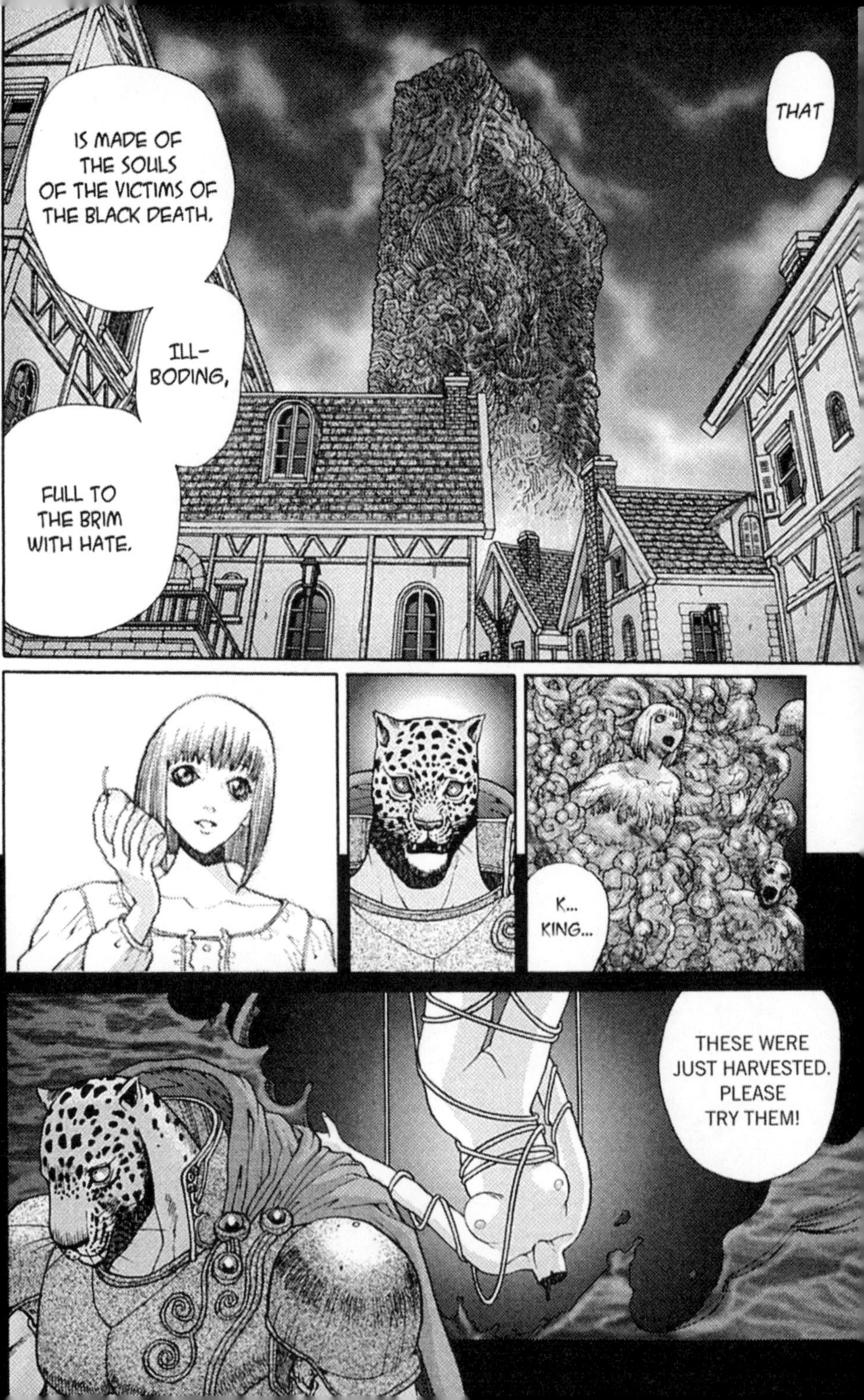
THAT
IS MADE OF THE SOULS OF THE VICTIMS OF THE BLACK DEATH.
ILL-BODING,
FULL TO THE BRIM WITH HATE.
K... KING...
THESE WERE JUST HARVESTED. PLEASE TRY THEM!

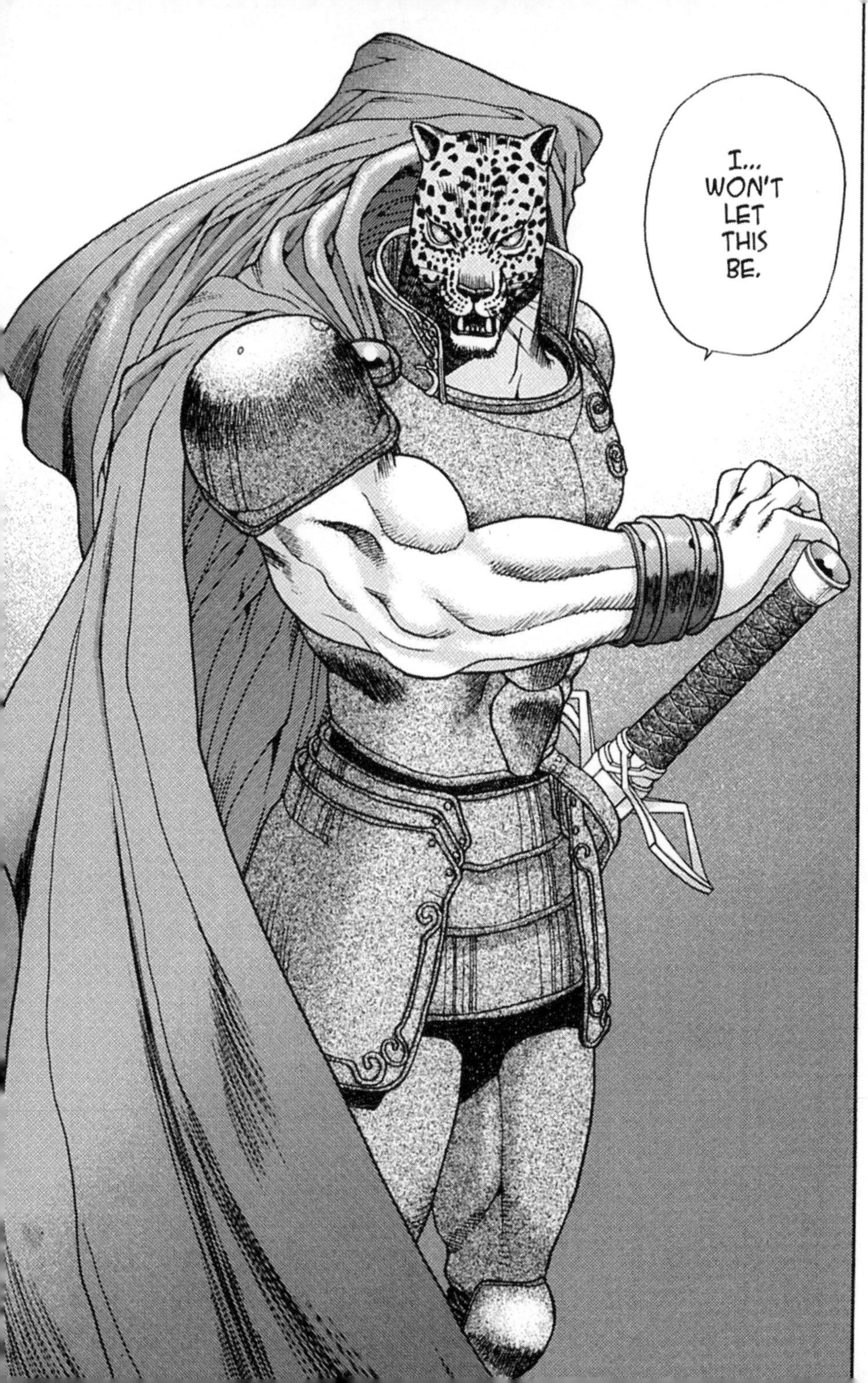
I... WON'T LET THIS BE.

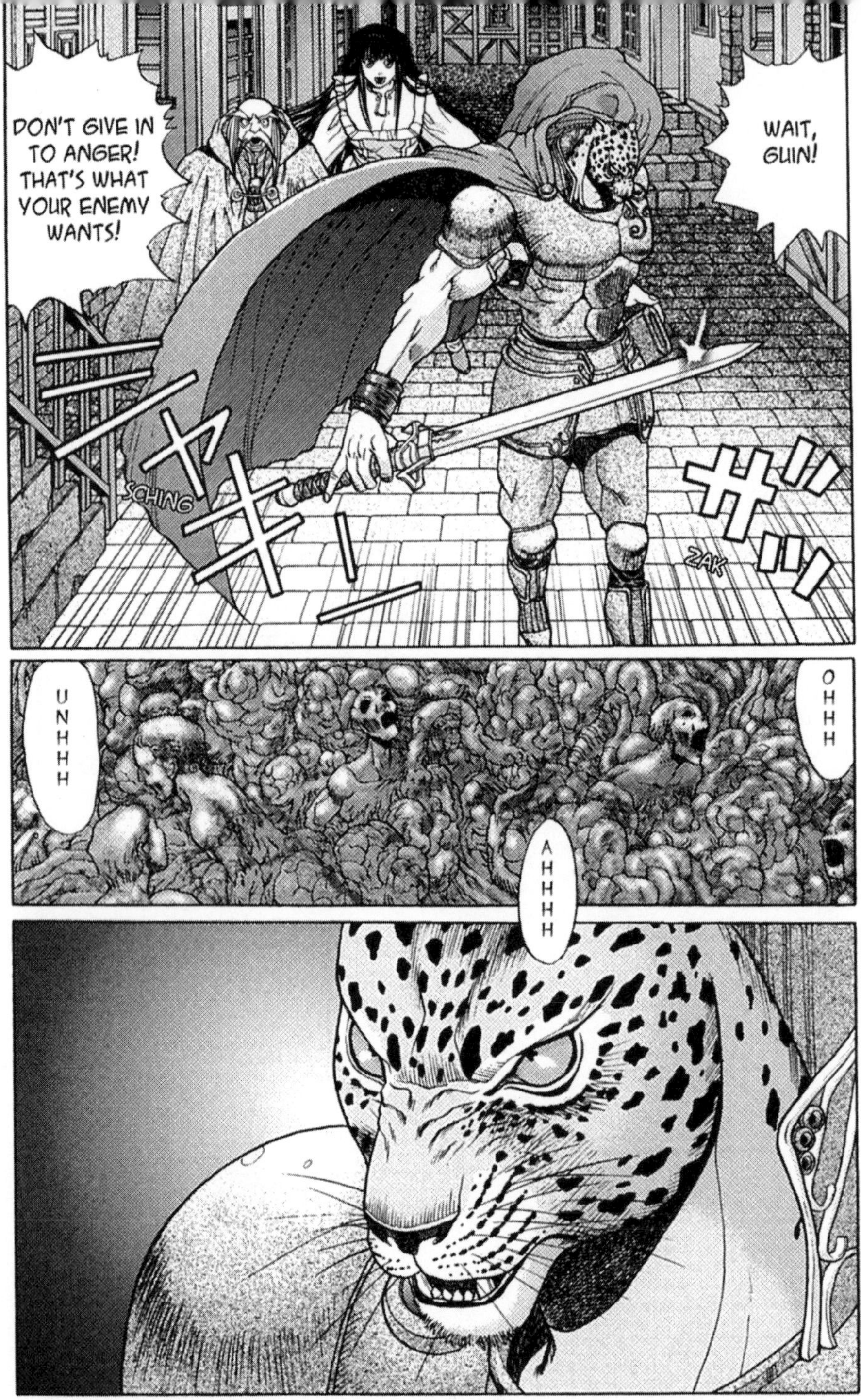
WAIT, GUIN!
DON'T GIVE IN TO ANGER! THAT'S WHAT YOUR ENEMY WANTS!
ザッ!
ZAK
シャキーン
SCHING
OHHH
UNHHH
AHHHH

CHAPTER 16

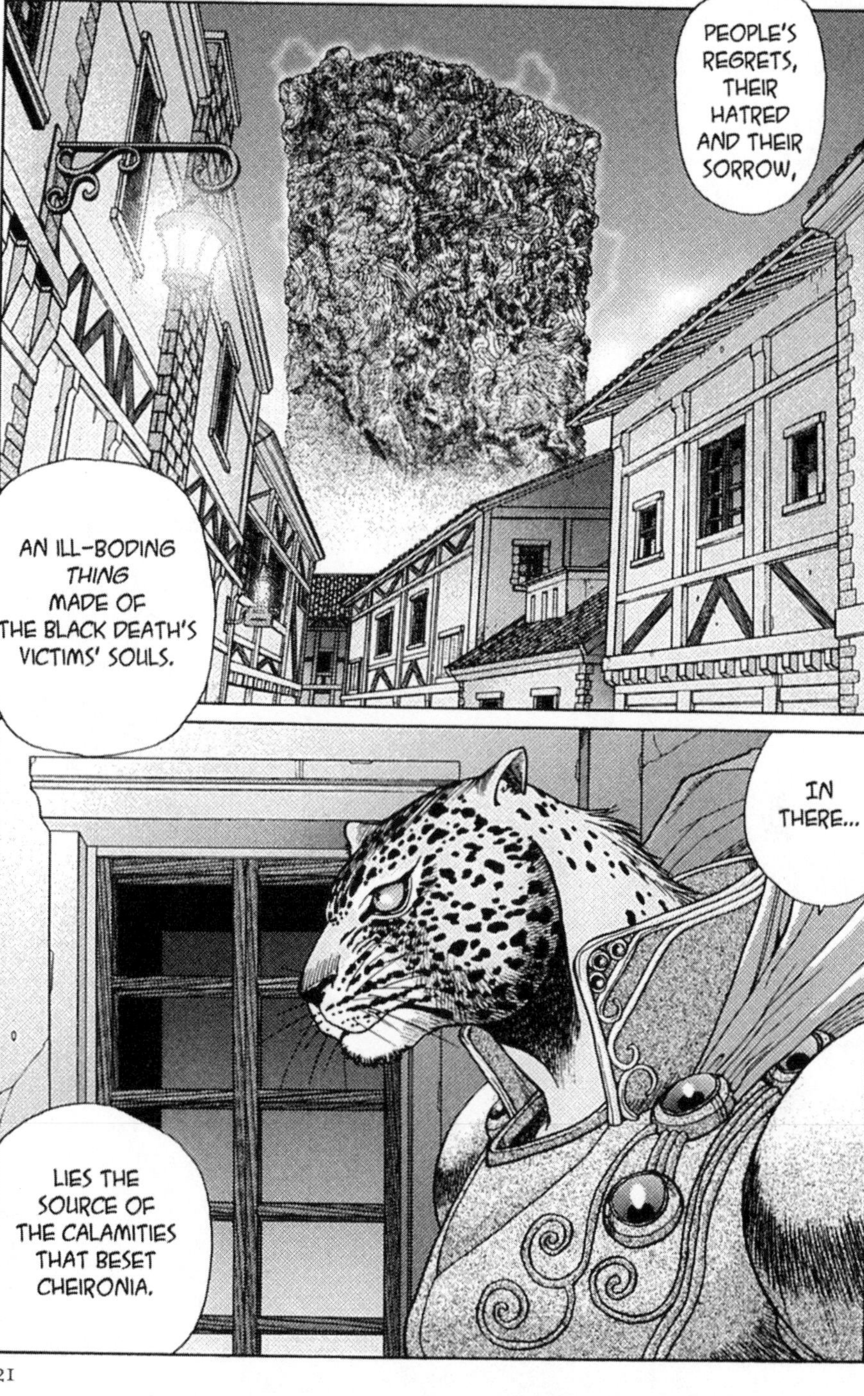

PEOPLE'S REGRETS, THEIR HATRED AND THEIR SORROW,
AN ILL-BODING *THING* MADE OF THE BLACK DEATH'S VICTIMS' SOULS.
IN THERE...
LIES THE SOURCE OF THE CALAMITIES THAT BESET CHEIRONIA.

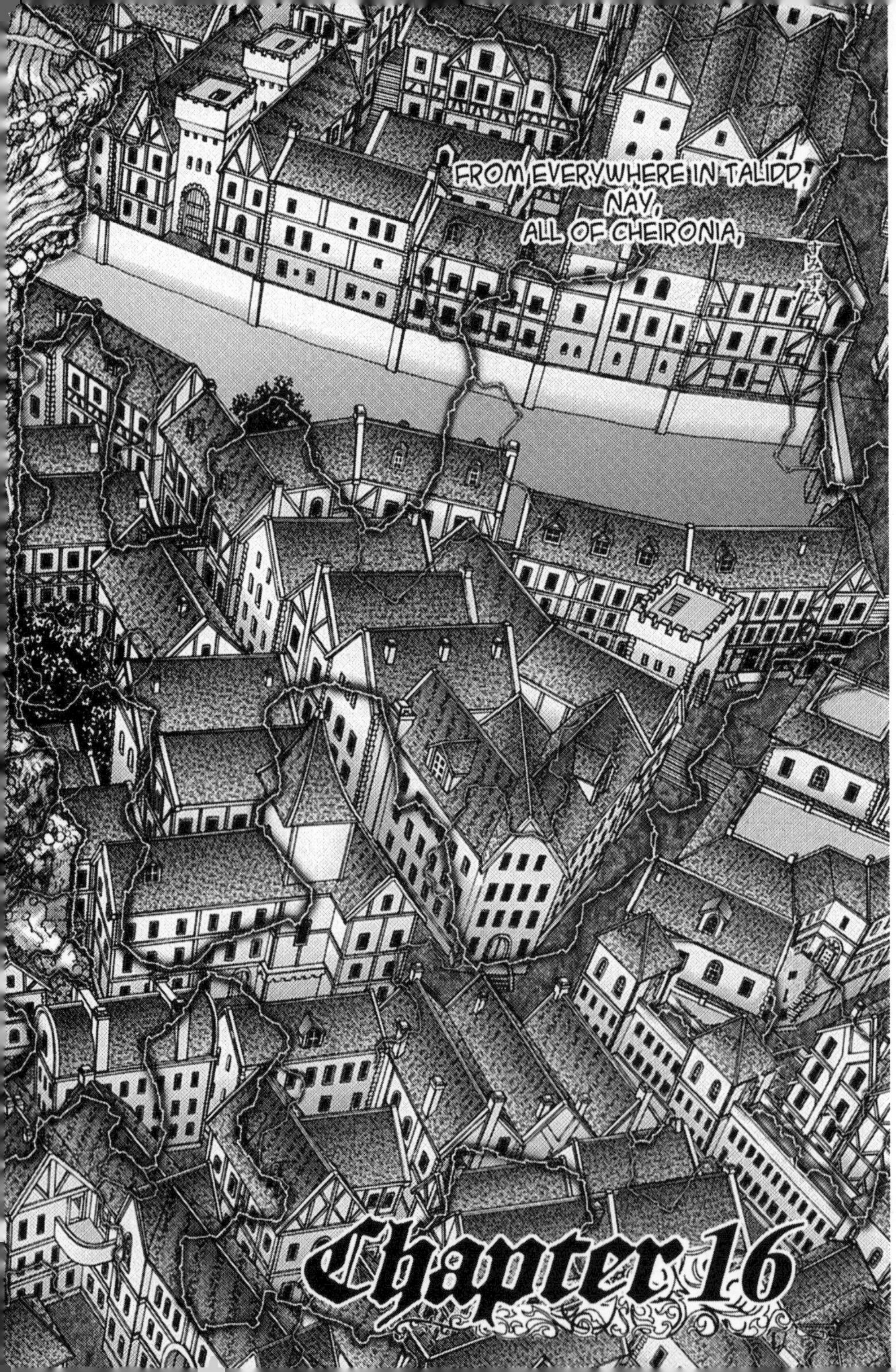
FROM EVERYWHERE IN TALIDD, NAY, ALL OF CHEIRONIA,
Chapter 16

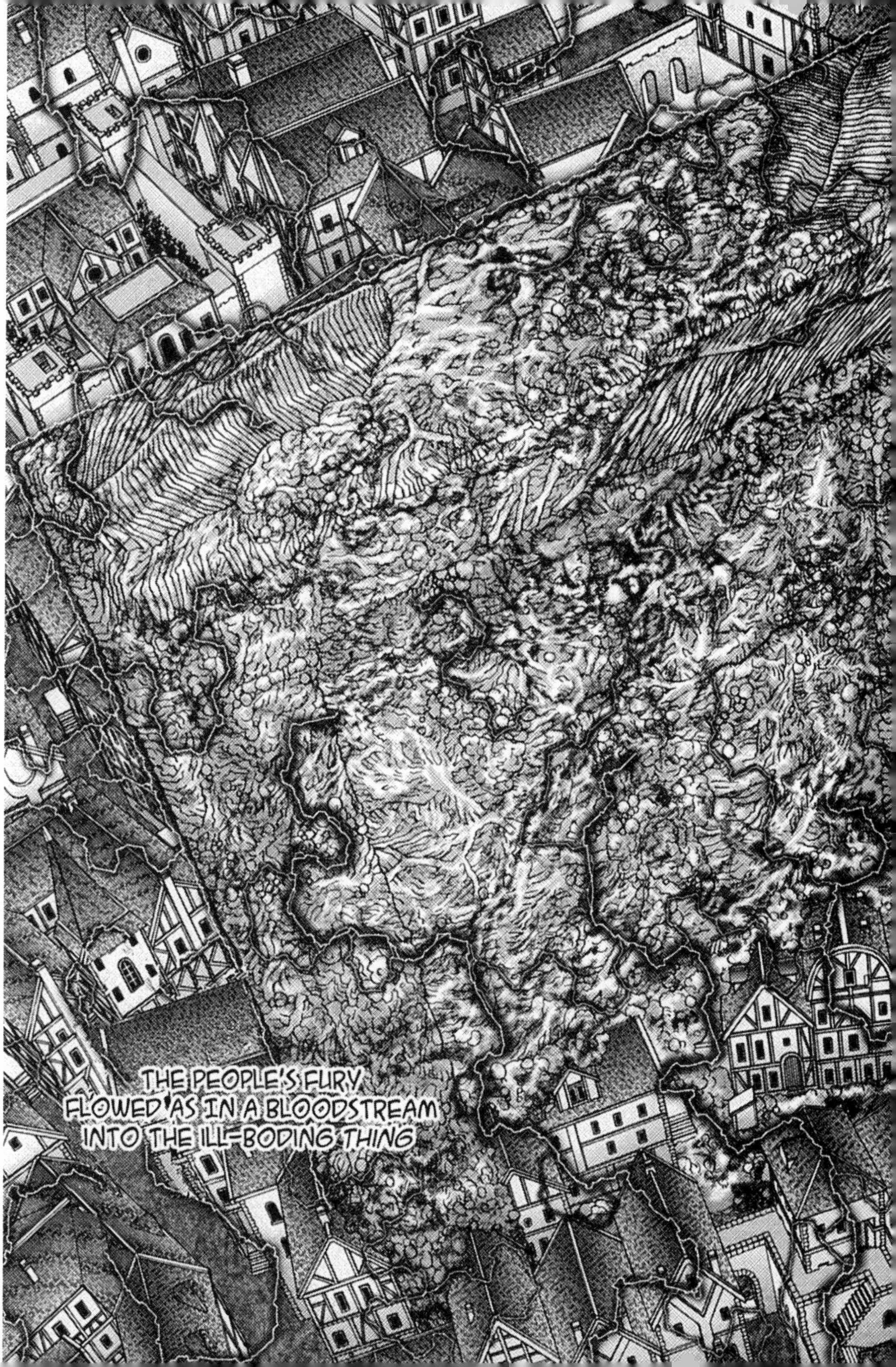
THE PEOPLE'S FURY FLOWED AS IN A BLOODSTREAM INTO THE ILL-BODING THING

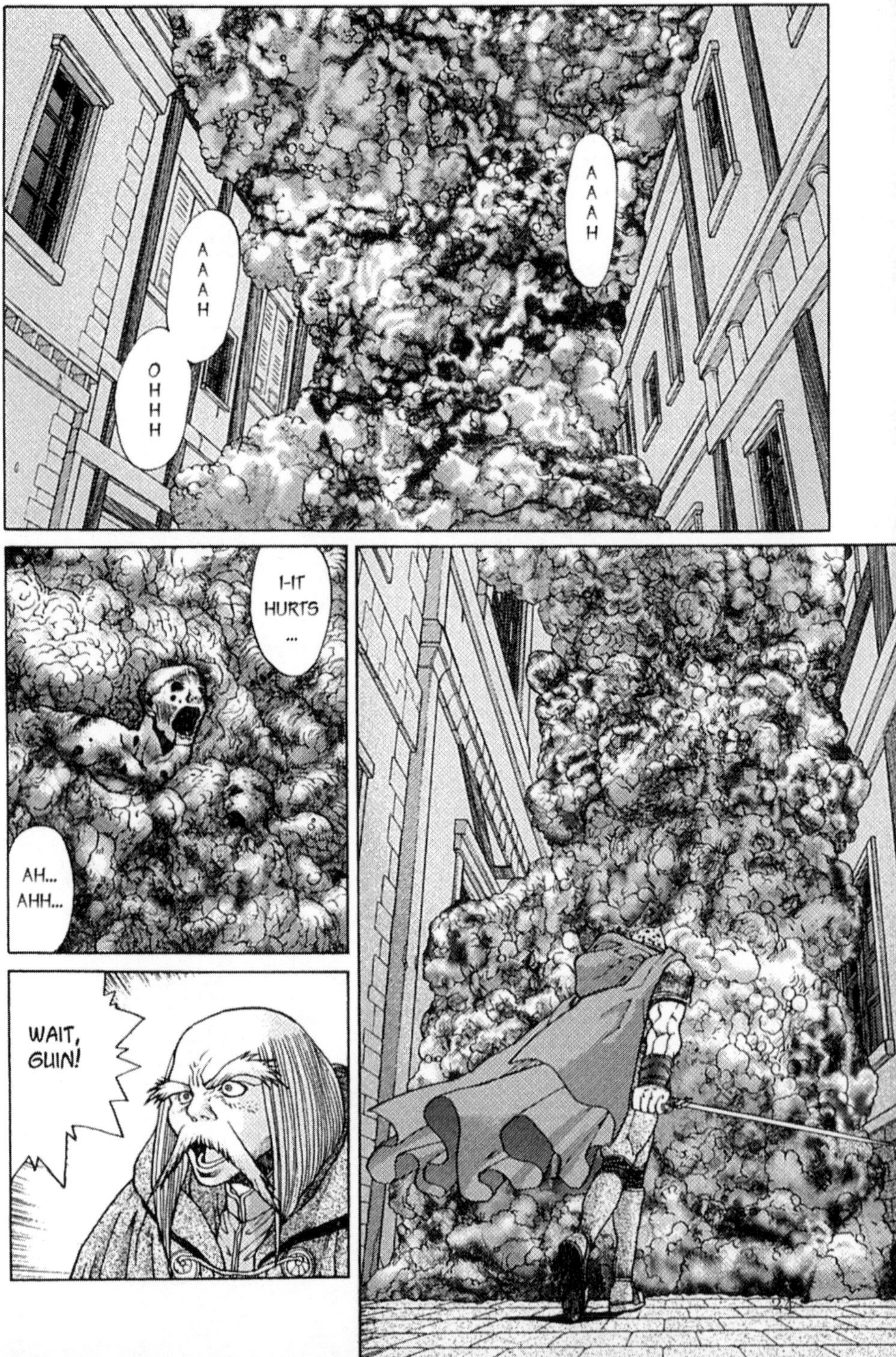
AAAH
AAAH
OHHH
I-IT HURTS...
AH... AHH...
WAIT, GUIN!

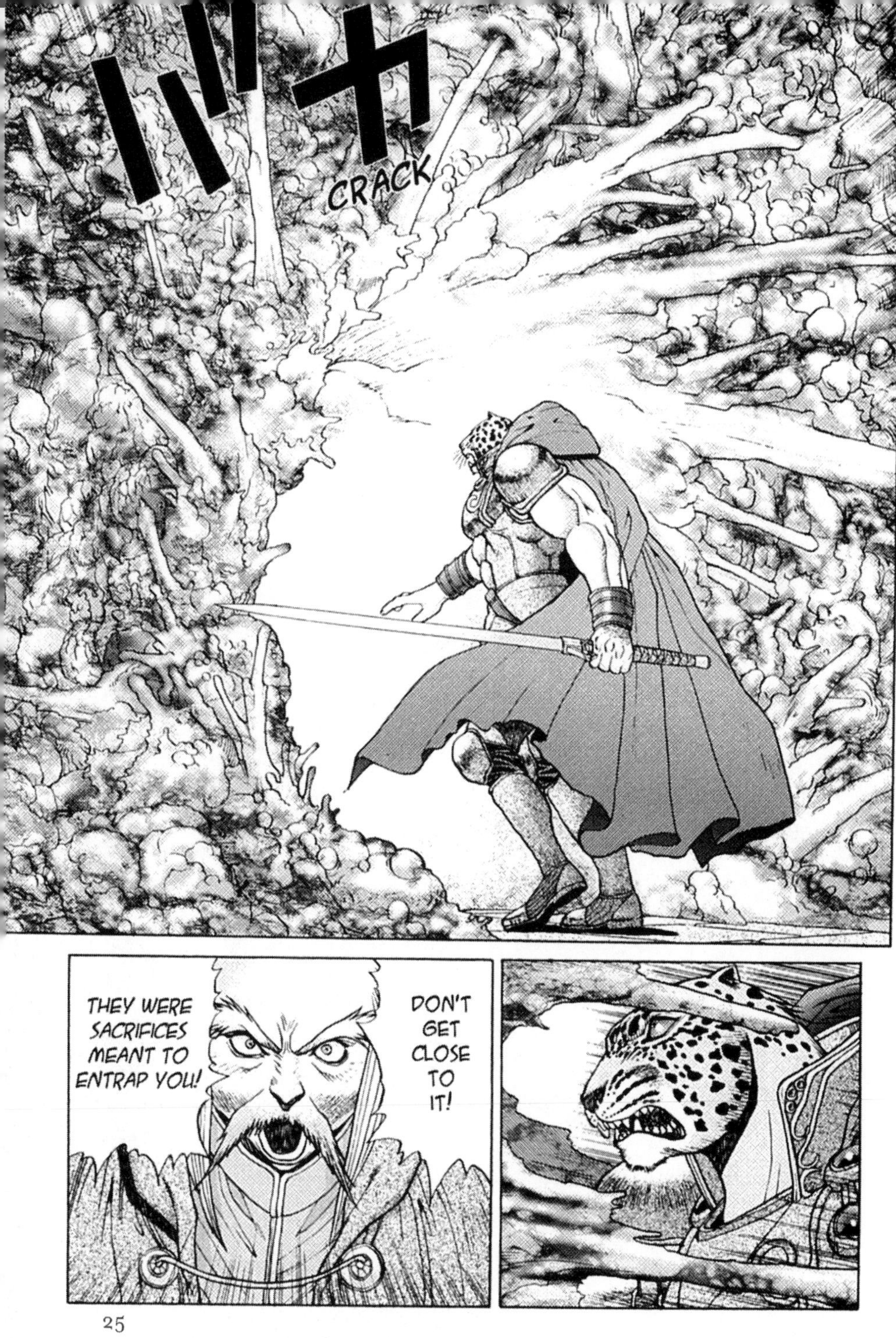
バカ
CRACK
DON'T GET CLOSE TO IT!
THEY WERE SACRIFICES MEANT TO ENTRAP YOU!

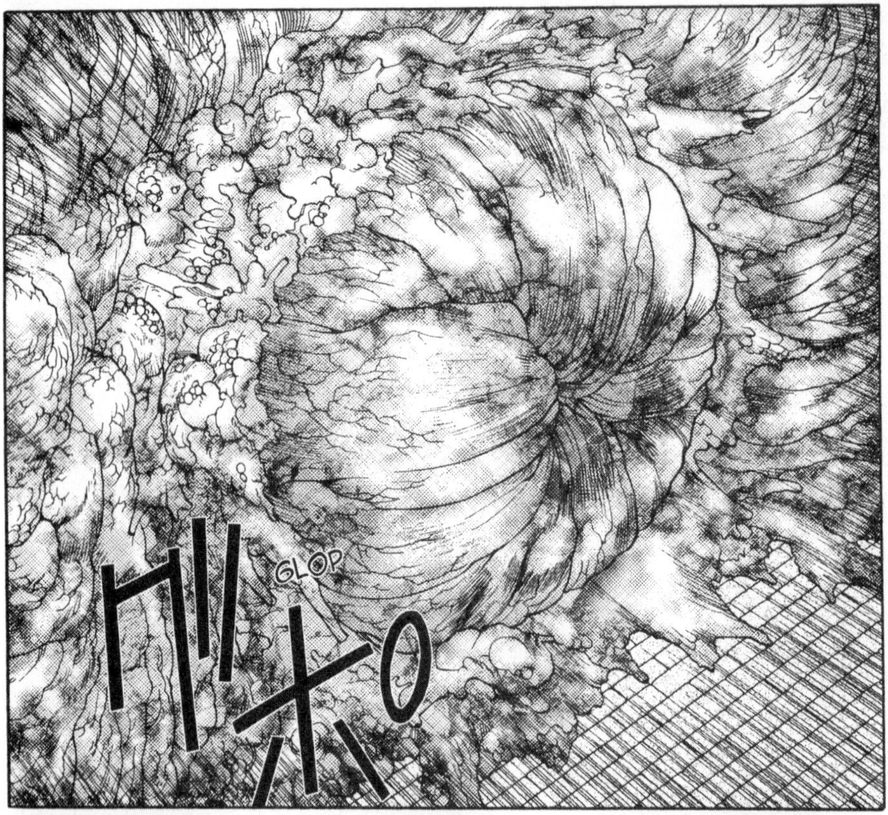
GLOP

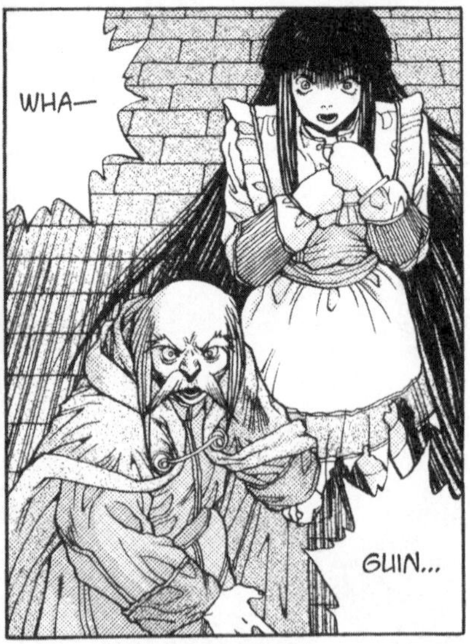
WHA—
GUIN...

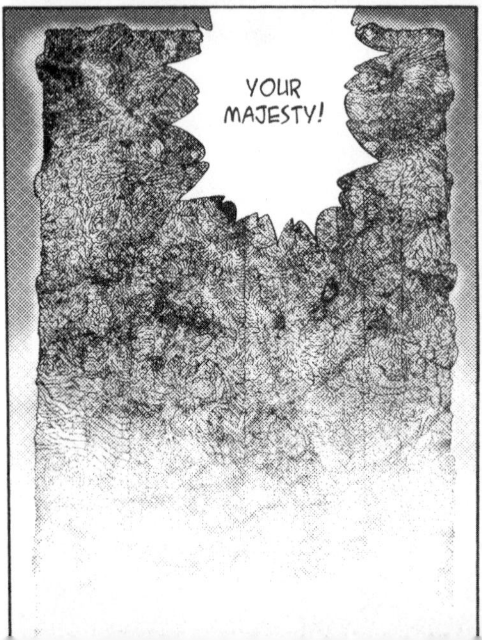
YOUR MAJESTY!

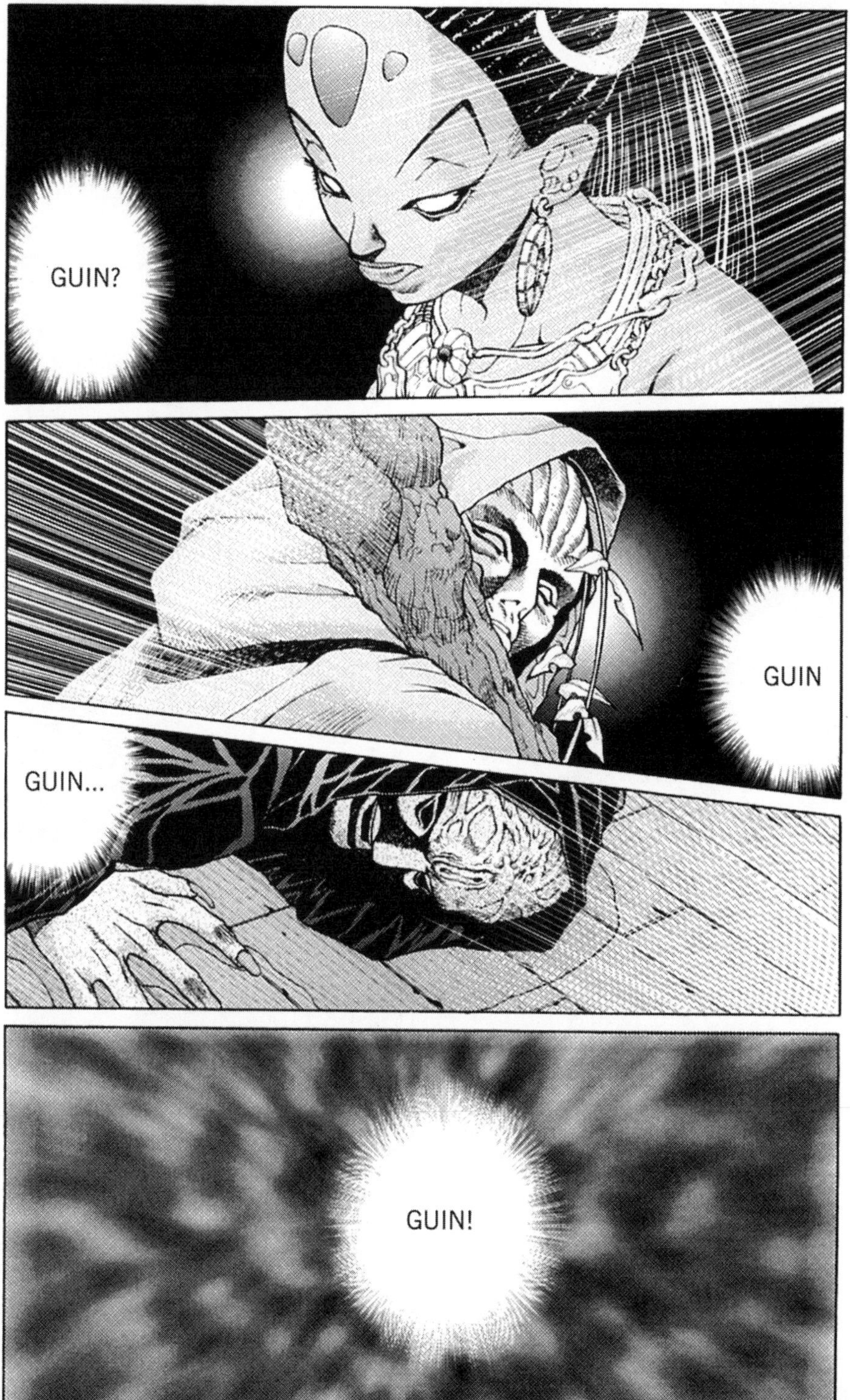
GUIN?
GUIN
GUIN...
GUIN!

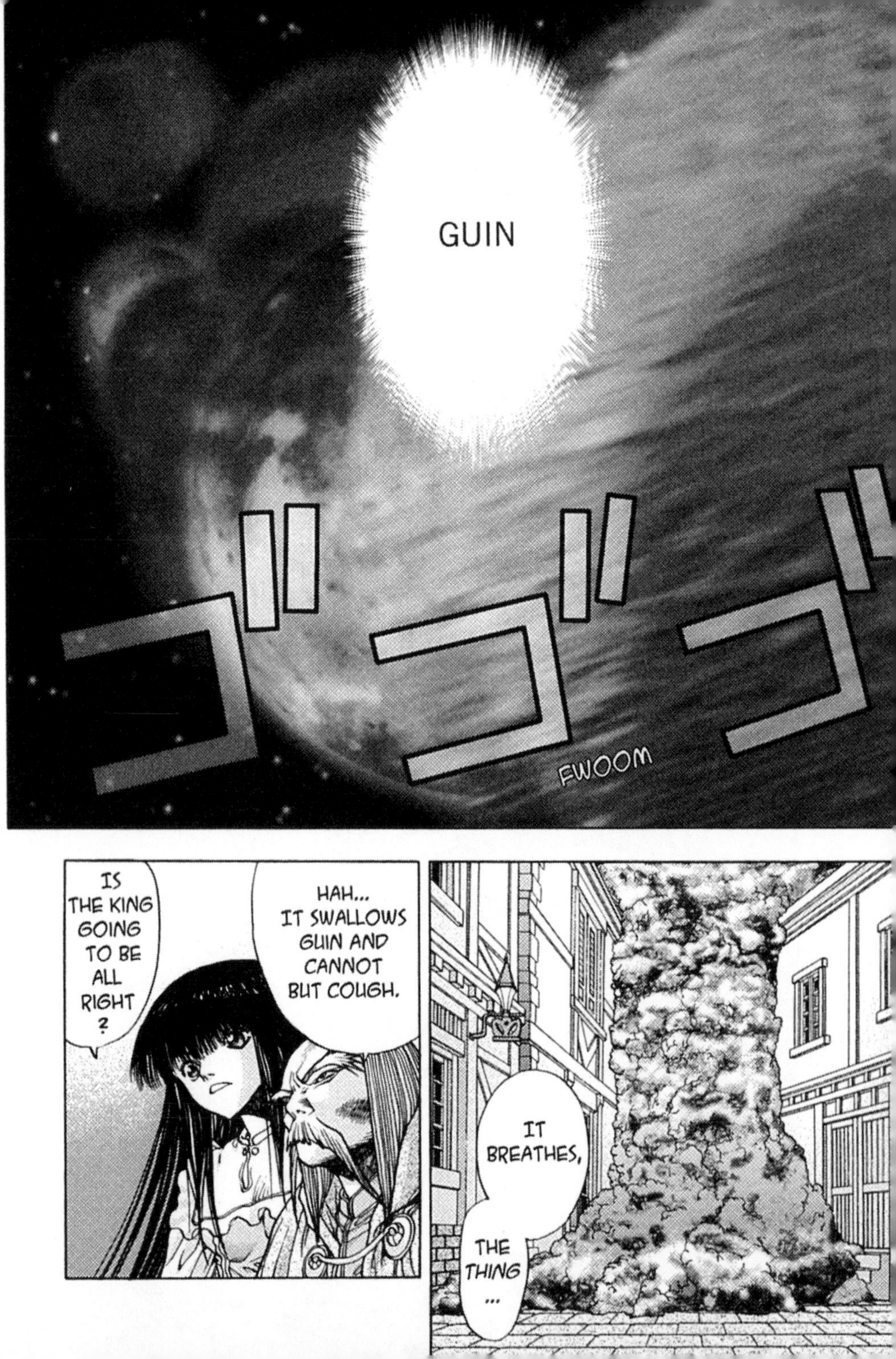
GUIN
ゴゴゴ
FWOOM
IT BREATHES,
THE THING...
HAH... IT SWALLOWS GUIN AND CANNOT BUT COUGH.
IS THE KING GOING TO BE ALL RIGHT?

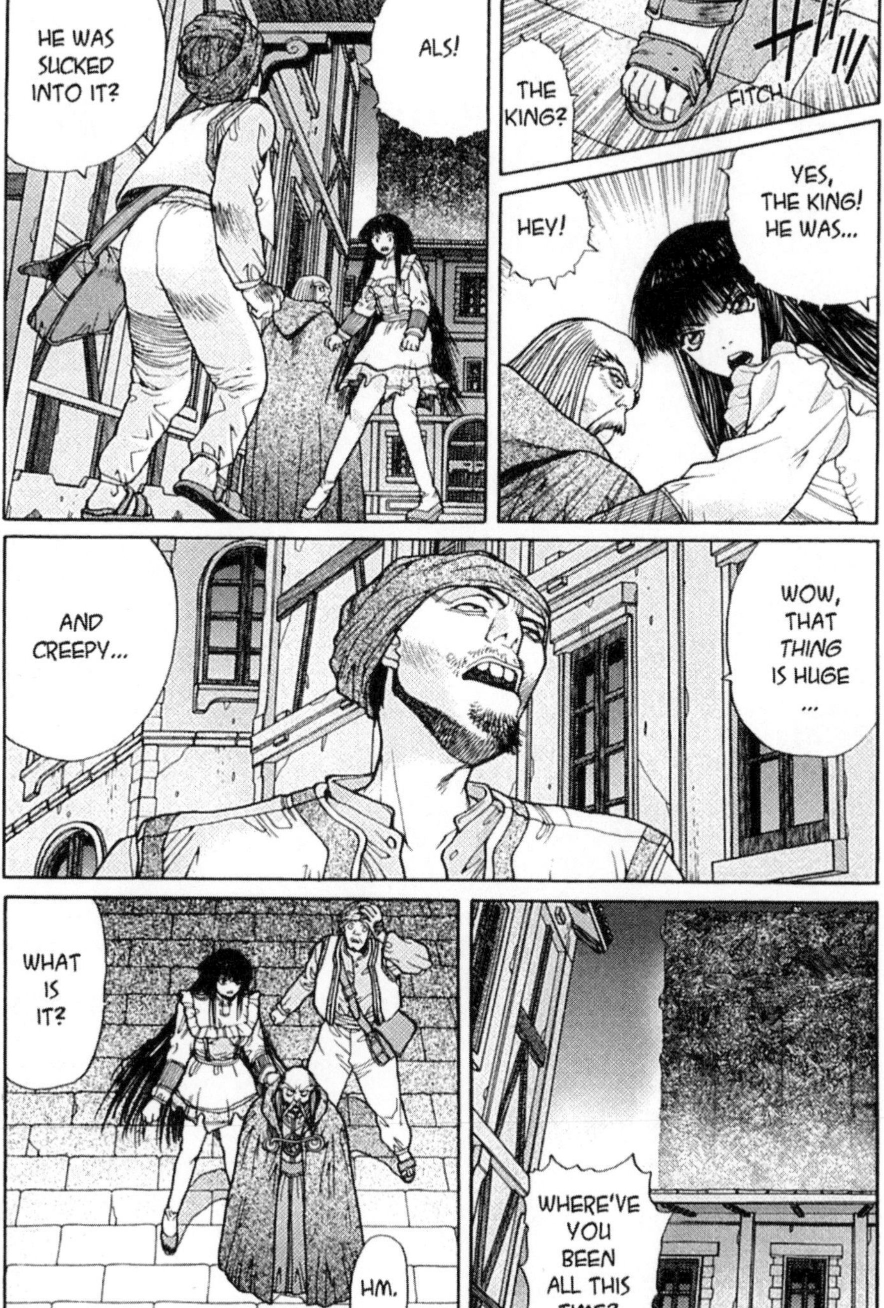
THE KING?
FITCH
YES, THE KING! HE WAS...
HEY!
ALS!
HE WAS SUCKED INTO IT?
WOW, THAT THING IS HUGE ...
AND CREEPY...
WHERE'VE YOU BEEN ALL THIS TIME?
WHAT IS IT?
HM.

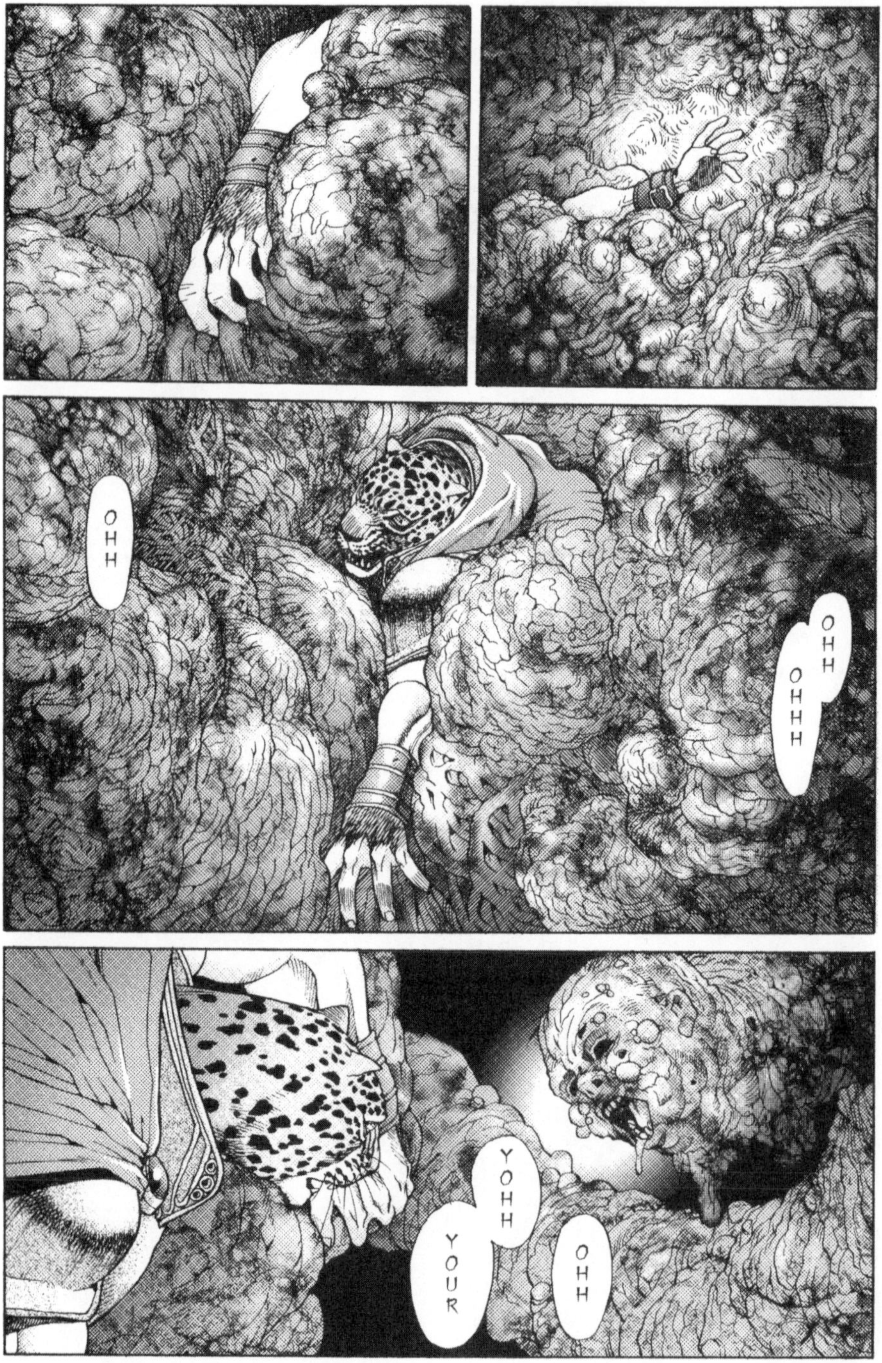
OHH
OHHH
OHH
OHH
YOHH
YOUR

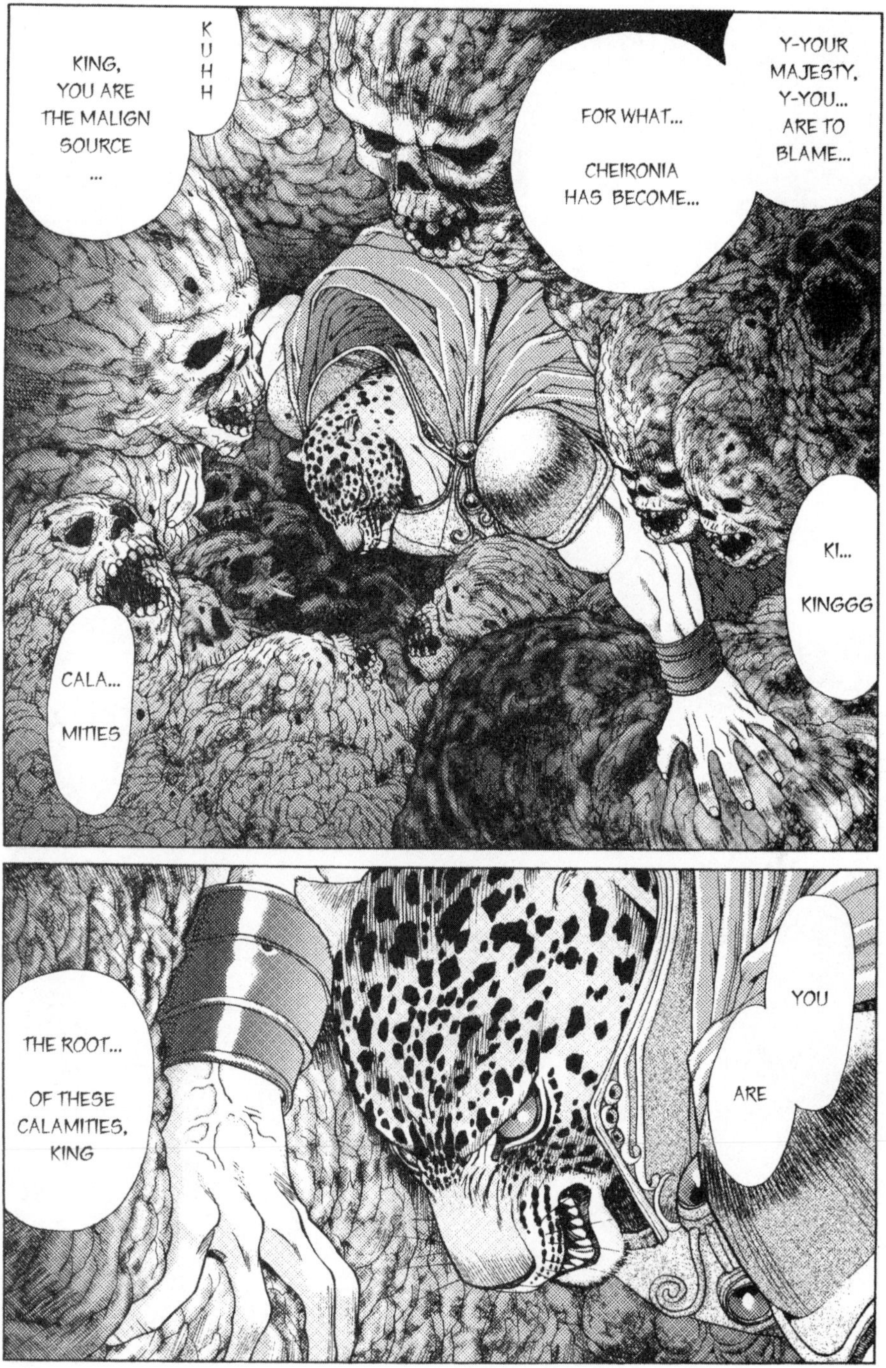
Y-YOUR MAJESTY, Y-YOU... ARE TO BLAME...
FOR WHAT... CHEIRONIA HAS BECOME...
KUHH
KING, YOU ARE THE MALIGN SOURCE ...
KI... KINGGG
CALA... MITIES
YOU ARE
THE ROOT... OF THESE CALAMITIES, KING

SO WHO LURED ME
IN HERE?

OH...
I SEE.

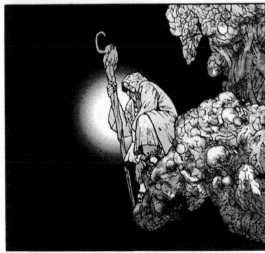

BOP

BOPP

BOP

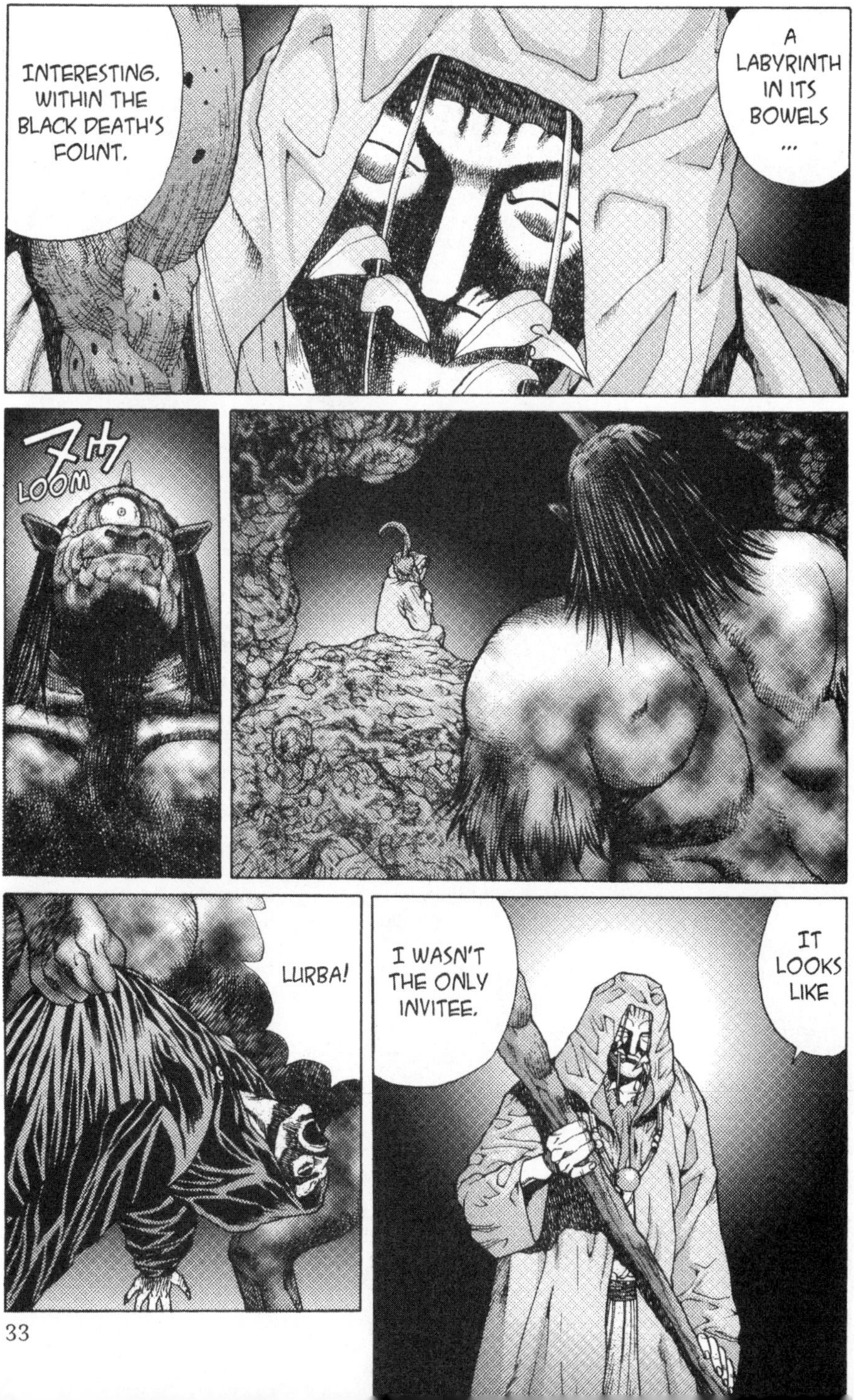
A LABYRINTH IN ITS BOWELS ...
INTERESTING. WITHIN THE BLACK DEATH'S FOUNT.
LOOM
IT LOOKS LIKE
I WASN'T THE ONLY INVITEE.
LURBA!

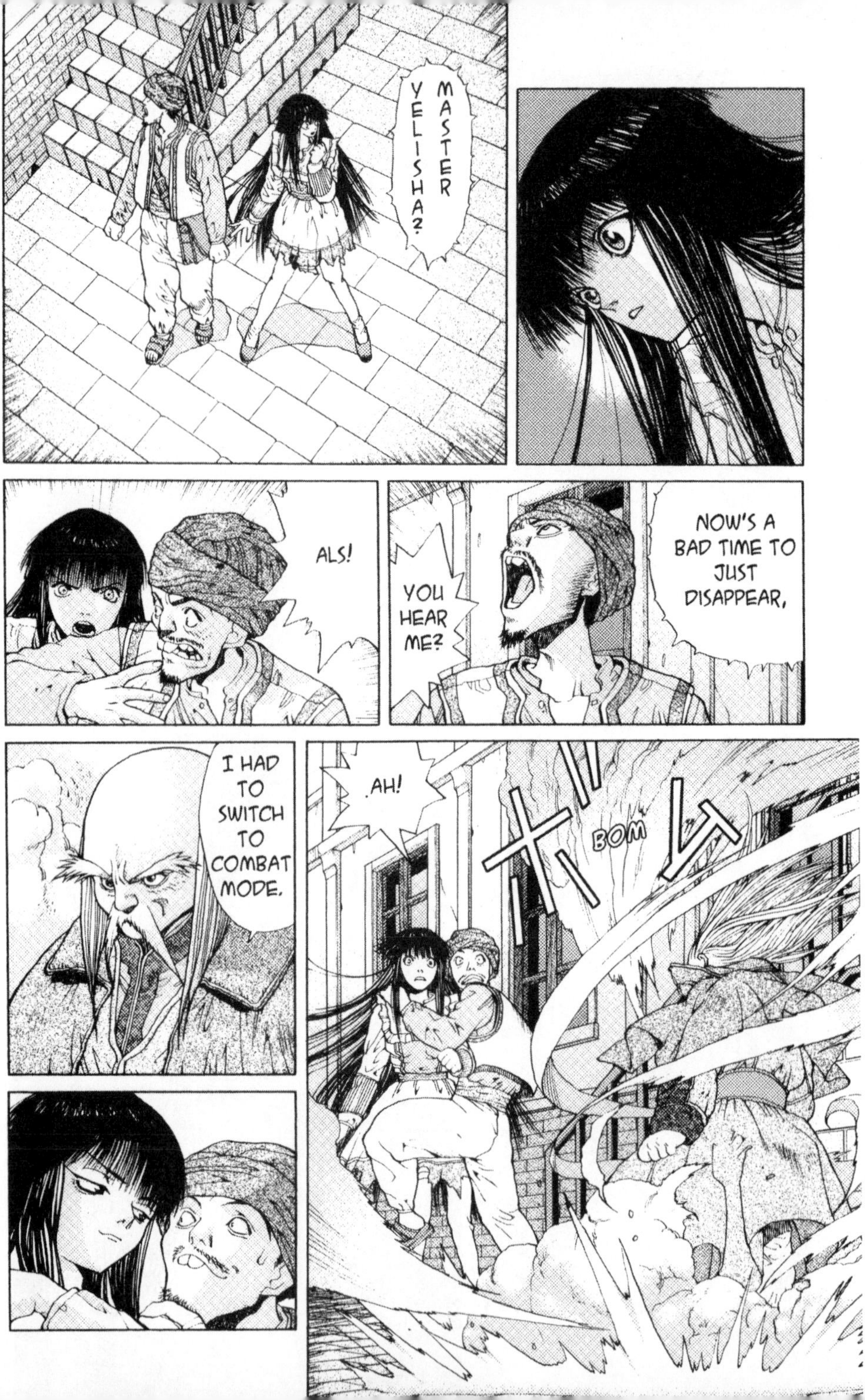
MASTER YELISHA?
NOW'S A BAD TIME TO JUST DISAPPEAR,
YOU HEAR ME?
ALS!
.AH!
BOM
I HAD TO SWITCH TO COMBAT MODE.

VALUSA...

DO YOU HAVE THE COURAGE TO ENTER THAT *THING,*

UGLY BEYOND WORDS?

AH HA.

THE KING MEANS—

OF COURSE I DO!

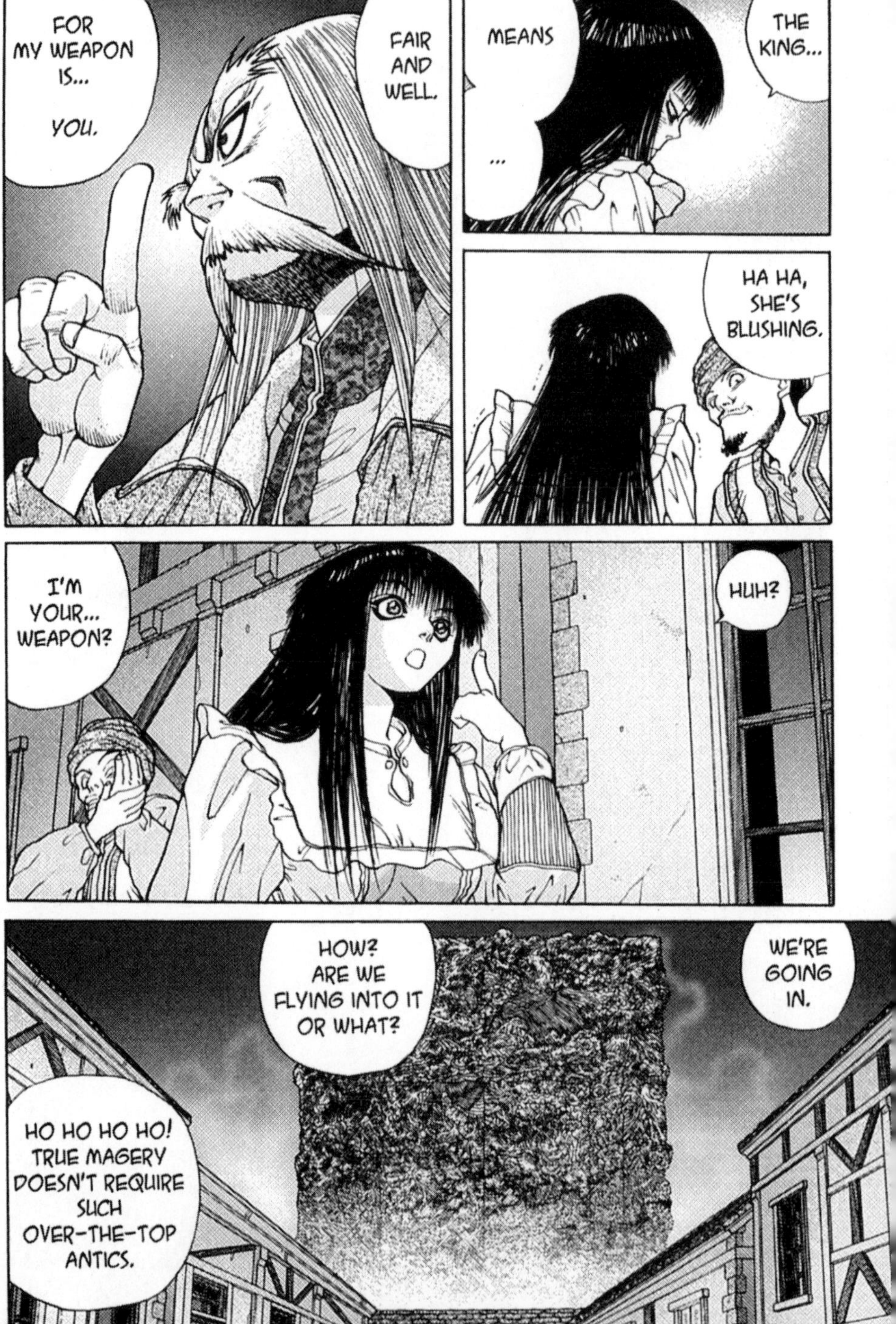
THE KING...
MEANS
...
HA HA, SHE'S BLUSHING.
FAIR AND WELL.
FOR MY WEAPON IS...
YOU.
HUH?
I'M YOUR... WEAPON?
WE'RE GOING IN.
HOW? ARE WE FLYING INTO IT OR WHAT?
HO HO HO HO! TRUE MAGERY DOESN'T REQUIRE SUCH OVER-THE-TOP ANTICS.

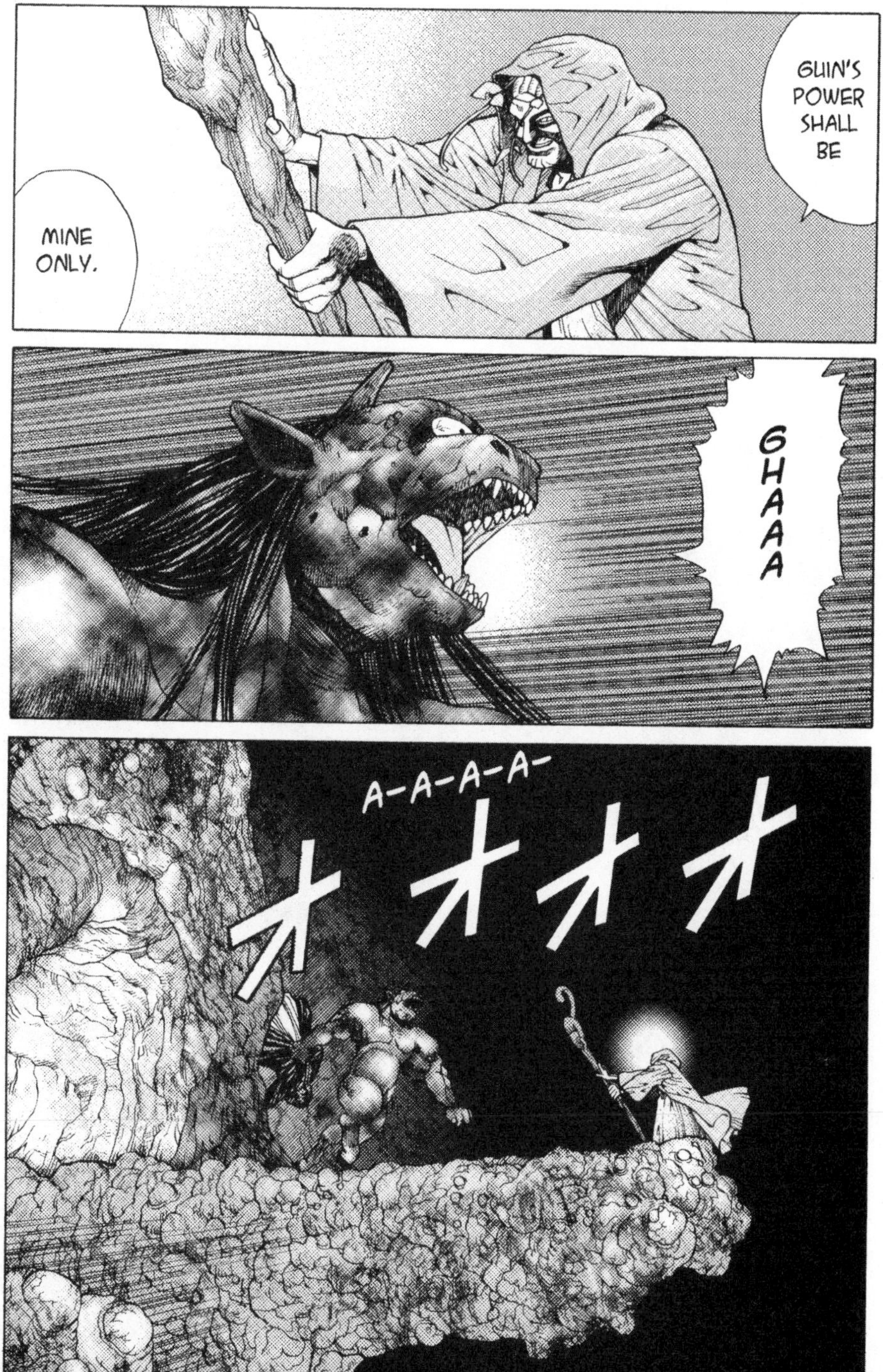
GUIN'S POWER SHALL BE
MINE ONLY.
GHAAAA
A-A-A-A-
オオオオ

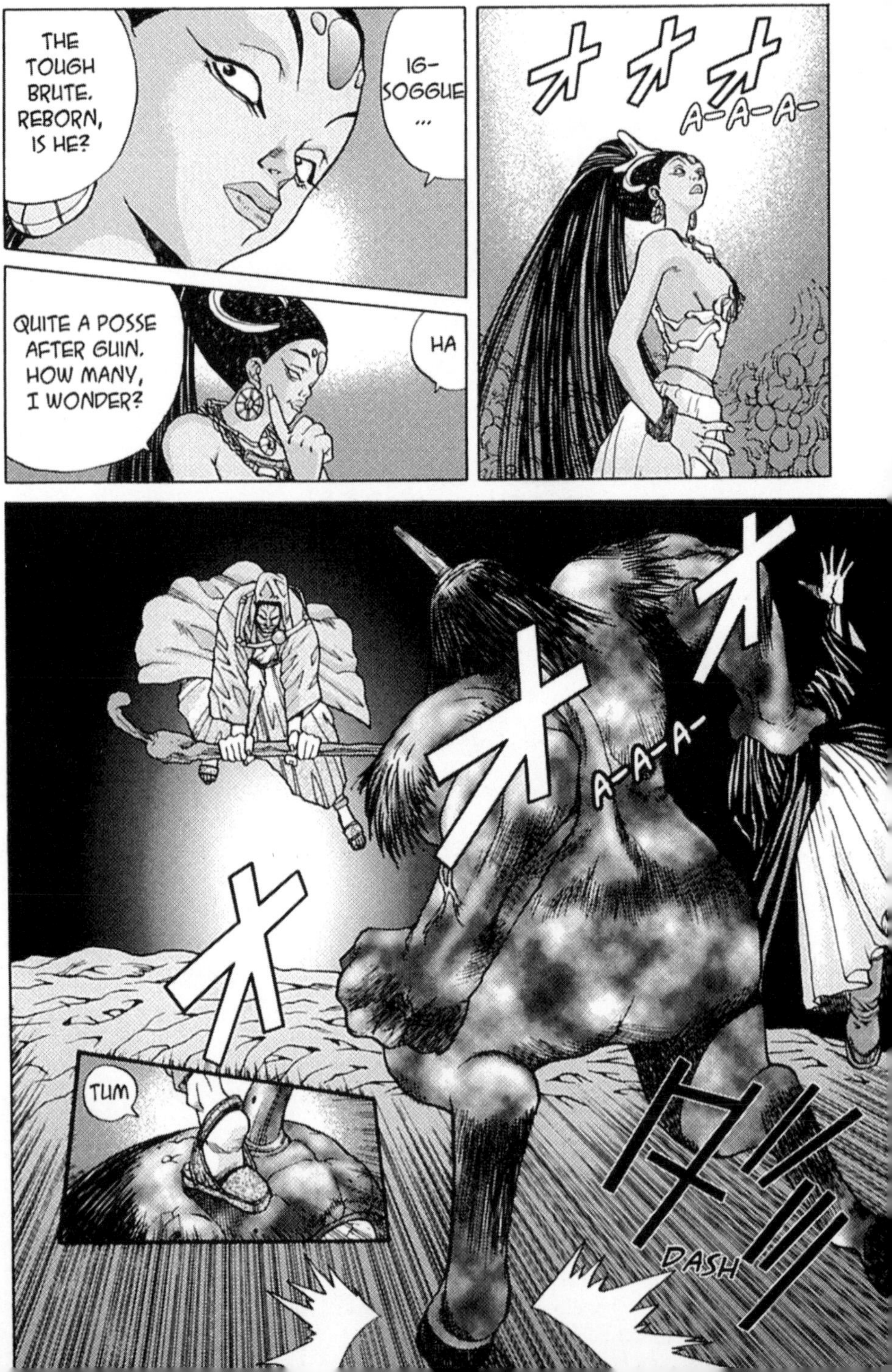
オオオ
A-A-A-
IG-SOGGUE ...
THE TOUGH BRUTE. REBORN, IS HE?
HA
QUITE A POSSE AFTER GUIN. HOW MANY, I WONDER?
オオオ
A-A-A-
ダッ
DASH
TUM

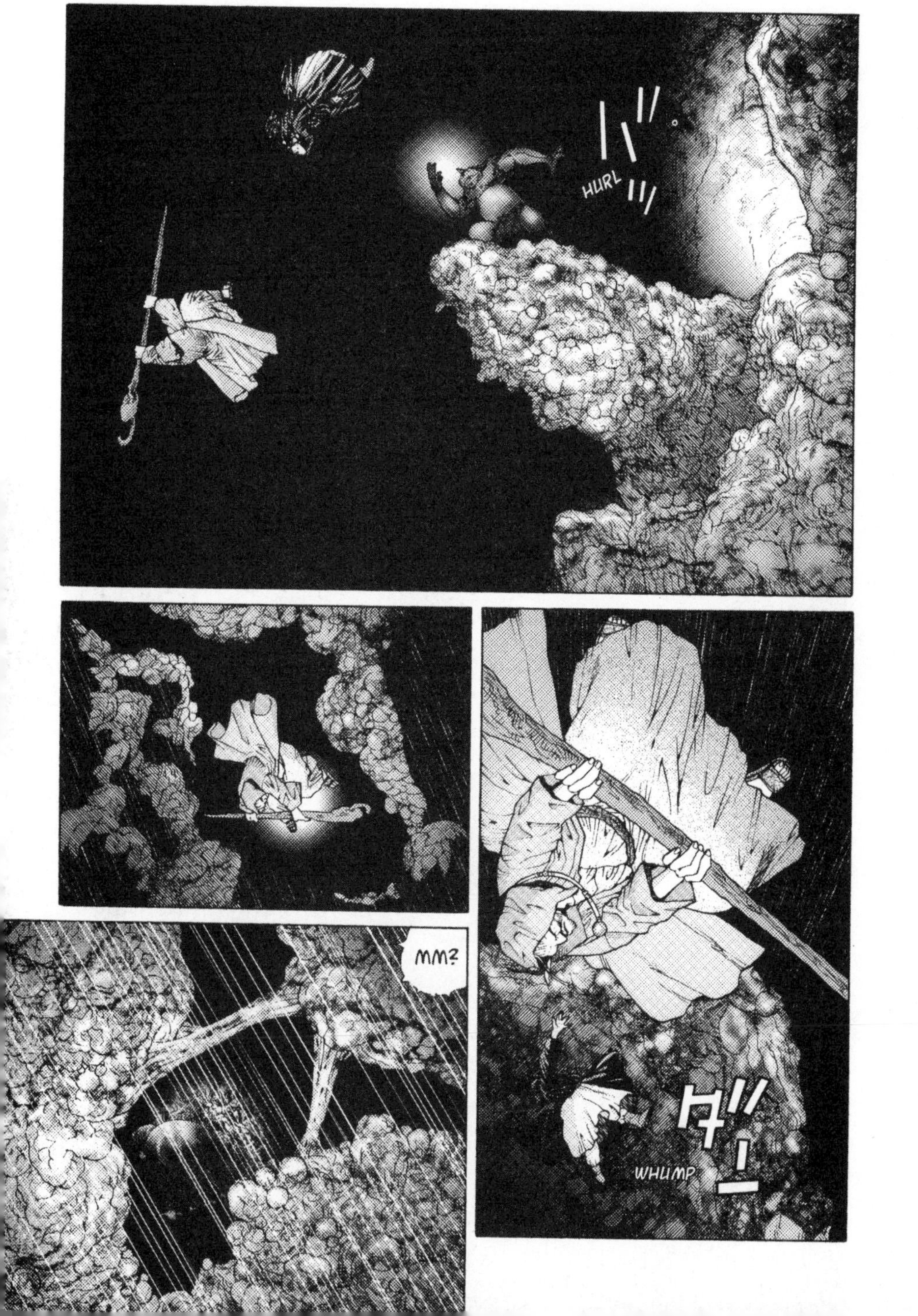
HURL
WHUMP
MM?

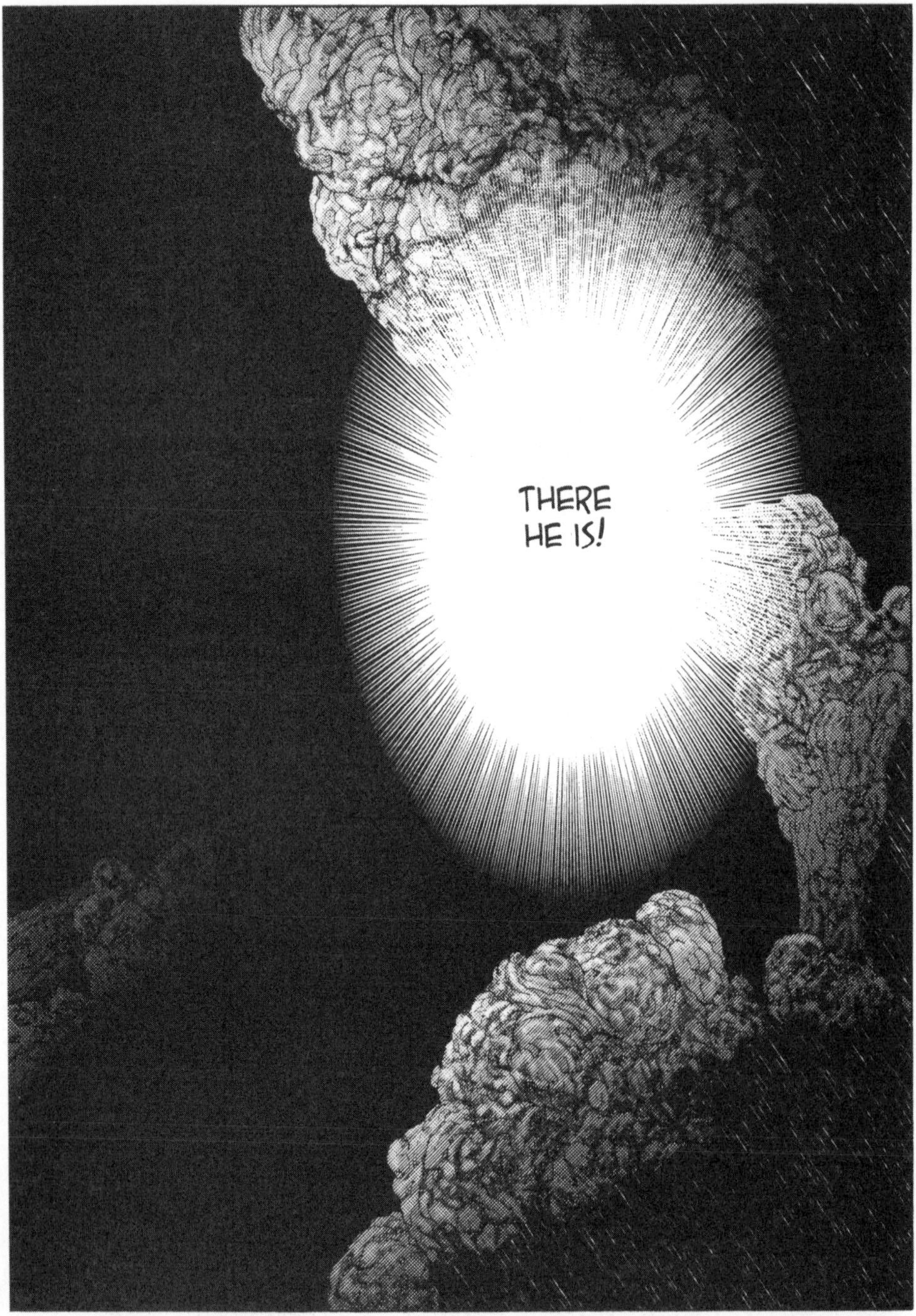
THERE HE IS!

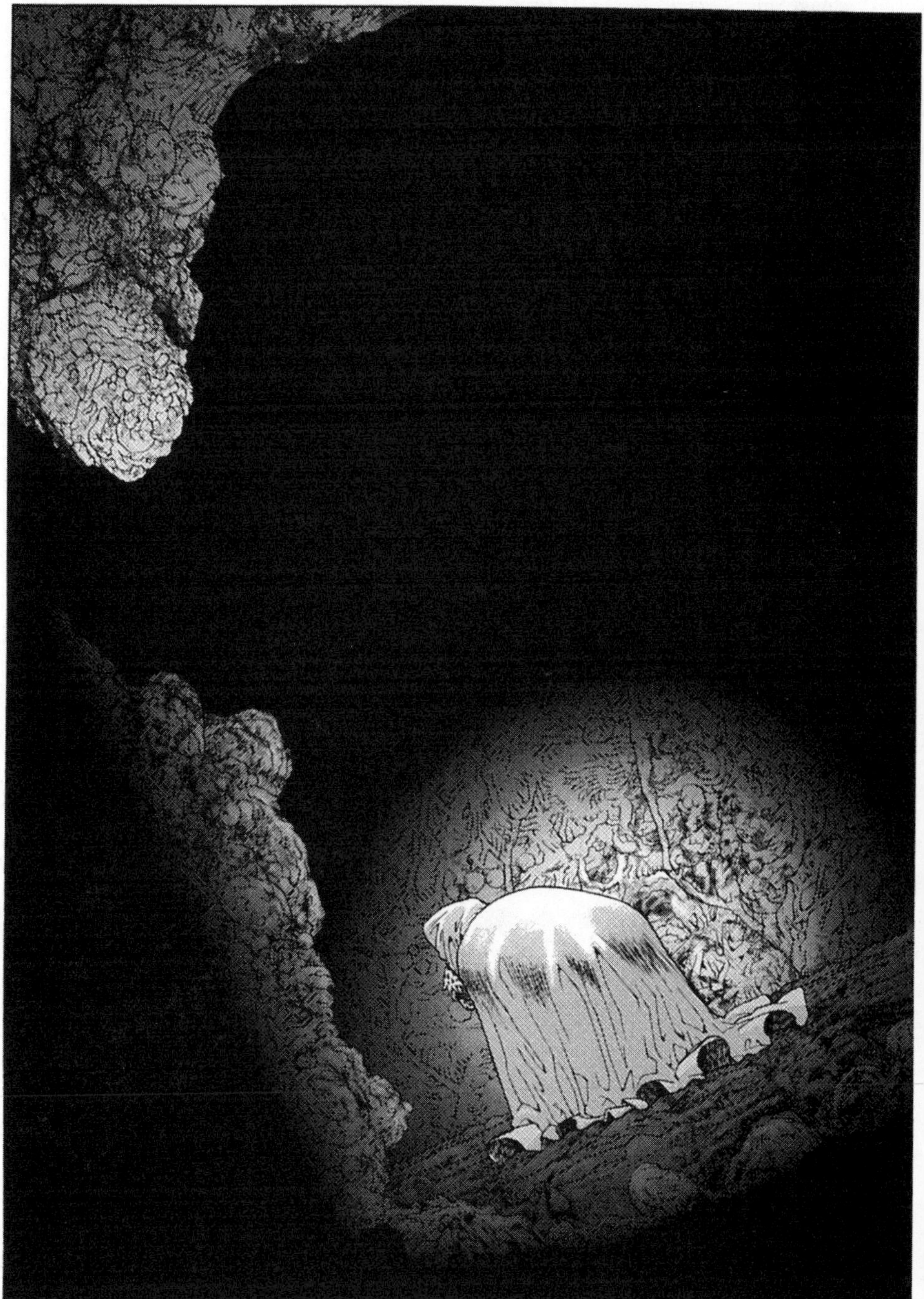

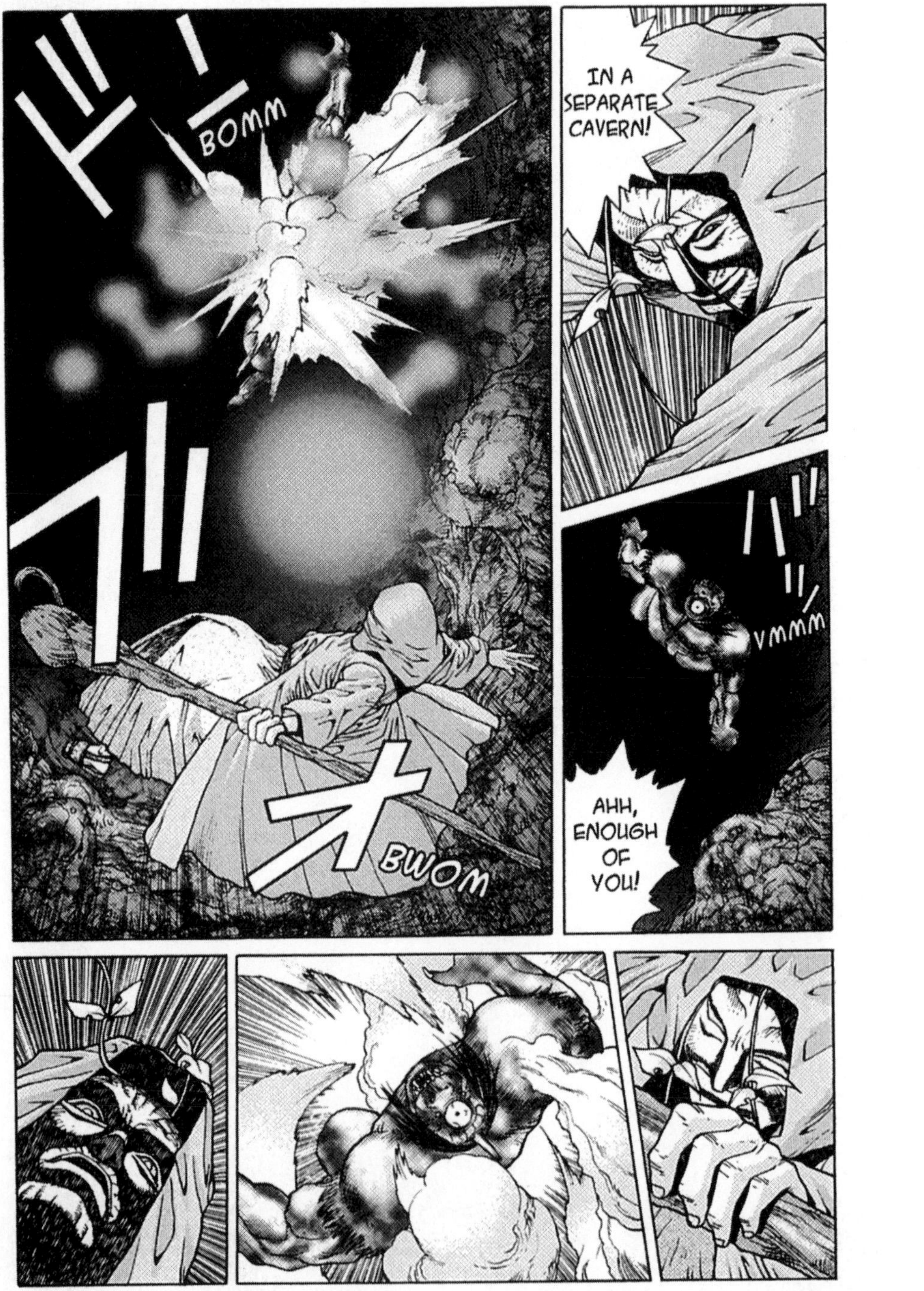
IN A SEPARATE CAVERN!
VMMM
AHH, ENOUGH OF YOU!
BOMM
BWOM

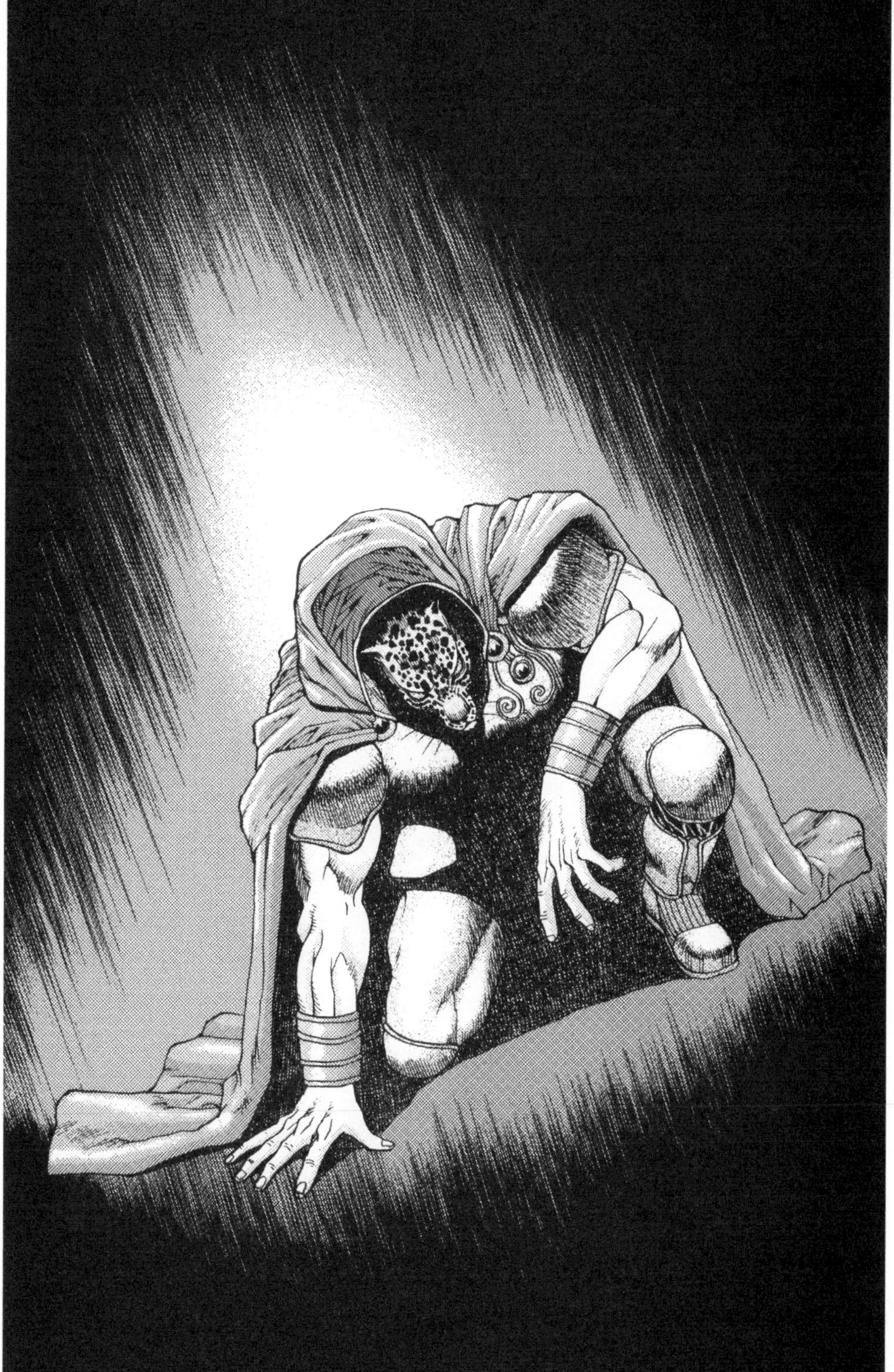

NOW, WHY DON'T YOU QUIT BEING KING?
WHY NOT LIVE EASY? I COULD HELP.
EIRAXA.

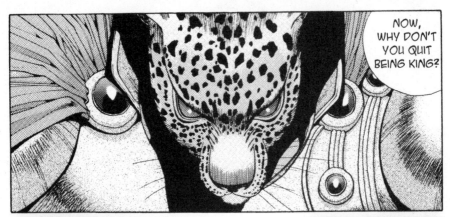

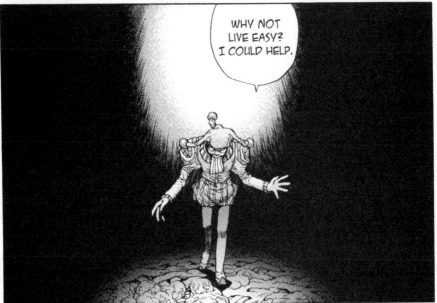

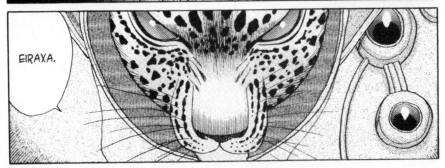

CHAPTER 17

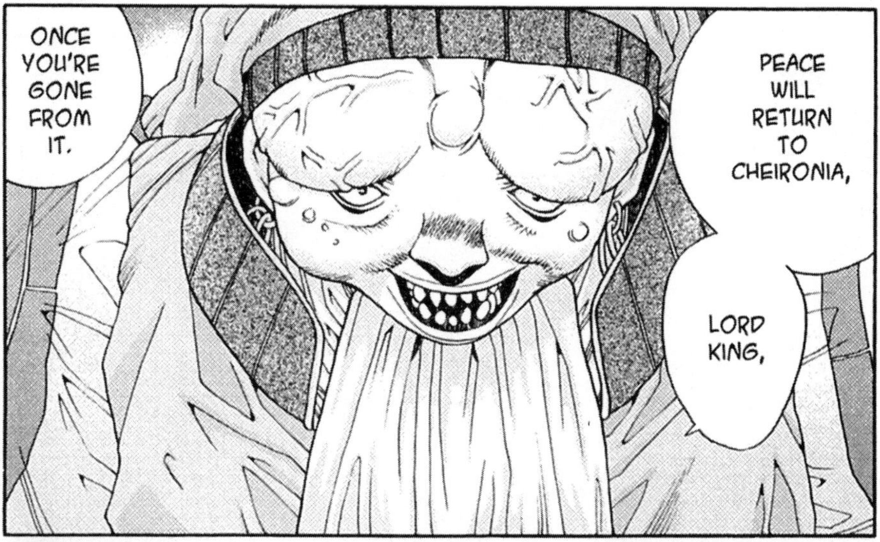
PEACE WILL RETURN TO CHEIRONIA,
LORD KING,
ONCE YOU'RE GONE FROM IT.

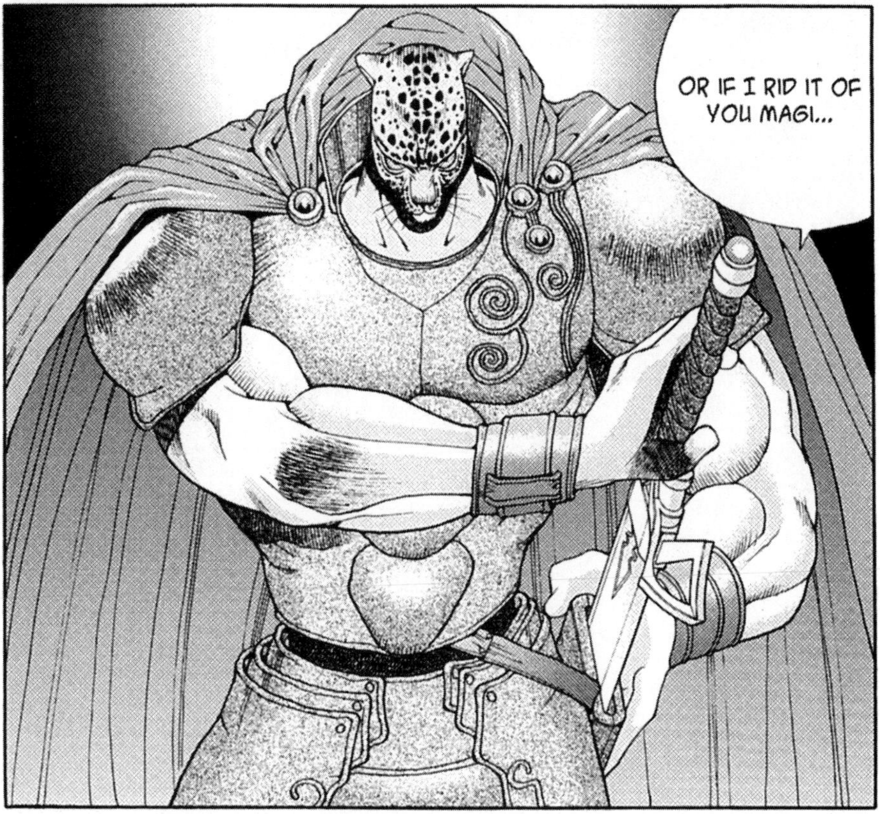
OR IF I RID IT OF YOU MAGI...

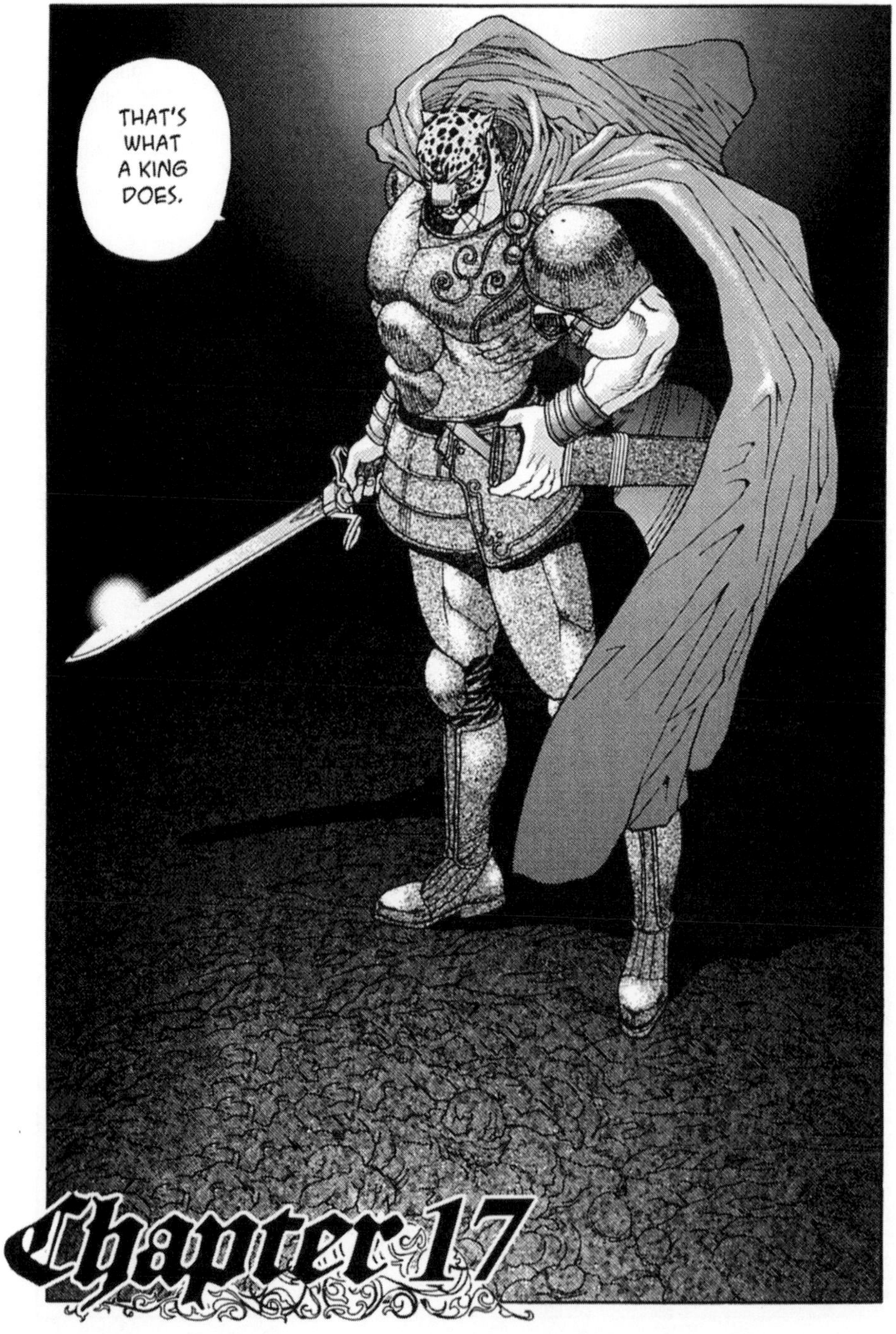
THAT'S WHAT A KING DOES.

Chapter 17

GUSH

THUMP

HM!

IT'S STARTED TO SPREAD!

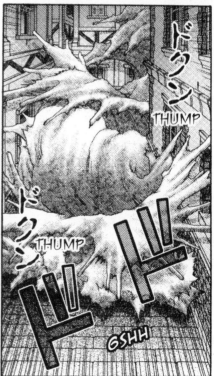

THUMP

THUMP

GSHH

THUMP

GUSH

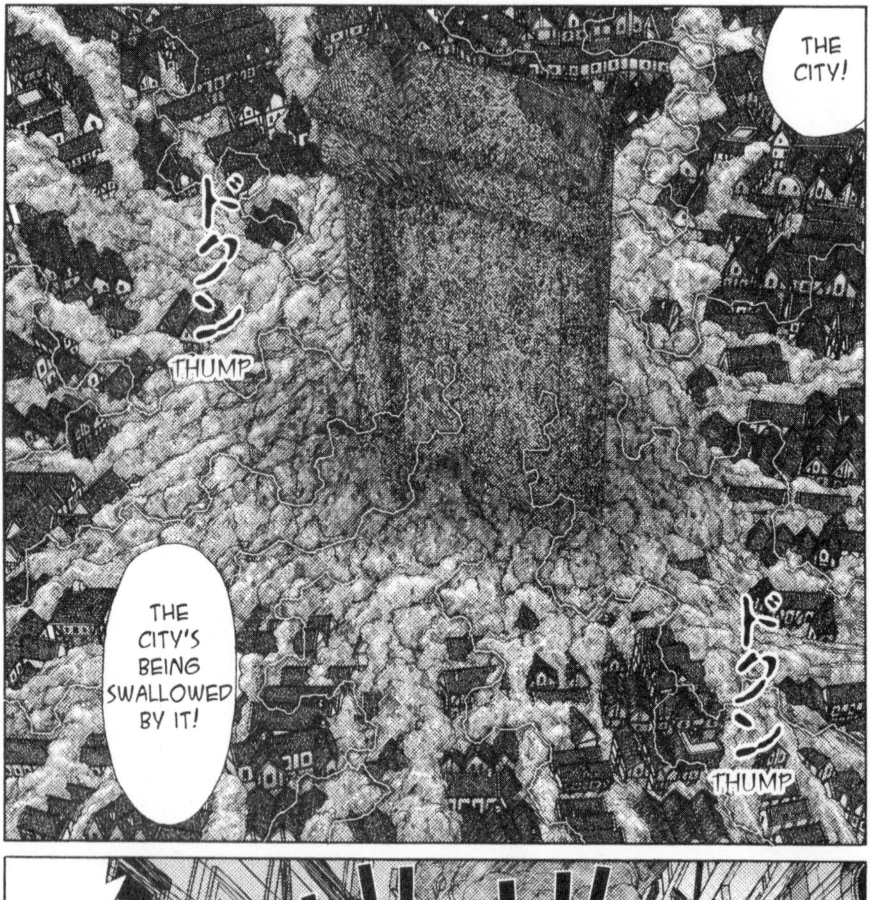
THE CITY!
THUMP
THE CITY'S BEING SWALLOWED BY IT!
THUMP

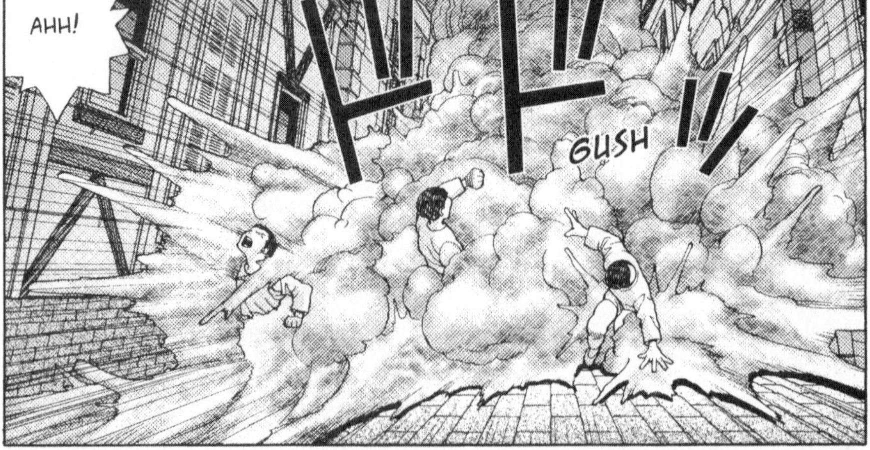
ドドドッ
GUSH
AHH!

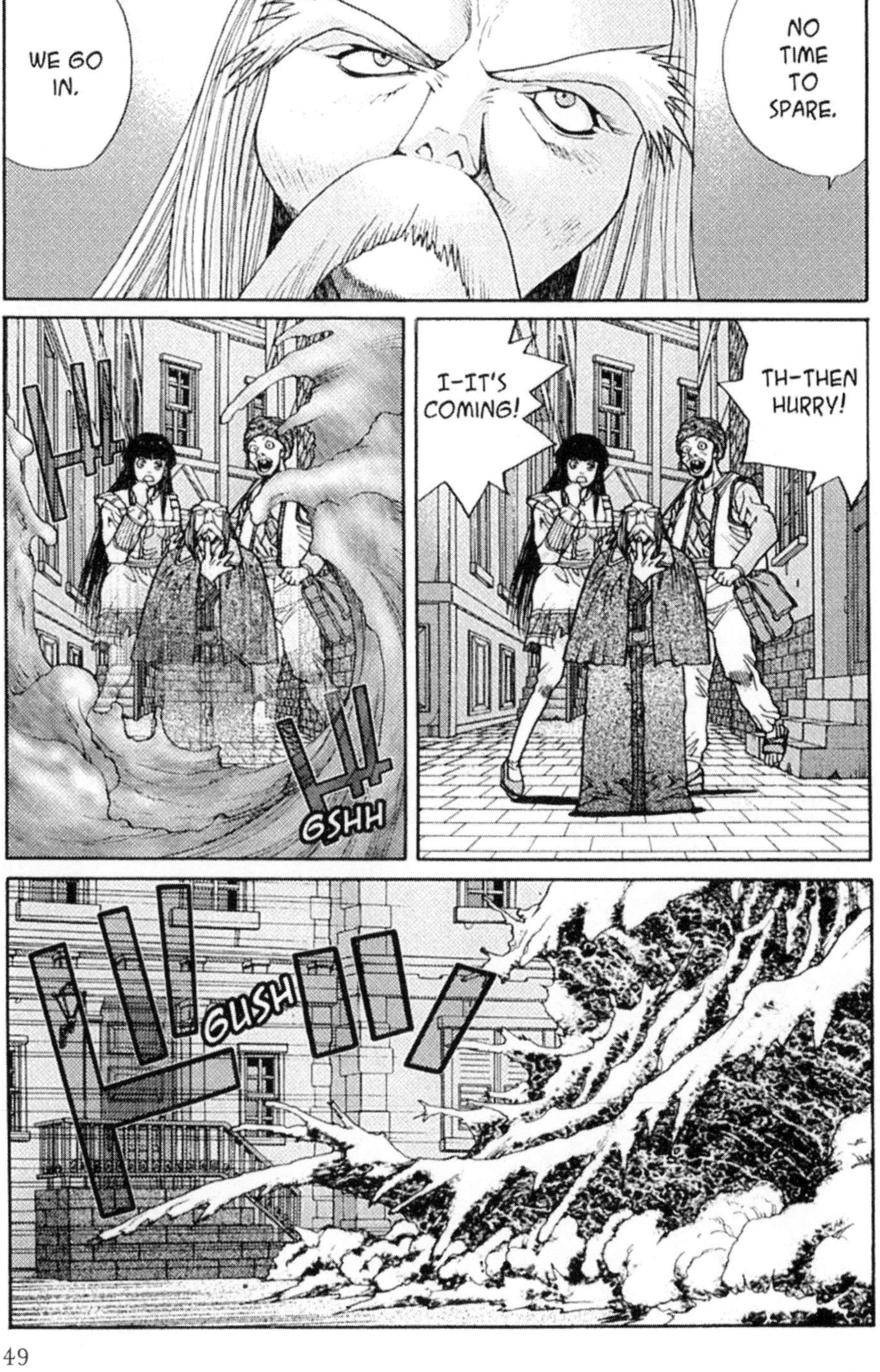
NO TIME TO SPARE.
WE GO IN.
TH-THEN HURRY!
I-IT'S COMING!
GSHH
GUSH

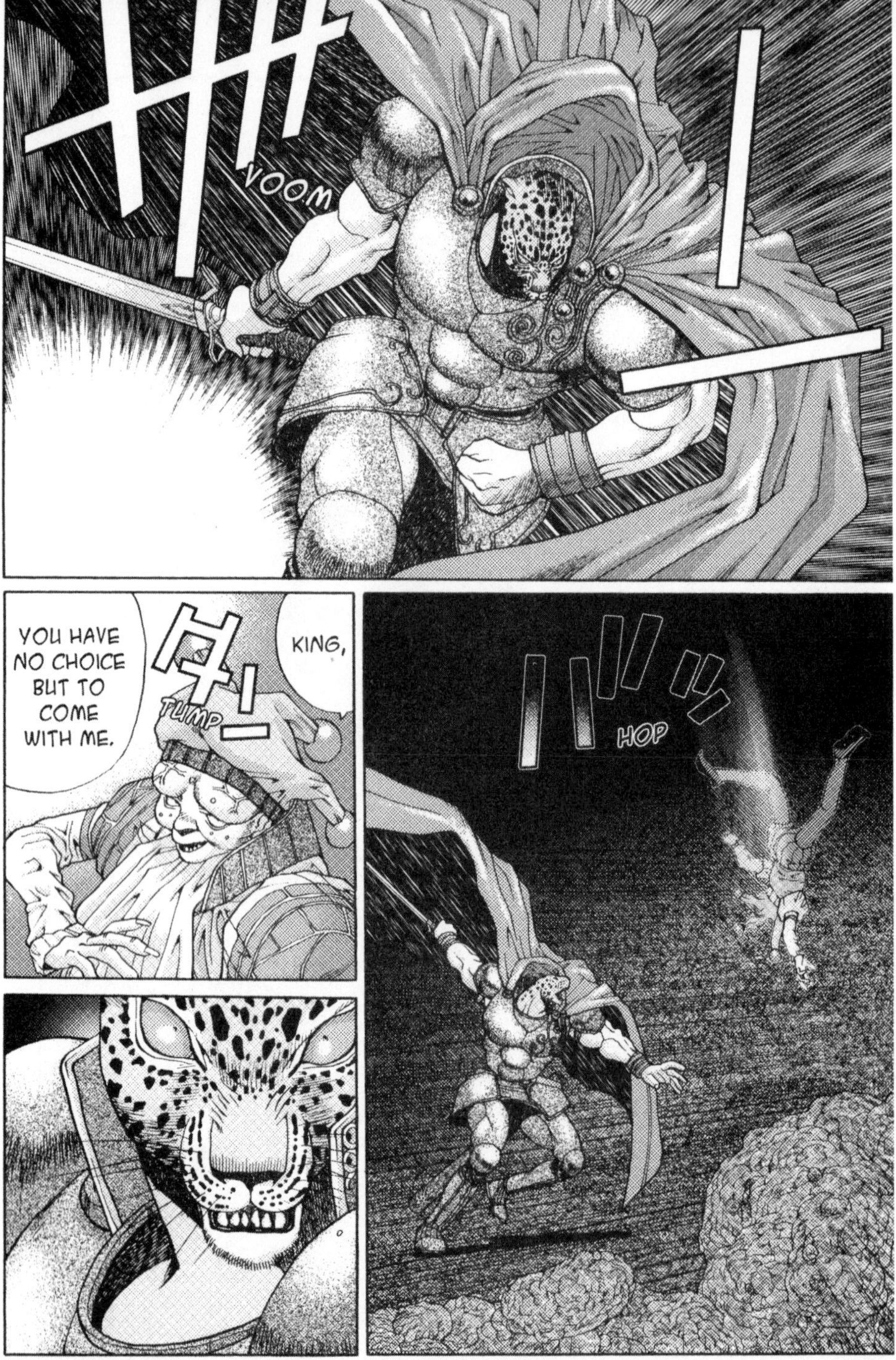
VOOM
HOP
KING,
TUMP
YOU HAVE NO CHOICE BUT TO COME WITH ME.

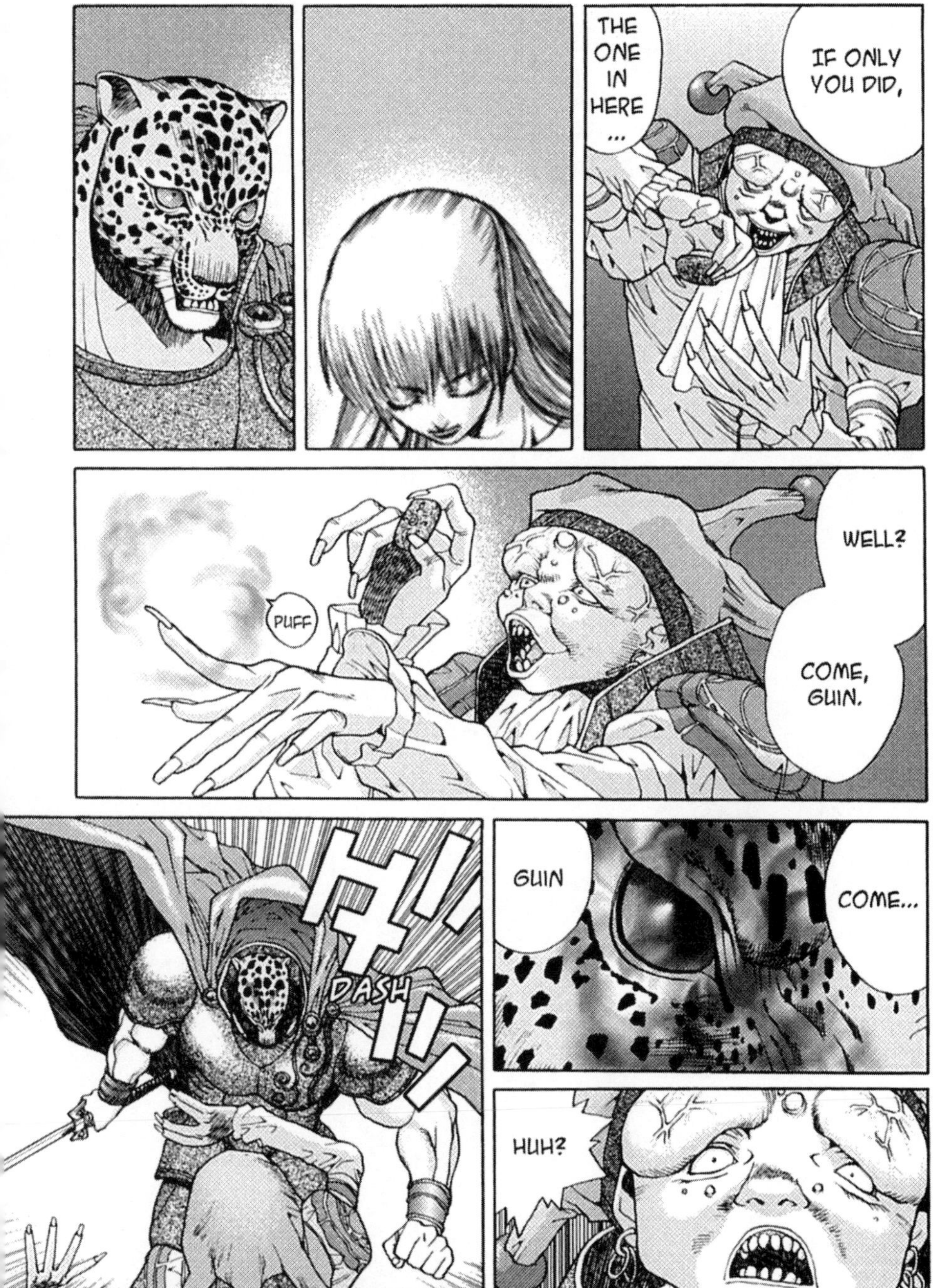

IF ONLY YOU DID,
THE ONE IN HERE ...
WELL?
COME, GUIN.
PUFF
COME...
GUIN
HUH?
DASH

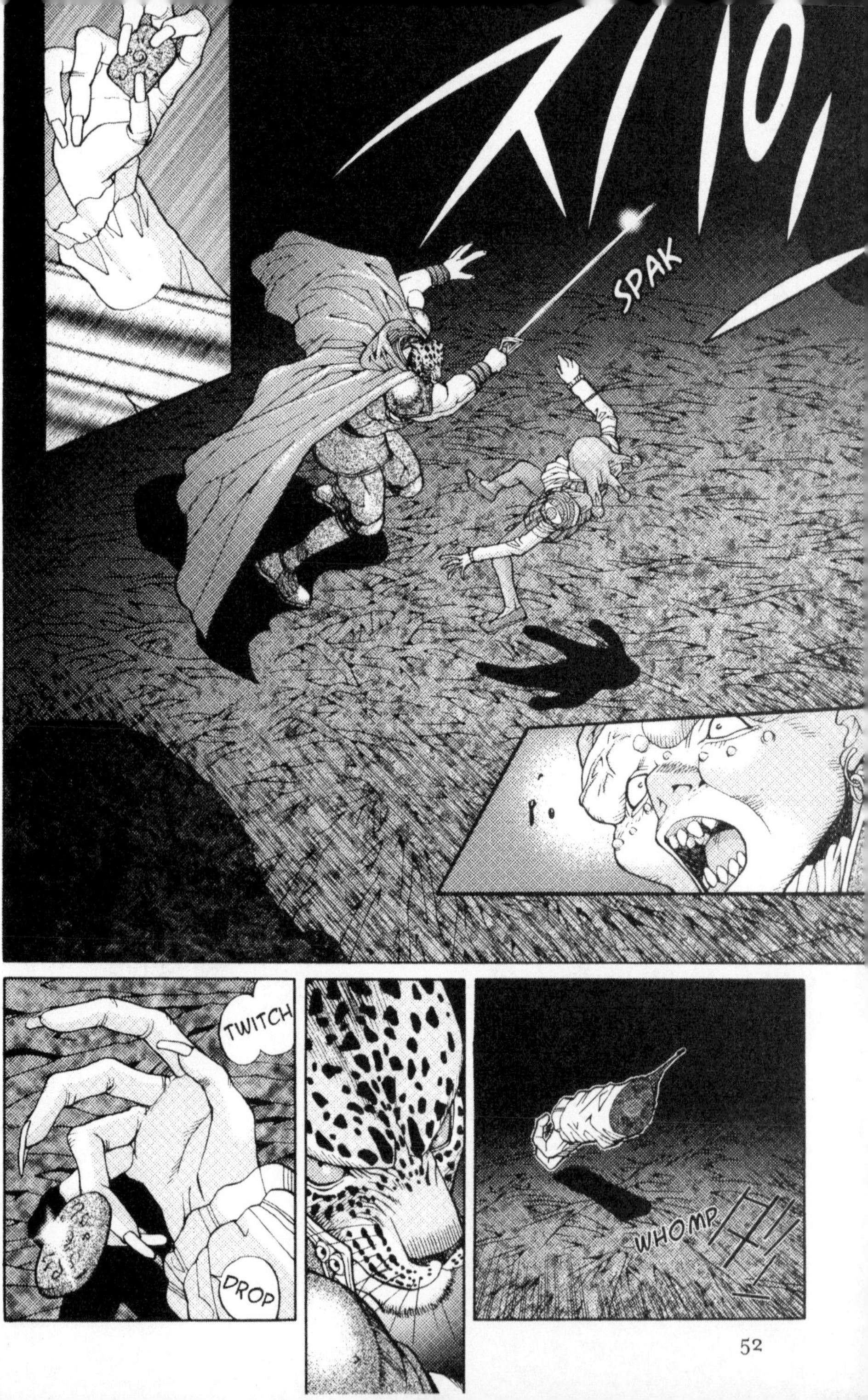
SPAK
WHOMP
TWITCH
DROP

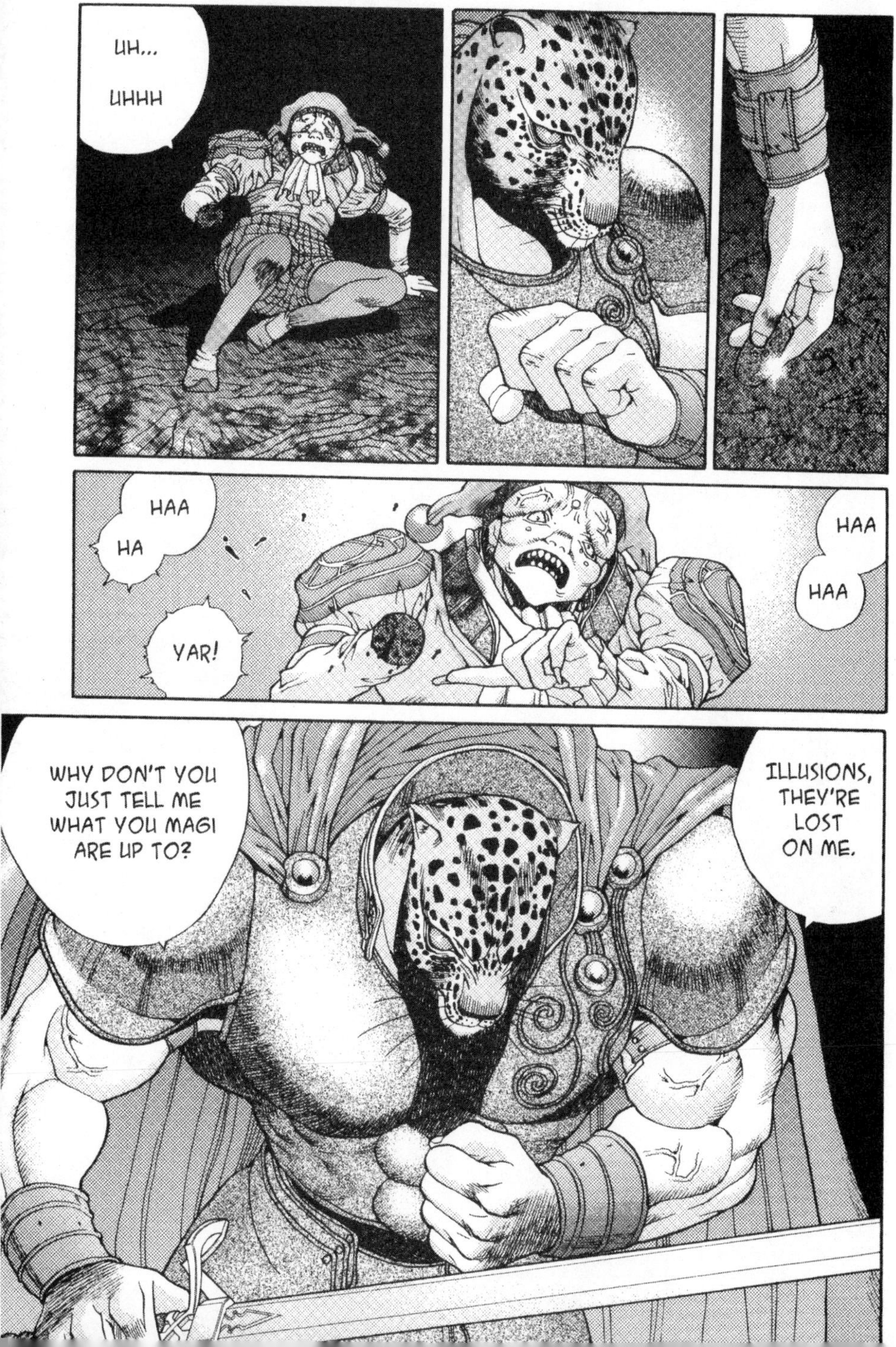
UH...
UHHH
HAA
HAA
HAA
HA
YAR!
ILLUSIONS, THEY'RE LOST ON ME.
WHY DON'T YOU JUST TELL ME WHAT YOU MAGI ARE UP TO?

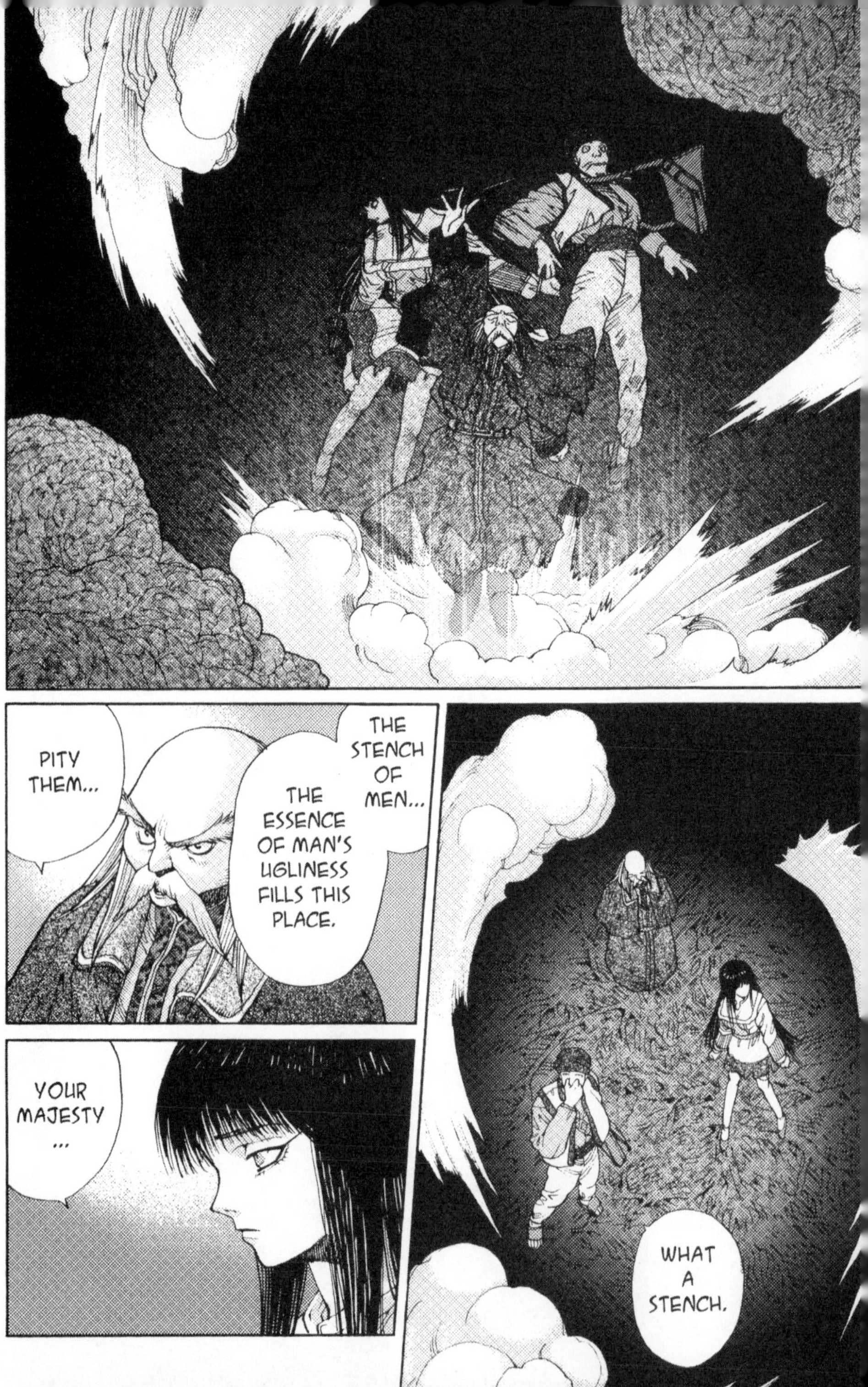

WHAT A STENCH.
THE STENCH OF MEN...
THE ESSENCE OF MAN'S UGLINESS FILLS THIS PLACE.
PITY THEM...
YOUR MAJESTY ...

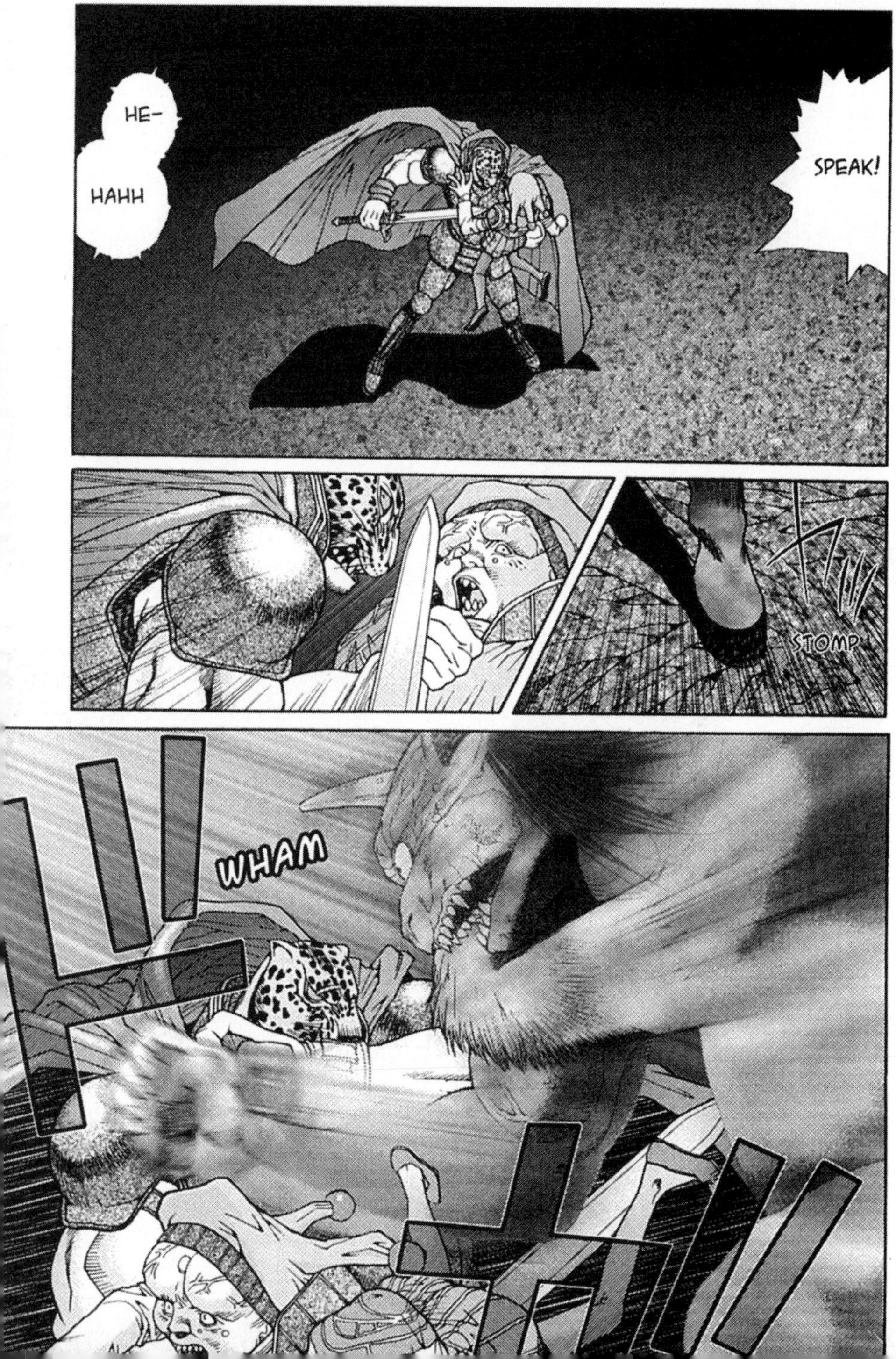
SPEAK!
HE-
HAHH
STOMP
WHAM

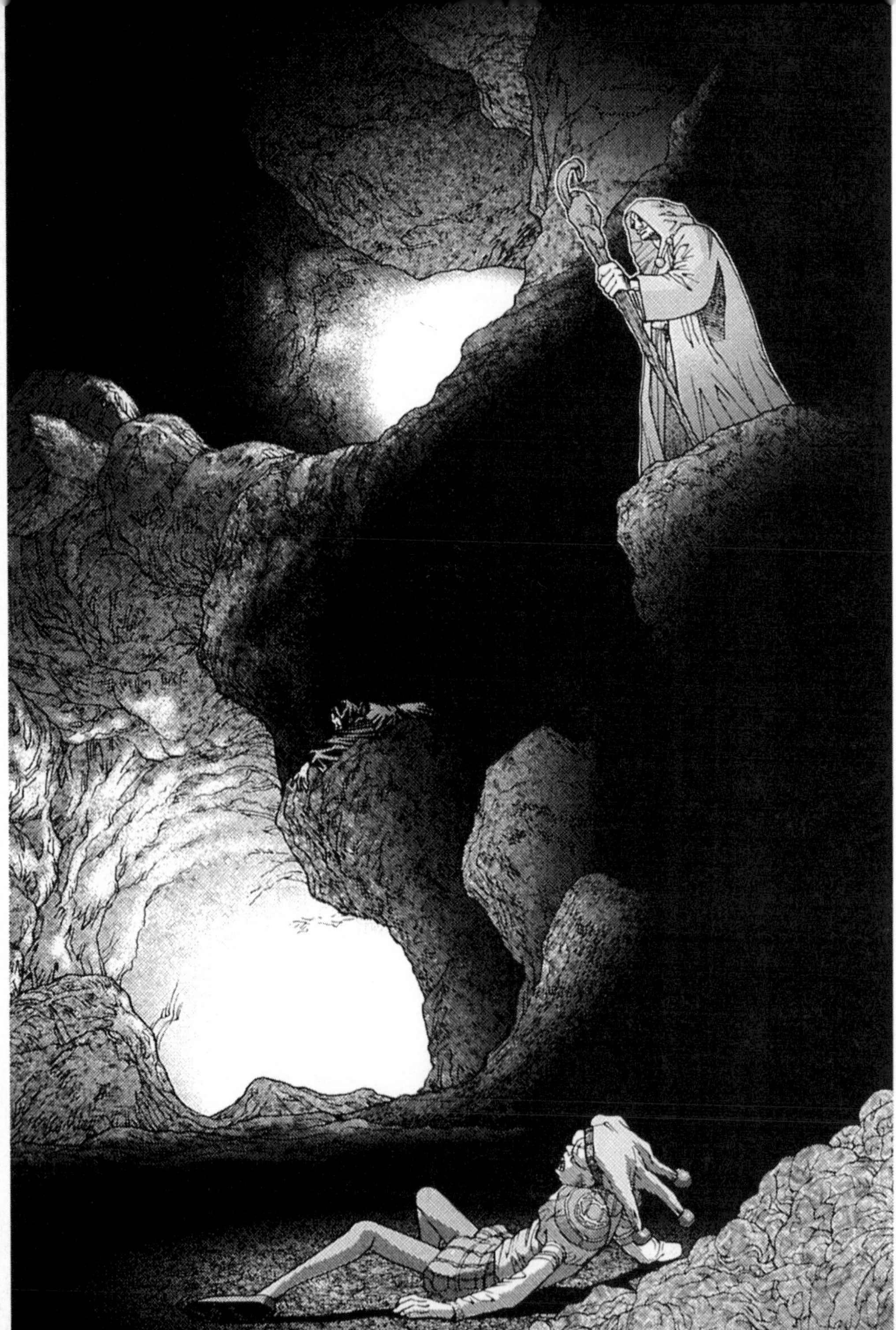

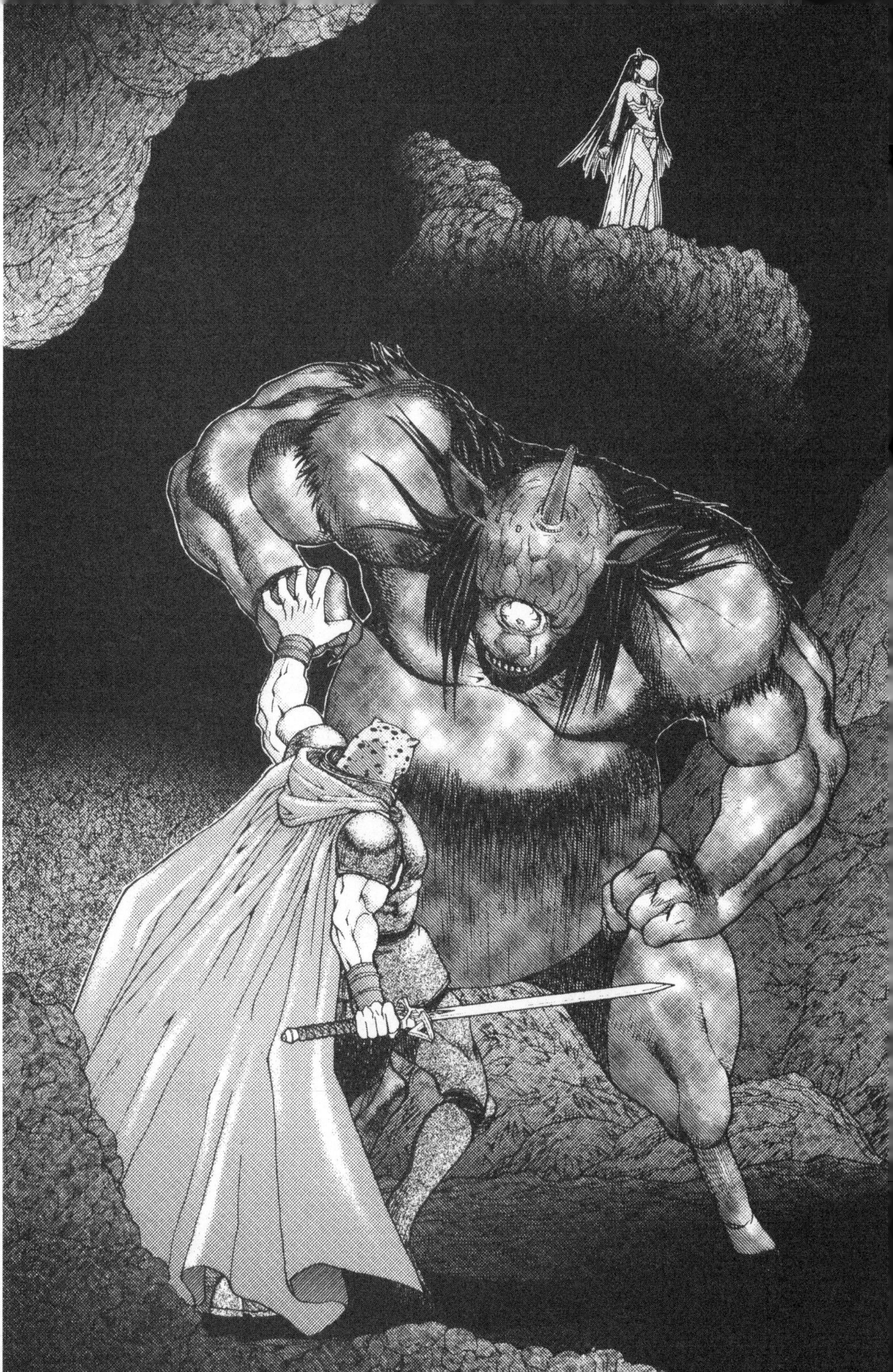

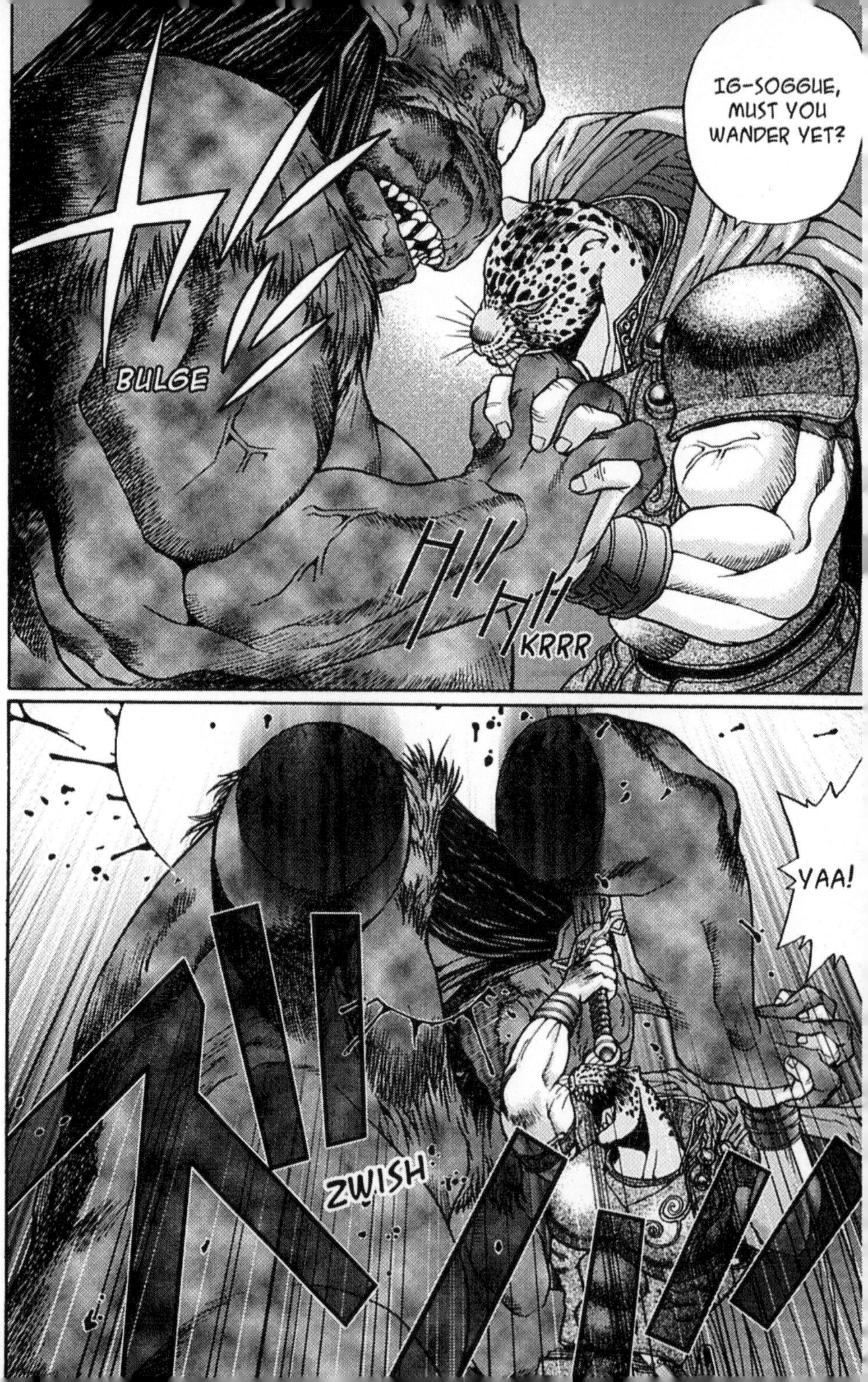
IG-SOGGUE, MUST YOU WANDER YET?
BULGE
KRRR
YAA!
ZWISH

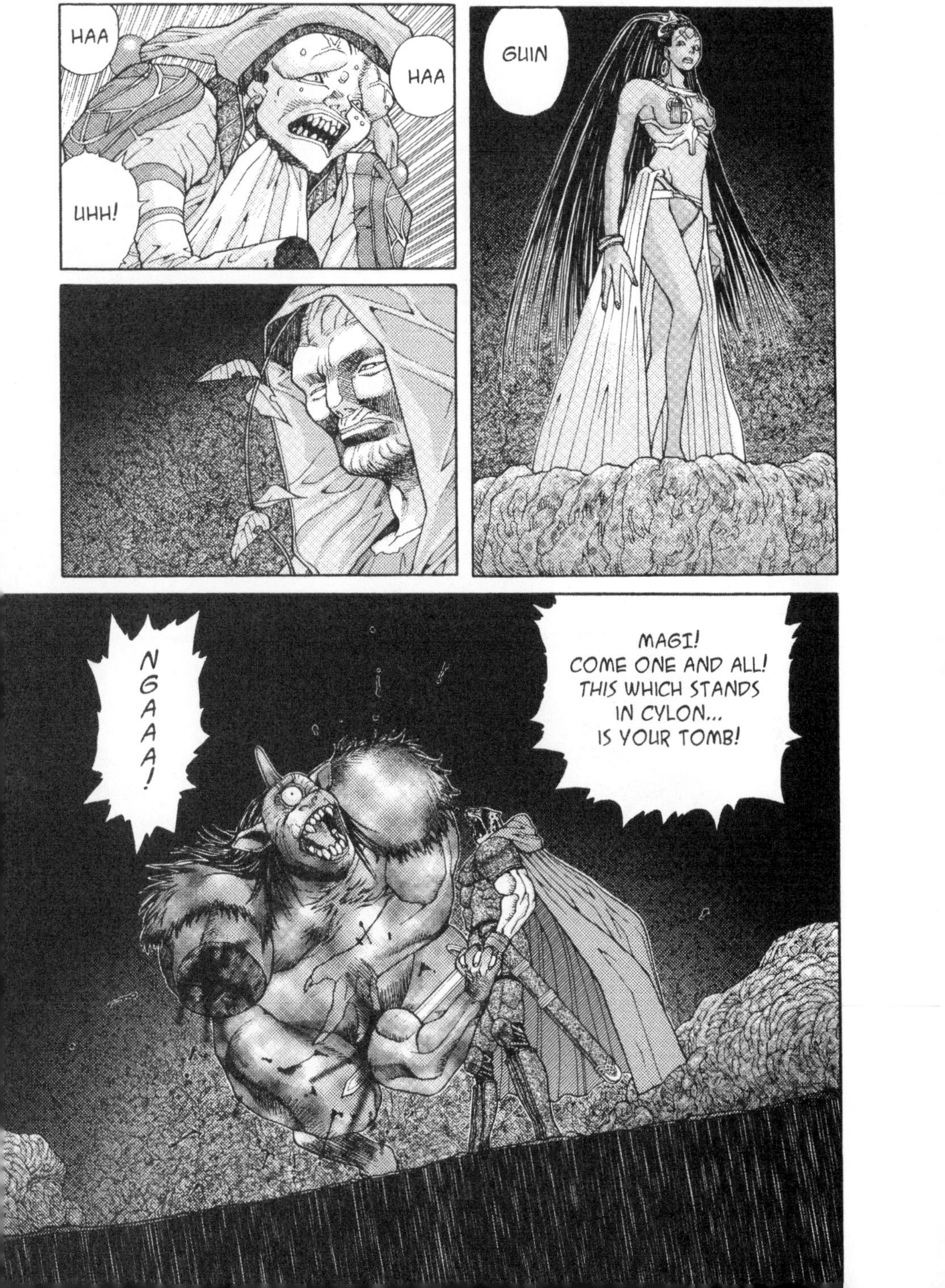
GUIN
HAA
HAA
UHH!
MAGI! COME ONE AND ALL! THIS WHICH STANDS IN CYLON... IS YOUR TOMB!
NGAAAA!

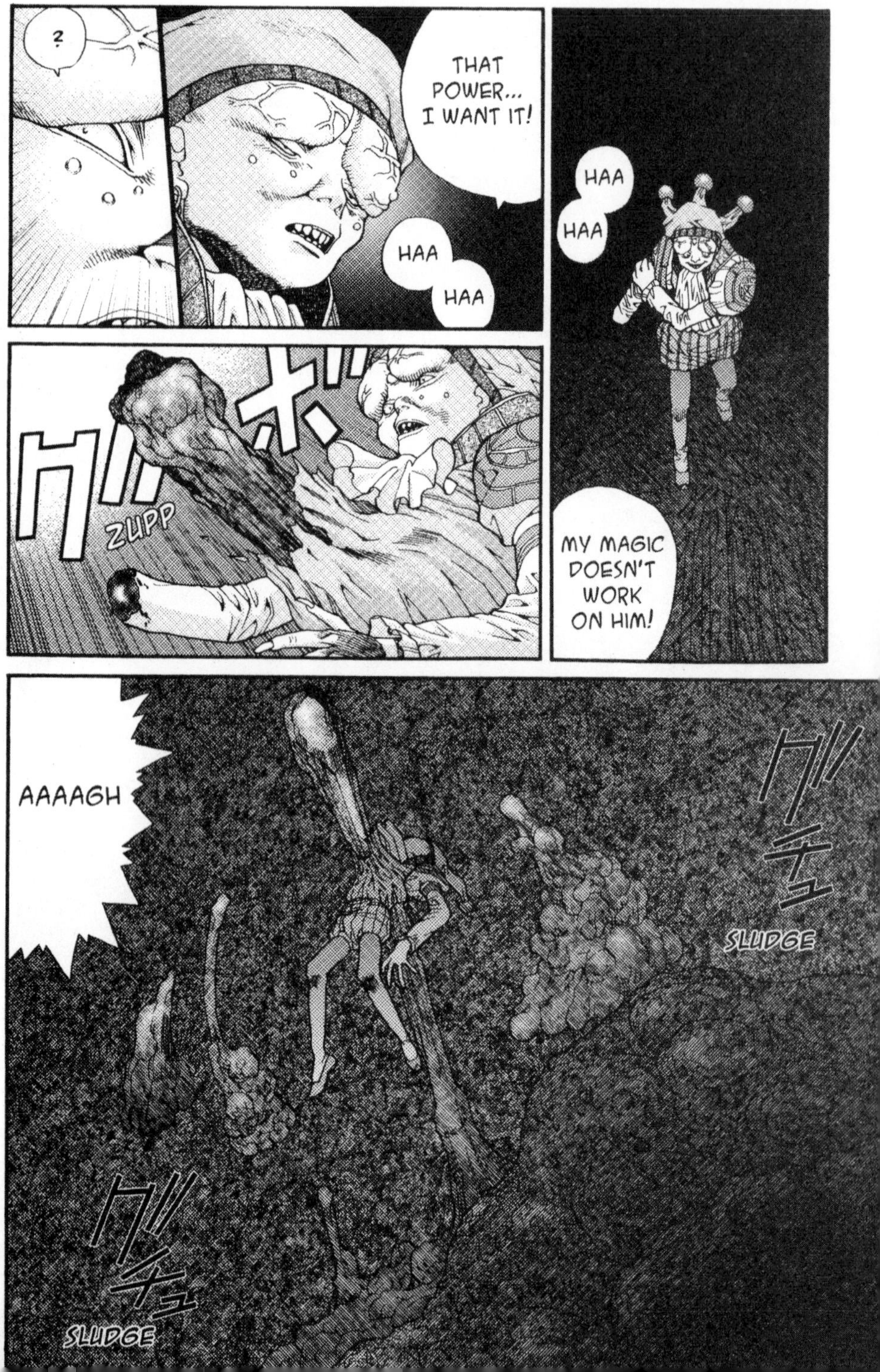
HAA
HAA
MY MAGIC DOESN'T WORK ON HIM!
?
THAT POWER... I WANT IT!
HAA
HAA
ZUPP
SLUDGE
AAAAGH
SLUDGE

CHAPTER 18

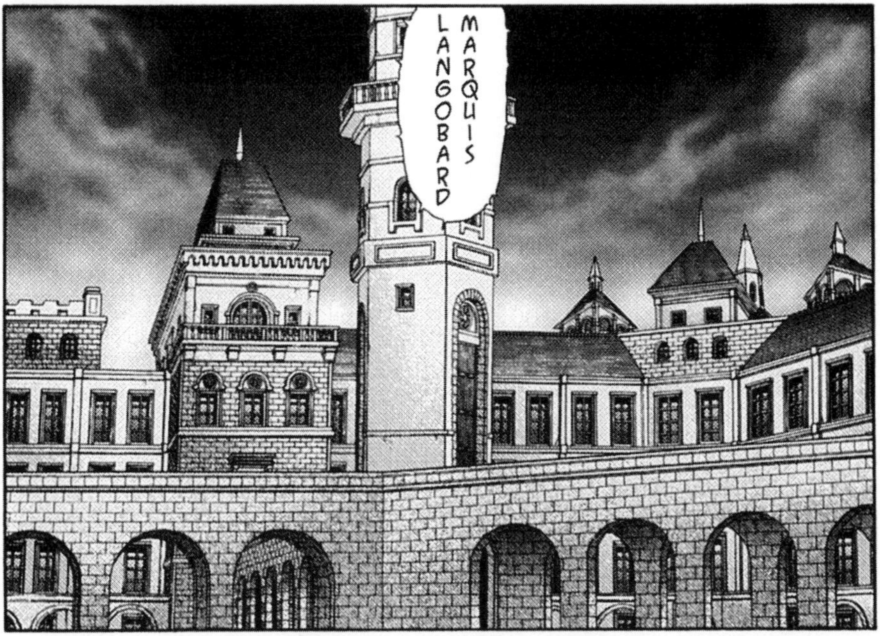
MARQUIS LANGOBARD

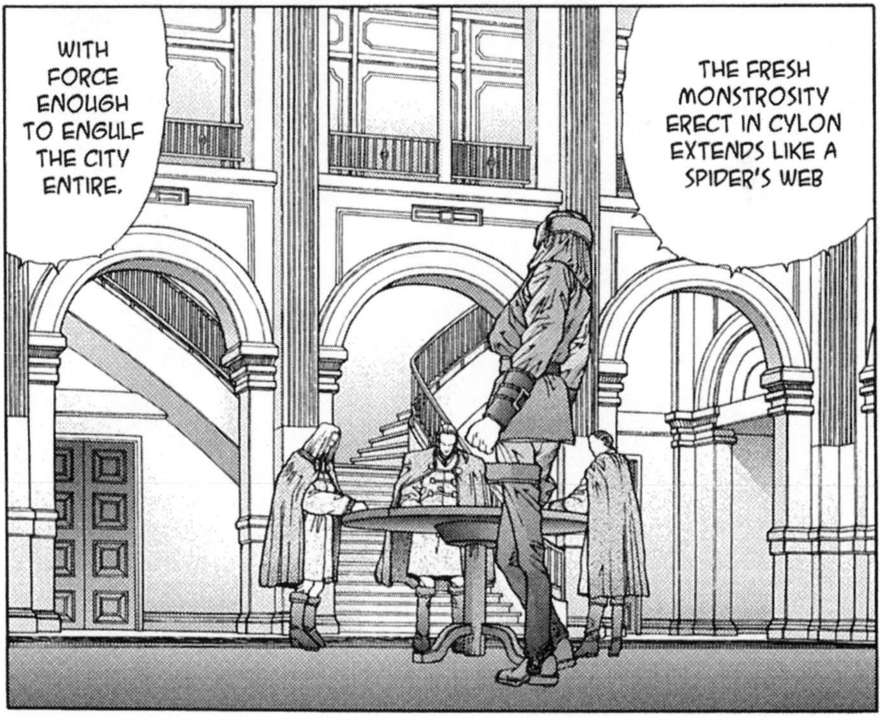
THE FRESH MONSTROSITY ERECT IN CYLON EXTENDS LIKE A SPIDER'S WEB
WITH FORCE ENOUGH TO ENGULF THE CITY ENTIRE.

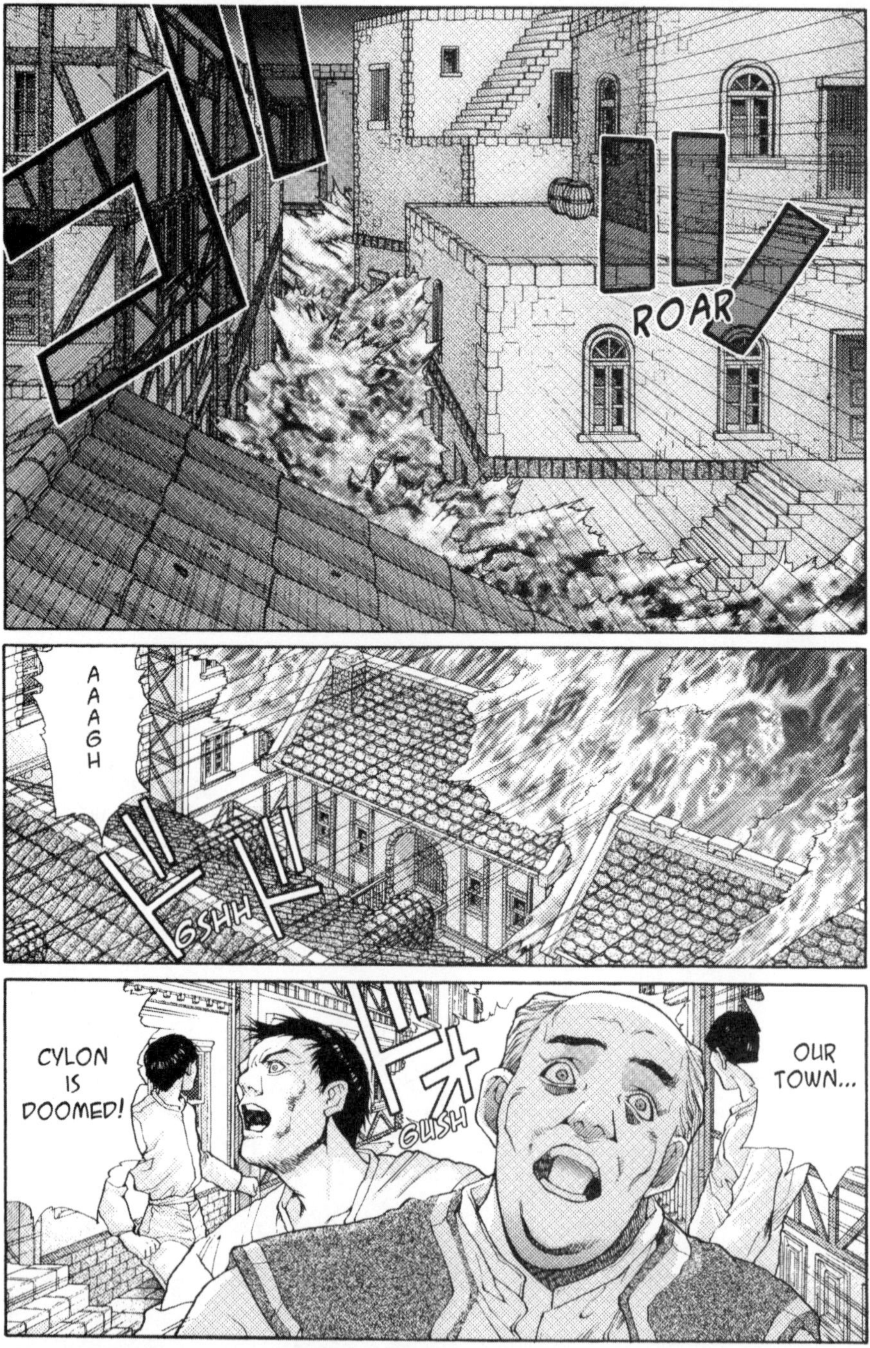
ROAR
AAAGH
GSHH
OUR TOWN...
GUSH
CYLON IS DOOMED!

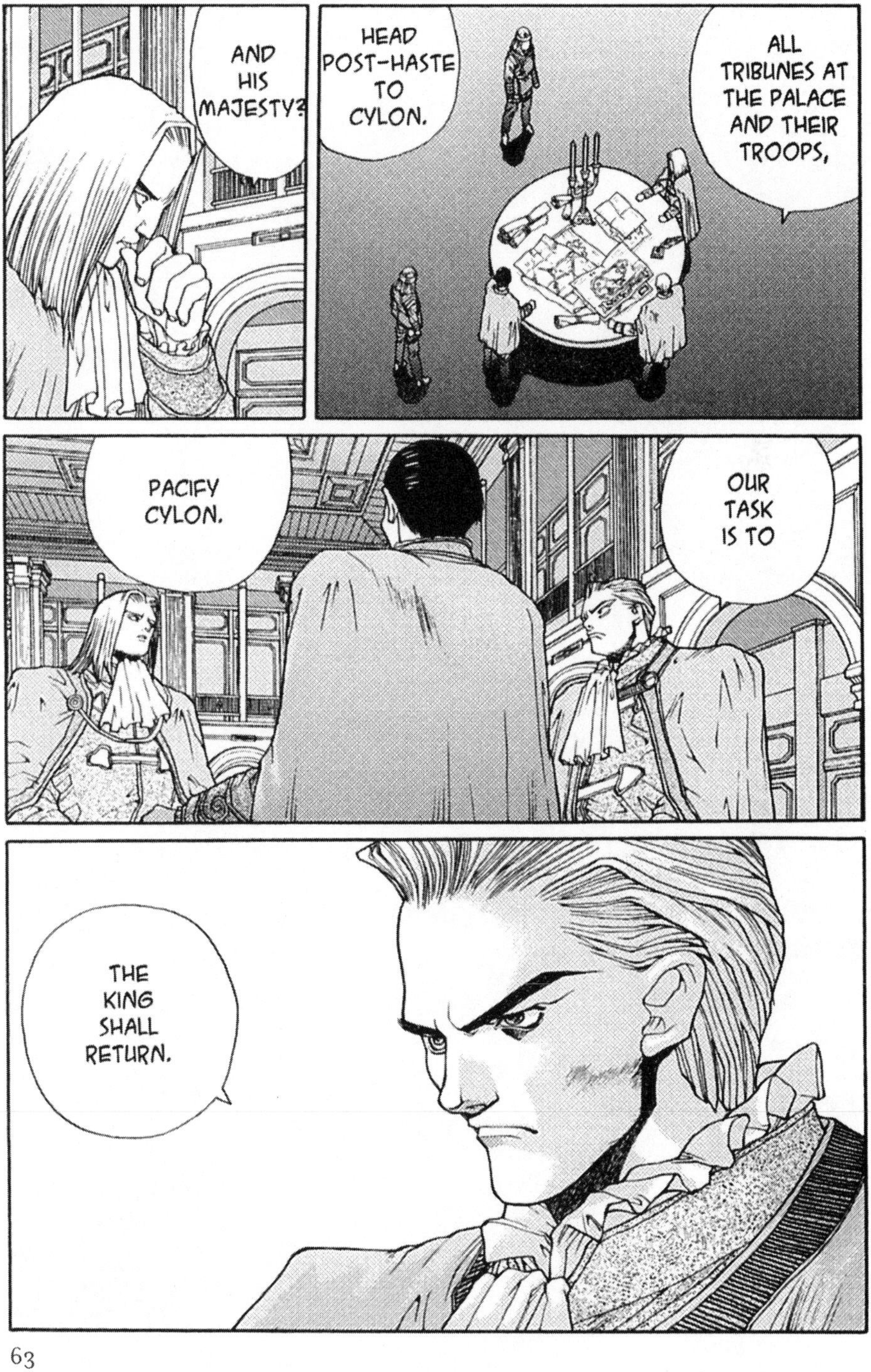
ALL TRIBUNES AT THE PALACE AND THEIR TROOPS,
HEAD POST-HASTE TO CYLON.
AND HIS MAJESTY?
OUR TASK IS TO
PACIFY CYLON.
THE KING SHALL RETURN.

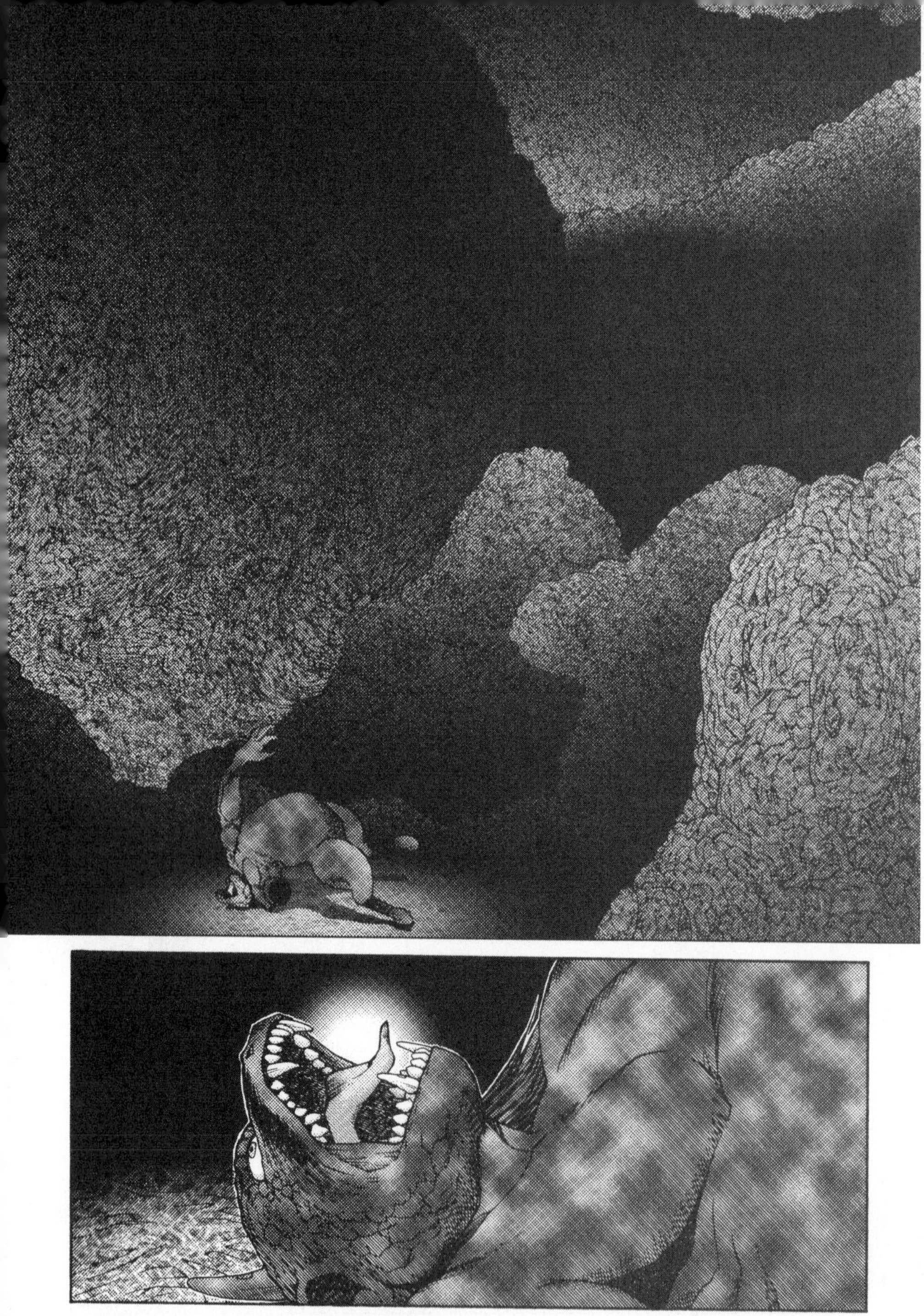

Chapter 18

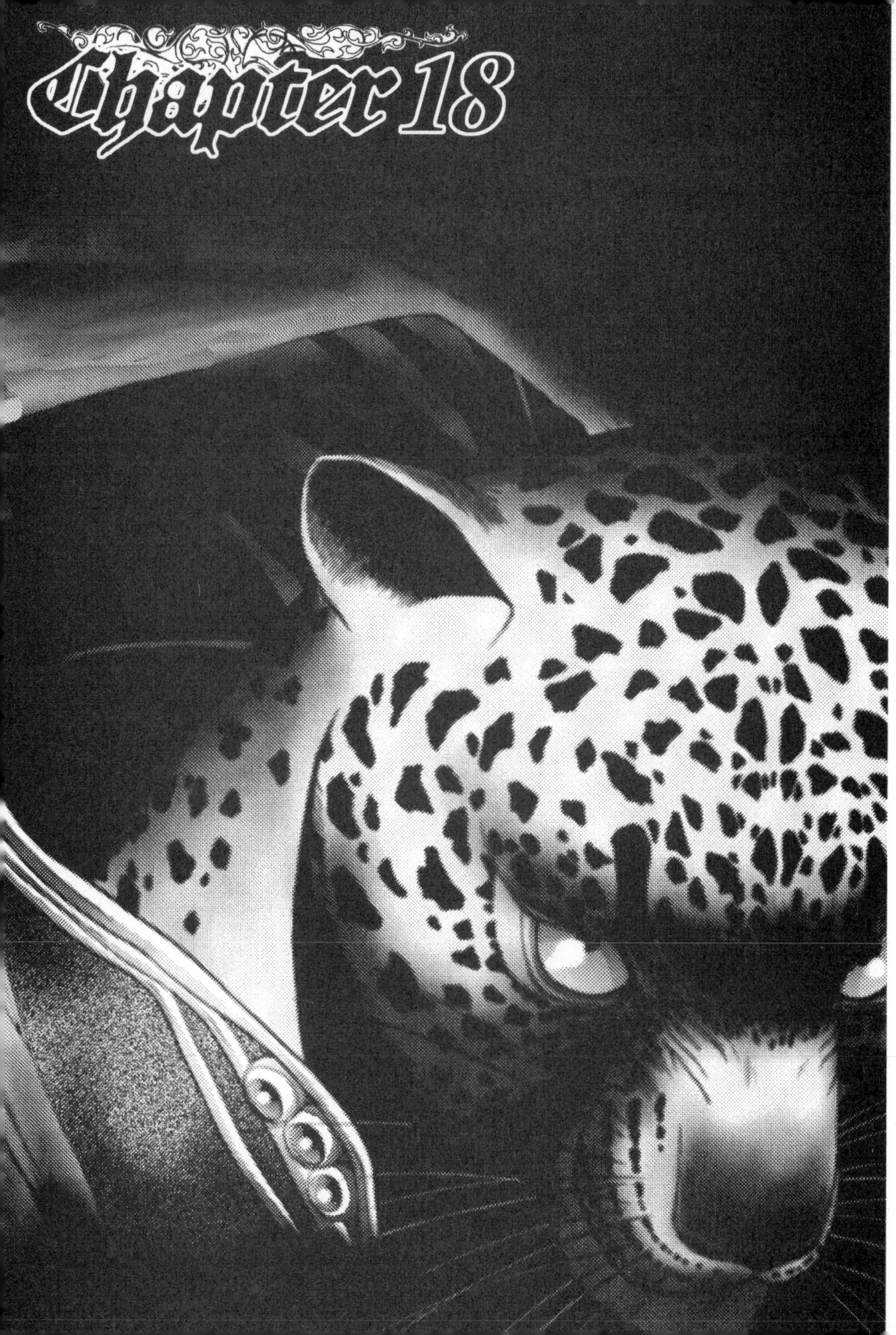

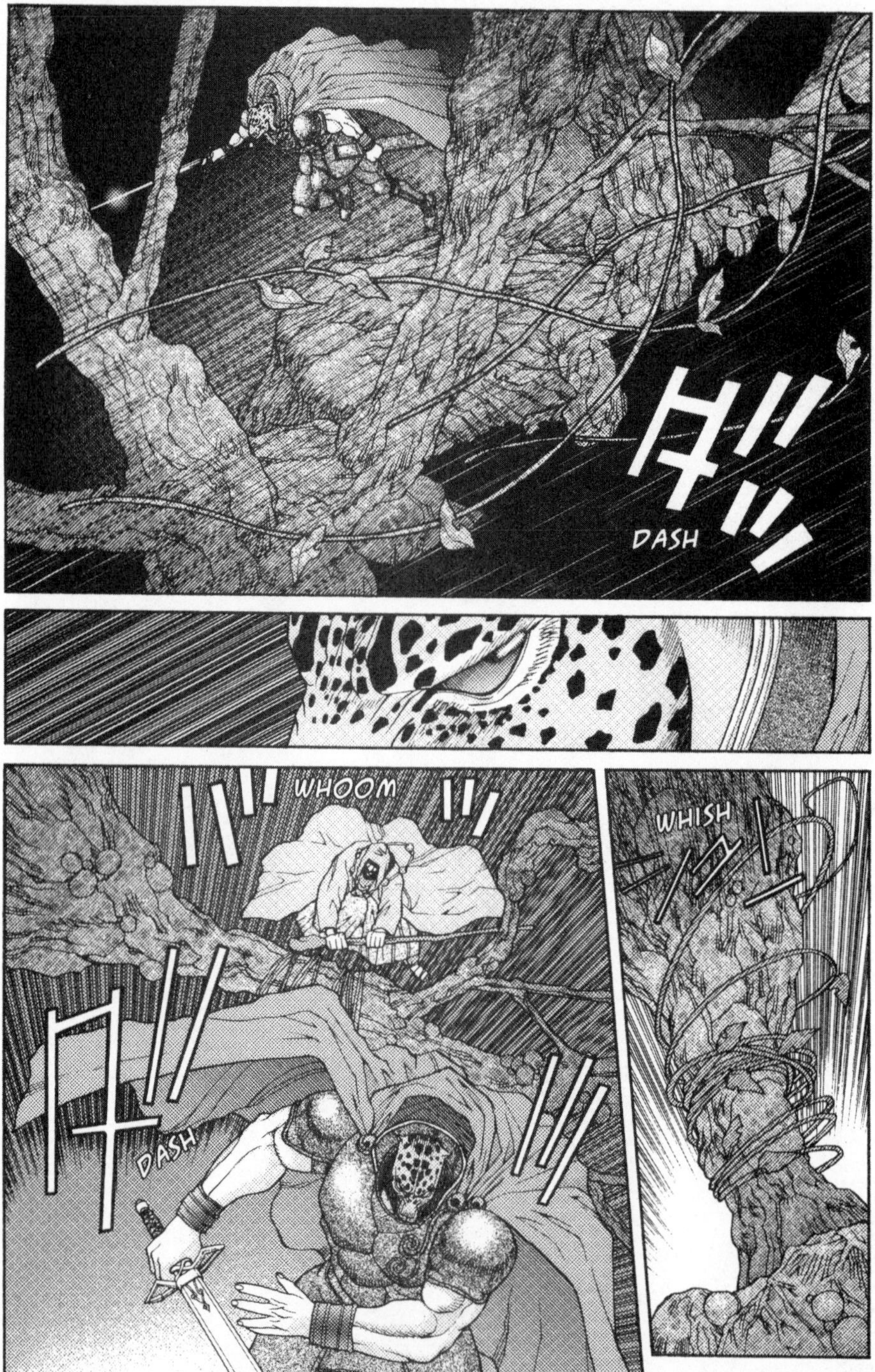
DASH
WHISH
WHOOM
DASH

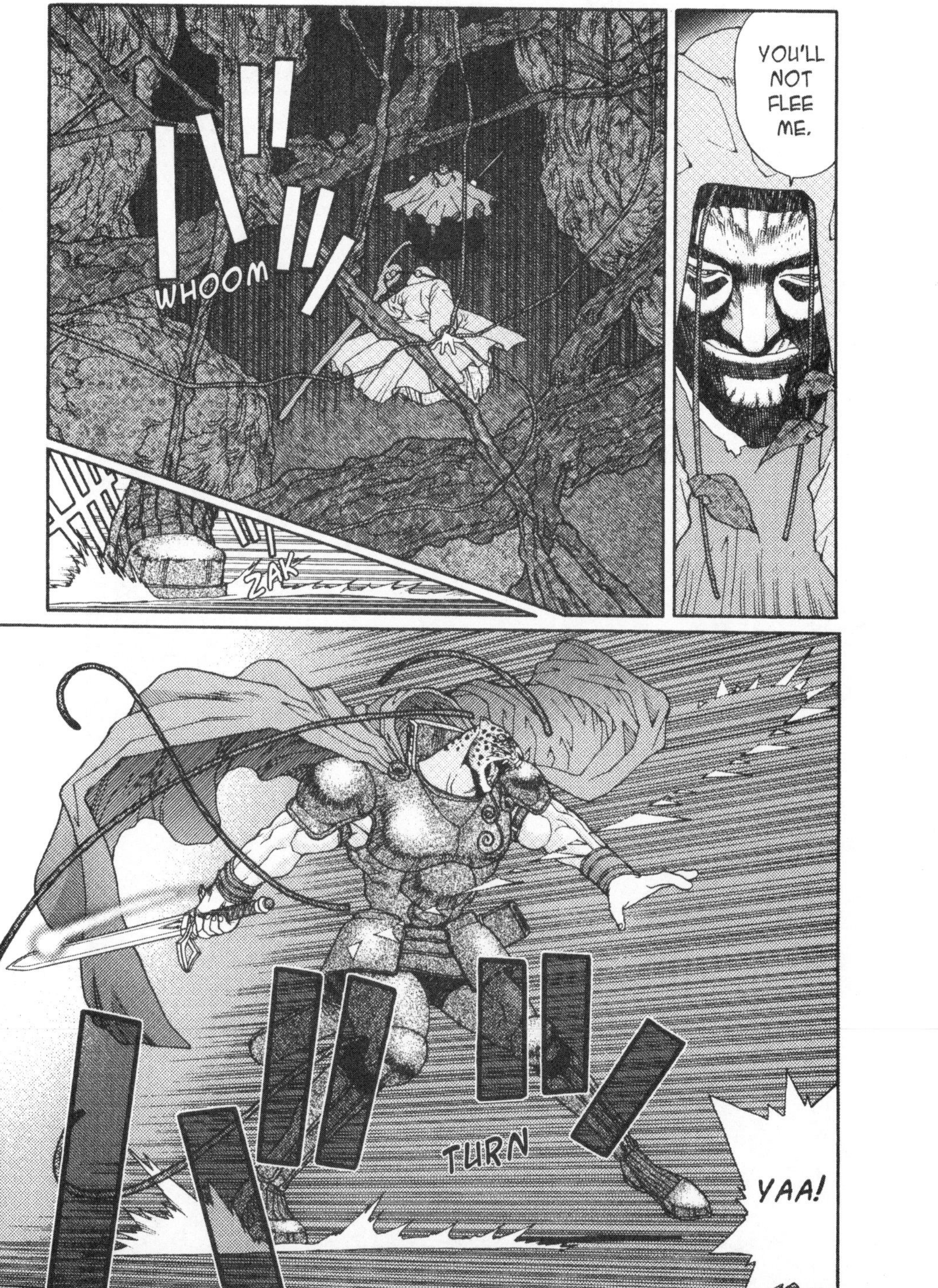
YOU'LL NOT FLEE ME.
WHOOM
ZAK
TURN
YAA!

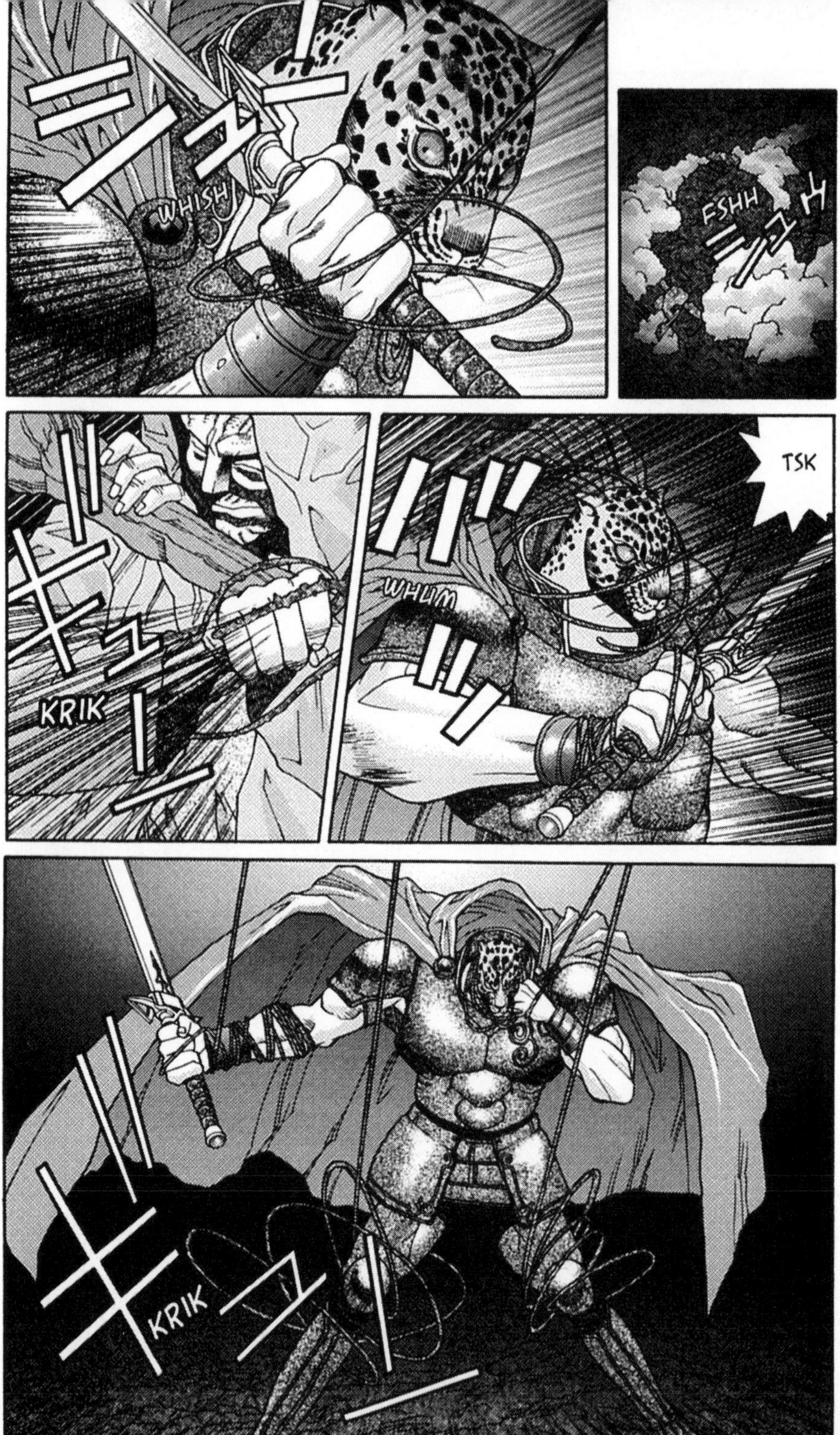
FSHH
WHISH
TSK
WHUM
KRIK
KRIK

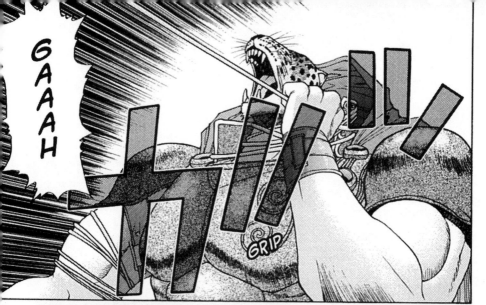

GAAAH

GRIP

THE HEAVY MOANS OF THIS FLESH-MOUND ARE ALL I HEAR.

THE KING...

WHAT'S WRONG?

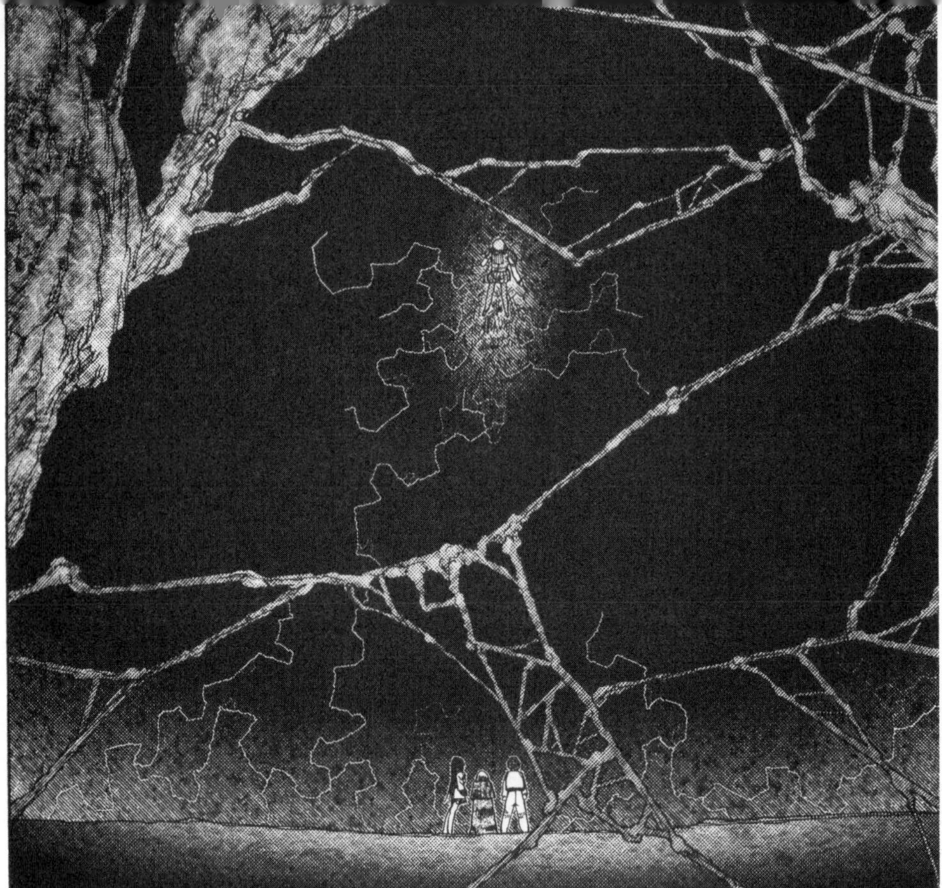

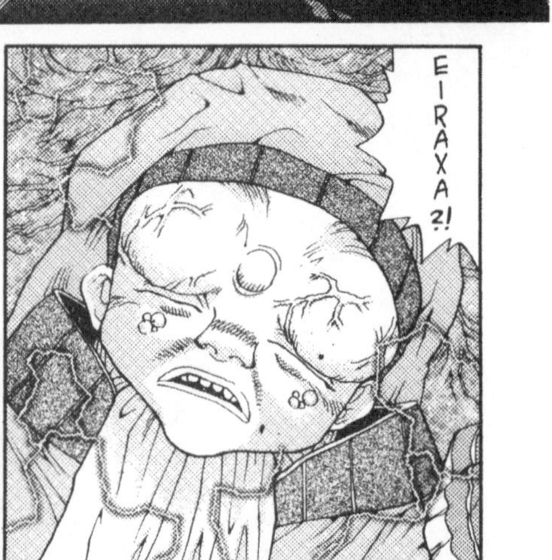
EIRAXA?!

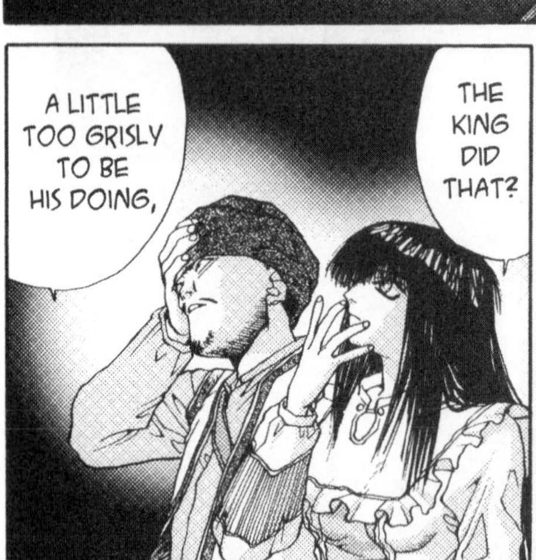
THE KING DID THAT?
A LITTLE TOO GRISLY TO BE HIS DOING,

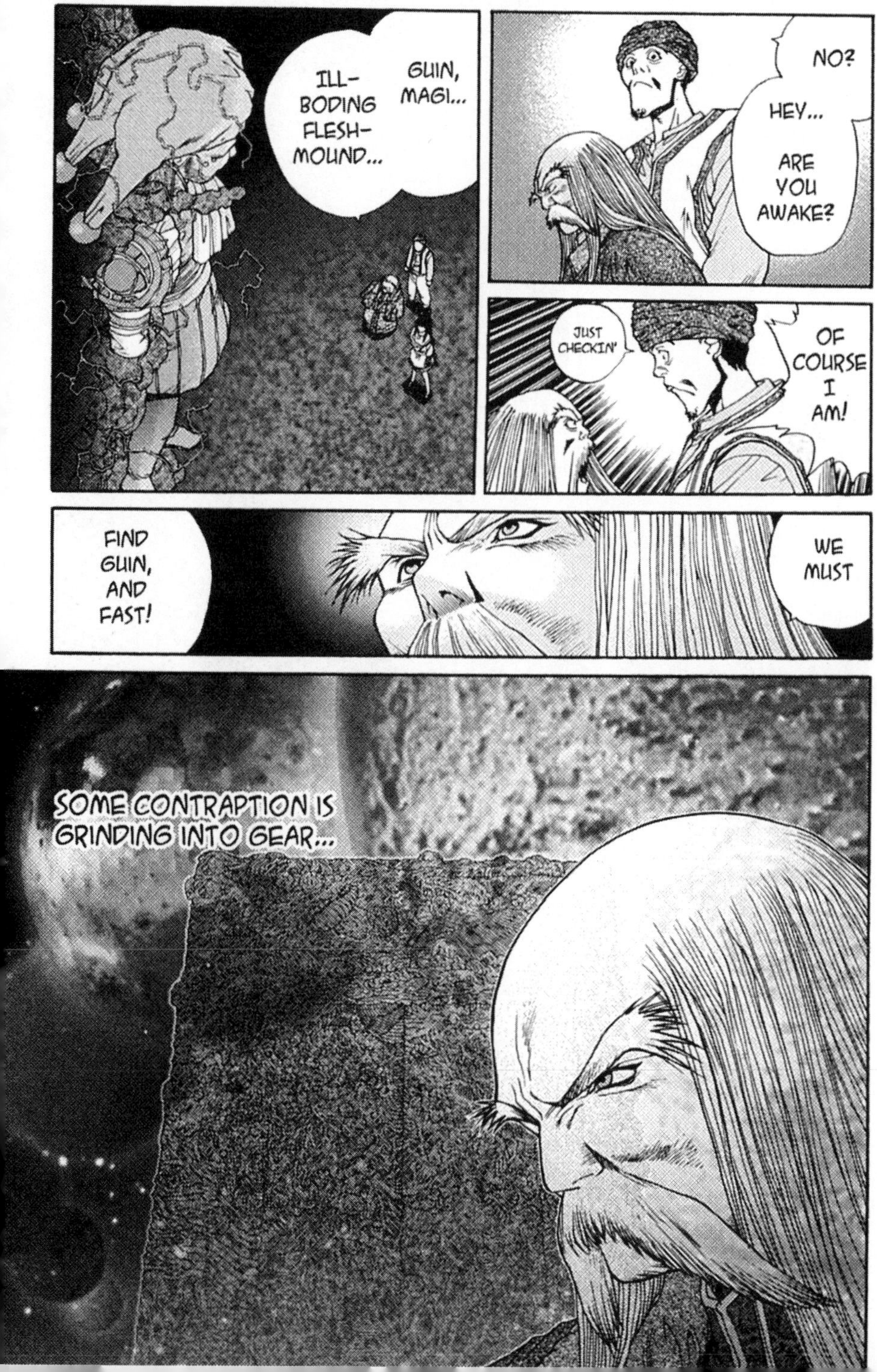
NO?
HEY...
ARE YOU AWAKE?
OF COURSE I AM!
JUST CHECKIN'
GUIN, MAGI...
ILL-BODING FLESH-MOUND...
WE MUST
FIND GUIN, AND FAST!
SOME CONTRAPTION IS GRINDING INTO GEAR...

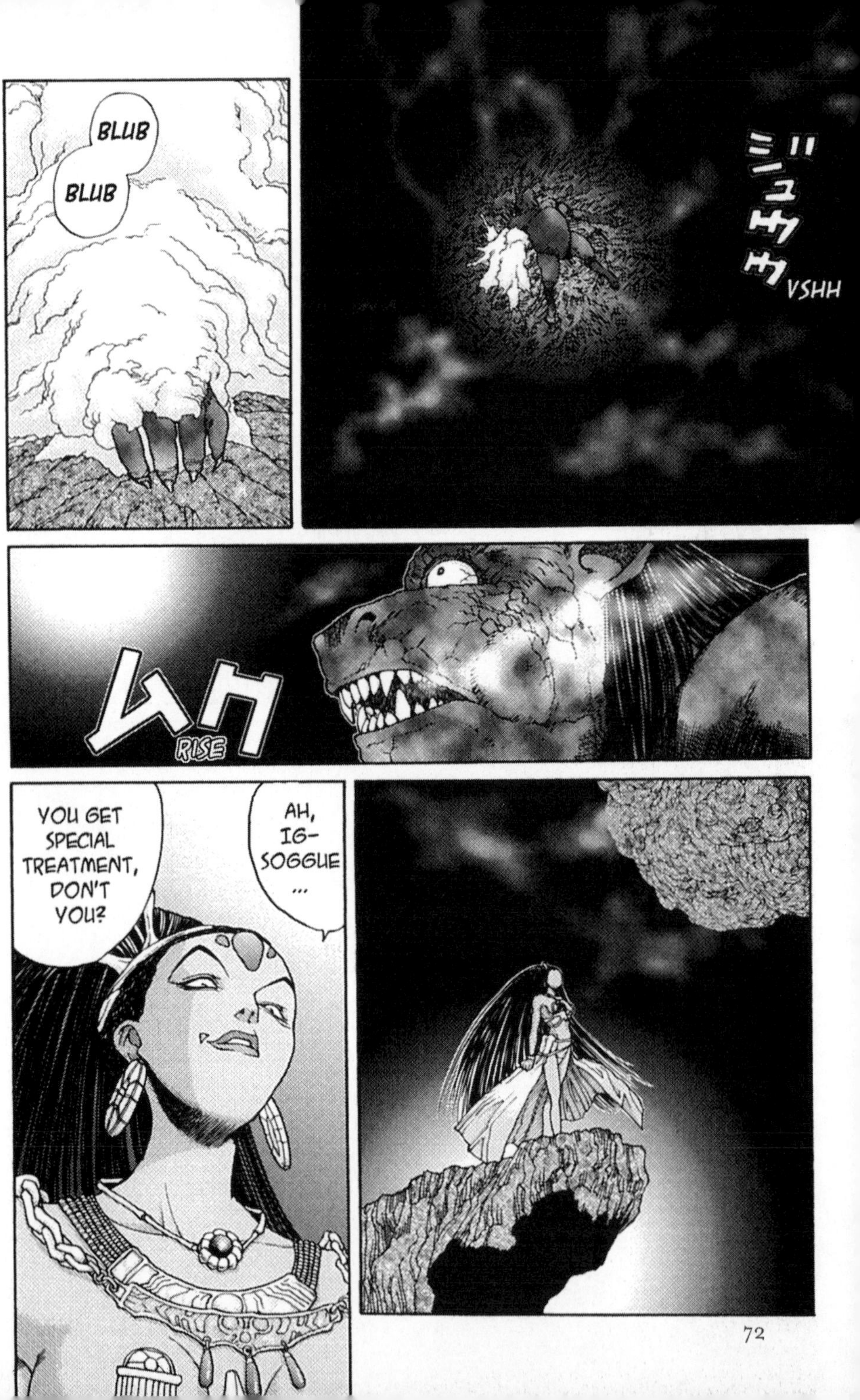
ジュウウ
VSHH
BLUB
BLUB
ムク
RISE
AH, IG-SOGGUE ...
YOU GET SPECIAL TREATMENT, DON'T YOU?

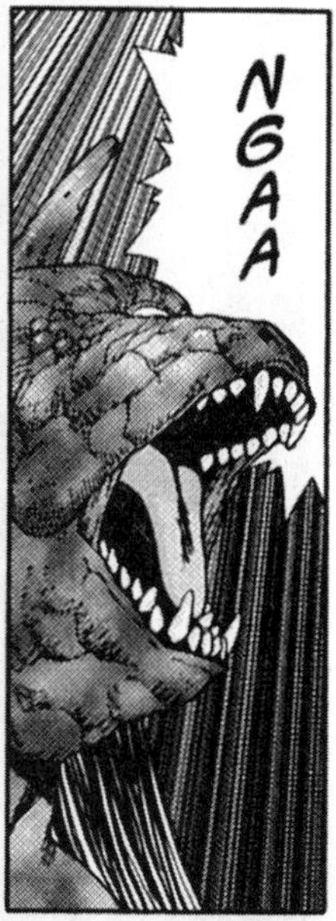
NGAA
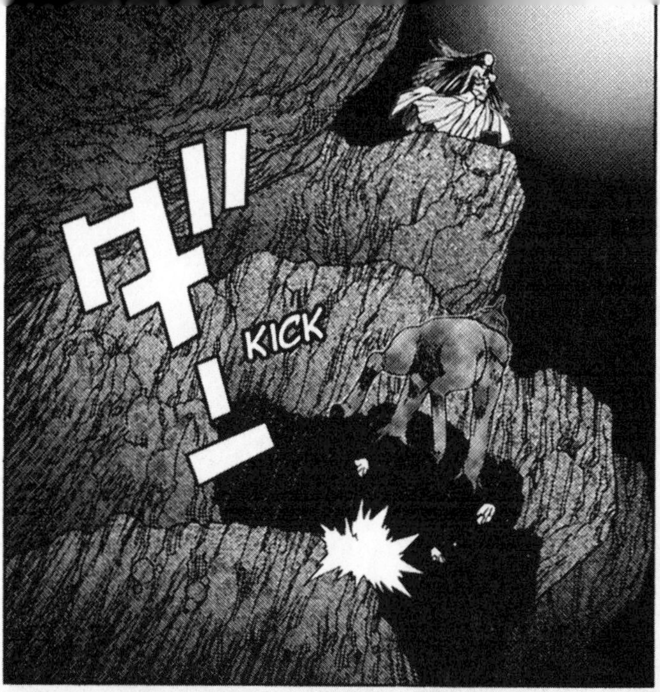
KICK
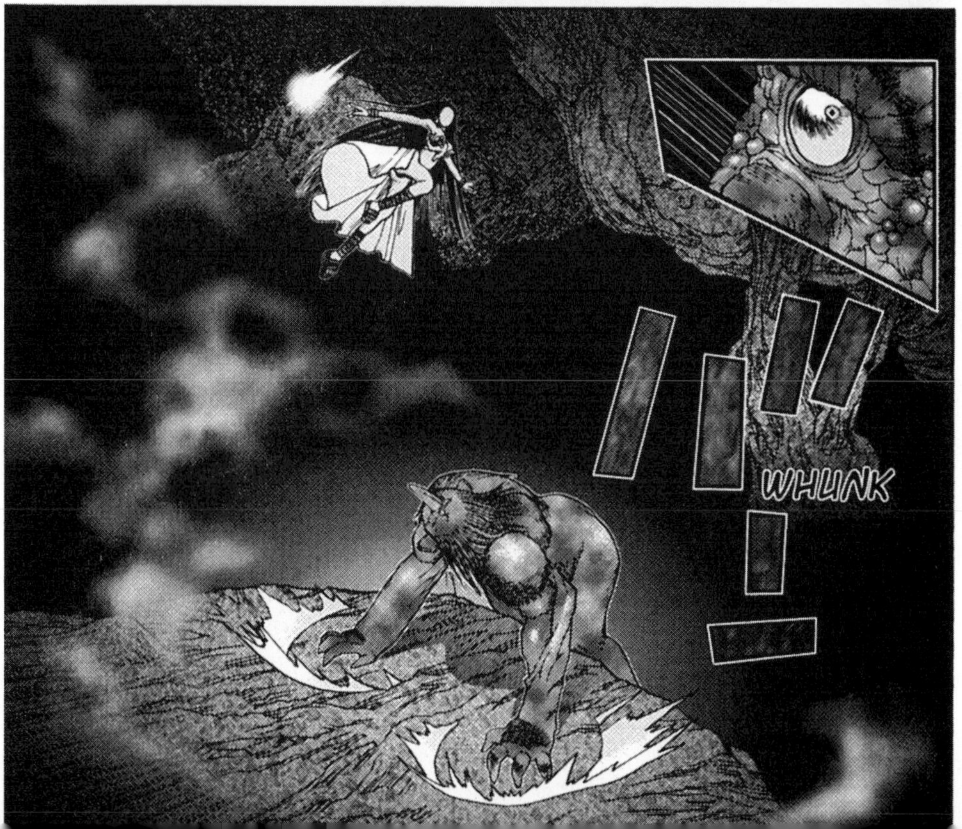
WHUNK

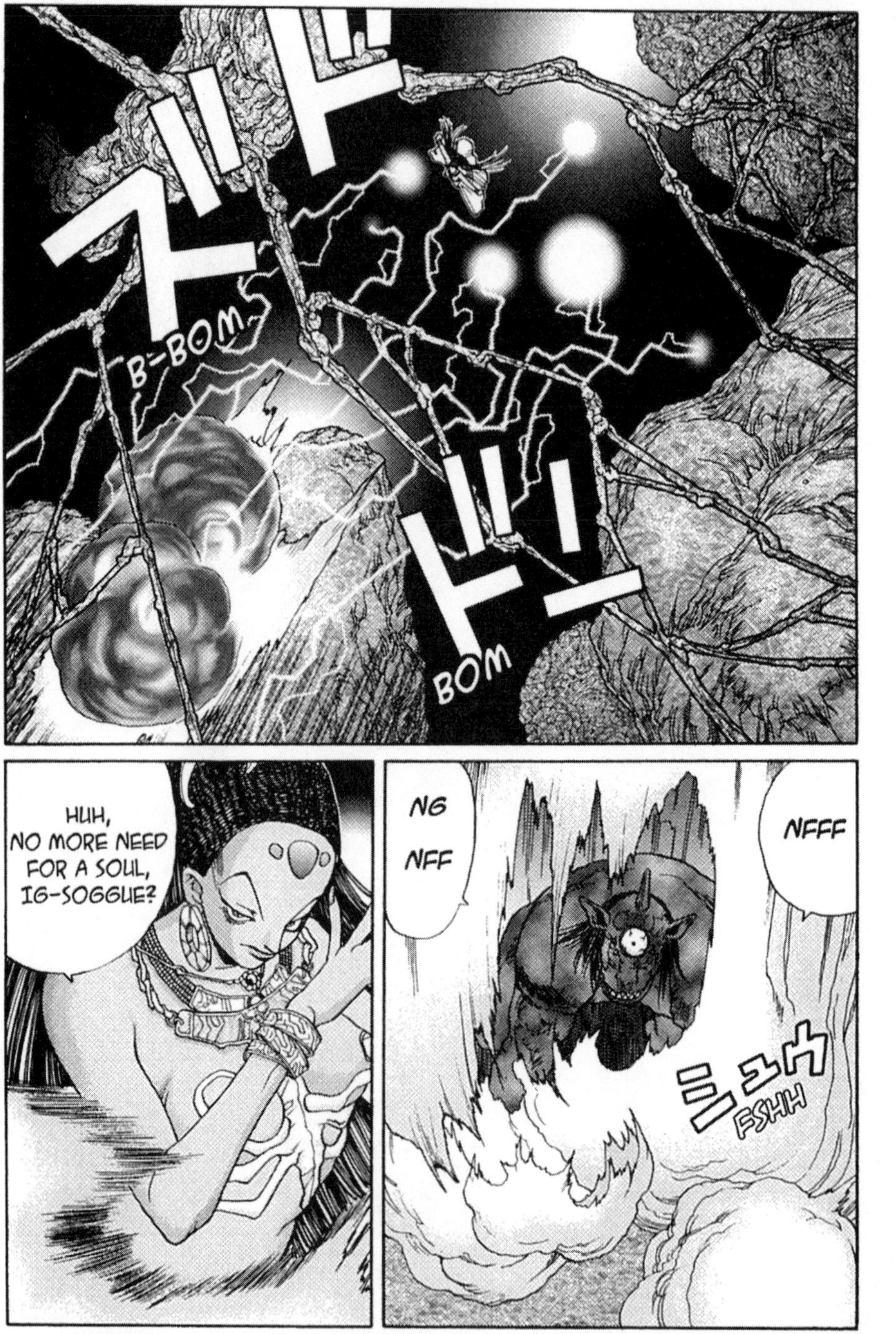
ズドド
B-BOM
ドドー
BOM
NFFF
NG NFF
シュウ
FSHH
HUH, NO MORE NEED FOR A SOUL, IG-SOGGUE?

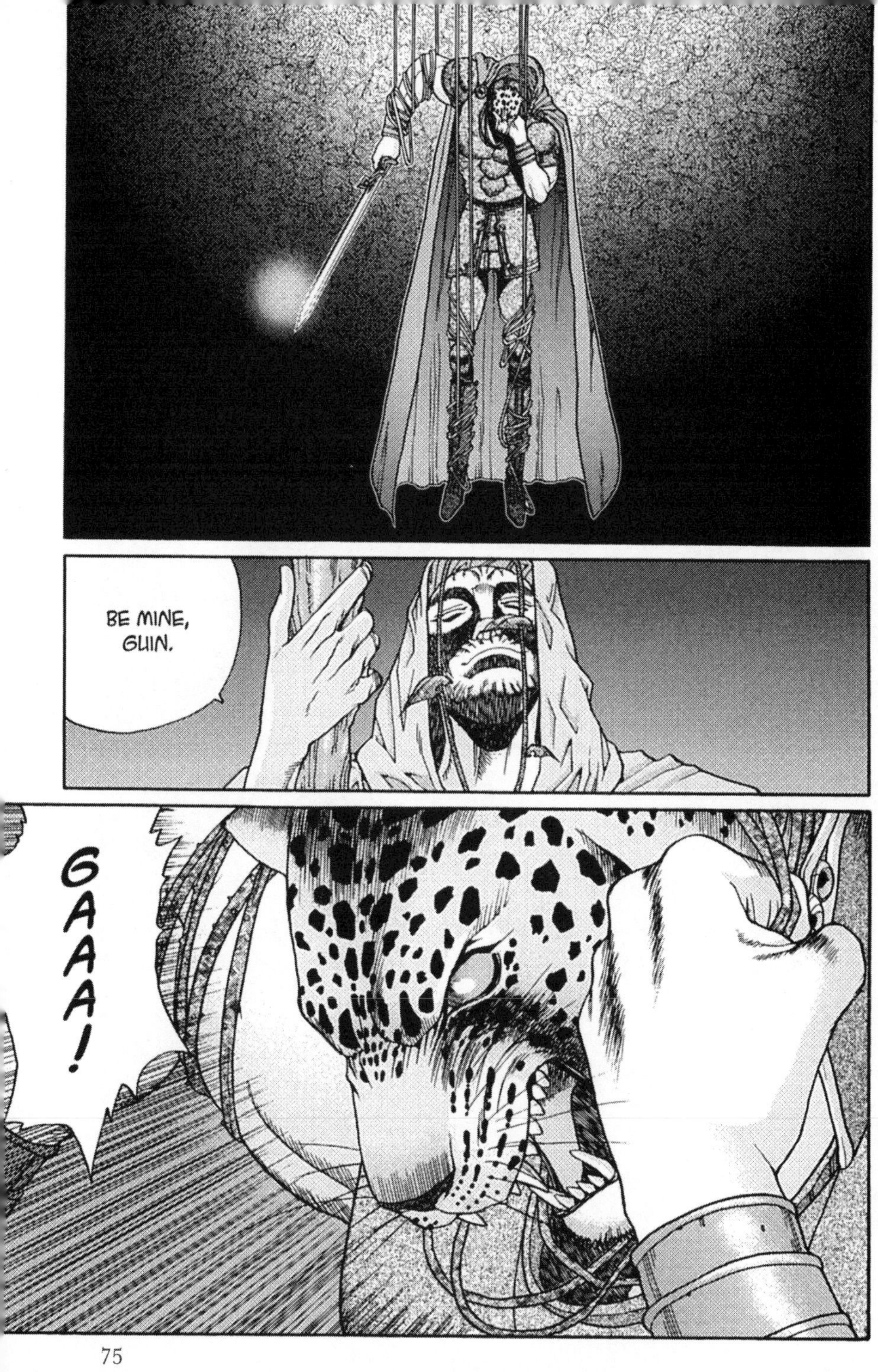
BE MINE, GUIN.
GAAAA!

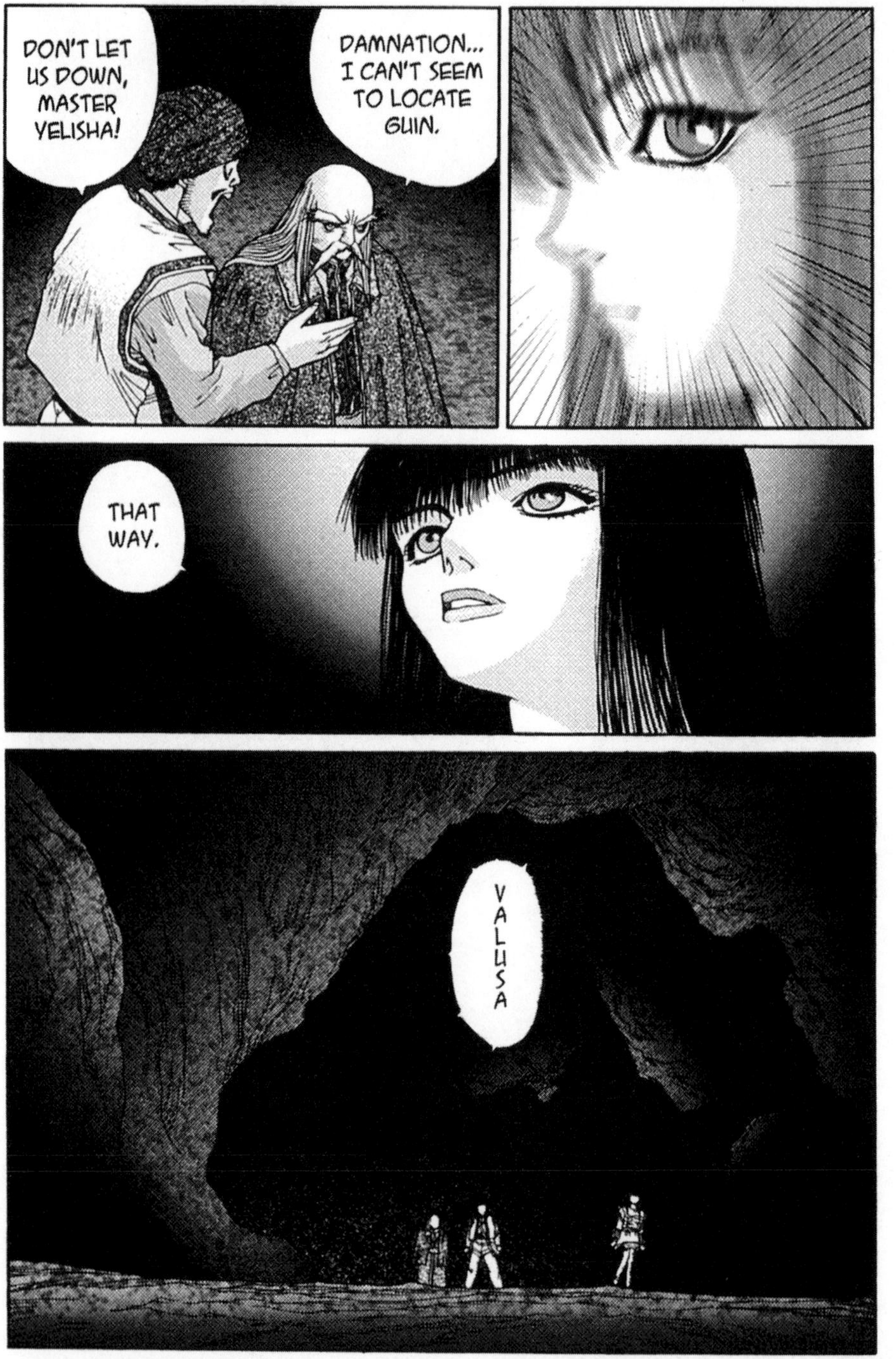
DAMNATION... I CAN'T SEEM TO LOCATE GUIN.
DON'T LET US DOWN, MASTER YELISHA!
THAT WAY.
VALUSA

CHAPTER 19

WAIT.
POM
THUMP

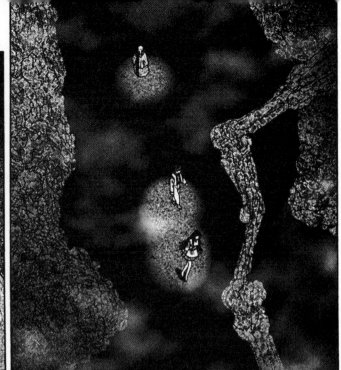

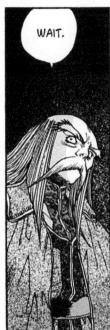

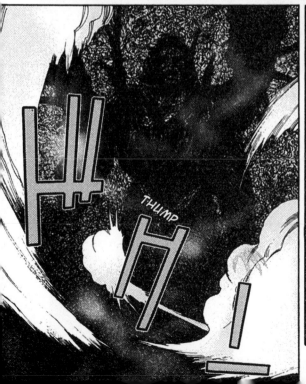

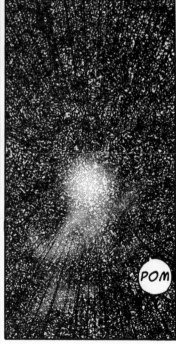

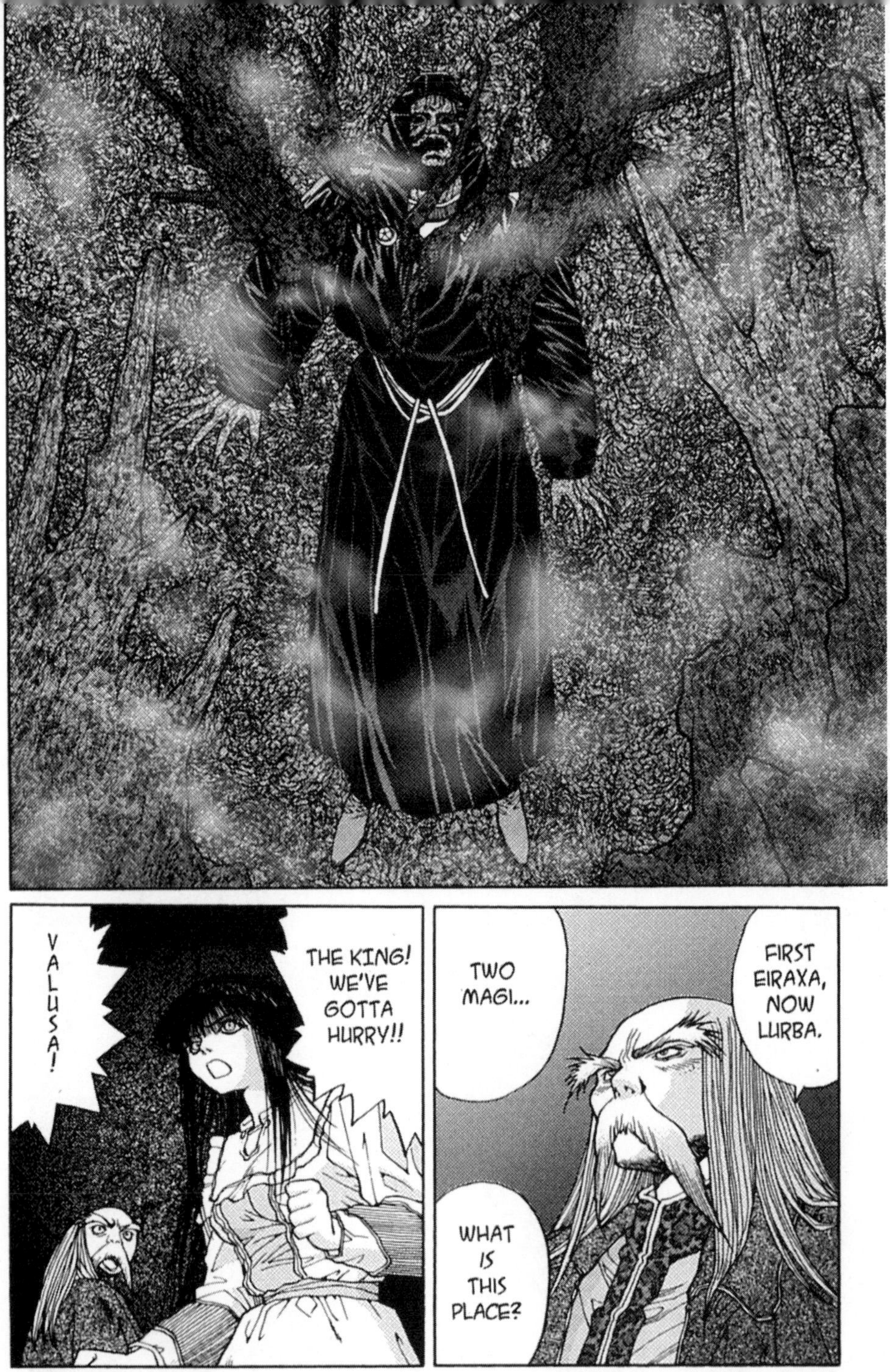
FIRST EIRAXA, NOW LURBA.
TWO MAGI...
WHAT IS THIS PLACE?
THE KING! WE'VE GOTTA HURRY!!
VALUSA!

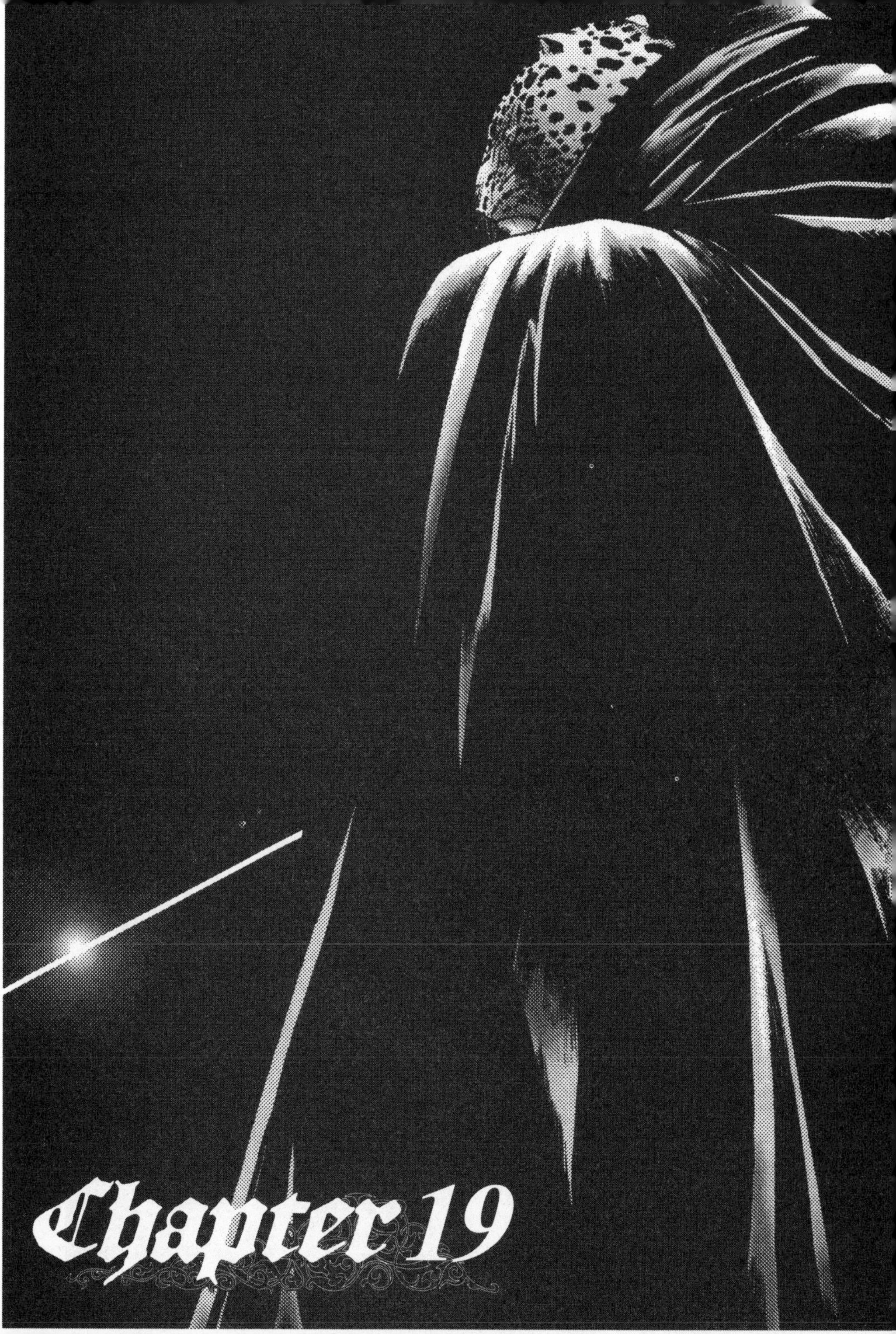
Chapter 19

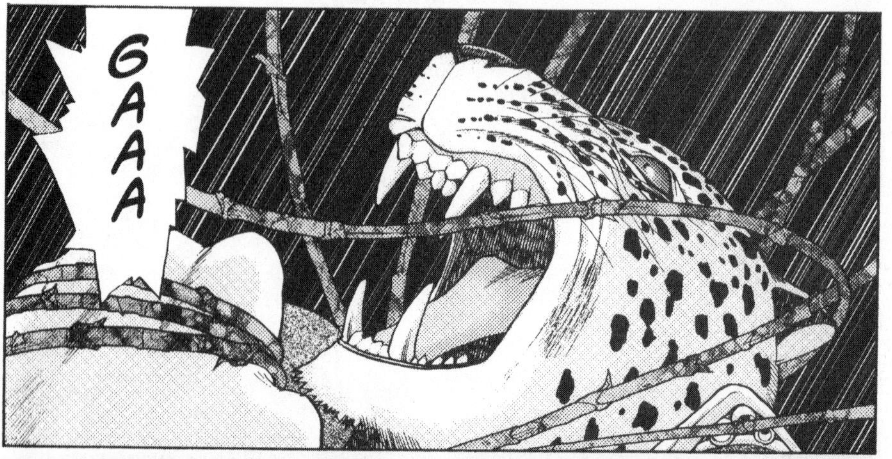
GAAAA

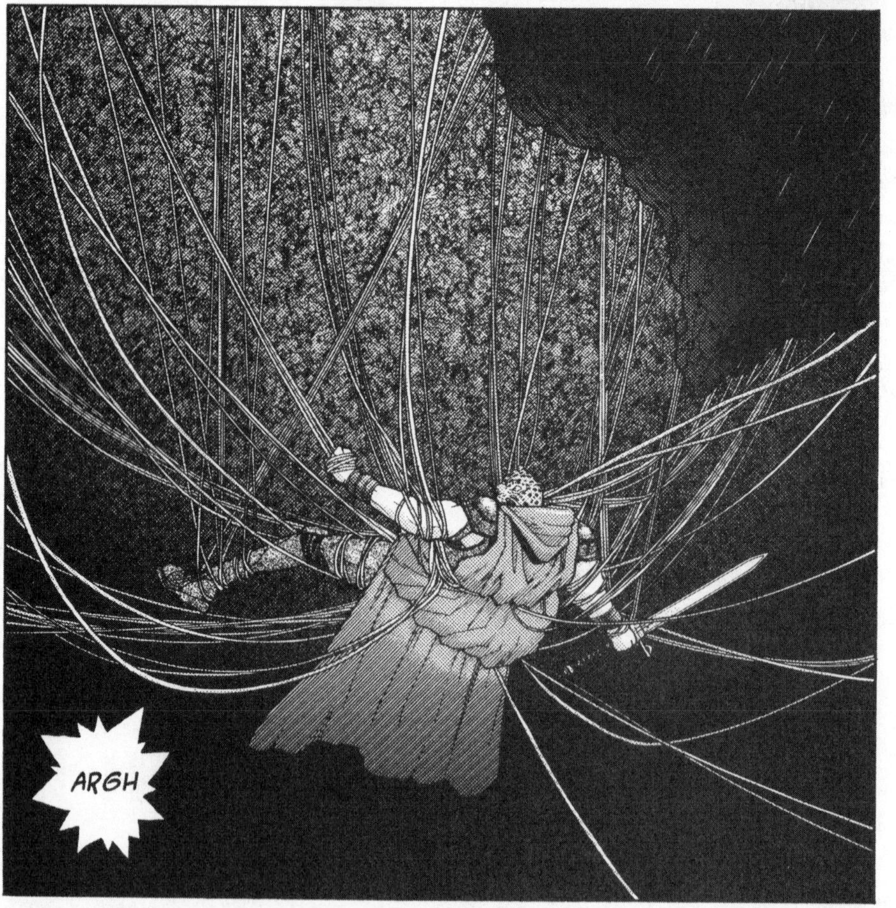
ARGH

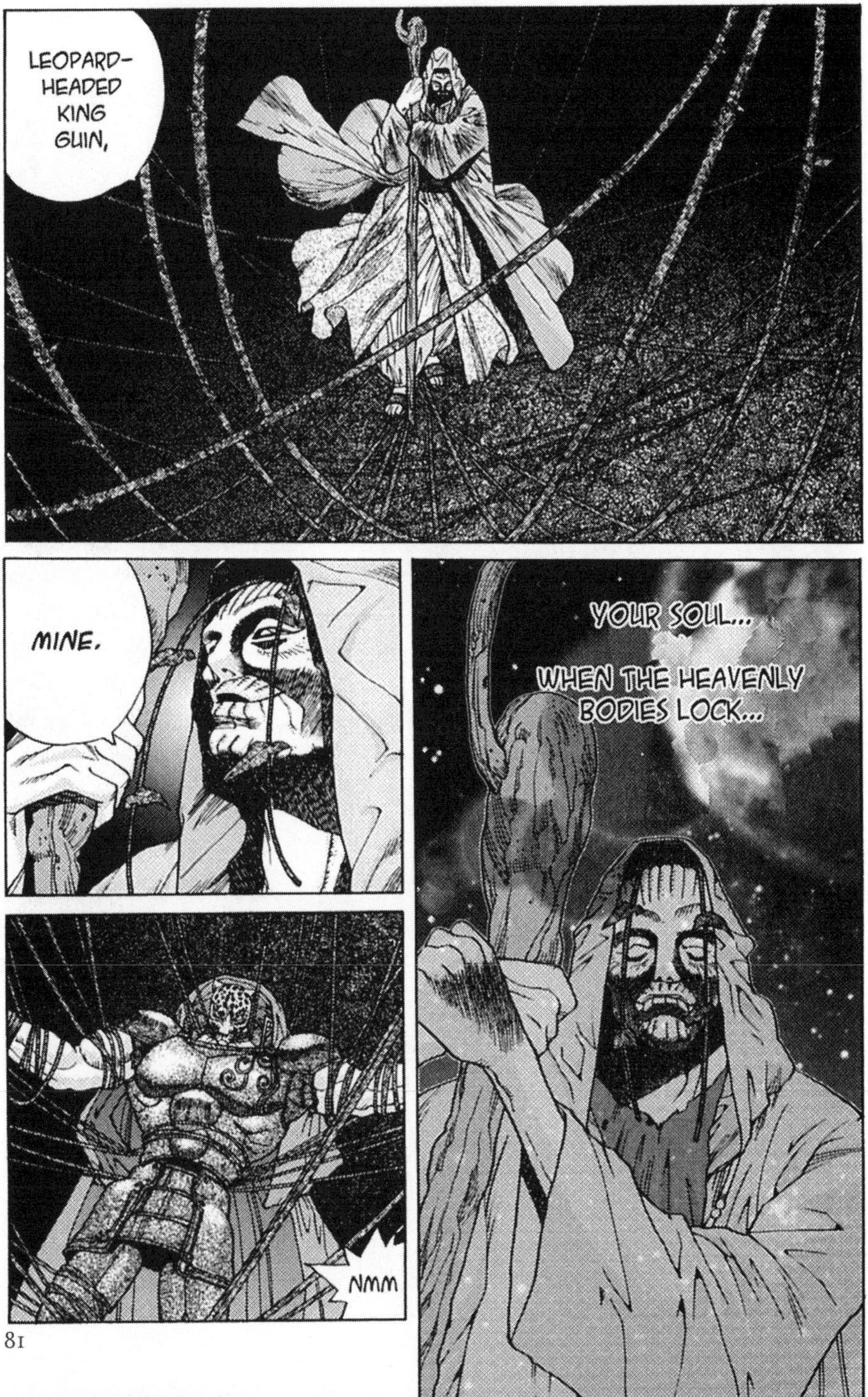
LEOPARD-HEADED KING GUIN,
YOUR SOUL...
WHEN THE HEAVENLY BODIES LOCK...
MINE.
NMM

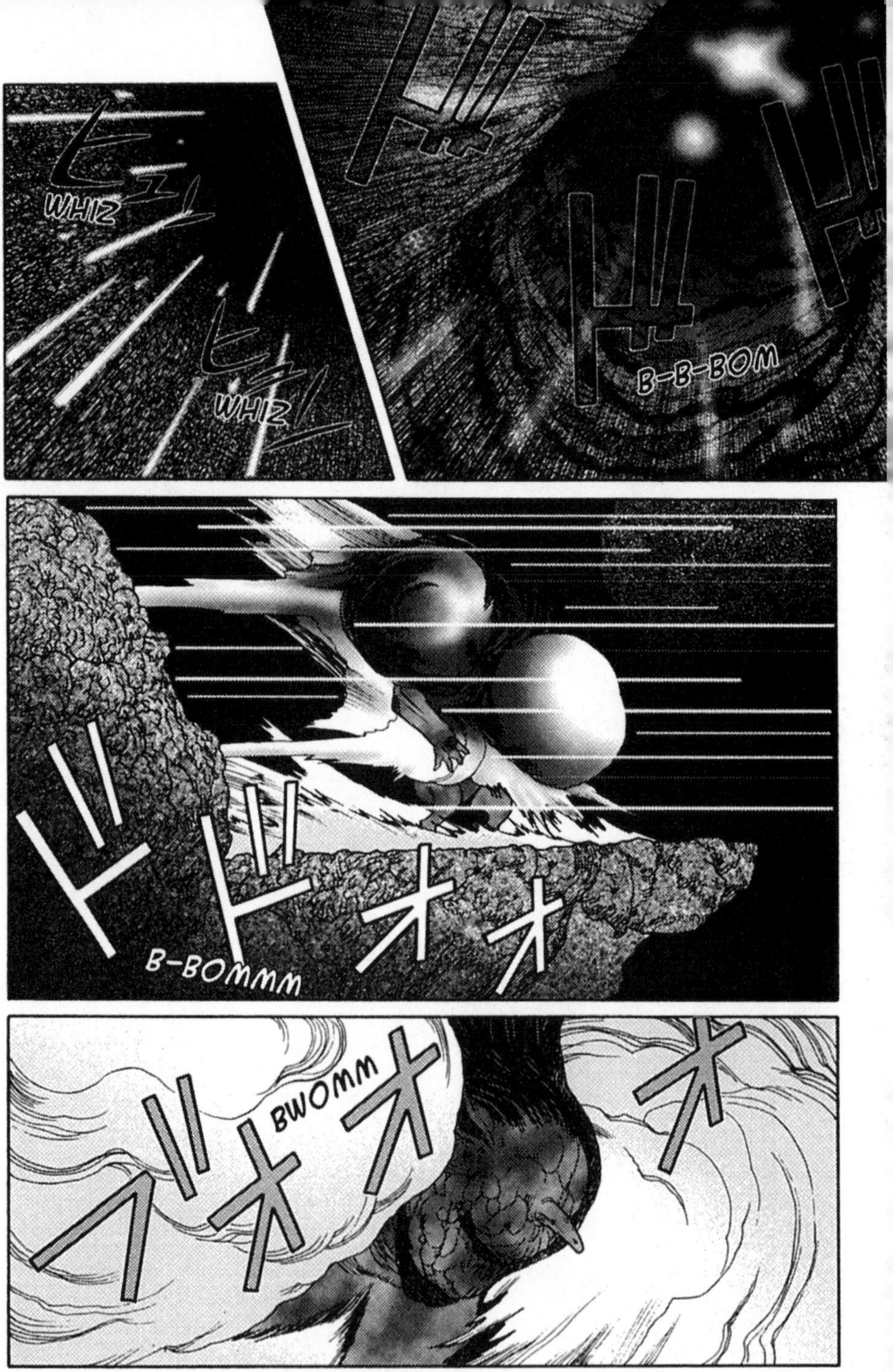
B-B-BOM
WHIZ
WHIZ
B-BOMMM
BWOMM

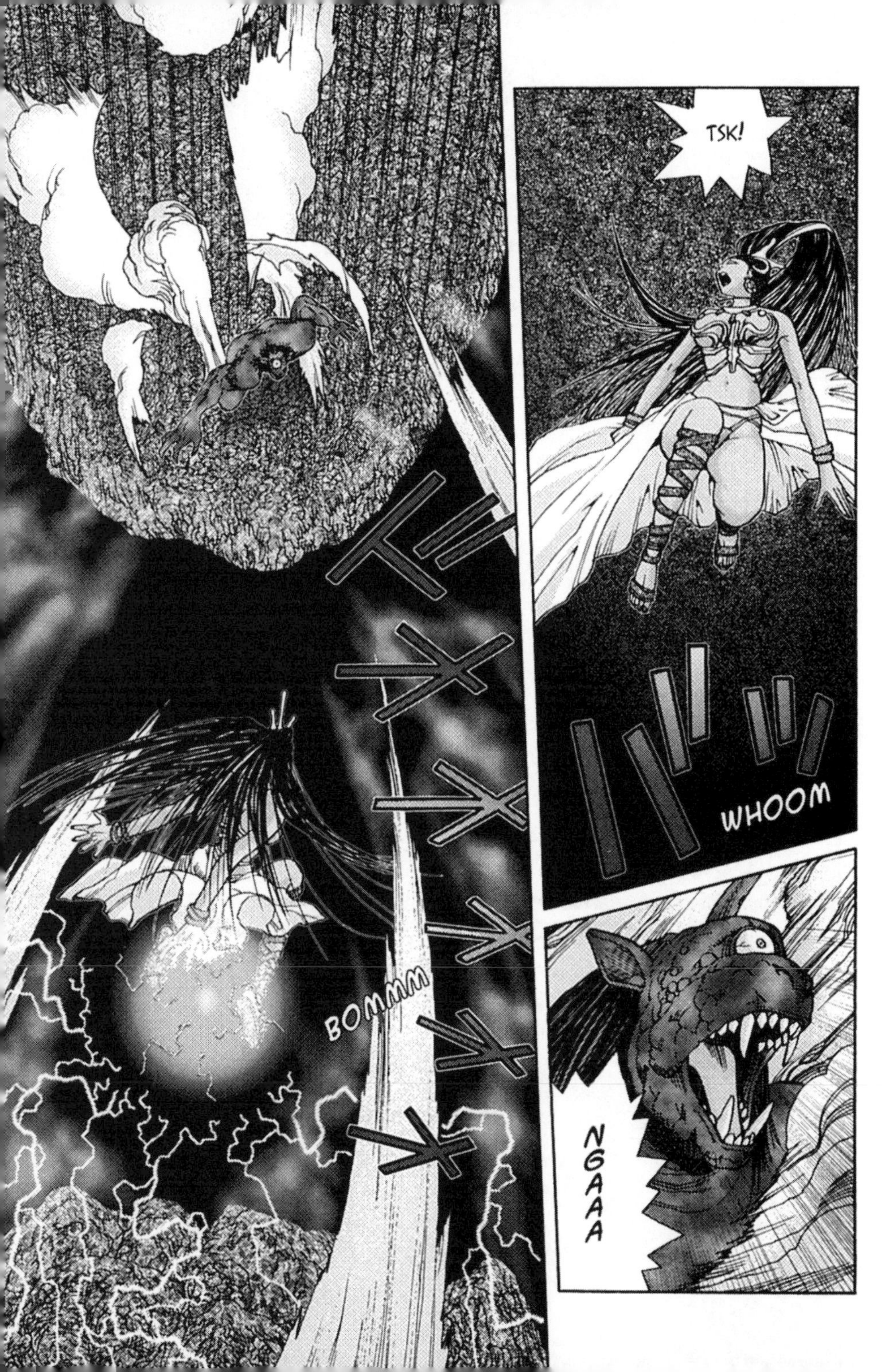
TSK!
WHOOM
NGAAA
BOMMM

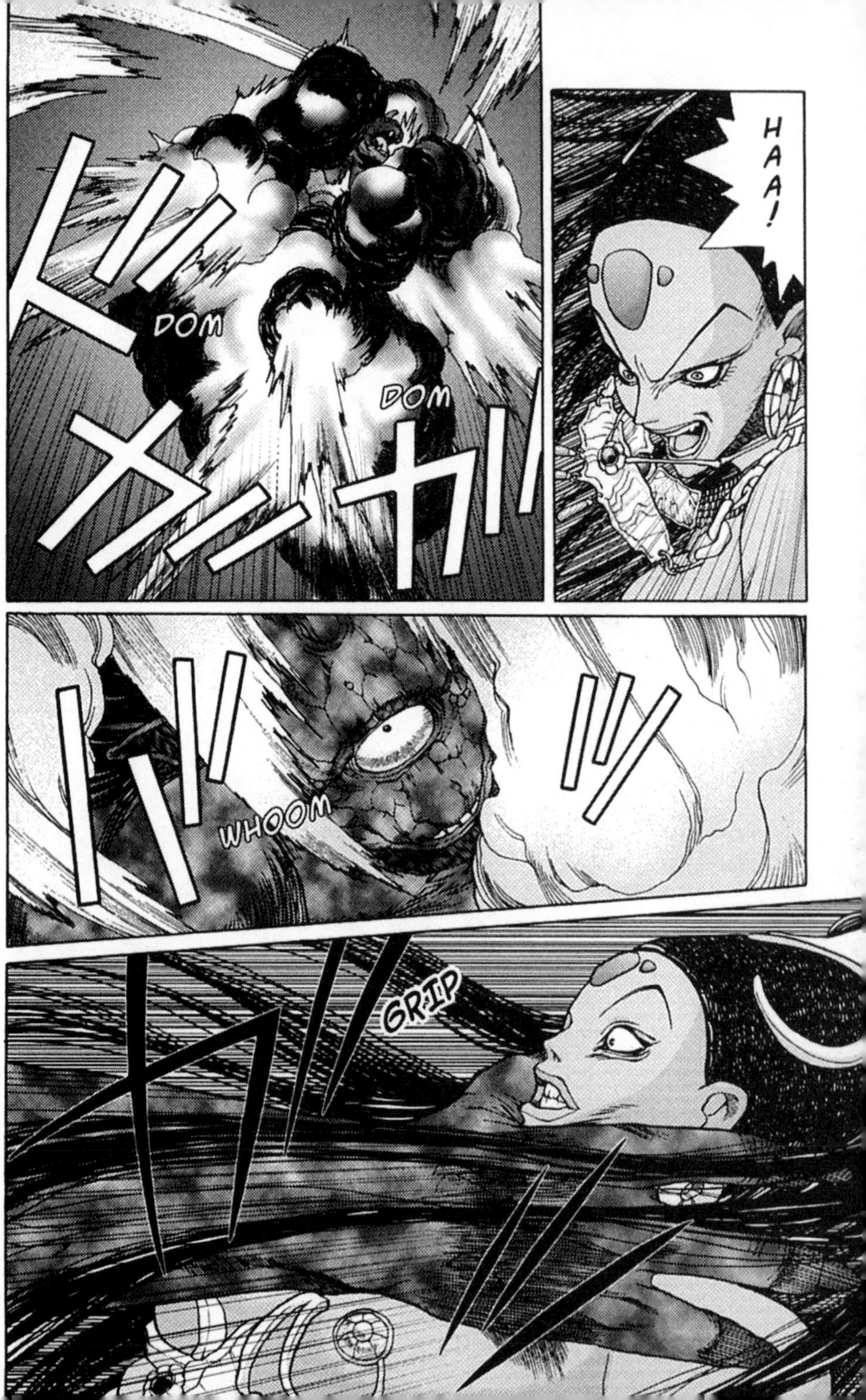
HAAA!
DOM
DOM
WHOOM
GRIP

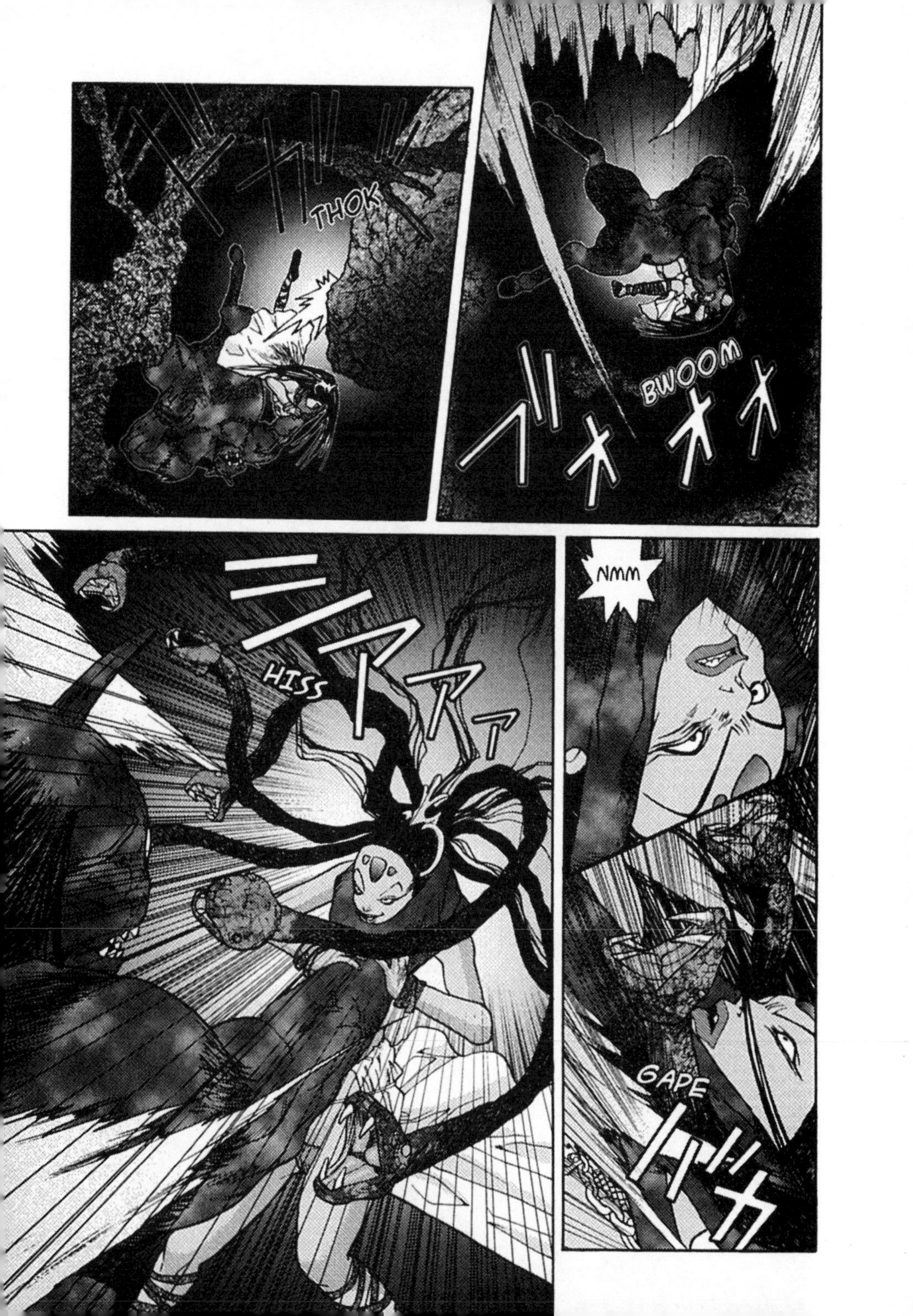
BWOOM
THOK
NMM
GAPE
HISS

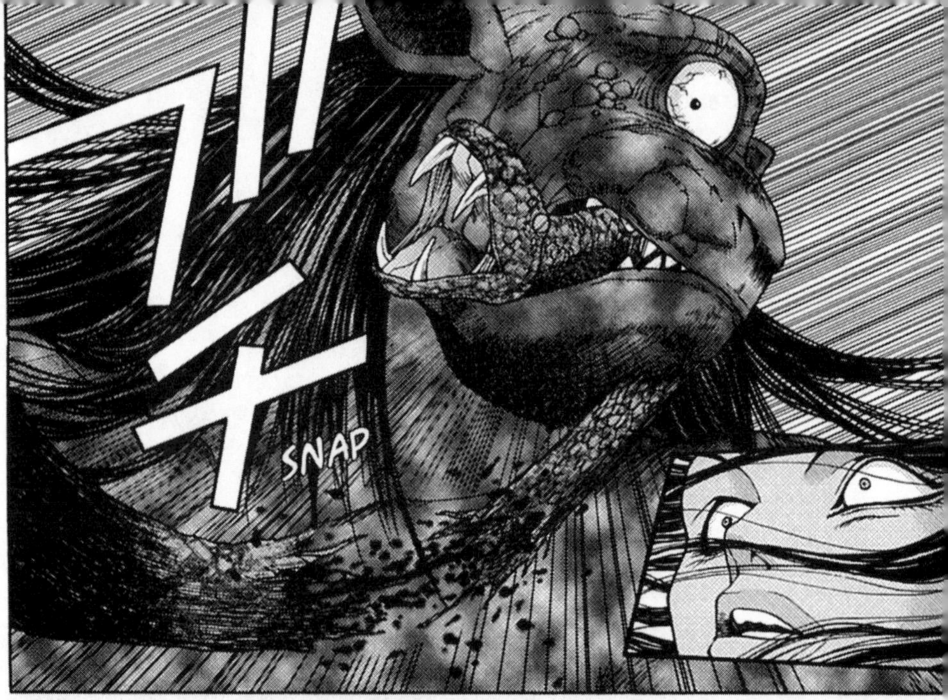
SNAP

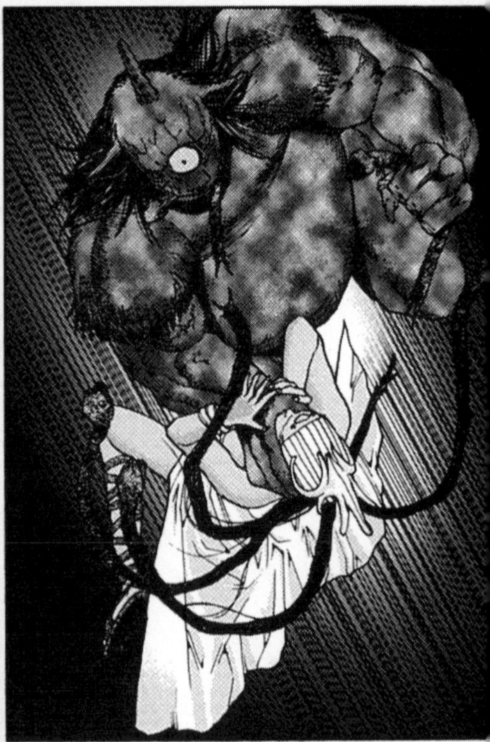

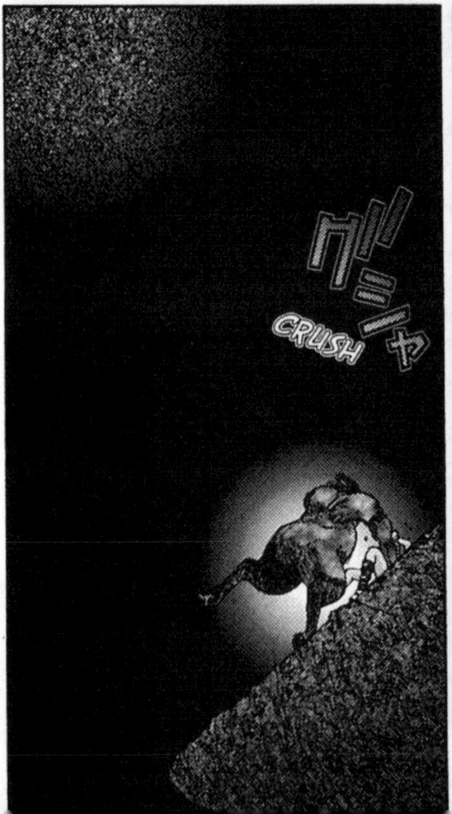
CRUSH

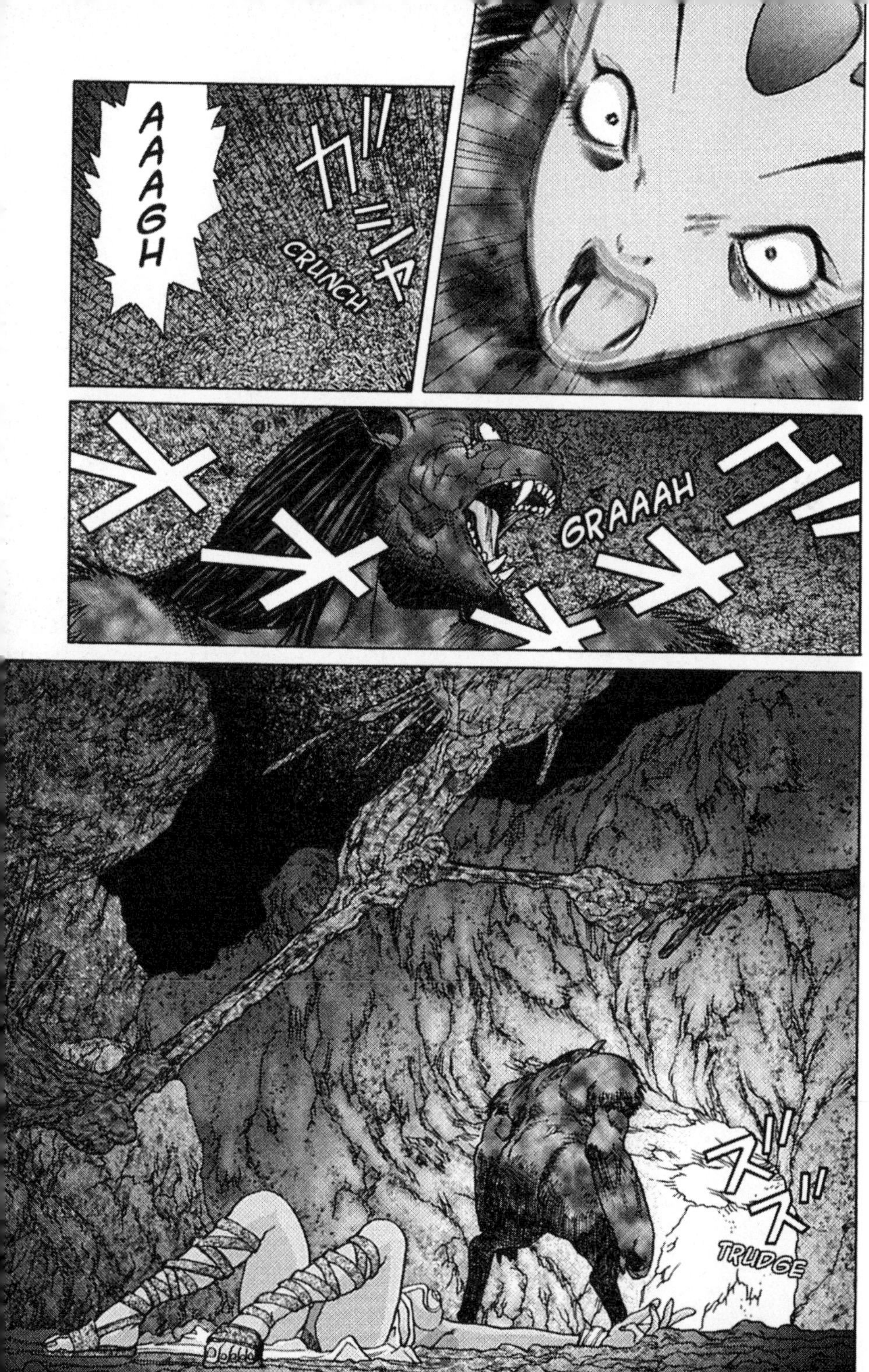
AAAAGH
CRUNCH
GRAAAH
TRUDGE

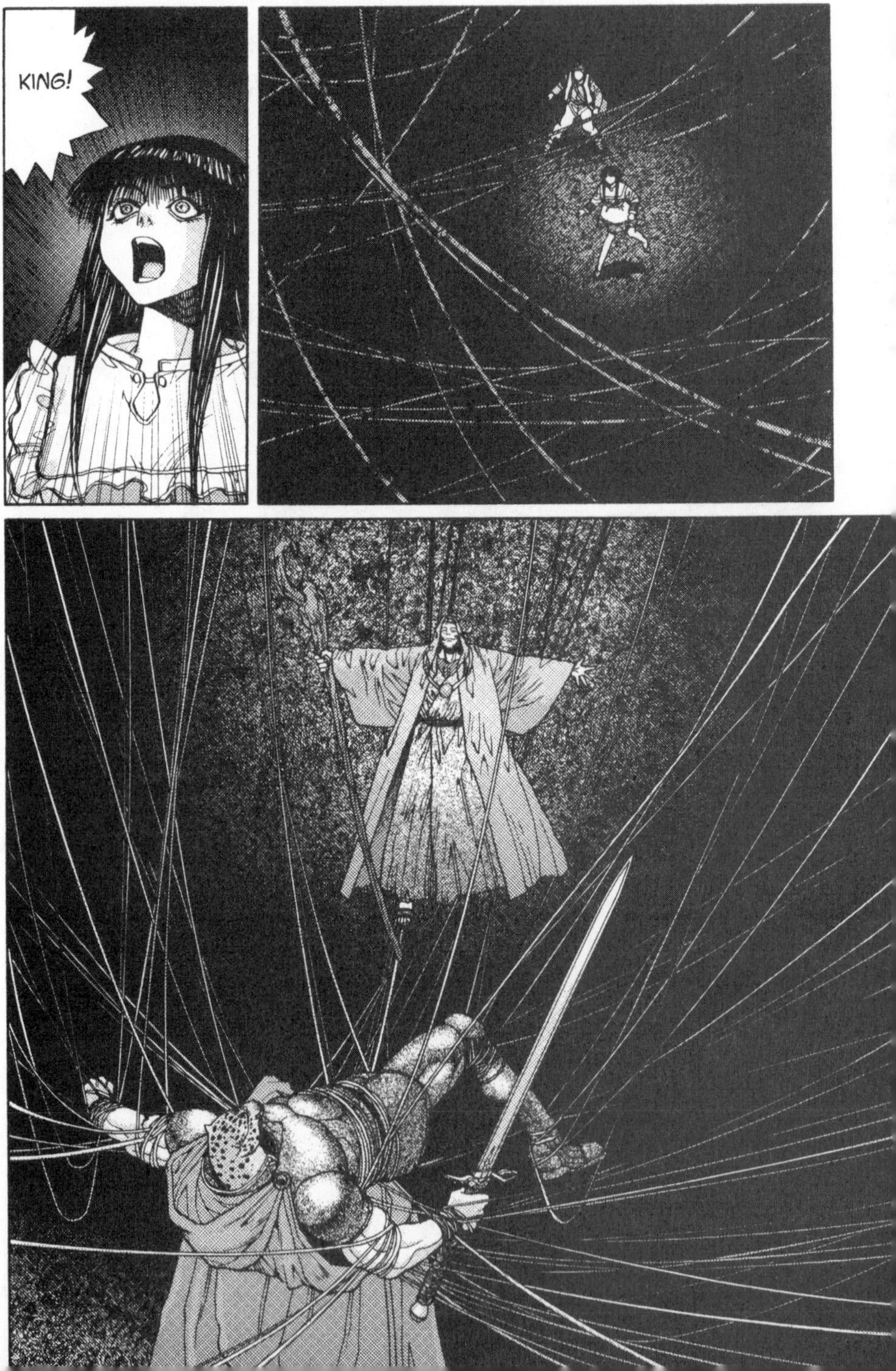
KING!

YANK

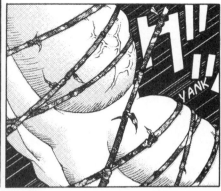

YANK

SWAY

BITE

NG

WHISK

HUH?

NOW, KING!

IT SEES US NOT...

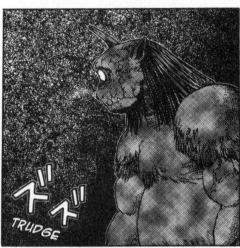

ズ ズ

TRUDGE

ズ

SLICE

ト゛ト゛

THUMP

ト゛ト゛

THUMP

ケ゛

GRAB

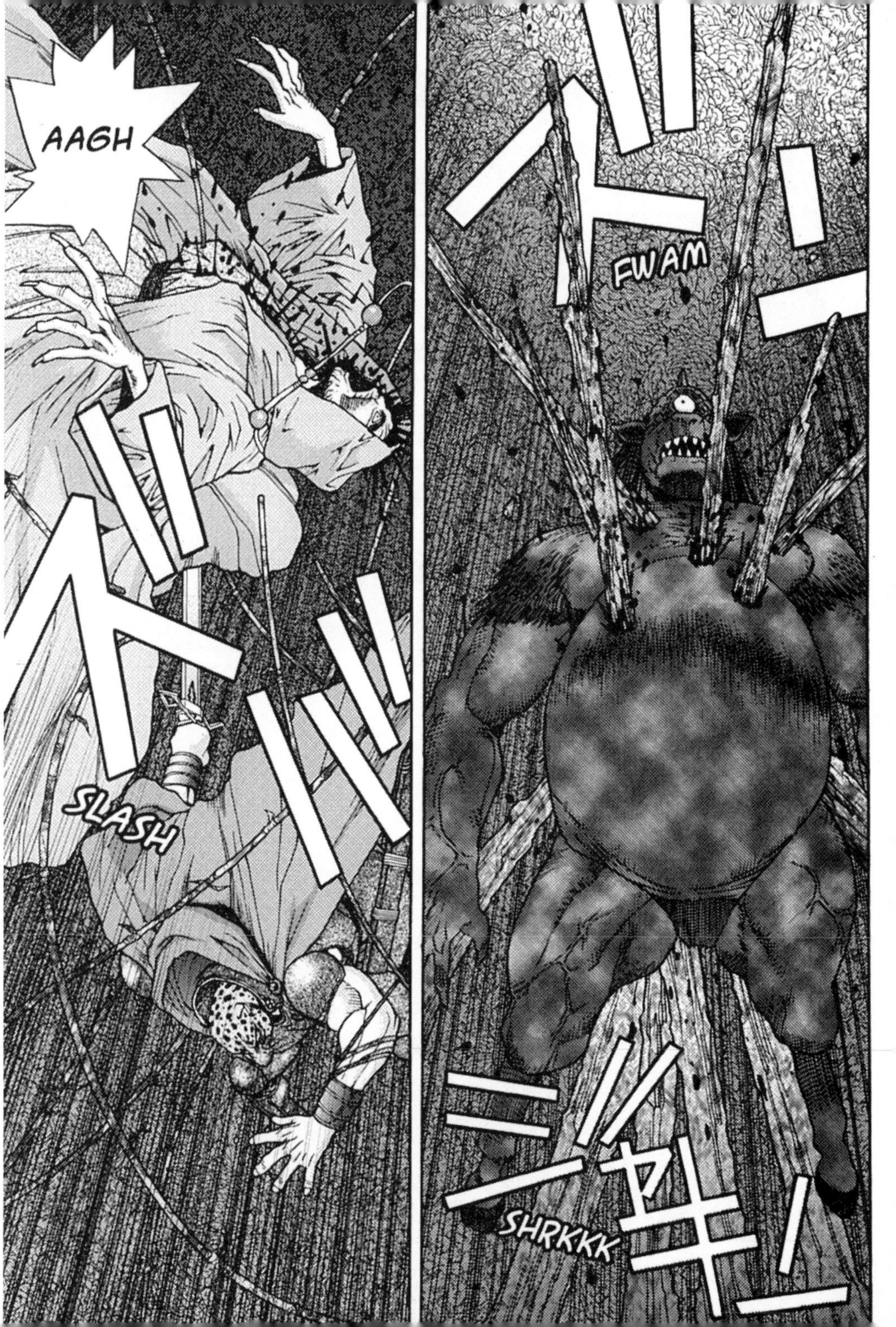
FWAM
SHRKKK
AAGH
SLASH

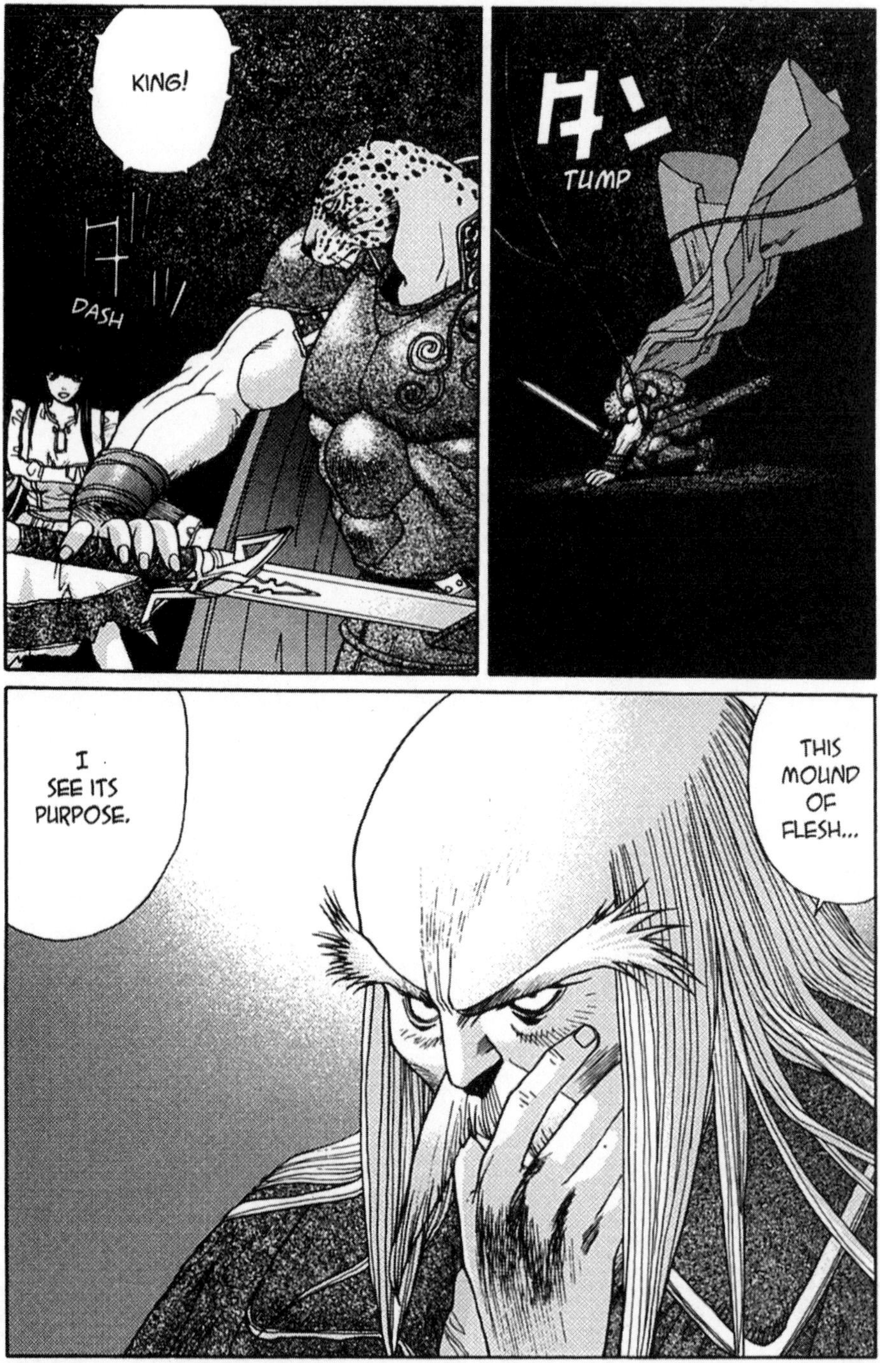
TUMP
KING!
DASH
THIS MOUND OF FLESH...
I SEE ITS PURPOSE.

CHAPTER 20

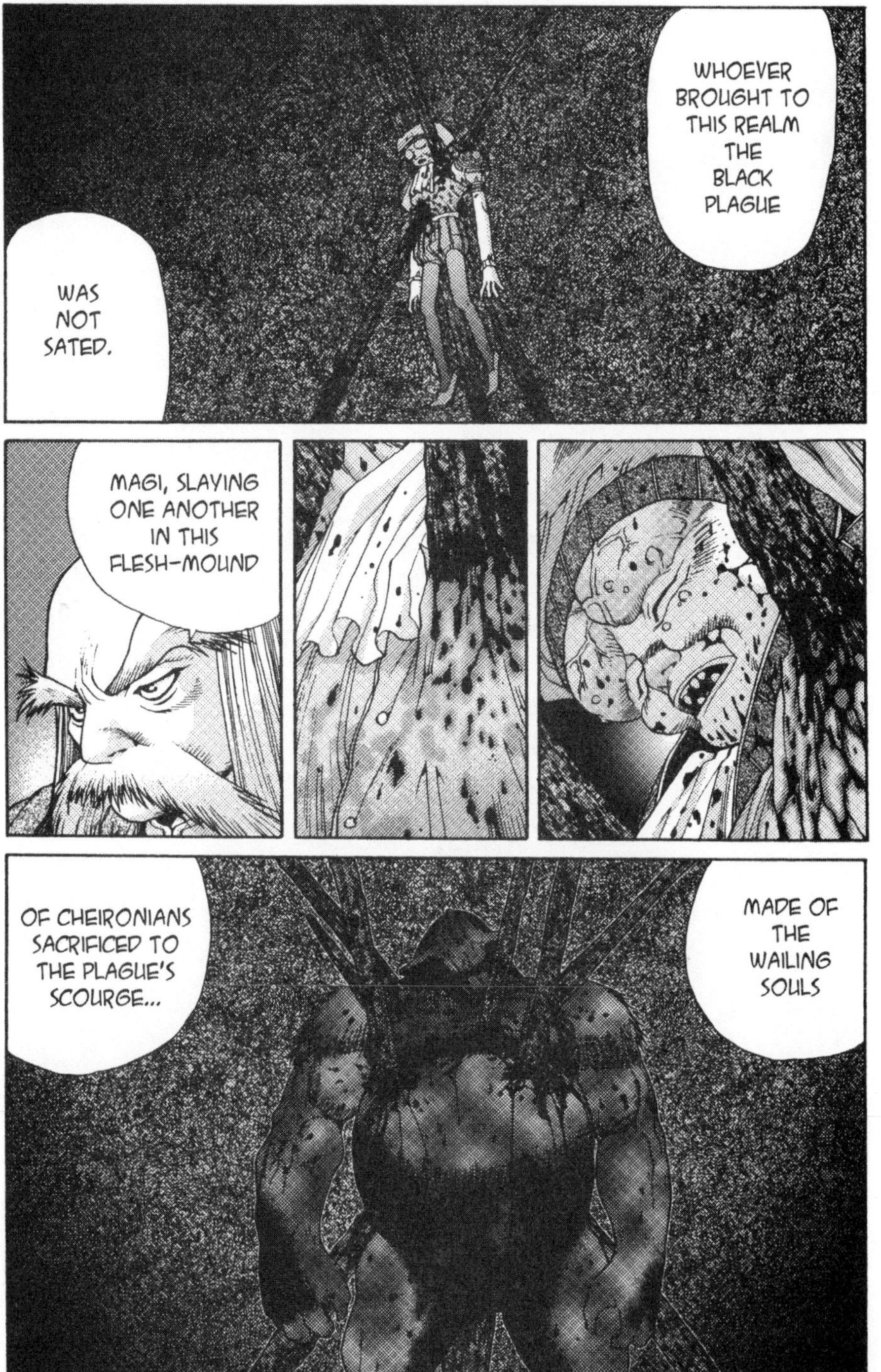
WHOEVER BROUGHT TO THIS REALM THE BLACK PLAGUE
WAS NOT SATED.
MAGI, SLAYING ONE ANOTHER IN THIS FLESH-MOUND
MADE OF THE WAILING SOULS
OF CHEIRONIANS SACRIFICED TO THE PLAGUE'S SCOURGE...

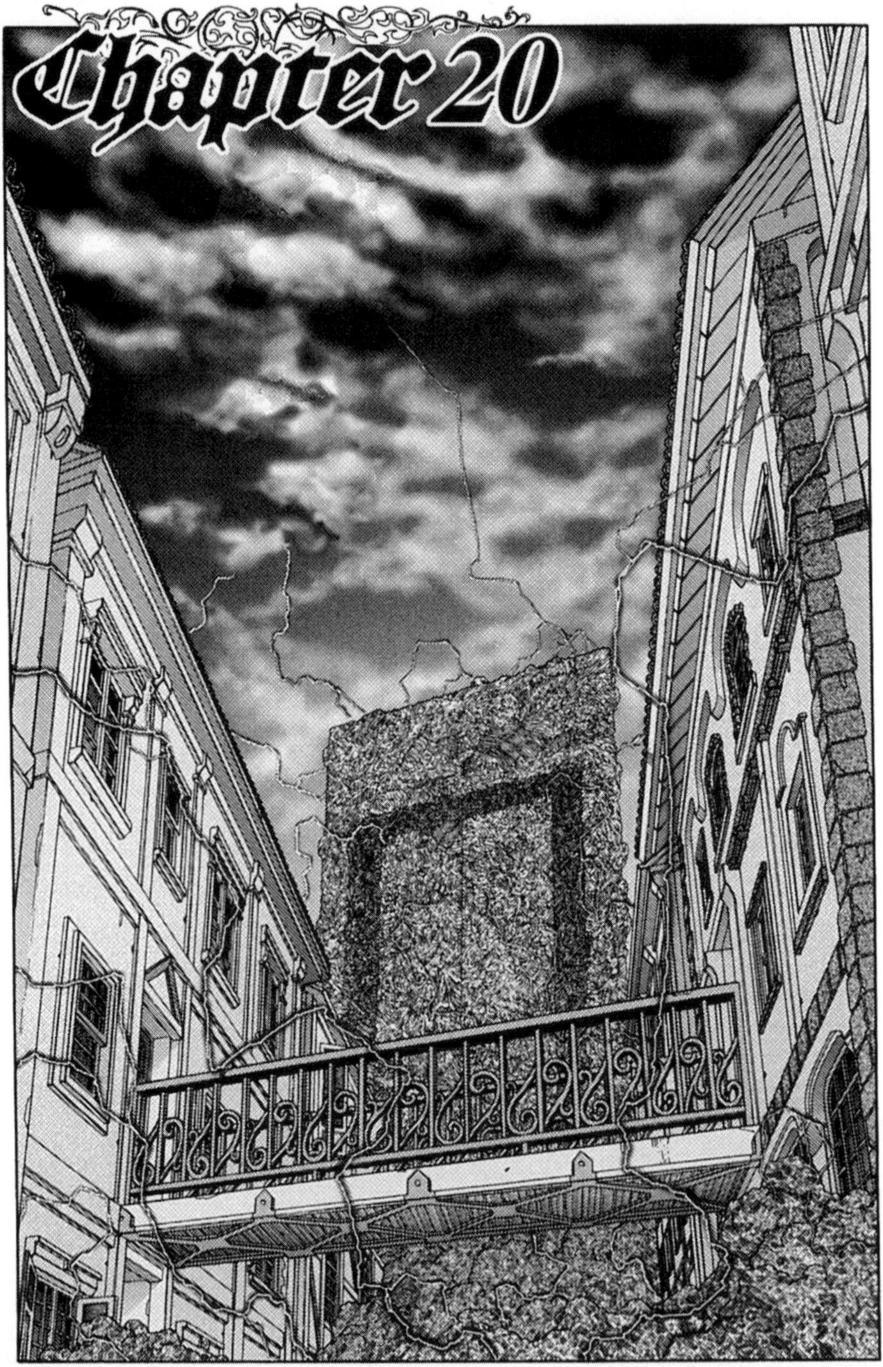
Chapter 20

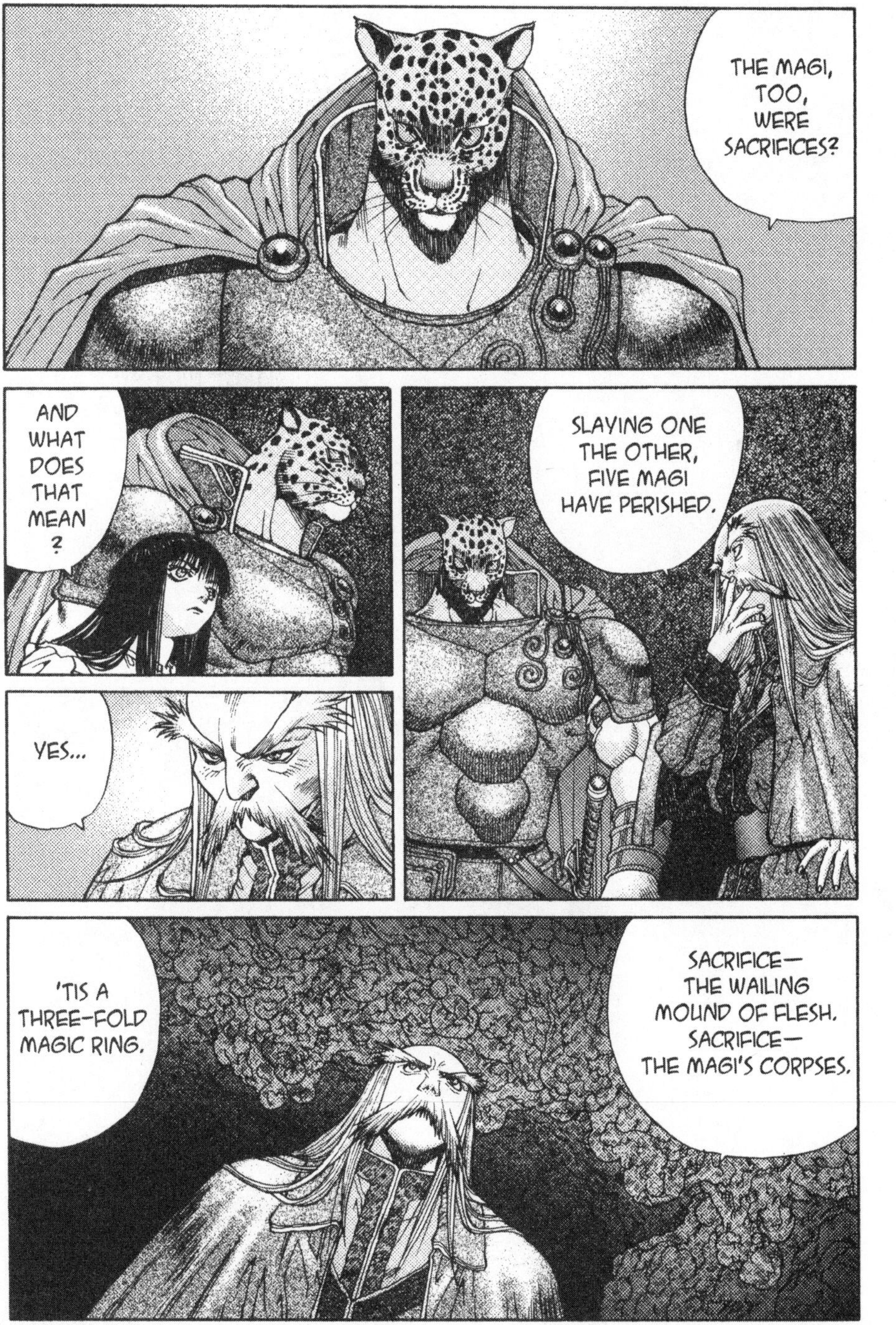
THE MAGI, TOO, WERE SACRIFICES?
SLAYING ONE THE OTHER, FIVE MAGI HAVE PERISHED.
AND WHAT DOES THAT MEAN ?
YES...
SACRIFICE— THE WAILING MOUND OF FLESH. SACRIFICE— THE MAGI'S CORPSES.
'TIS A THREE-FOLD MAGIC RING.

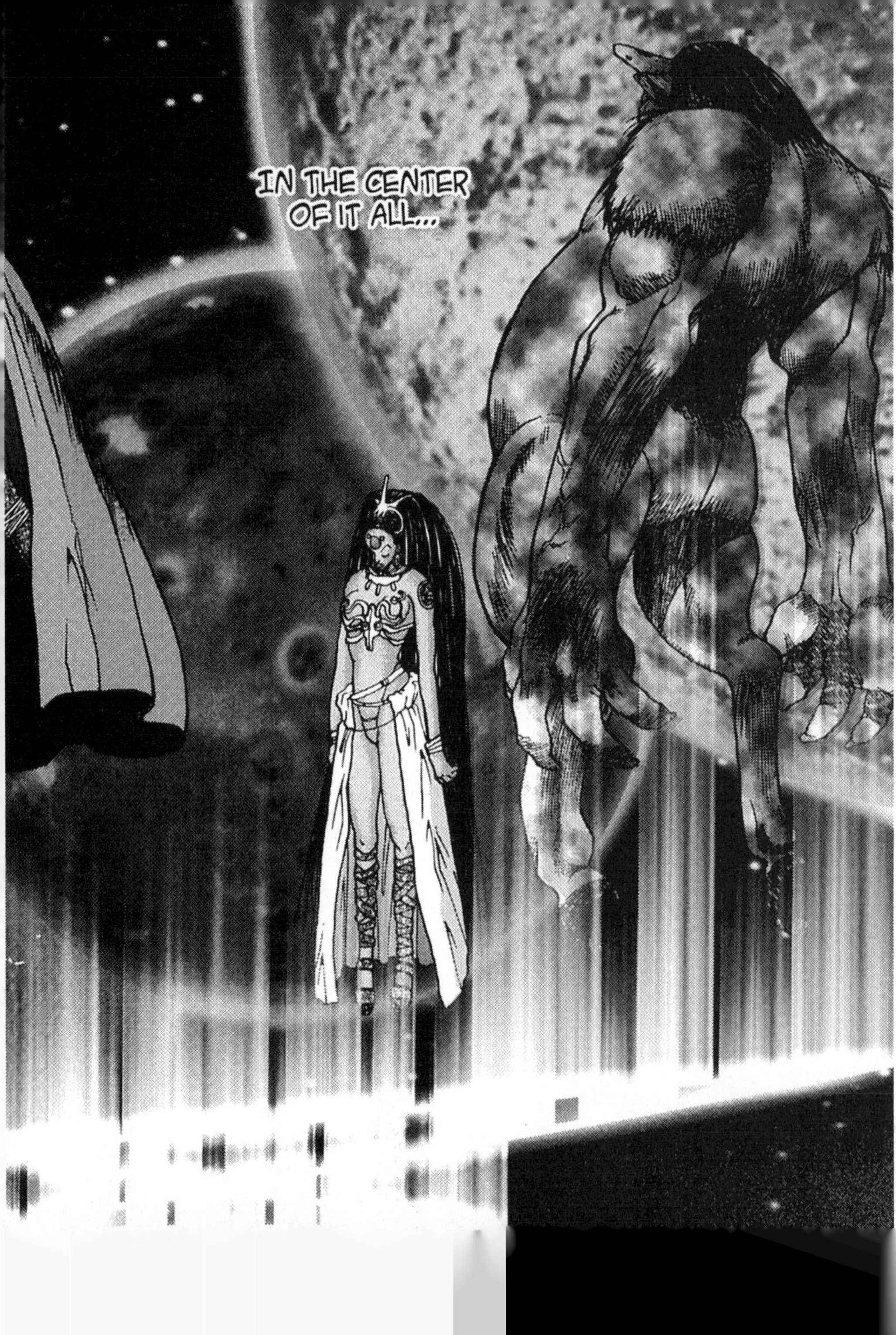
IN THE CENTER OF IT ALL...

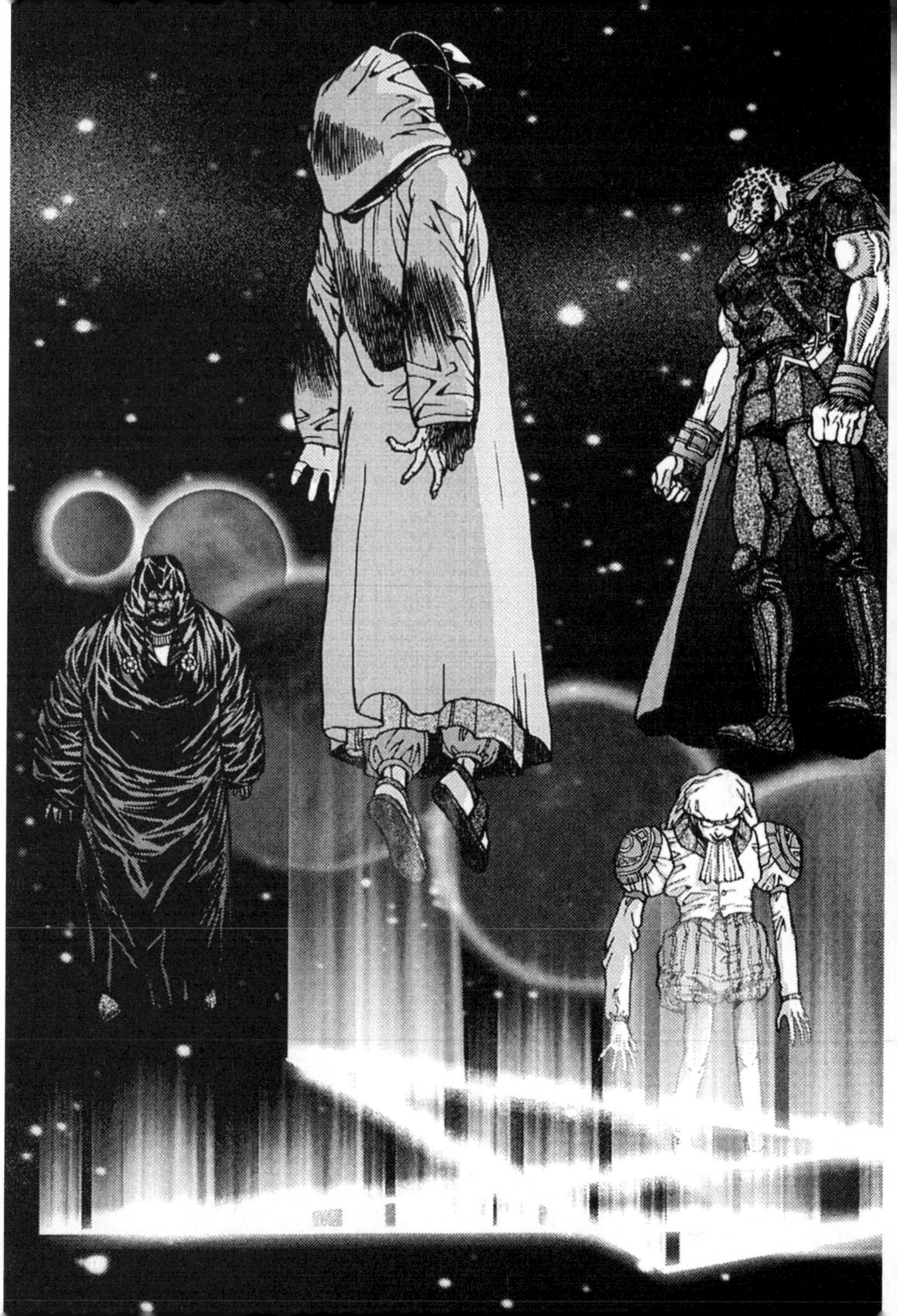

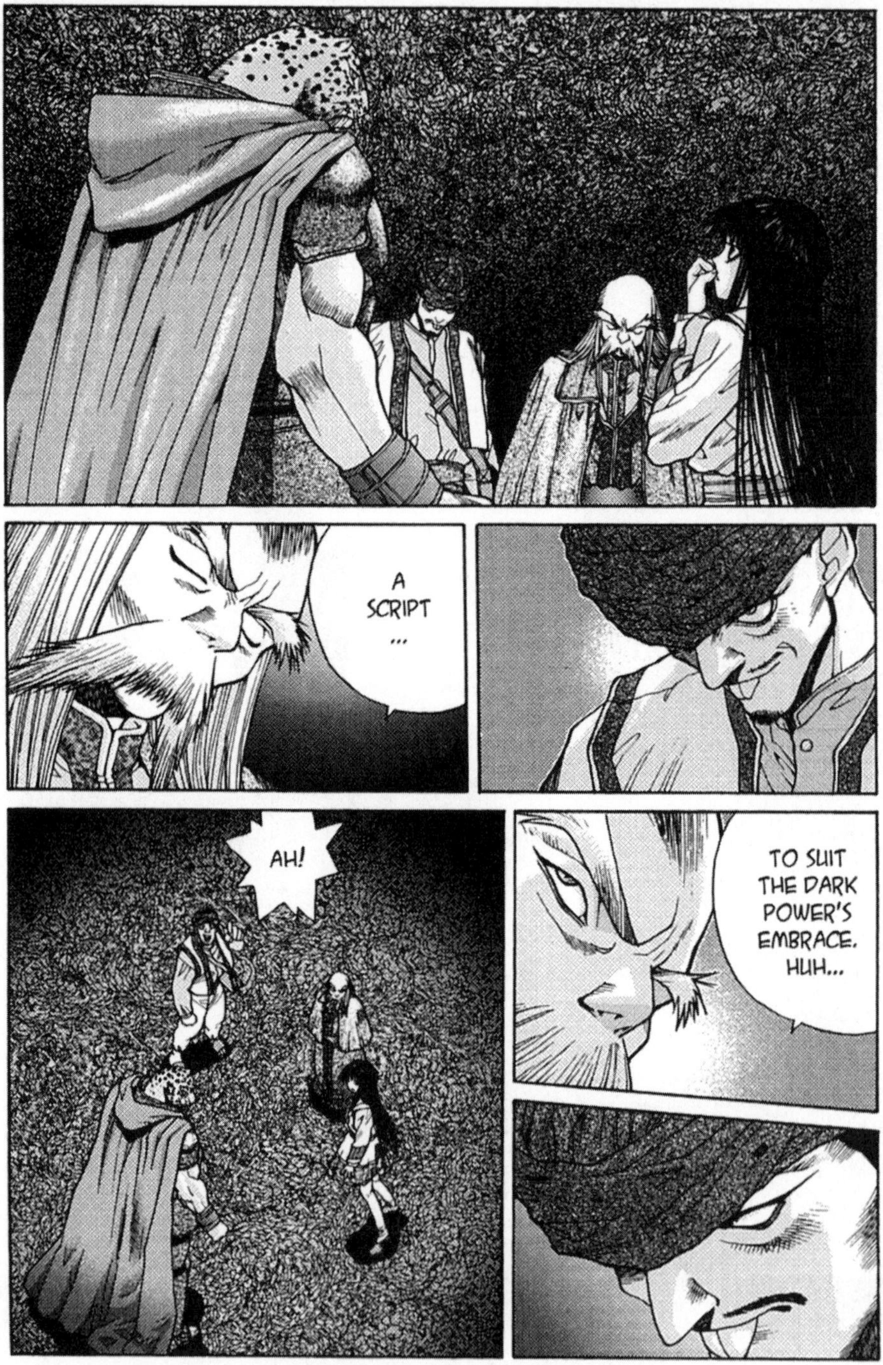
A SCRIPT ...
TO SUIT THE DARK POWER'S EMBRACE. HUH...
AH!

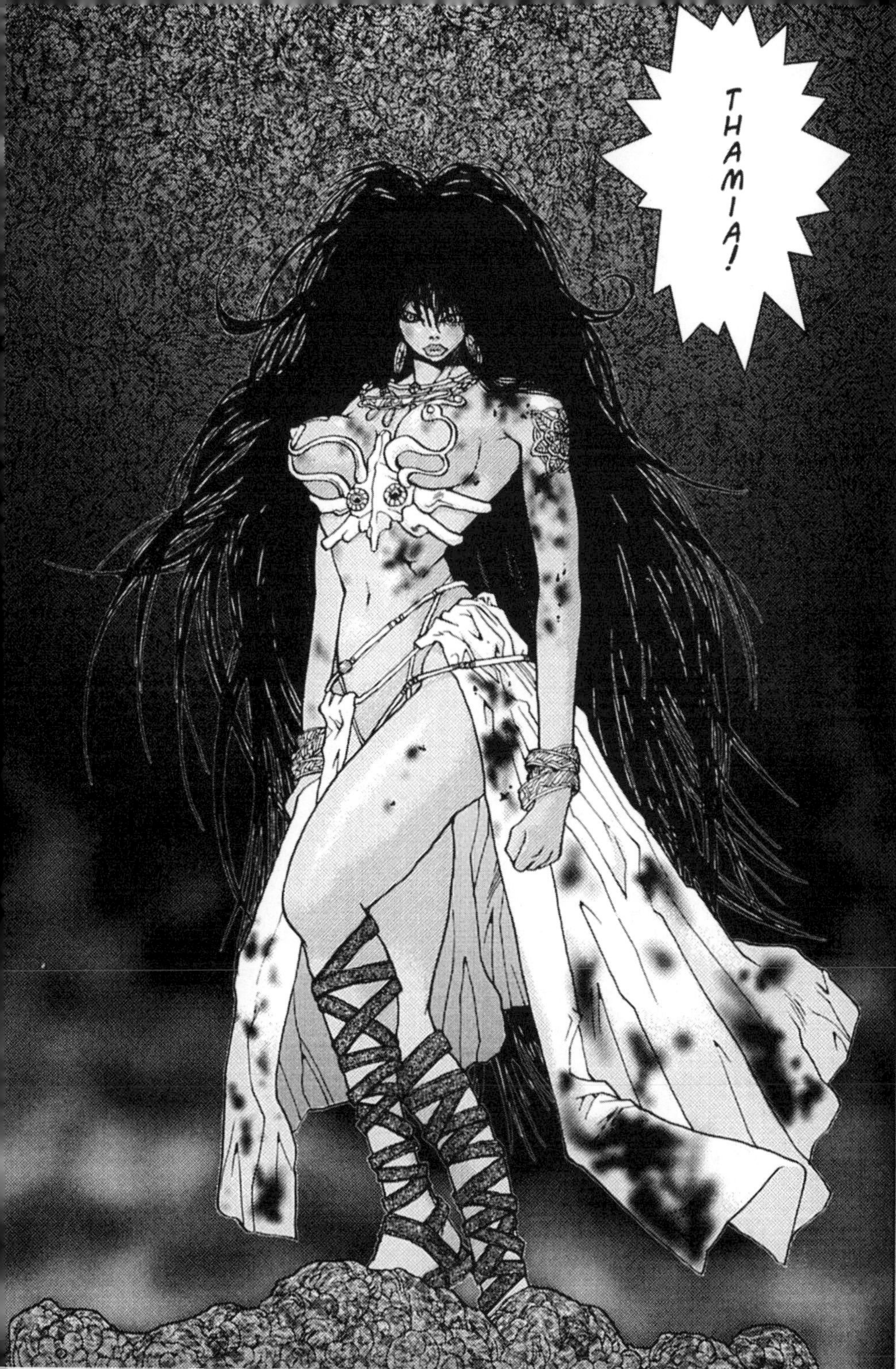
THAMIA!

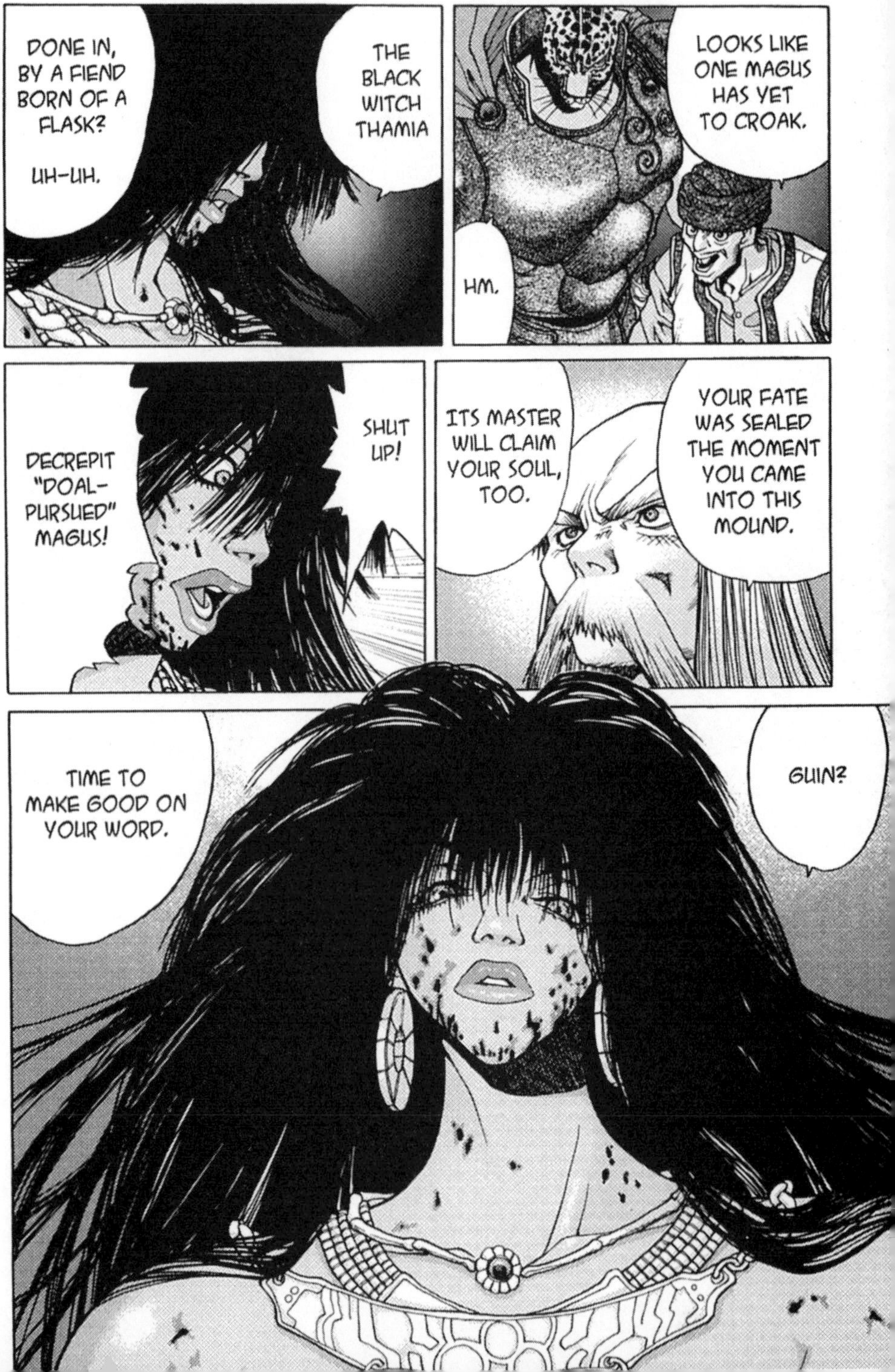
LOOKS LIKE ONE MAGUS HAS YET TO CROAK.
HM.
THE BLACK WITCH THAMIA
DONE IN, BY A FIEND BORN OF A FLASK?
UH-UH.
YOUR FATE WAS SEALED THE MOMENT YOU CAME INTO THIS MOUND.
ITS MASTER WILL CLAIM YOUR SOUL, TOO.
SHUT UP!
DECREPIT "DOAL-PURSUED" MAGUS!
GUIN?
TIME TO MAKE GOOD ON YOUR WORD.

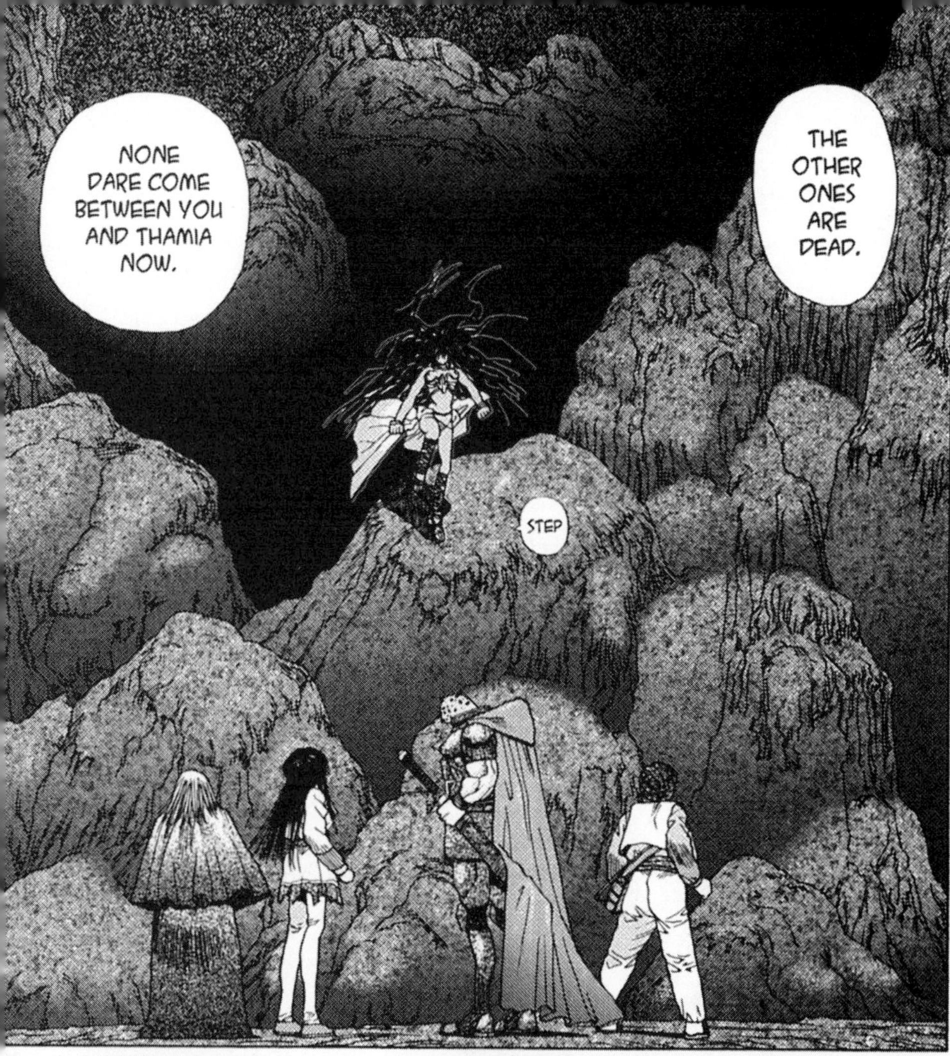
THE OTHER ONES ARE DEAD.
NONE DARE COME BETWEEN YOU AND THAMIA NOW.
STEP

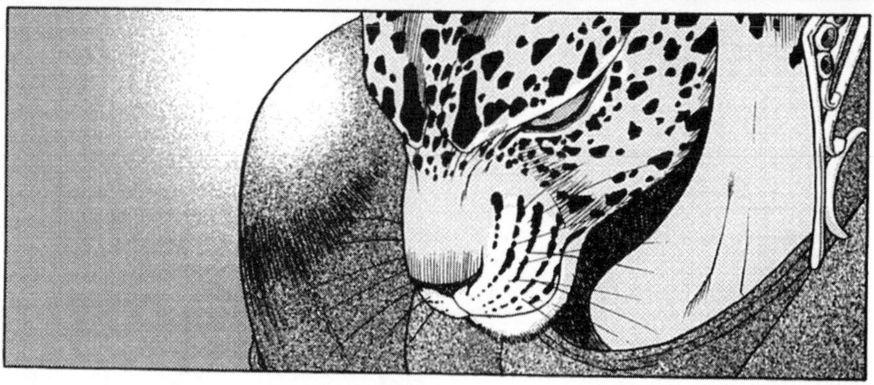

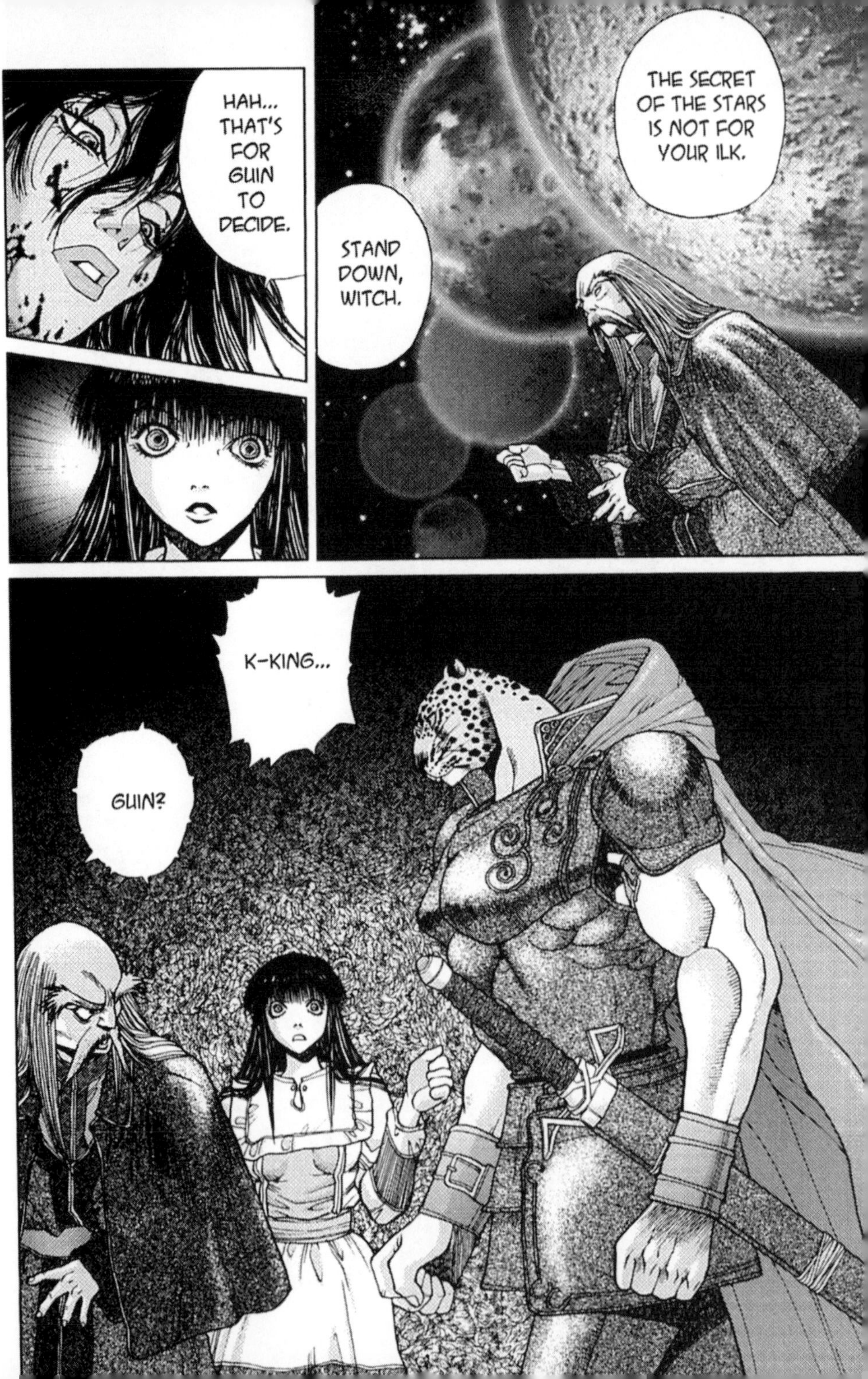
THE SECRET OF THE STARS IS NOT FOR YOUR ILK.
STAND DOWN, WITCH.
HAH... THAT'S FOR GUIN TO DECIDE.
K-KING...
GUIN?

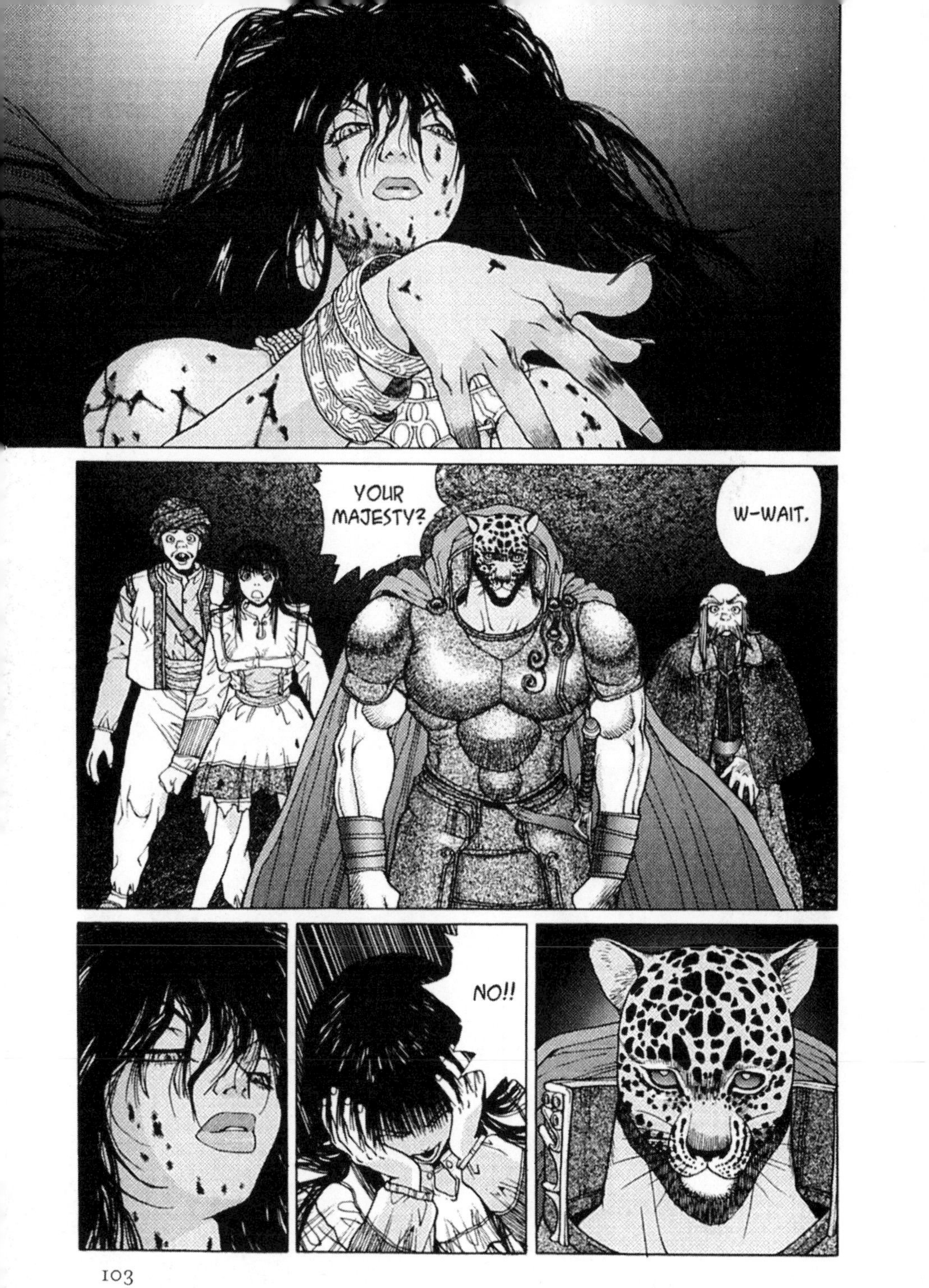
W-WAIT.
YOUR MAJESTY?
NO!!

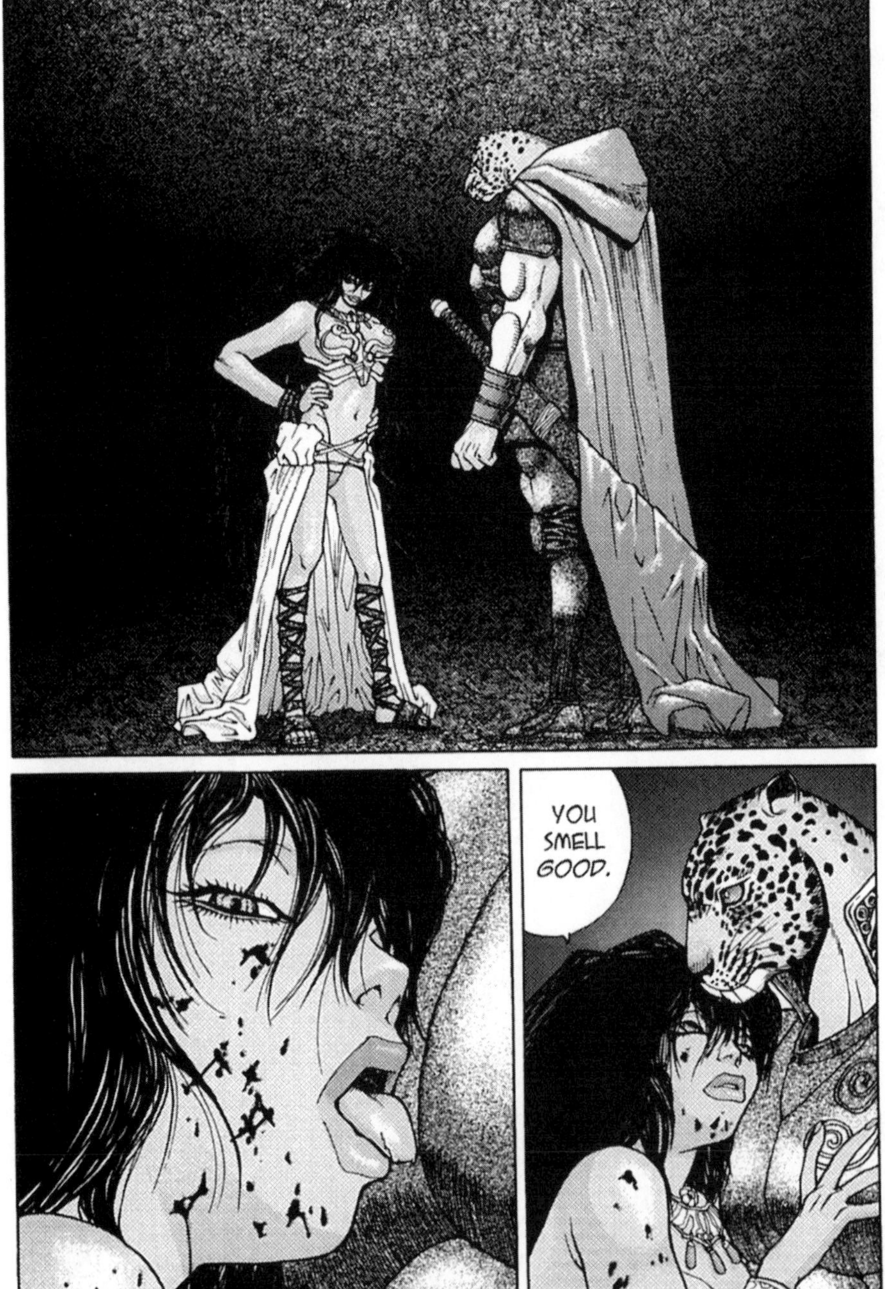
YOU SMELL GOOD.

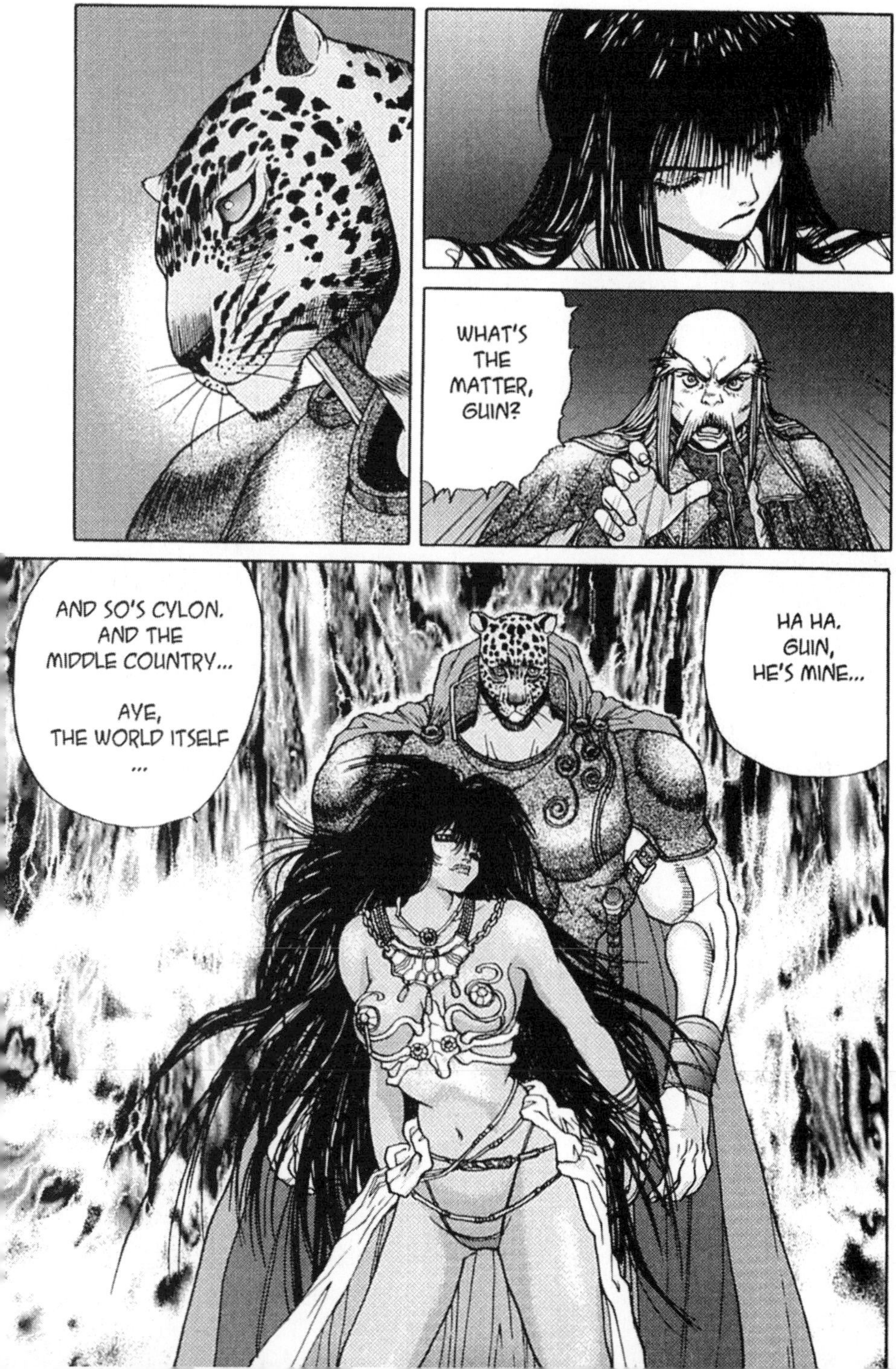
WHAT'S THE MATTER, GUIN?
HA HA. GUIN, HE'S MINE...
AND SO'S CYLON. AND THE MIDDLE COUNTRY...
AYE, THE WORLD ITSELF ...

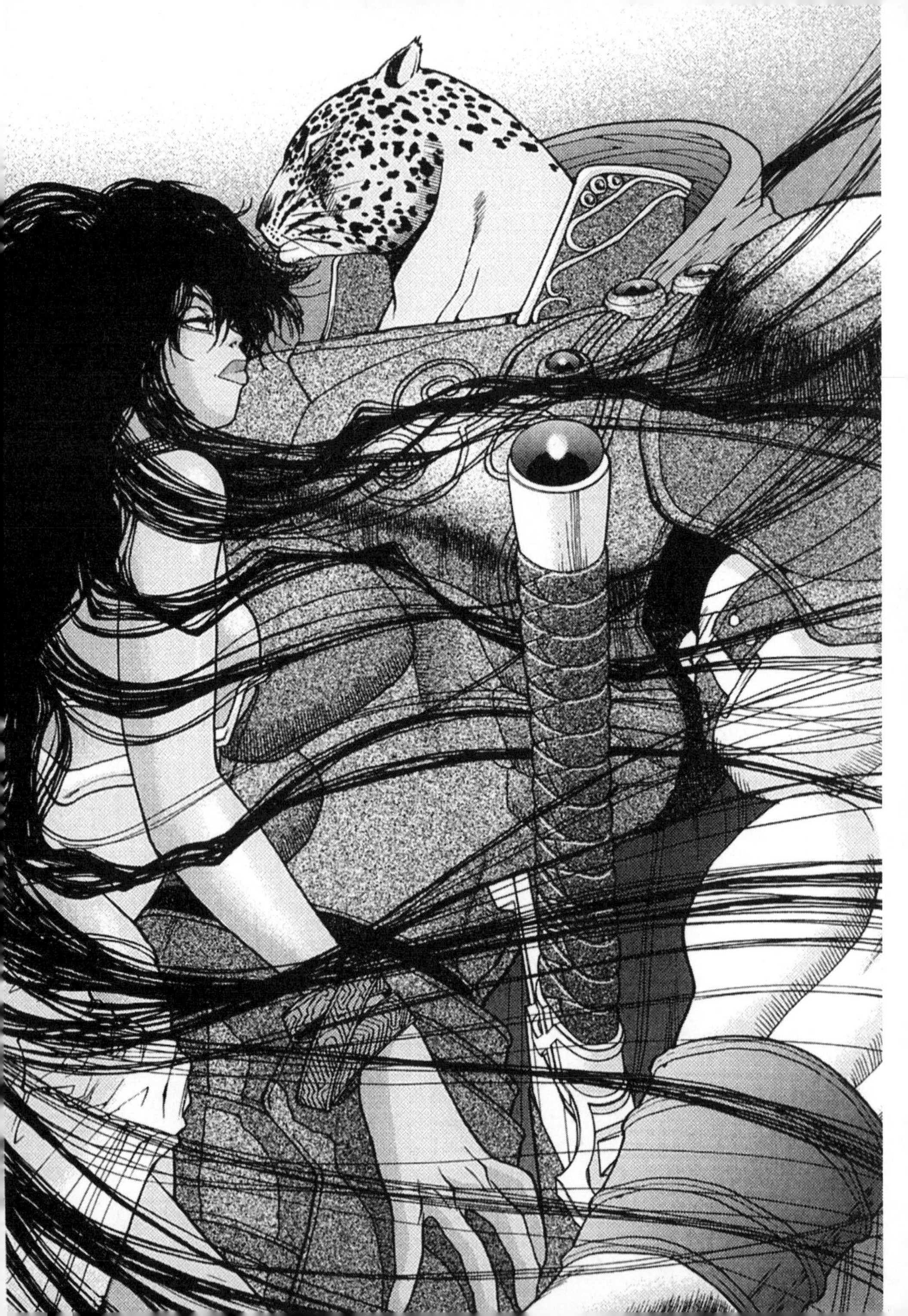

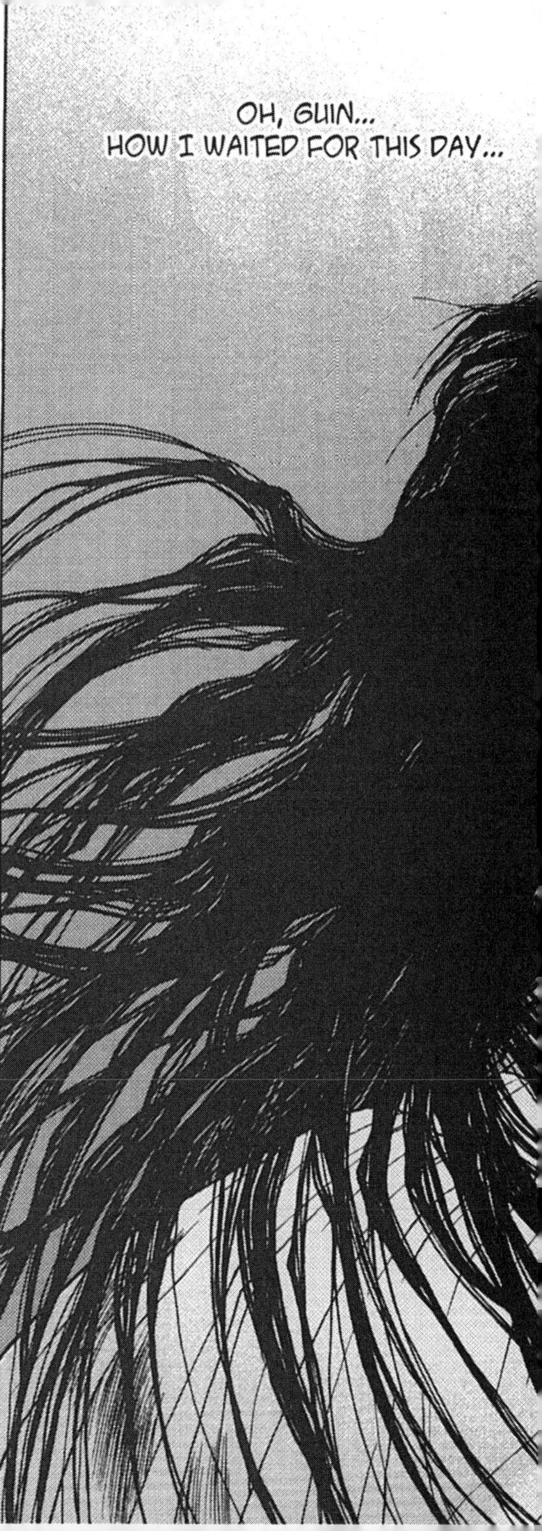
OH, GUIN...
HOW I WAITED FOR THIS DAY...

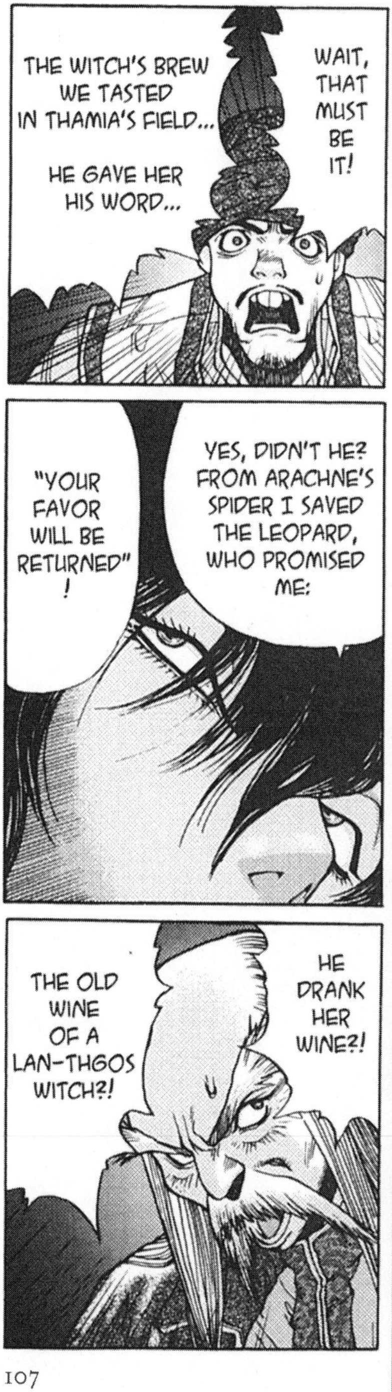
WAIT, THAT MUST BE IT!
THE WITCH'S BREW WE TASTED IN THAMIA'S FIELD...
HE GAVE HER HIS WORD...
YES, DIDN'T HE? FROM ARACHNE'S SPIDER I SAVED THE LEOPARD, WHO PROMISED ME:
"YOUR FAVOR WILL BE RETURNED" !
HE DRANK HER WINE?!
THE OLD WINE OF A LAN-THGOS WITCH?!

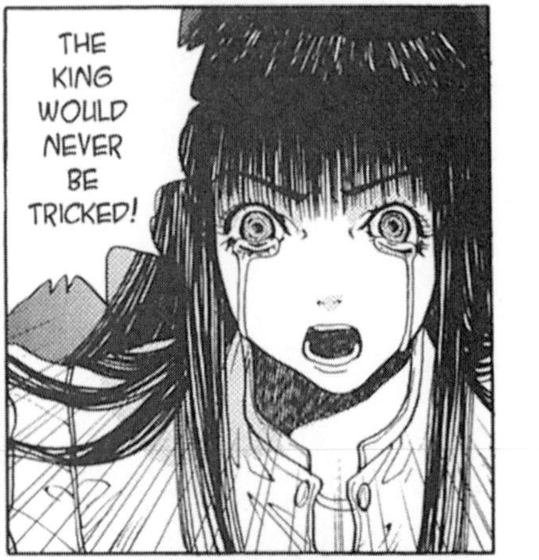
THE KING WOULD NEVER BE TRICKED!

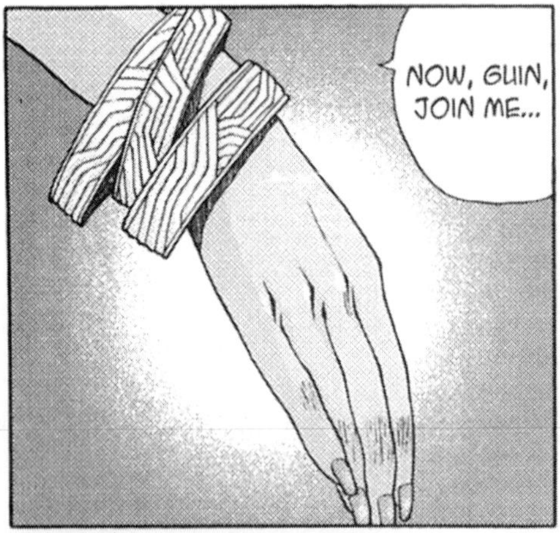
NOW, GUIN, JOIN ME...

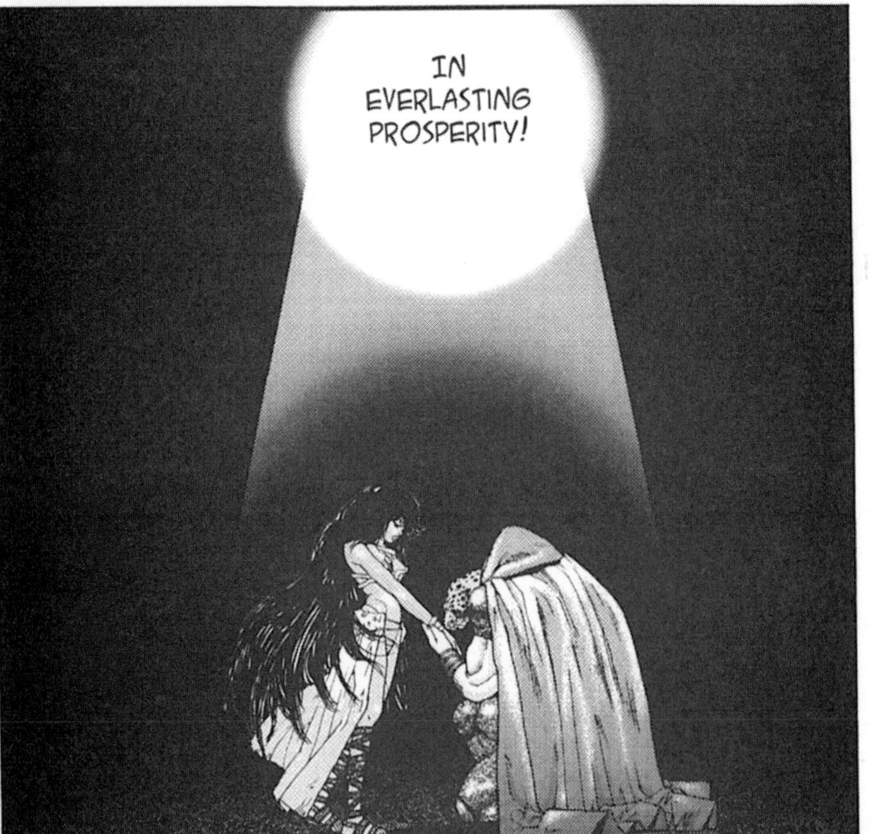
IN EVERLASTING PROSPERITY!

CHAPTER 21

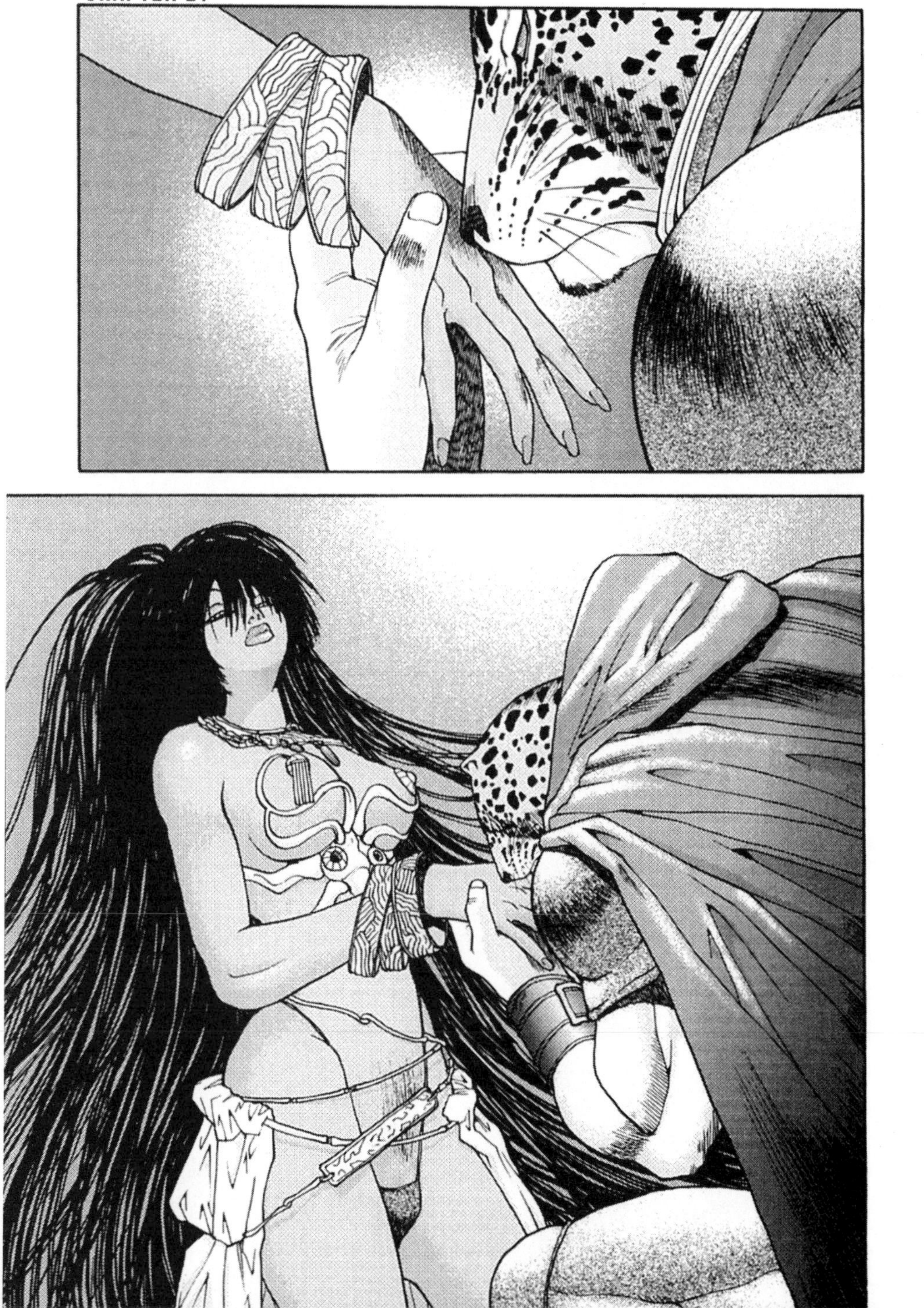

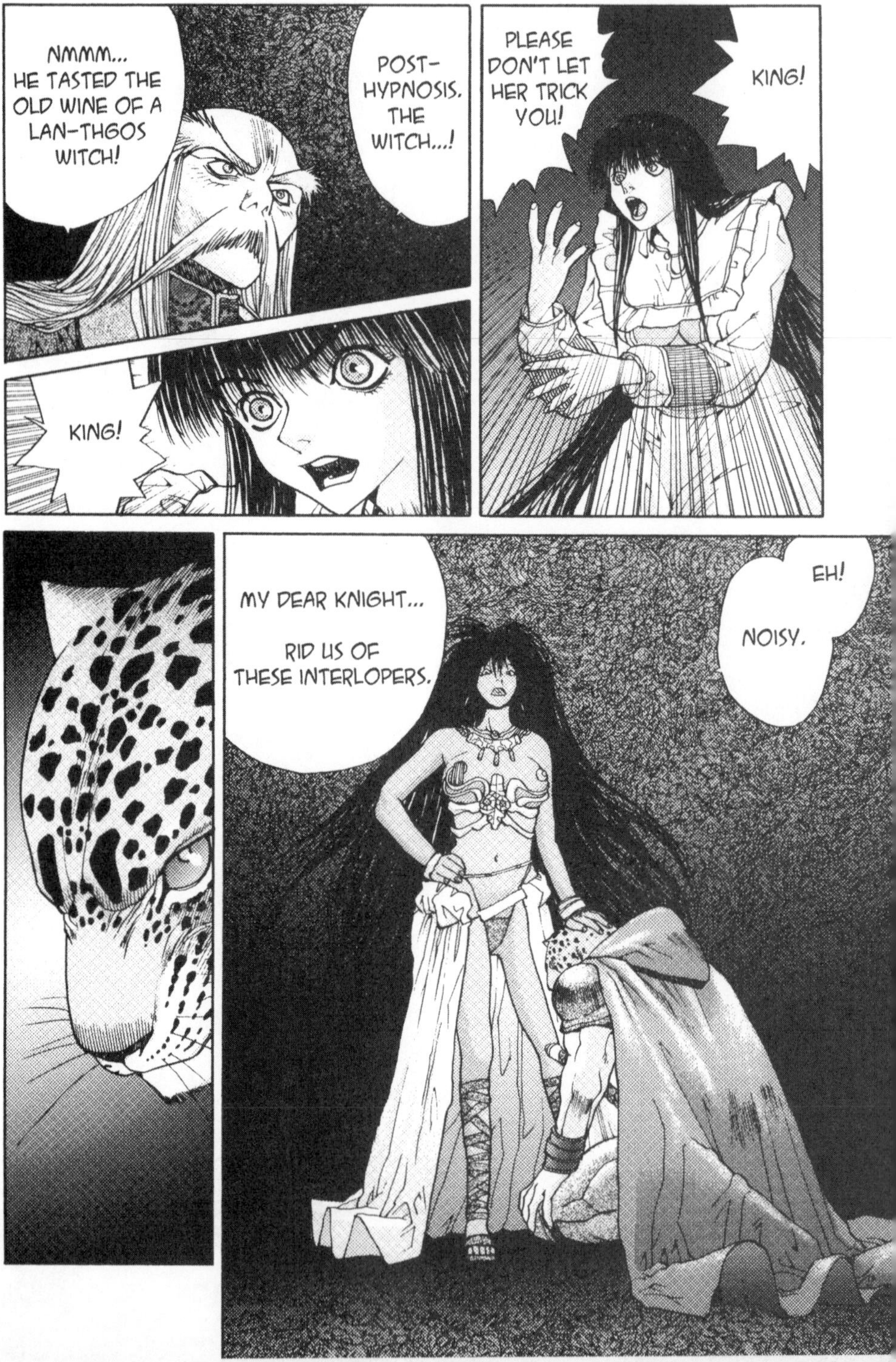
KING!
PLEASE DON'T LET HER TRICK YOU!
POST-HYPNOSIS. THE WITCH...!
NMMM... HE TASTED THE OLD WINE OF A LAN-THGOS WITCH!
KING!
EH!
NOISY.
MY DEAR KNIGHT...
RID US OF THESE INTERLOPERS.

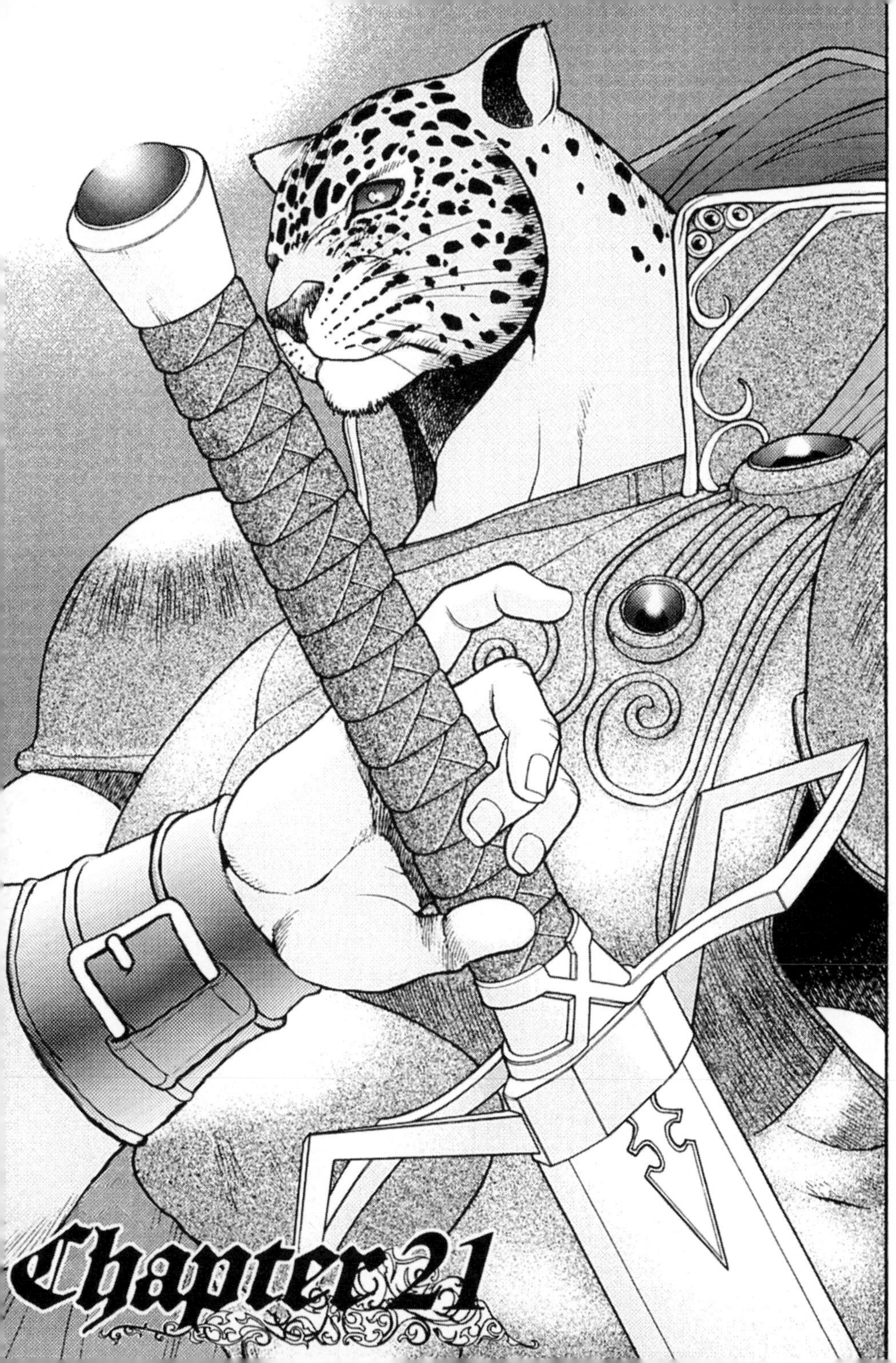
Chapter 21

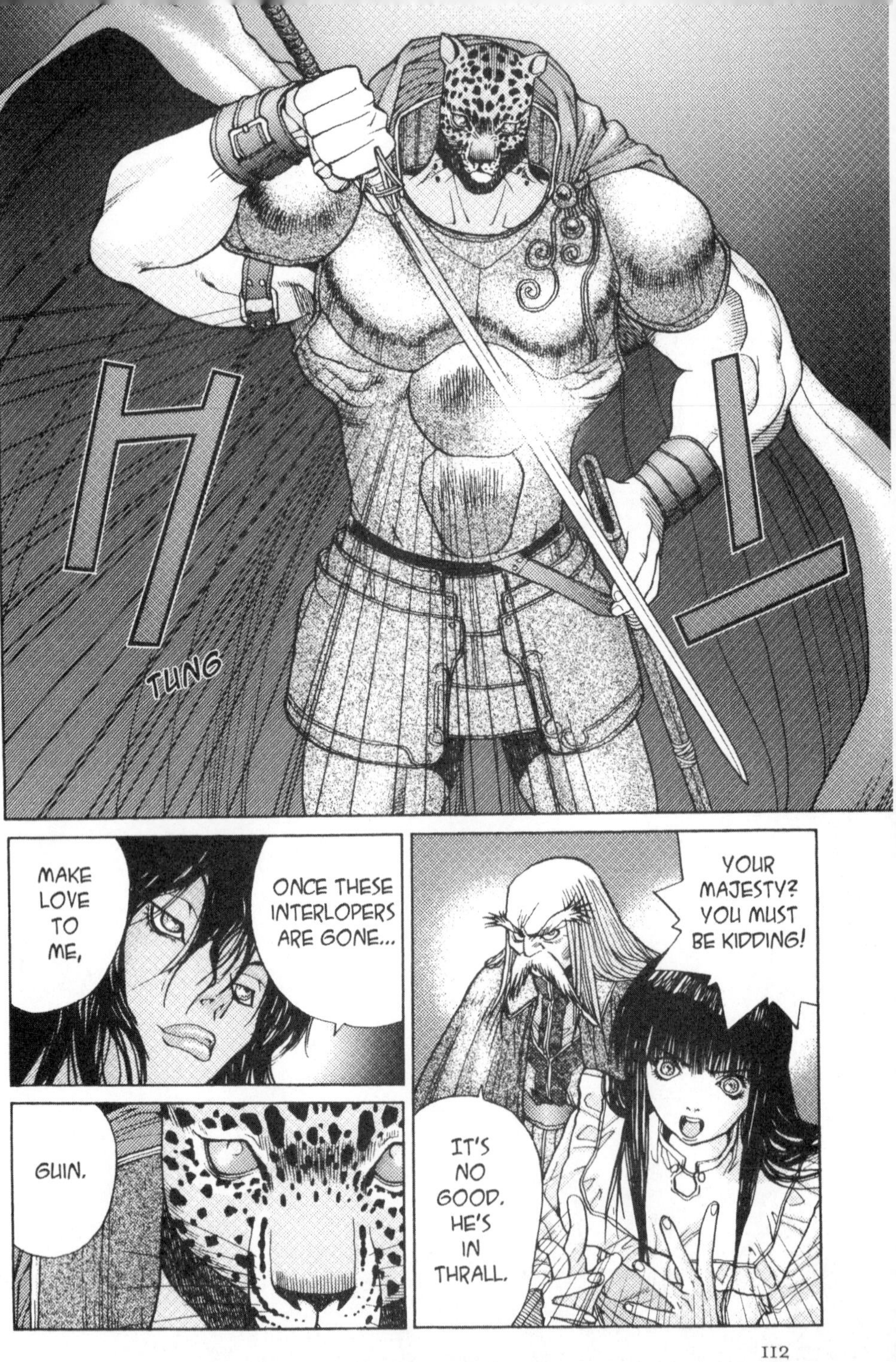
TUNG
YOUR MAJESTY? YOU MUST BE KIDDING!
IT'S NO GOOD. HE'S IN THRALL.
ONCE THESE INTERLOPERS ARE GONE...
MAKE LOVE TO ME,
GUIN.

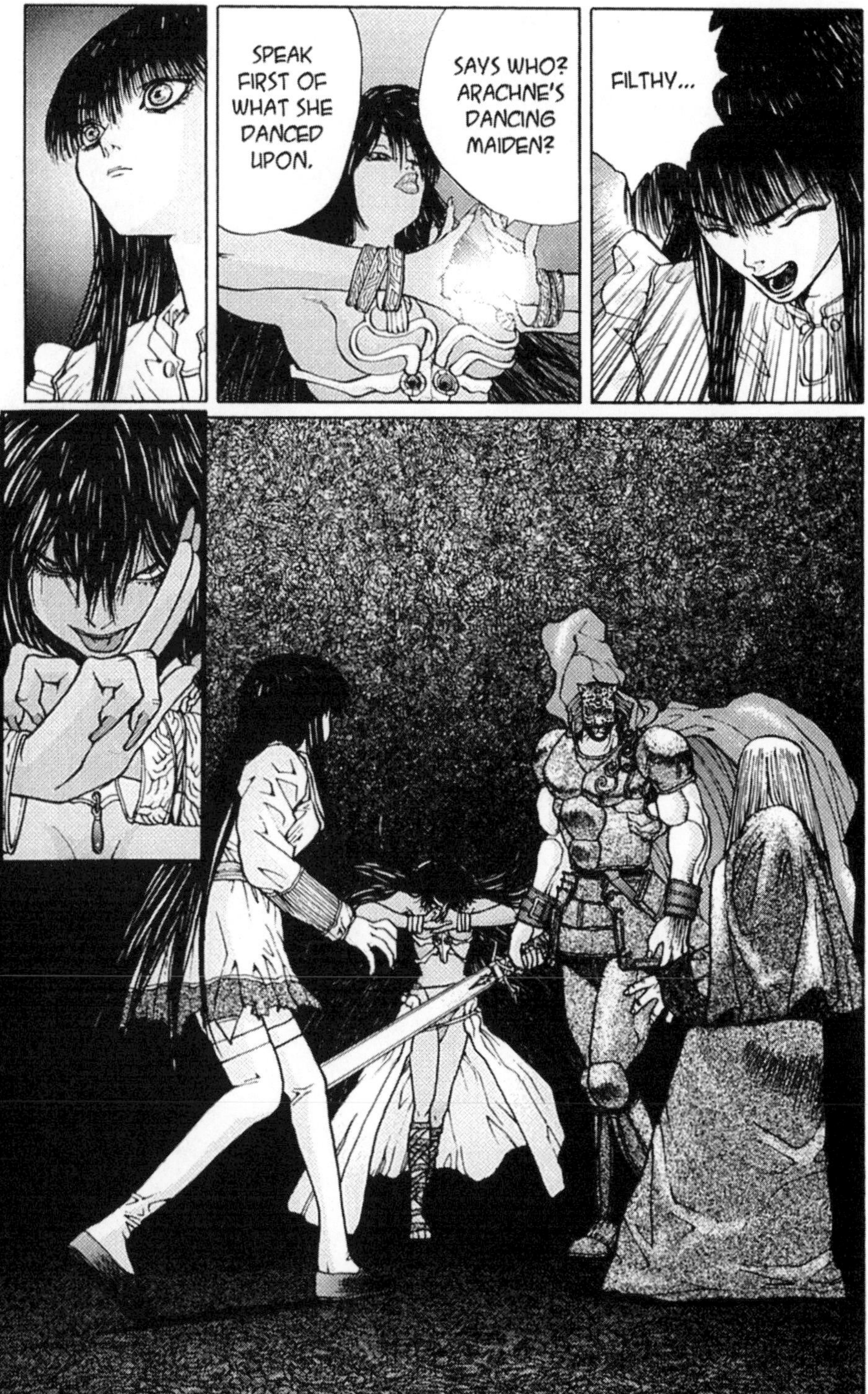
FILTHY...
SAYS WHO? ARACHNE'S DANCING MAIDEN?
SPEAK FIRST OF WHAT SHE DANCED UPON.

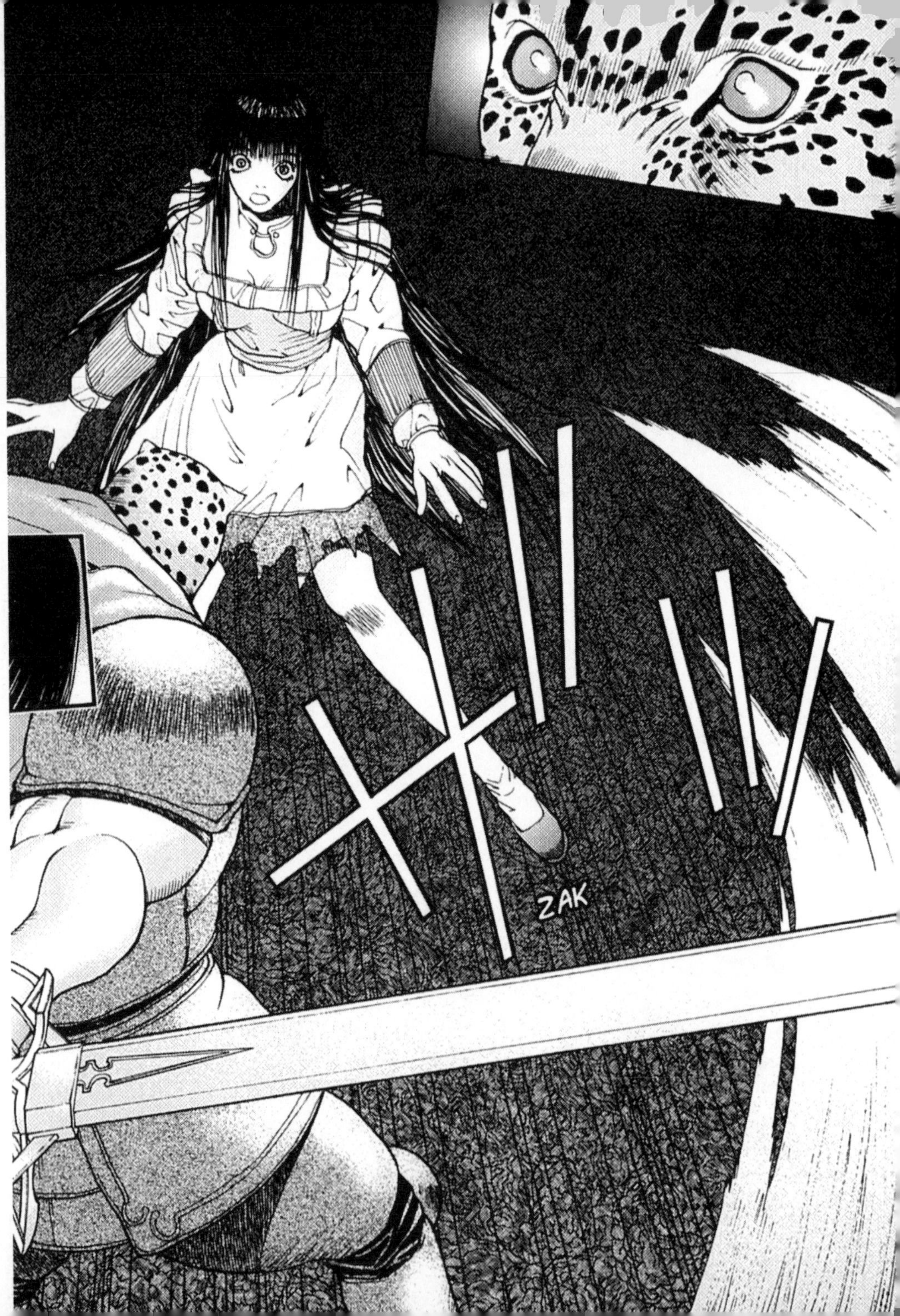
ZAK

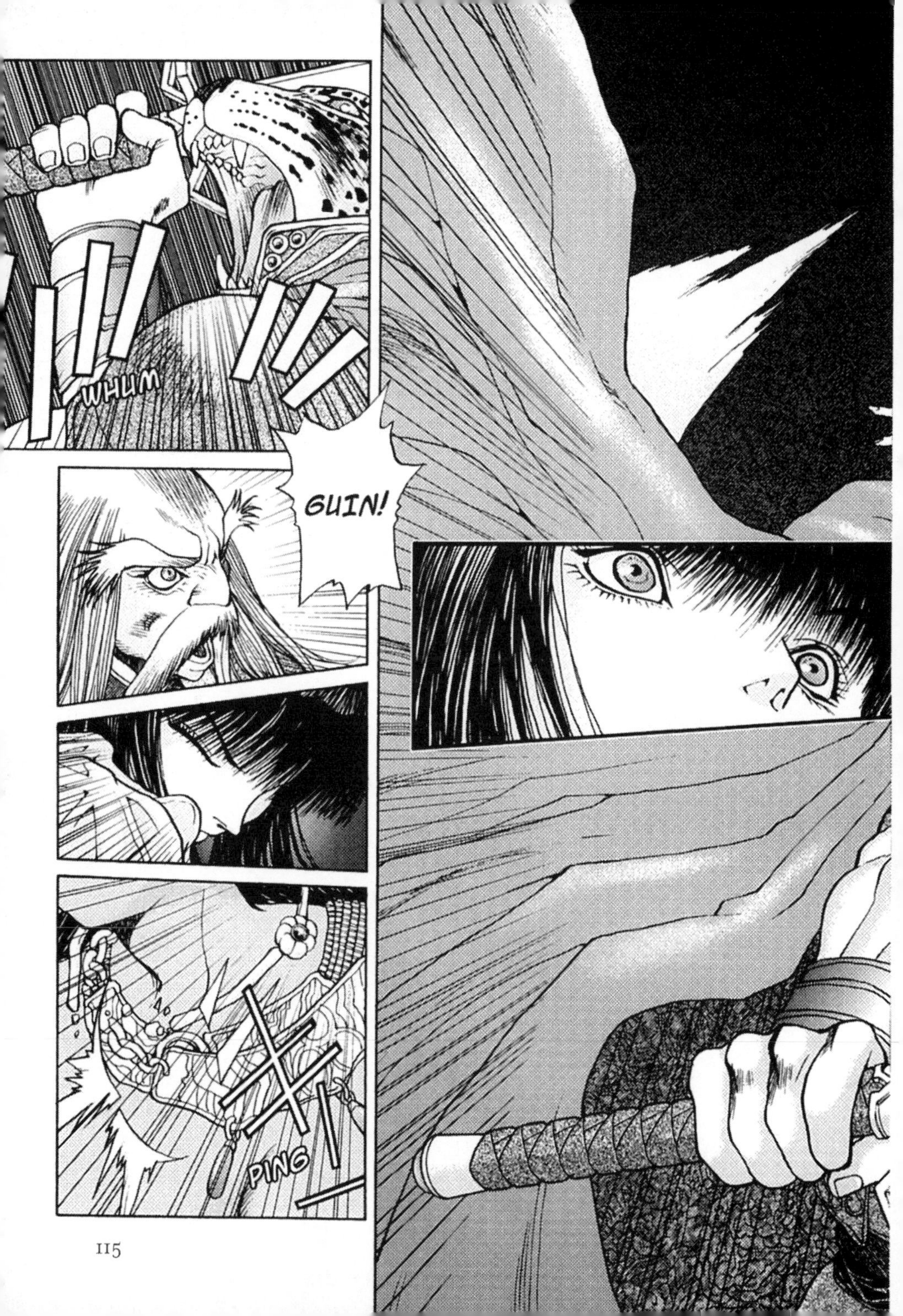
WHUM
GUIN!
PING

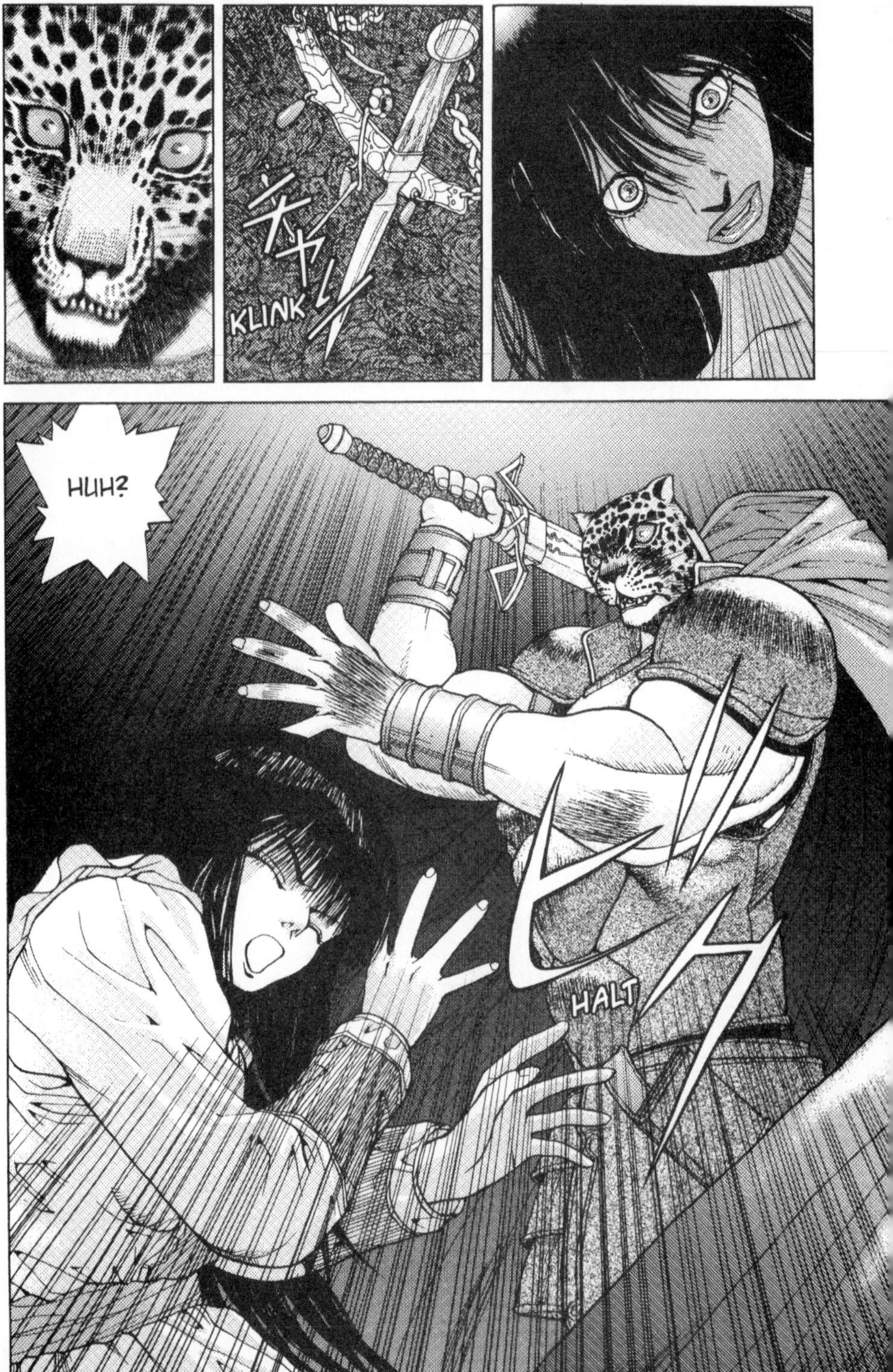
KLINK
HUH?
HALT

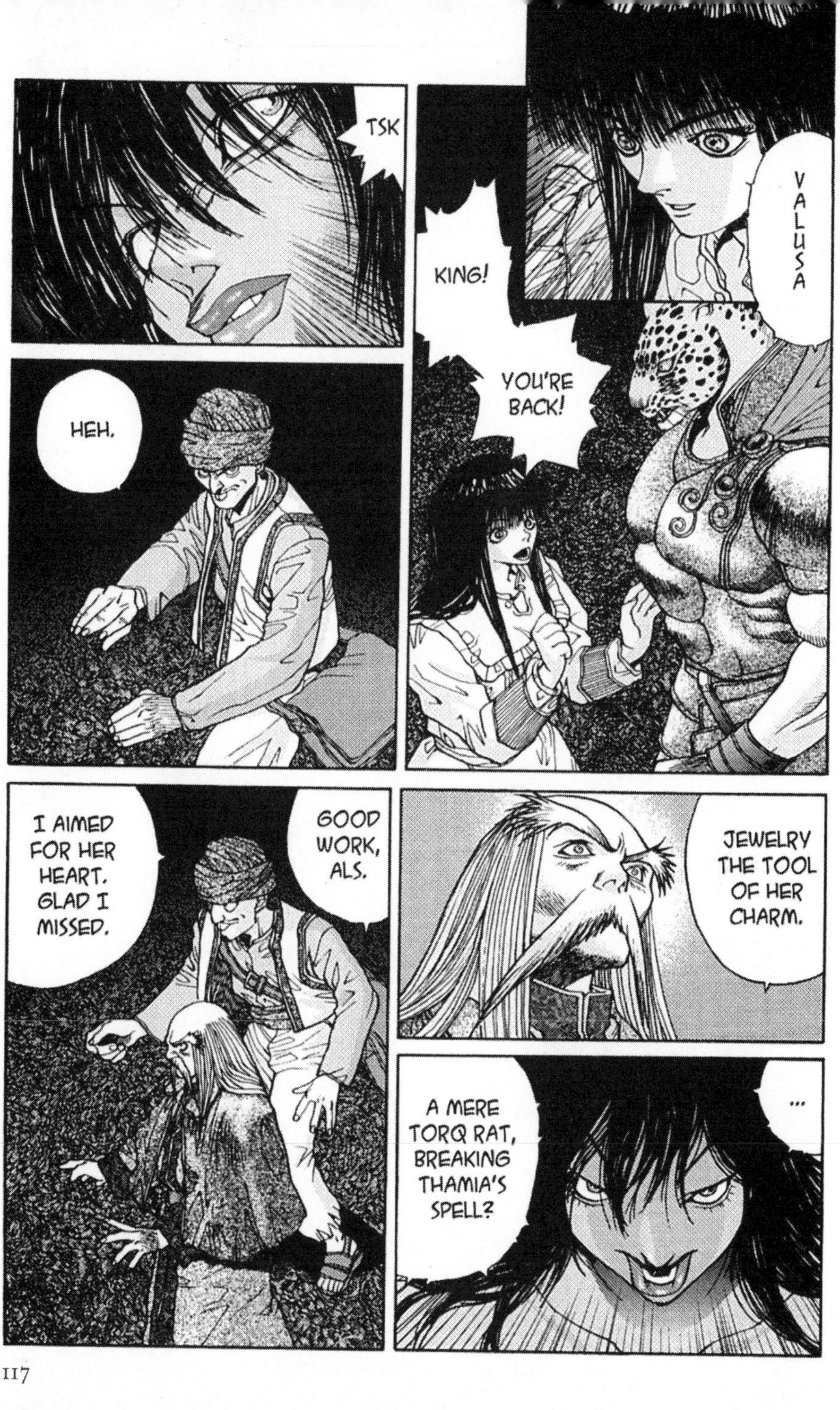
VALUSA
TSK
KING!
YOU'RE BACK!
HEH.
JEWELRY THE TOOL OF HER CHARM.
...
A MERE TORQ RAT, BREAKING THAMIA'S SPELL?
GOOD WORK, ALS.
I AIMED FOR HER HEART. GLAD I MISSED.

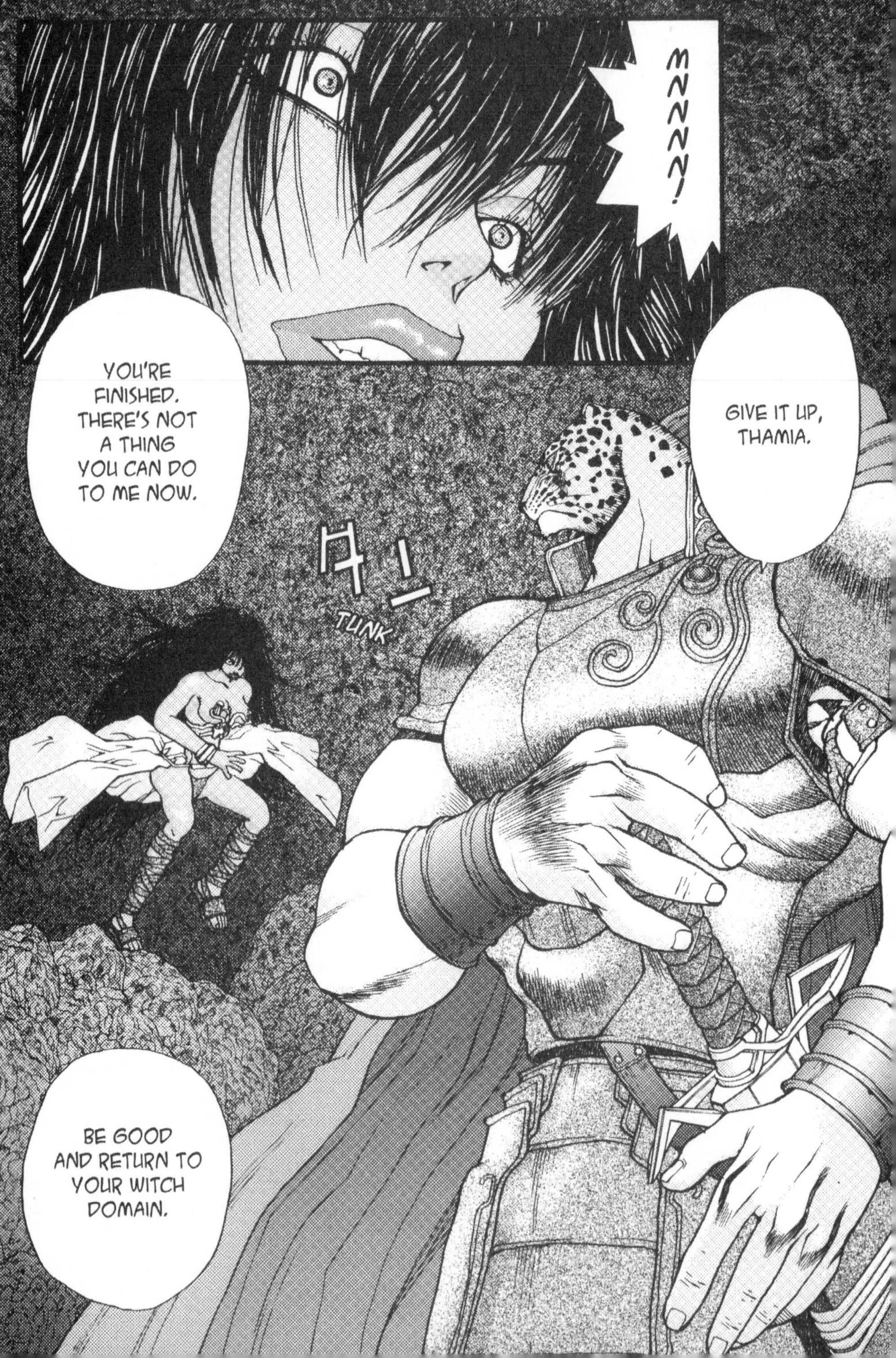
MNNNN!
GIVE IT UP, THAMIA.
YOU'RE FINISHED. THERE'S NOT A THING YOU CAN DO TO ME NOW.
TUNK
BE GOOD AND RETURN TO YOUR WITCH DOMAIN.

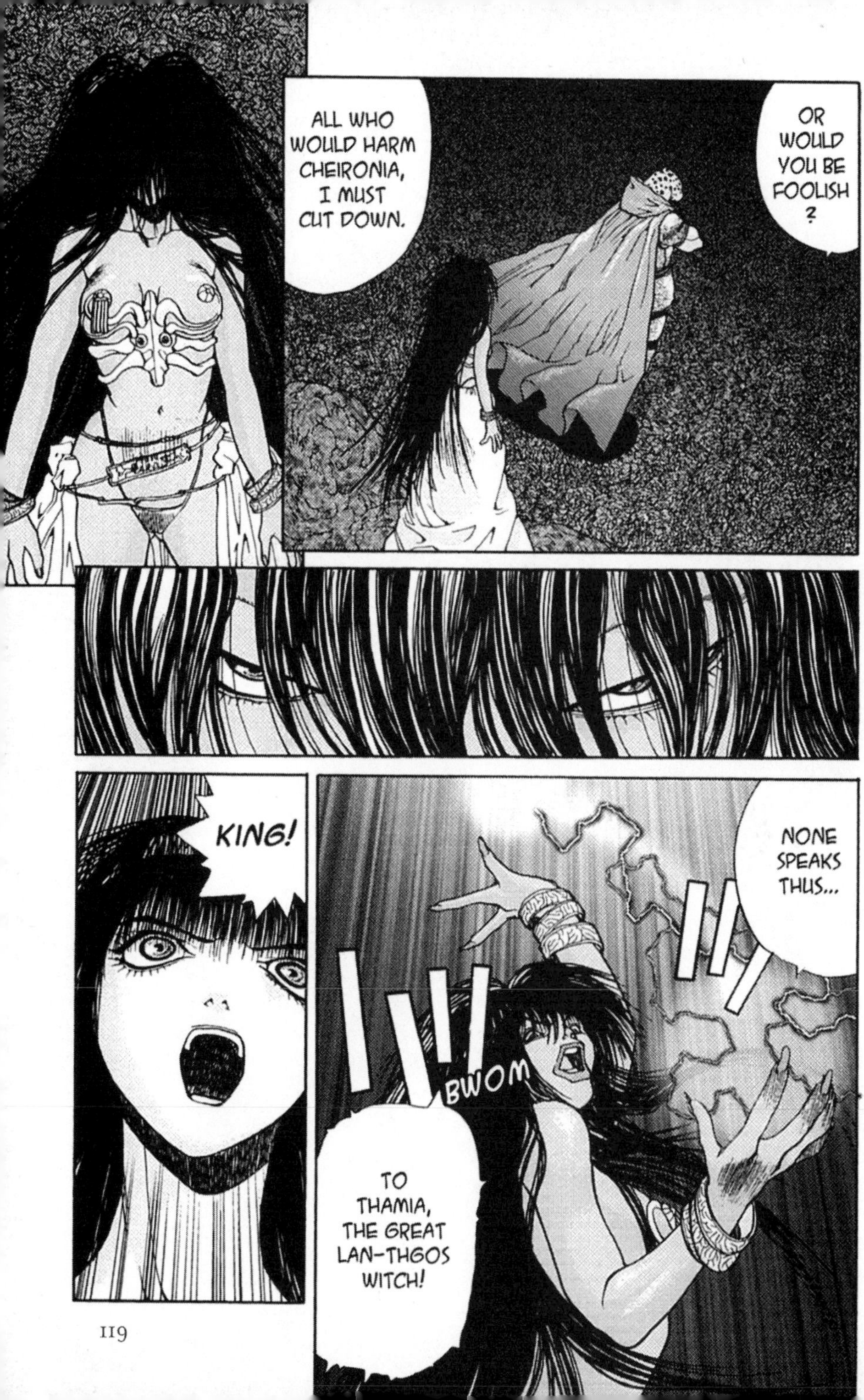
OR WOULD YOU BE FOOLISH?
ALL WHO WOULD HARM CHEIRONIA, I MUST CUT DOWN.
NONE SPEAKS THUS...
BWOM
TO THAMIA, THE GREAT LAN-THGOS WITCH!
KING!

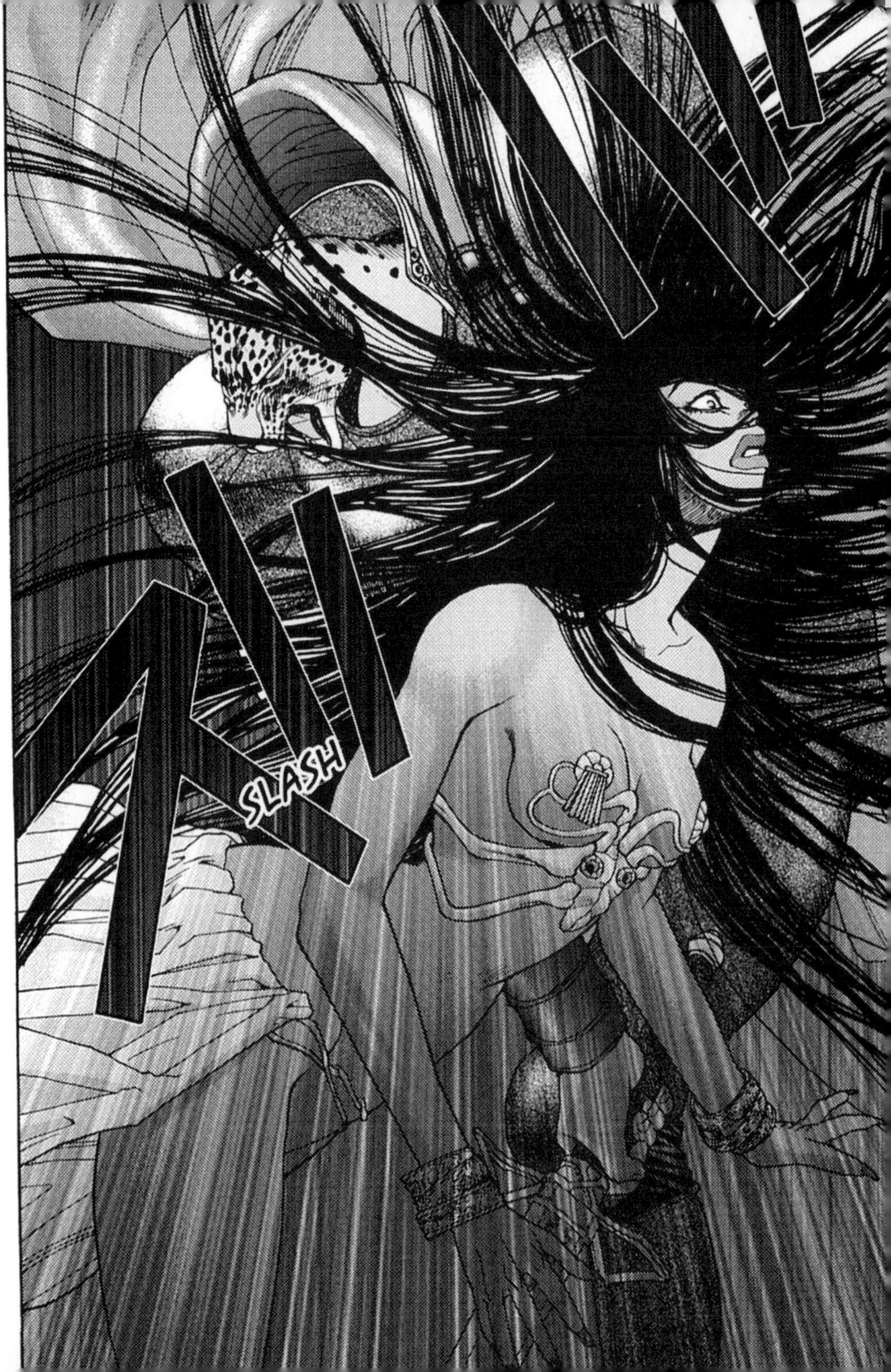
SLASH

CHAPTER 22

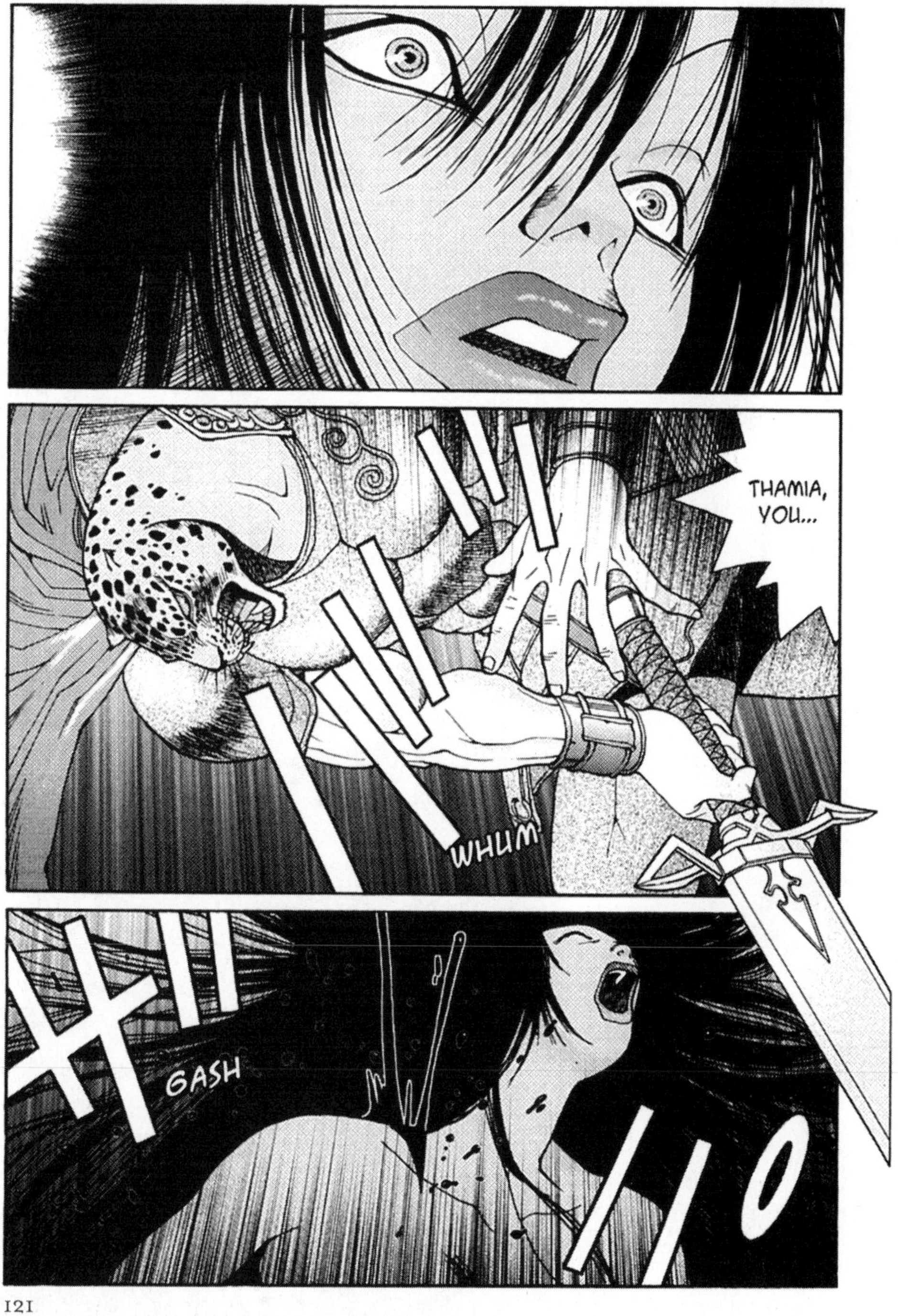
THAMIA, YOU...
WHUM
GASH

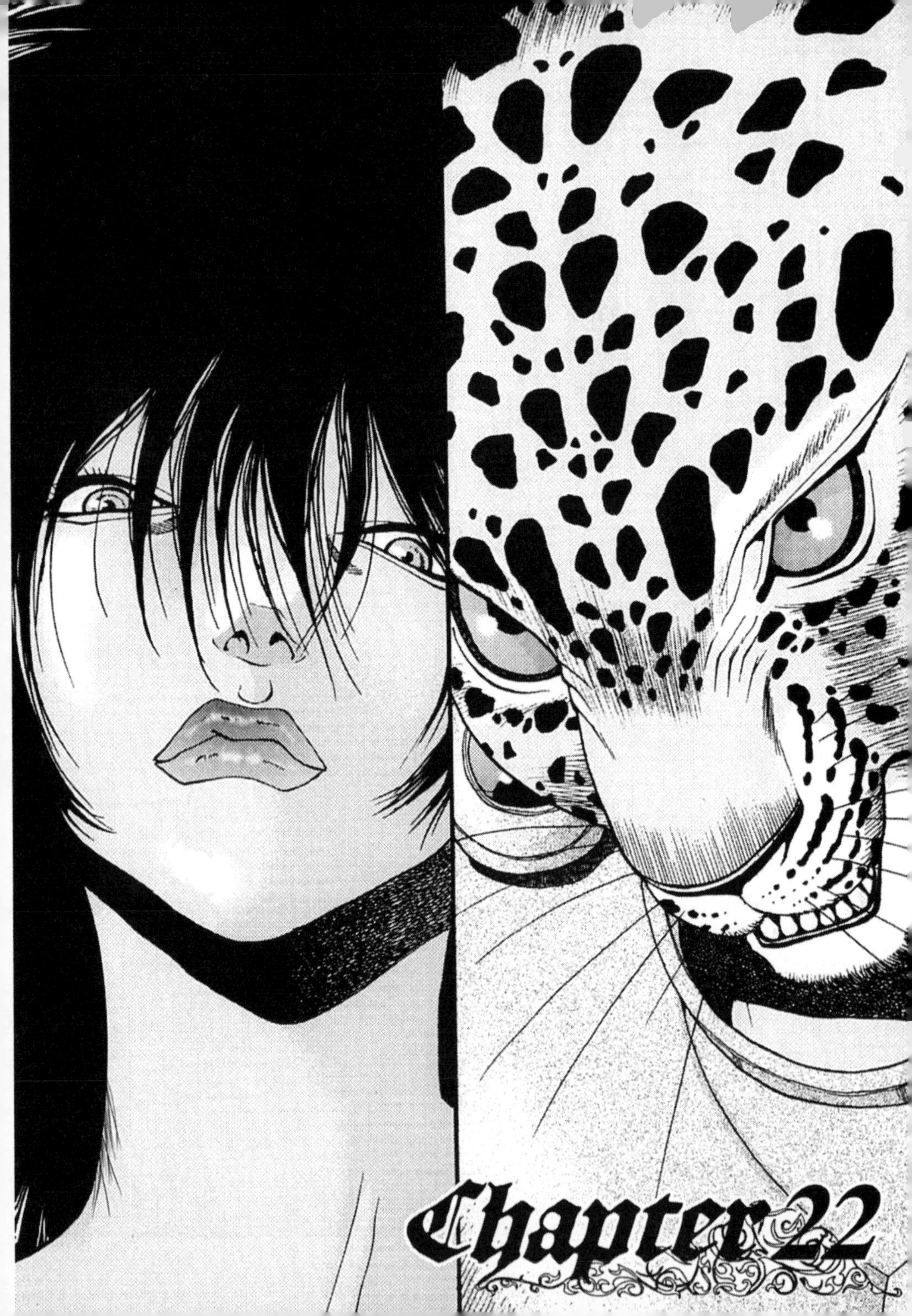
Chapter 22

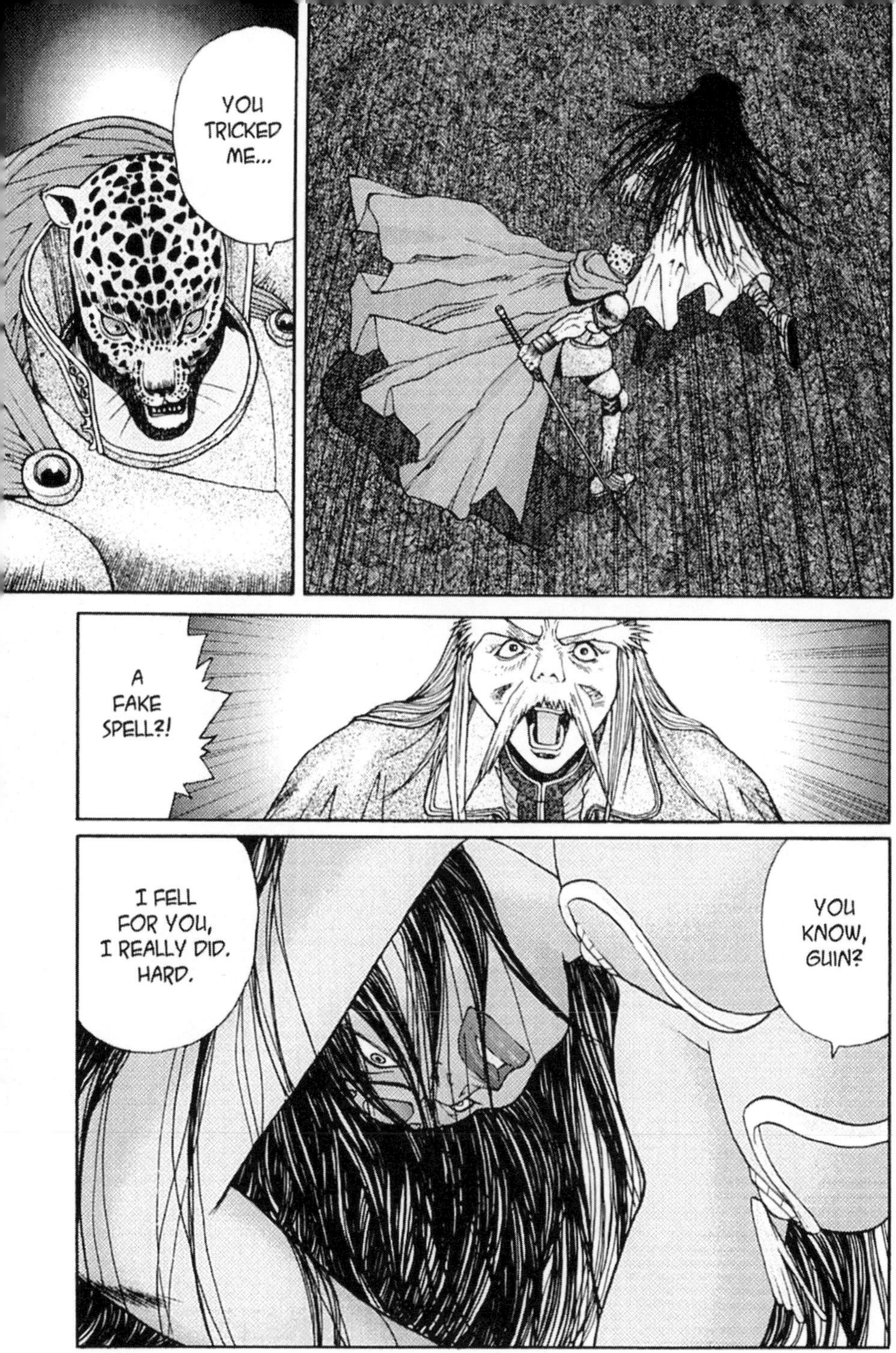
YOU TRICKED ME...
A FAKE SPELL?!
YOU KNOW, GUIN?
I FELL FOR YOU, I REALLY DID. HARD.

THERE'S NO GOING BACK,

スリ スリ
CRAWL

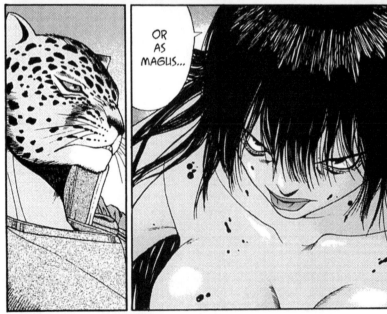

OR AS MAGUS...

AS WOMAN

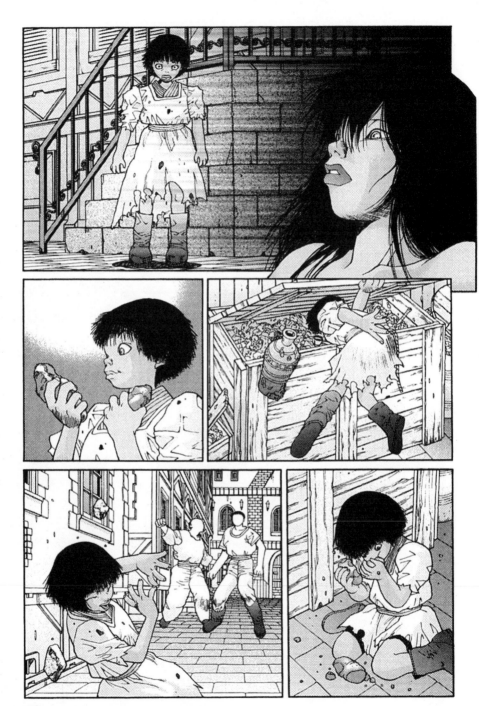

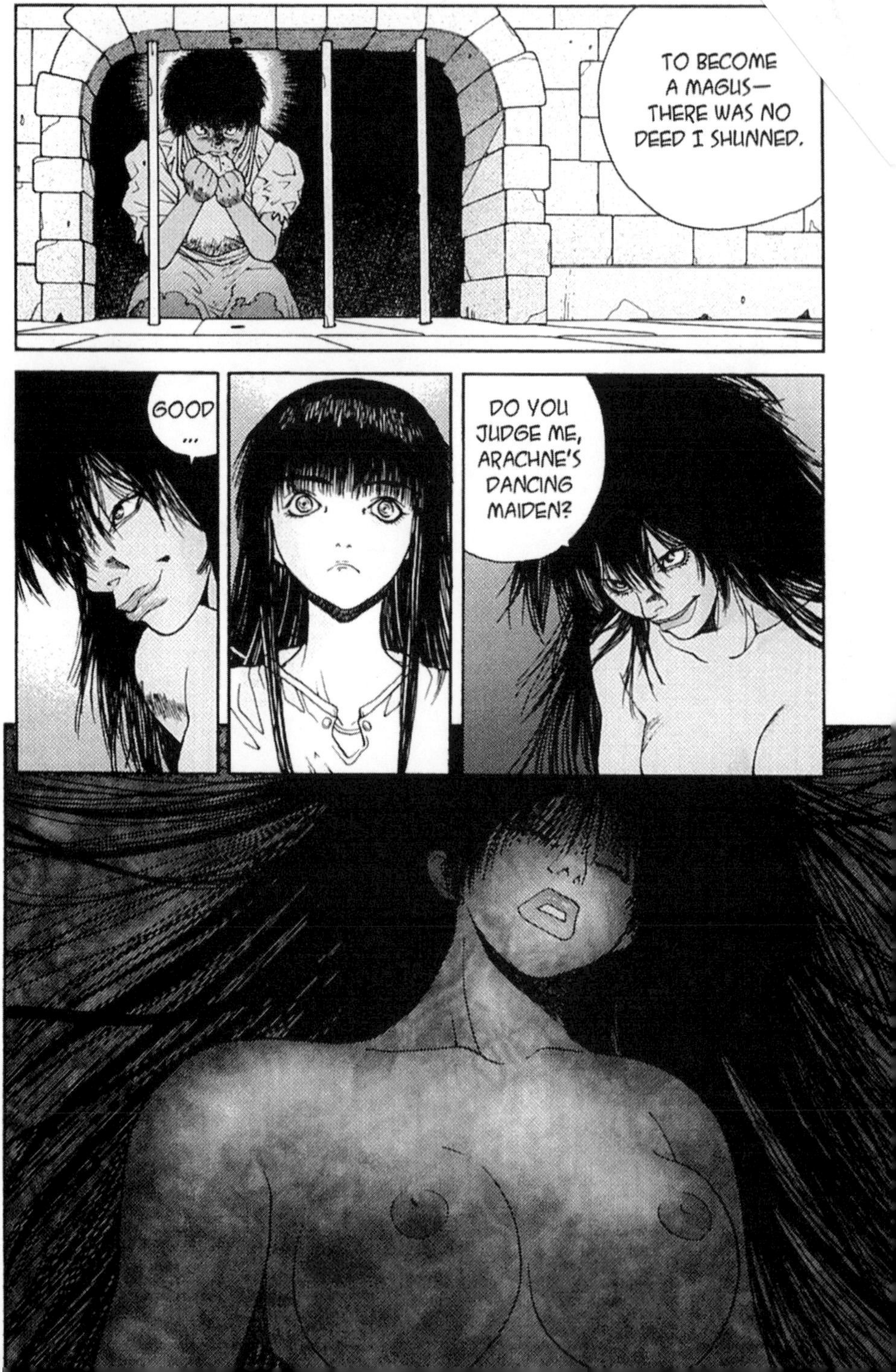
TO BECOME A MAGUS— THERE WAS NO DEED I SHUNNED.
DO YOU JUDGE ME, ARACHNE'S DANCING MAIDEN?
GOOD ...

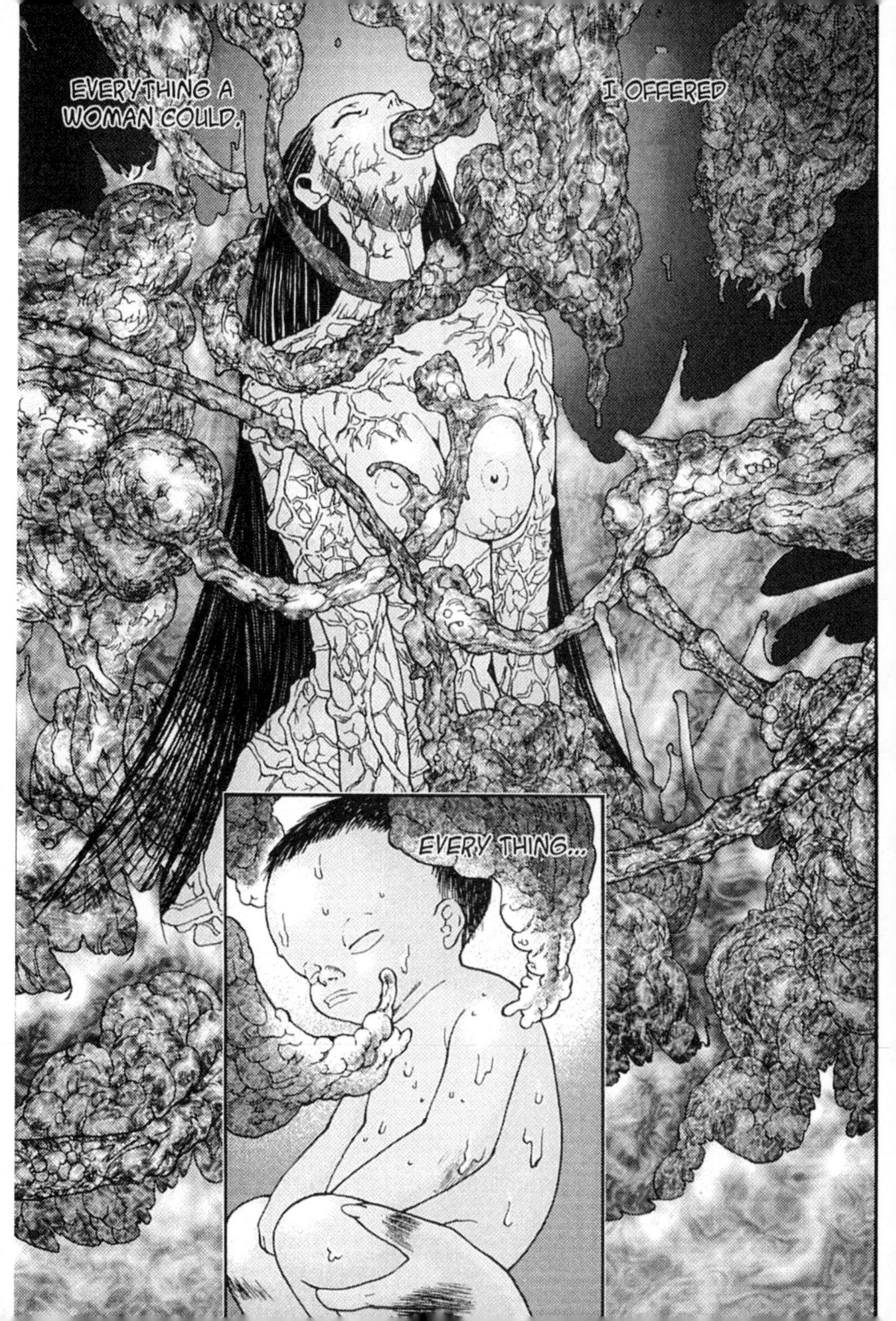
I OFFERED
EVERYTHING A WOMAN COULD.
EVERY THING...

BE THE ONE...

TO PUT ME TO...

HAH

HAH

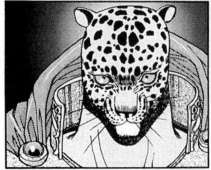

GRANT ME A WISH, GUIN.

THE FINAL WISH OF THAMIA THE MAGUS.

HAHH

AT LEAST,

GUIN.

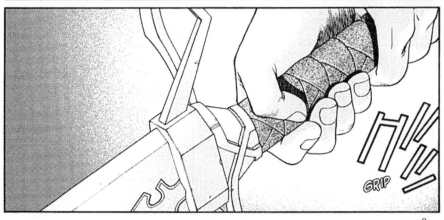

GRIP

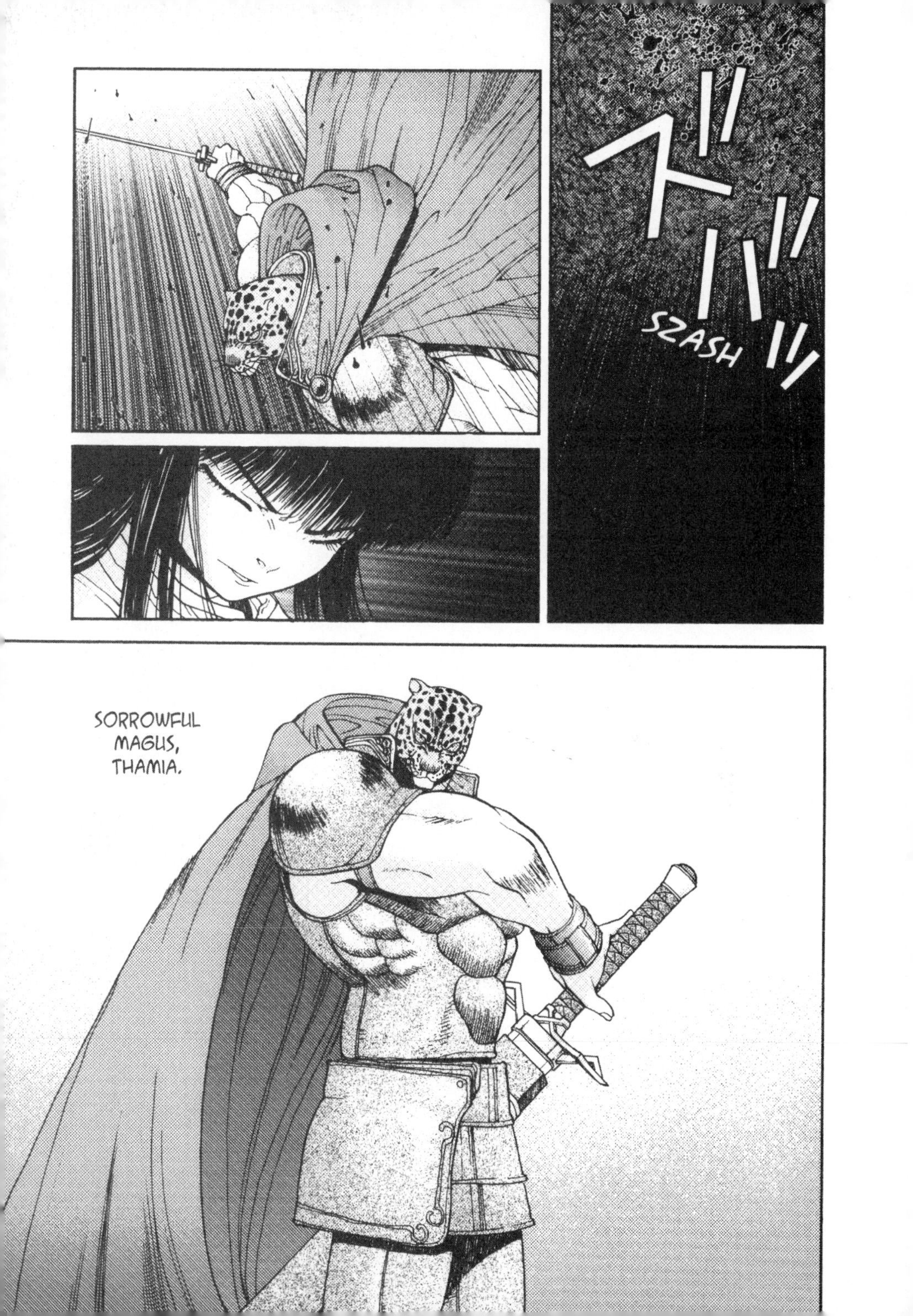
ズバーッ
SZASH
SORROWFUL MAGUS, THAMIA.

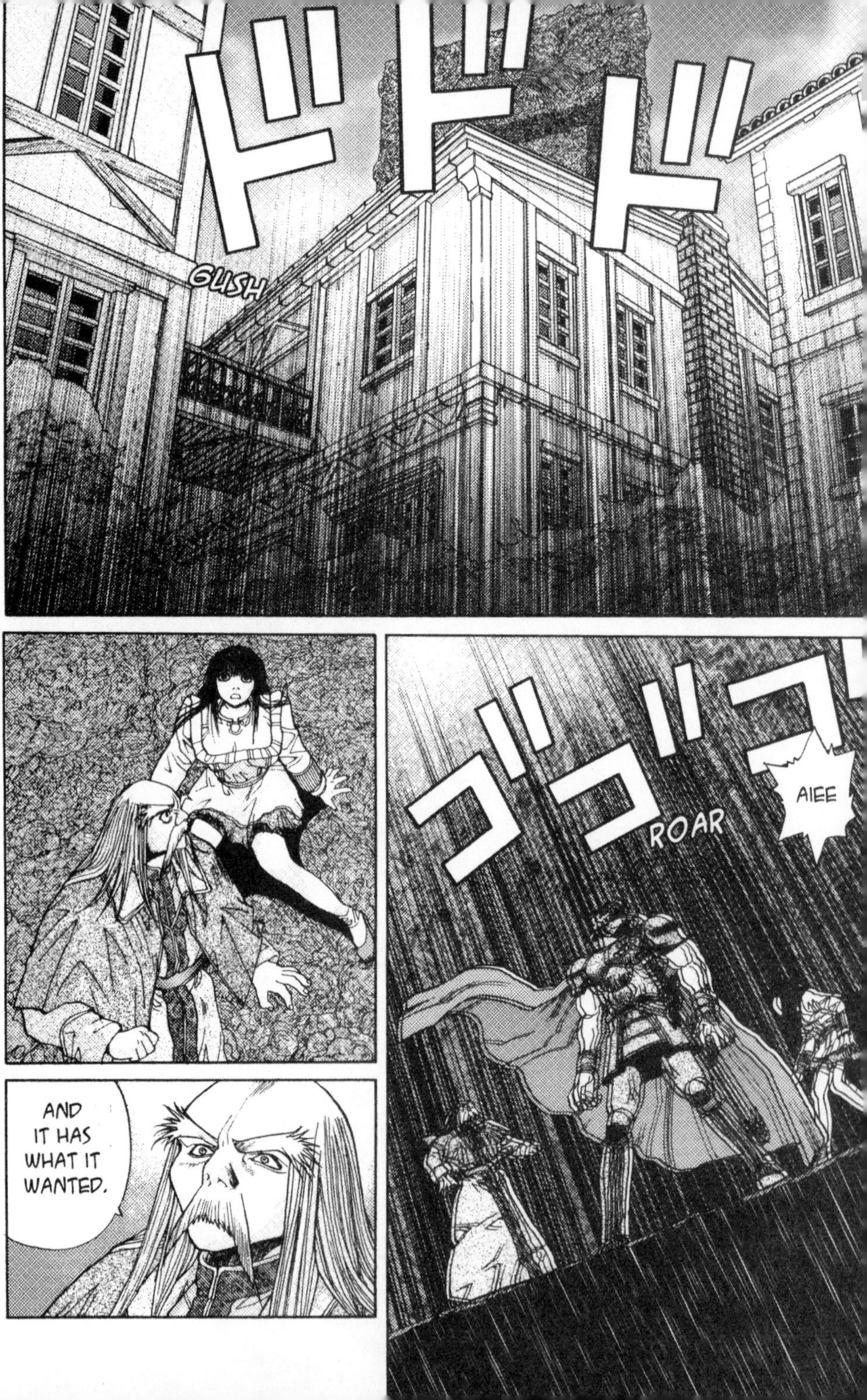
ドドド
GUSH
ゴゴゴ
ROAR
AIEE
AND IT HAS WHAT IT WANTED.

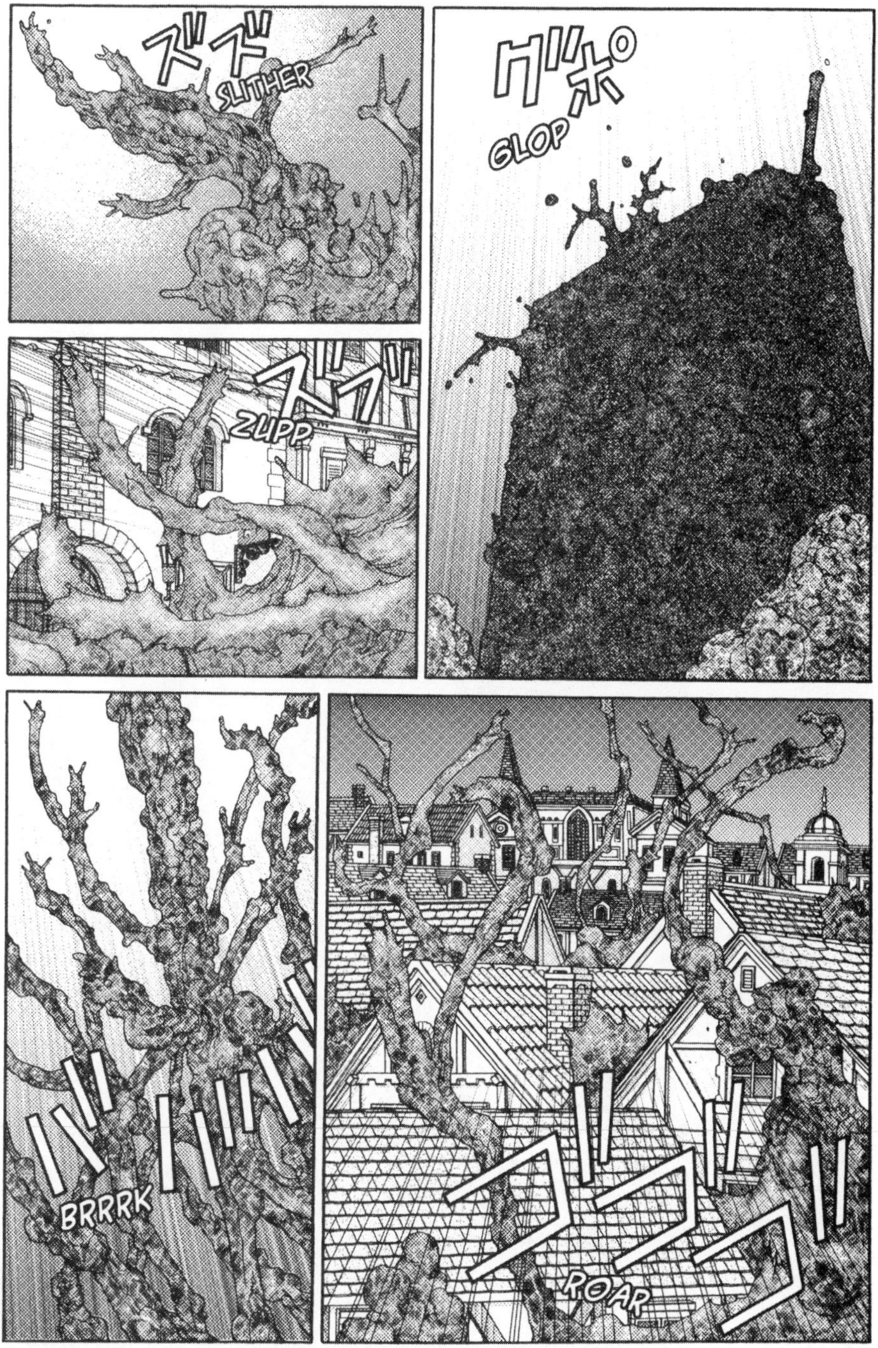
グポ
GLOP
ズズ
SLITHER
ズブ
ZUPP
ゴゴゴ
ROAR
BRRRK

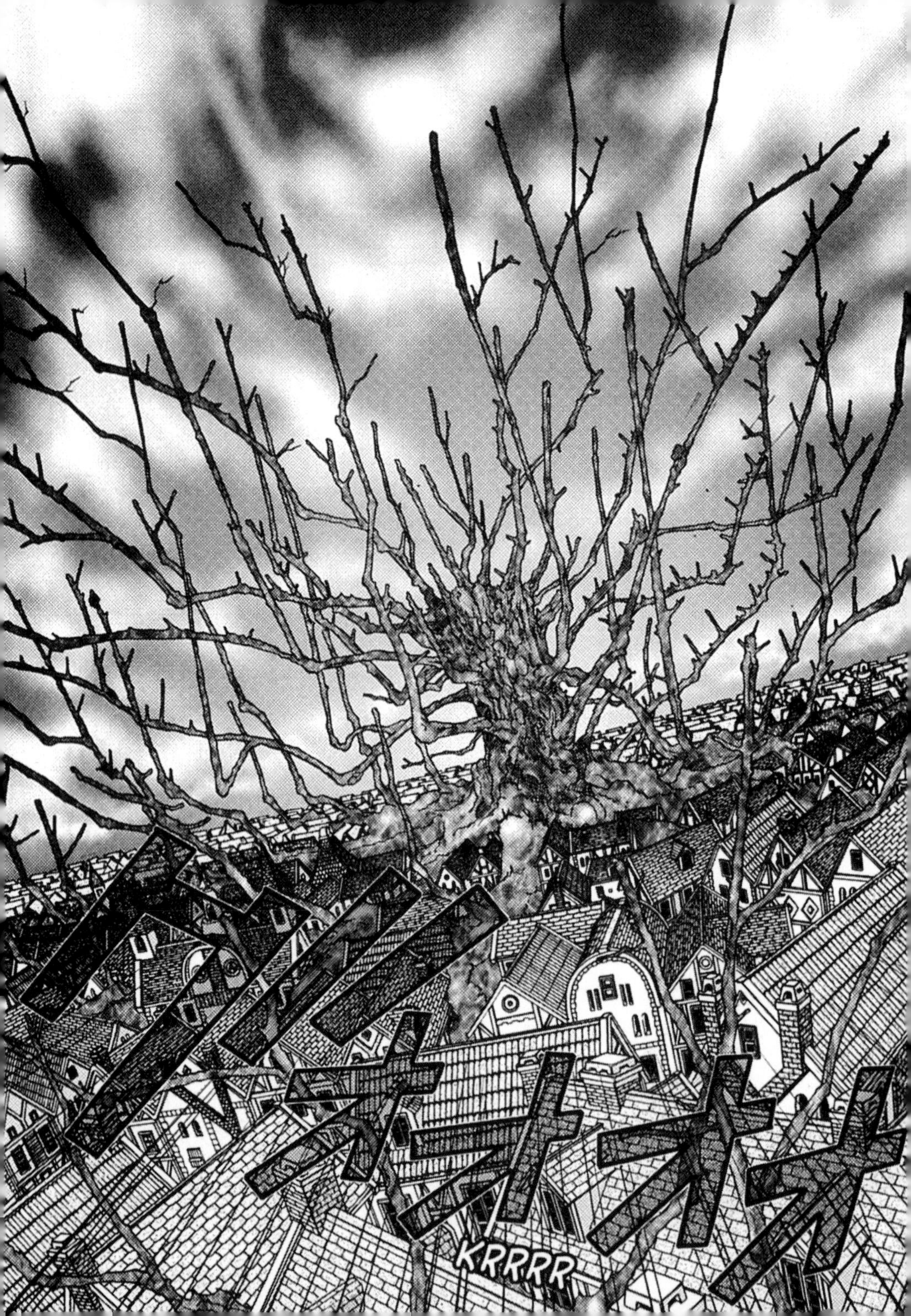
KRRRR

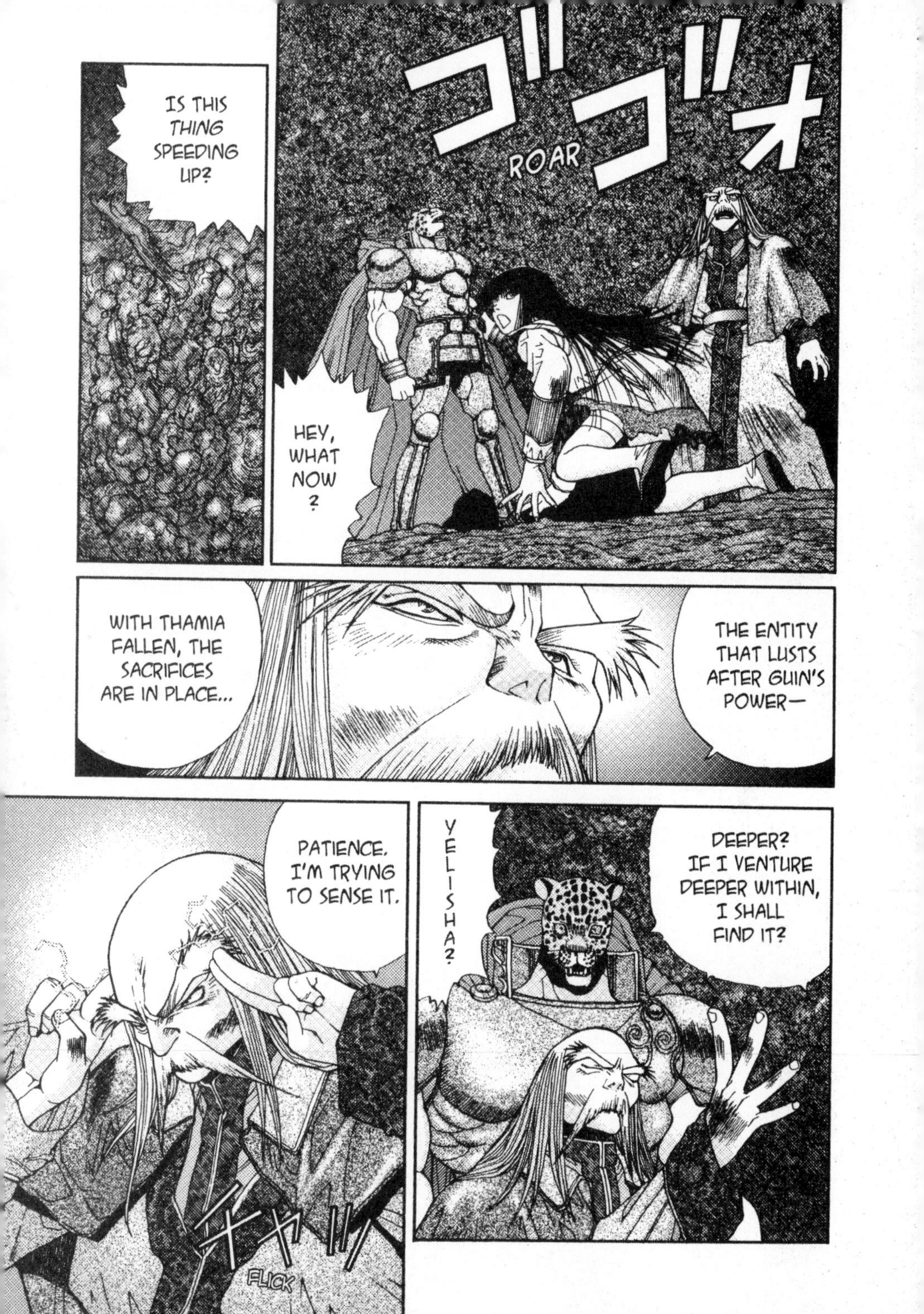
ゴゴオ
ROAR
HEY, WHAT NOW?
IS THIS THING SPEEDING UP?
THE ENTITY THAT LUSTS AFTER GUIN'S POWER—
WITH THAMIA FALLEN, THE SACRIFICES ARE IN PLACE...
DEEPER? IF I VENTURE DEEPER WITHIN, I SHALL FIND IT?
YELISHA?
PATIENCE. I'M TRYING TO SENSE IT.
FLICK

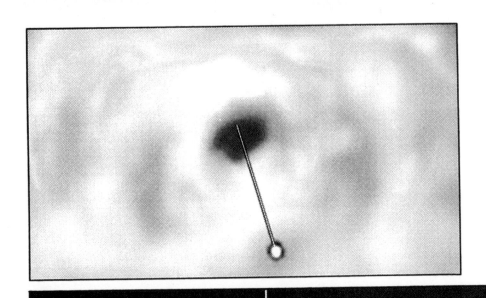

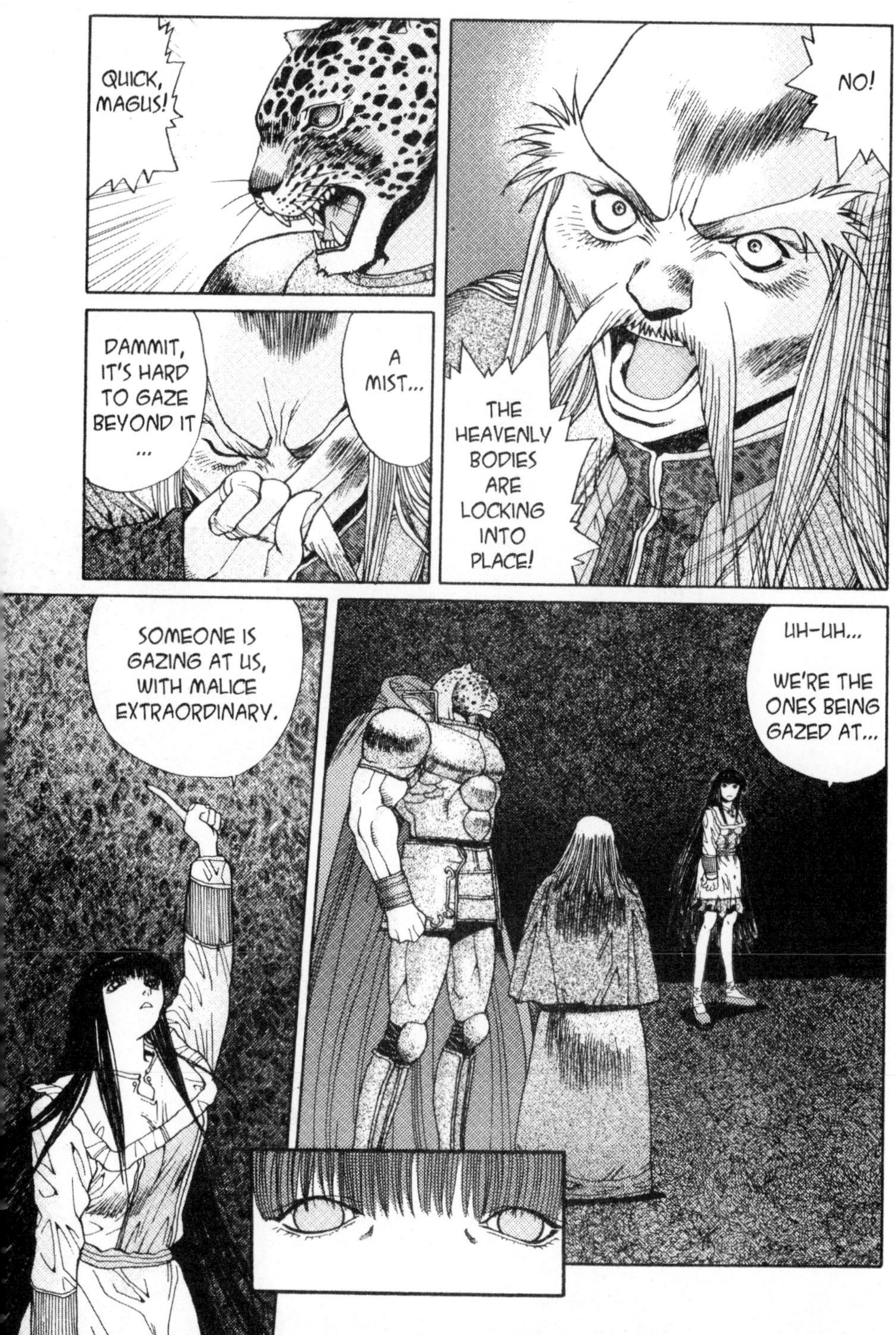
QUICK, MAGUS!
A MIST...
DAMMIT, IT'S HARD TO GAZE BEYOND IT ...
NO!
THE HEAVENLY BODIES ARE LOCKING INTO PLACE!
SOMEONE IS GAZING AT US, WITH MALICE EXTRAORDINARY.
UH-UH...
WE'RE THE ONES BEING GAZED AT...

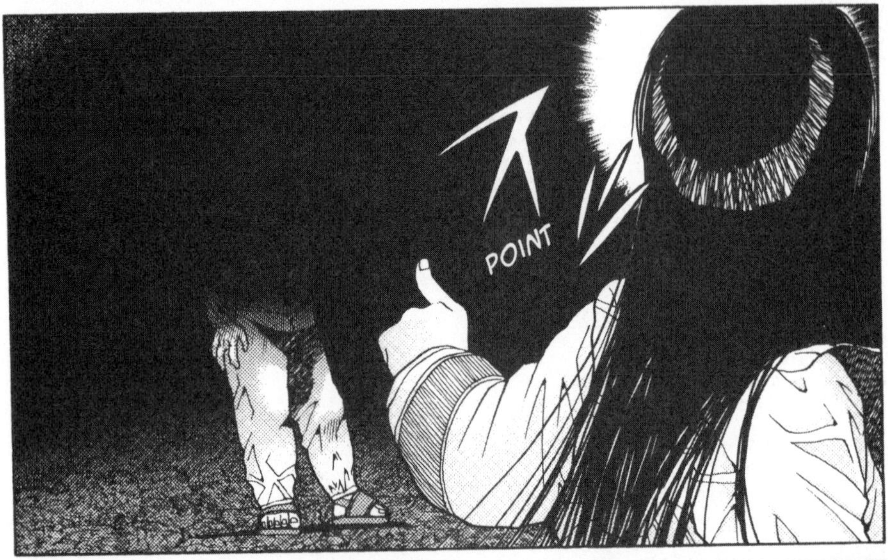
POINT
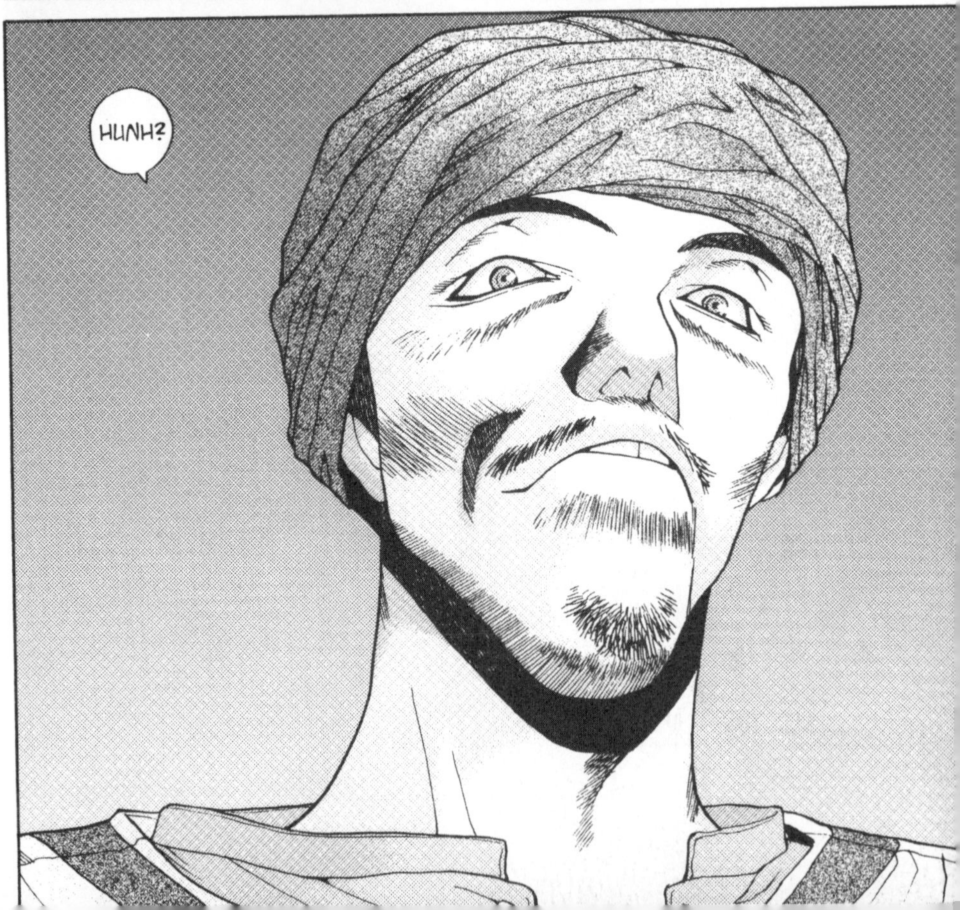
HUNH?

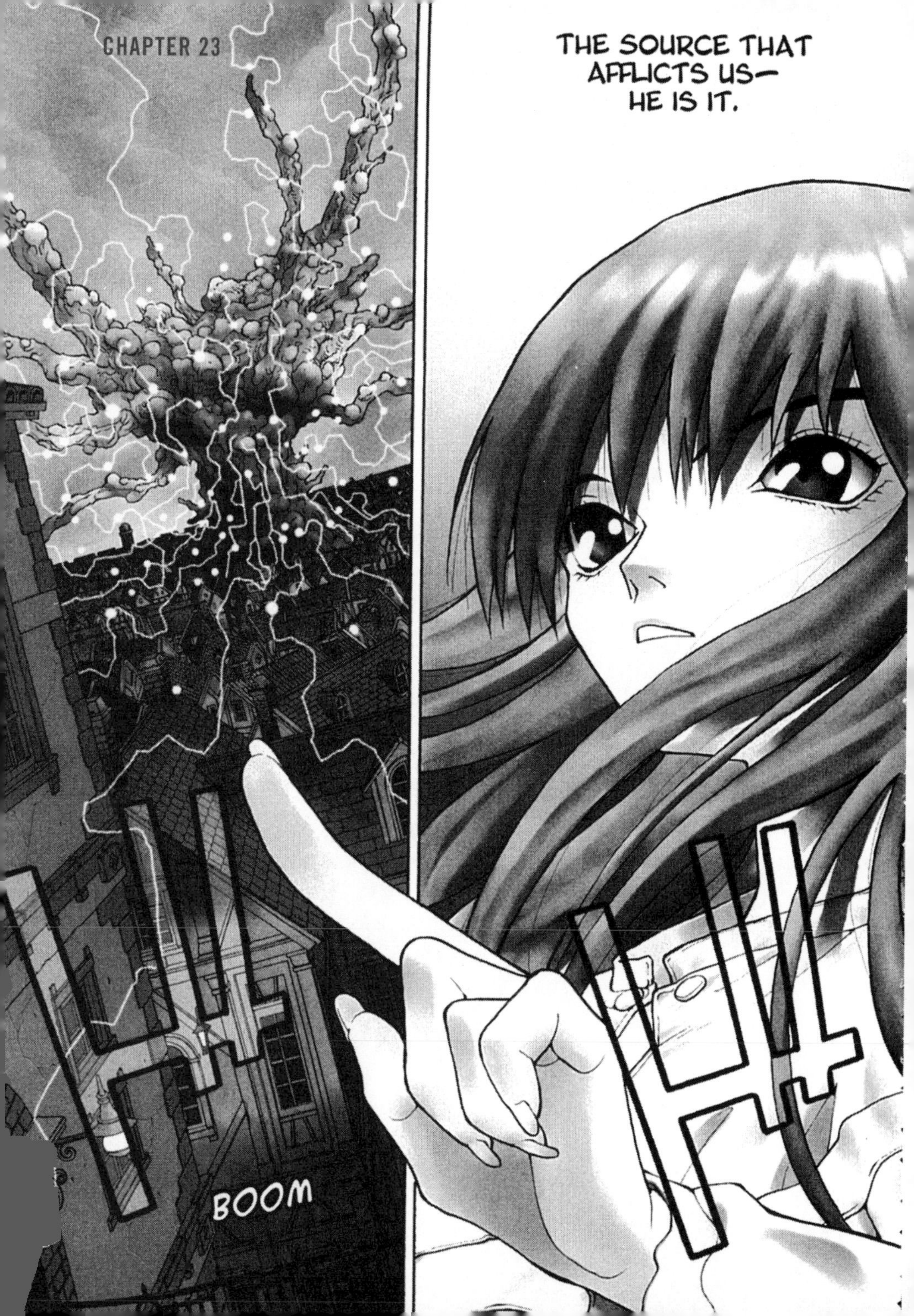
THE SOURCE THAT AFFLICTS US—
HE IS IT.
CHAPTER 23
BOOM

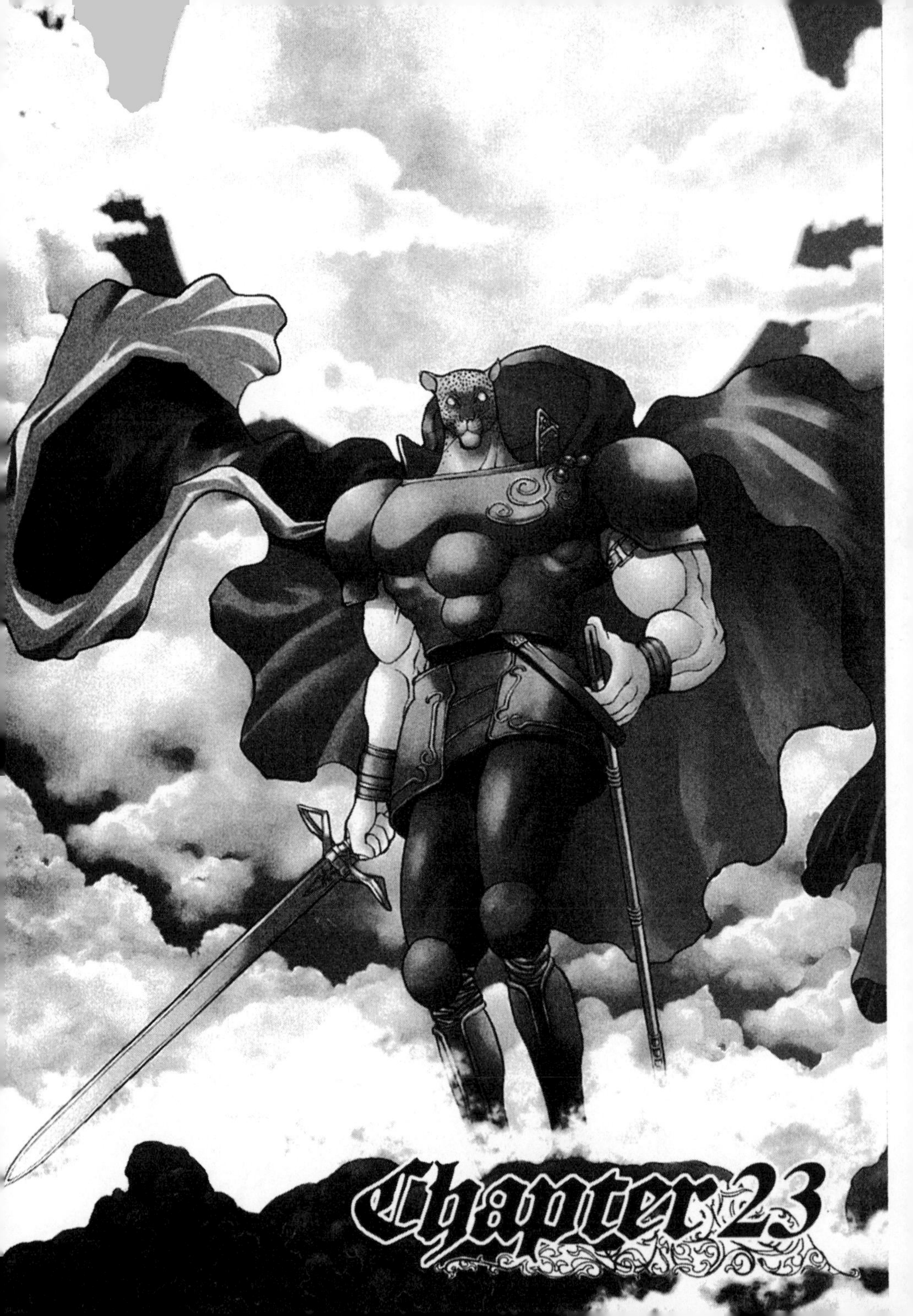
Chapter 23

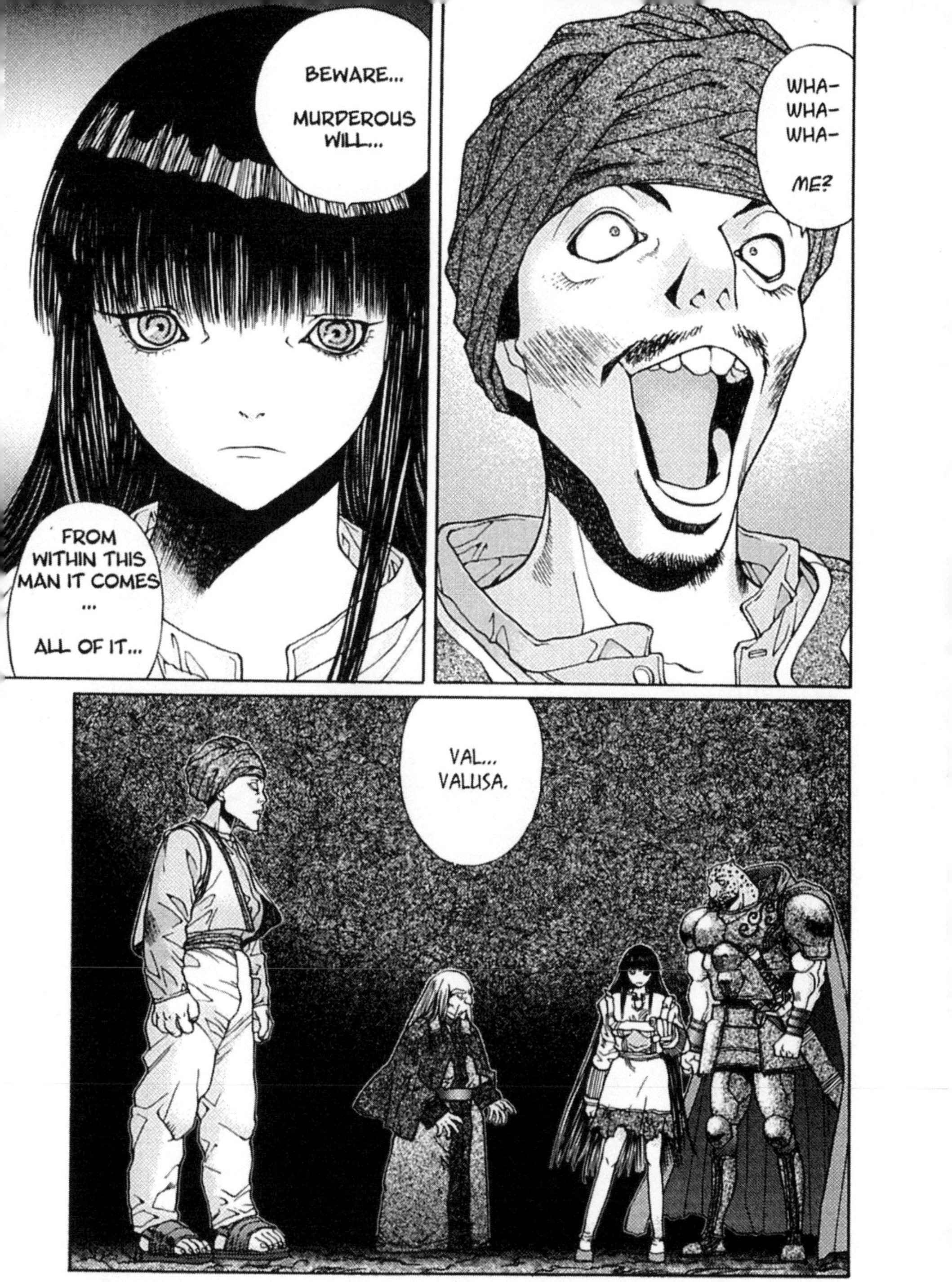
WHA-
WHA-
WHA-
ME?
BEWARE...
MURDEROUS WILL...
FROM WITHIN THIS MAN IT COMES ...
ALL OF IT...
VAL... VALUSA.

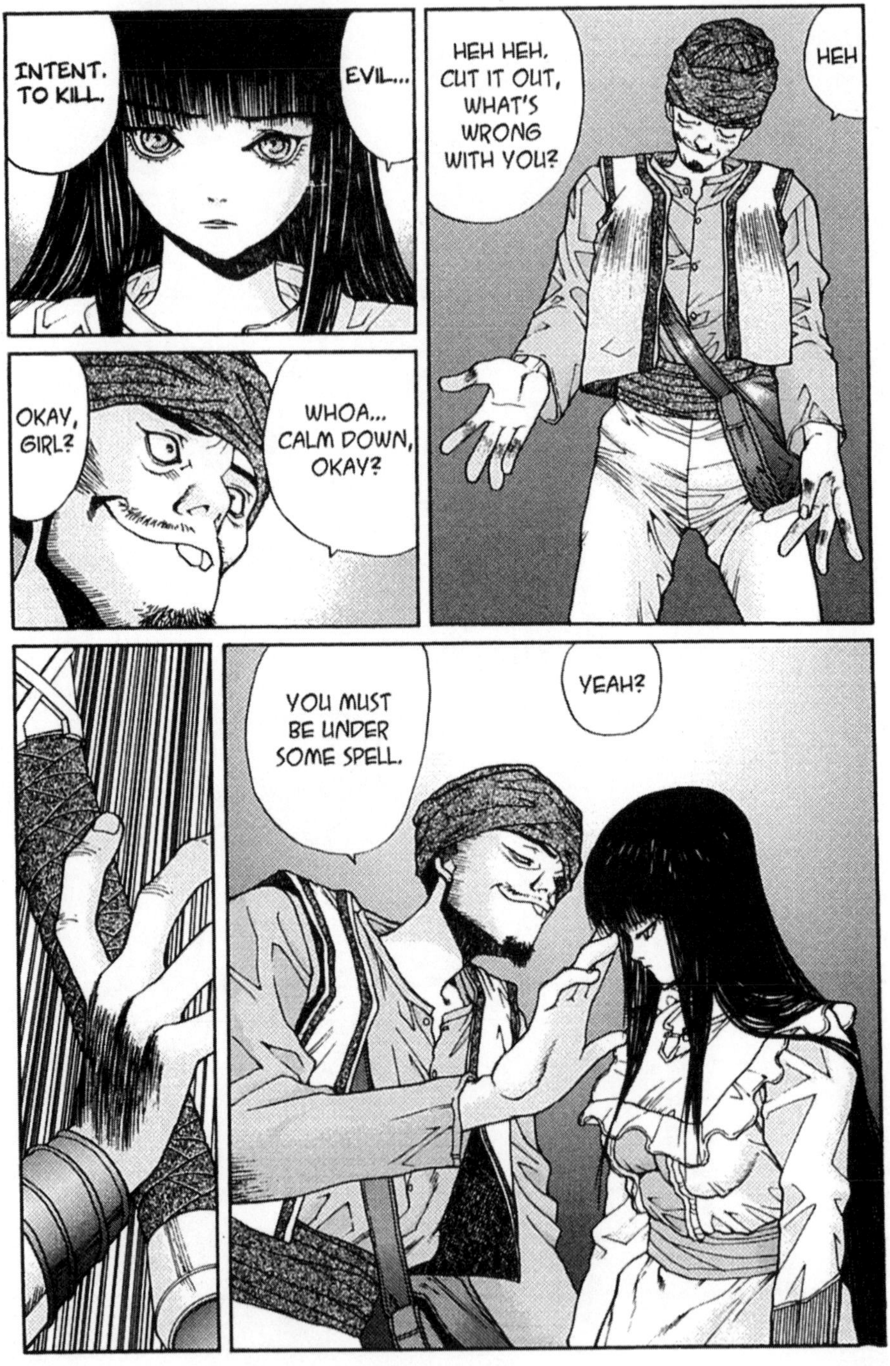
HEH
HEH HEH. CUT IT OUT, WHAT'S WRONG WITH YOU?
EVIL...
INTENT. TO KILL.
WHOA... CALM DOWN, OKAY?
OKAY, GIRL?
YEAH?
YOU MUST BE UNDER SOME SPELL.

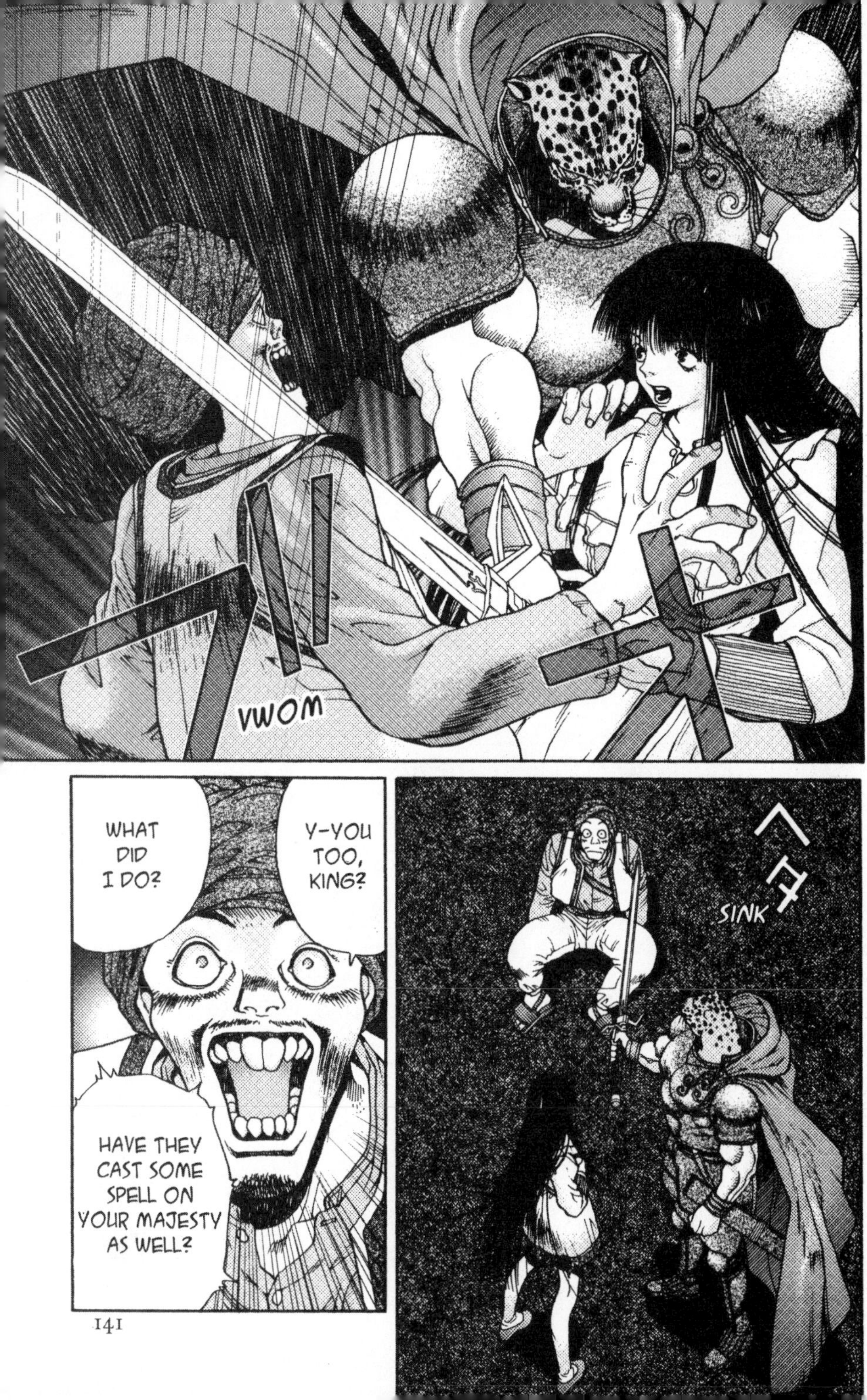
VWOM
SINK
Y-YOU TOO, KING?
WHAT DID I DO?
HAVE THEY CAST SOME SPELL ON YOUR MAJESTY AS WELL?

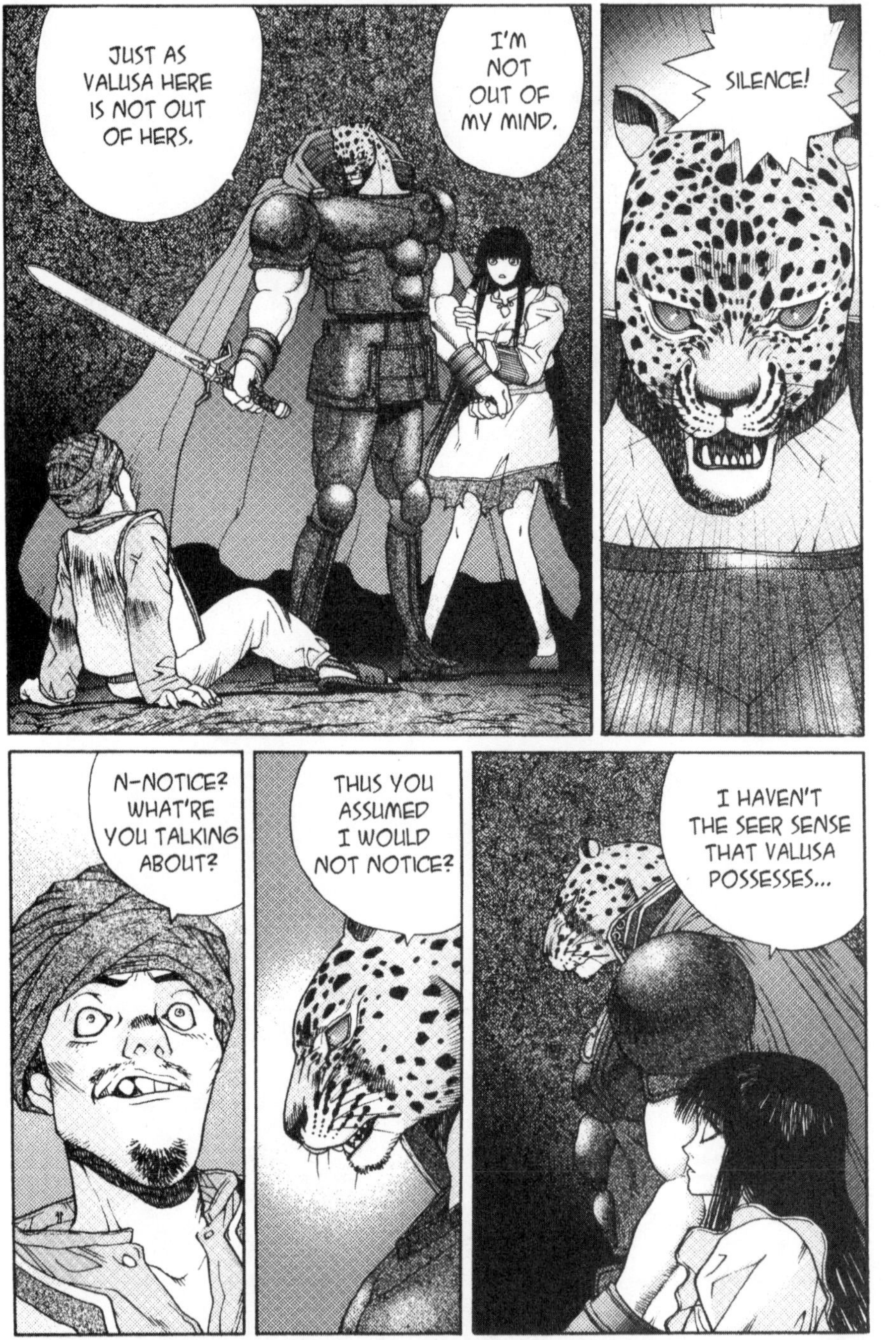
SILENCE!
I'M NOT OUT OF MY MIND.
JUST AS VALUSA HERE IS NOT OUT OF HERS.
I HAVEN'T THE SEER SENSE THAT VALUSA POSSESSES...
THUS YOU ASSUMED I WOULD NOT NOTICE?
N-NOTICE? WHAT'RE YOU TALKING ABOUT?

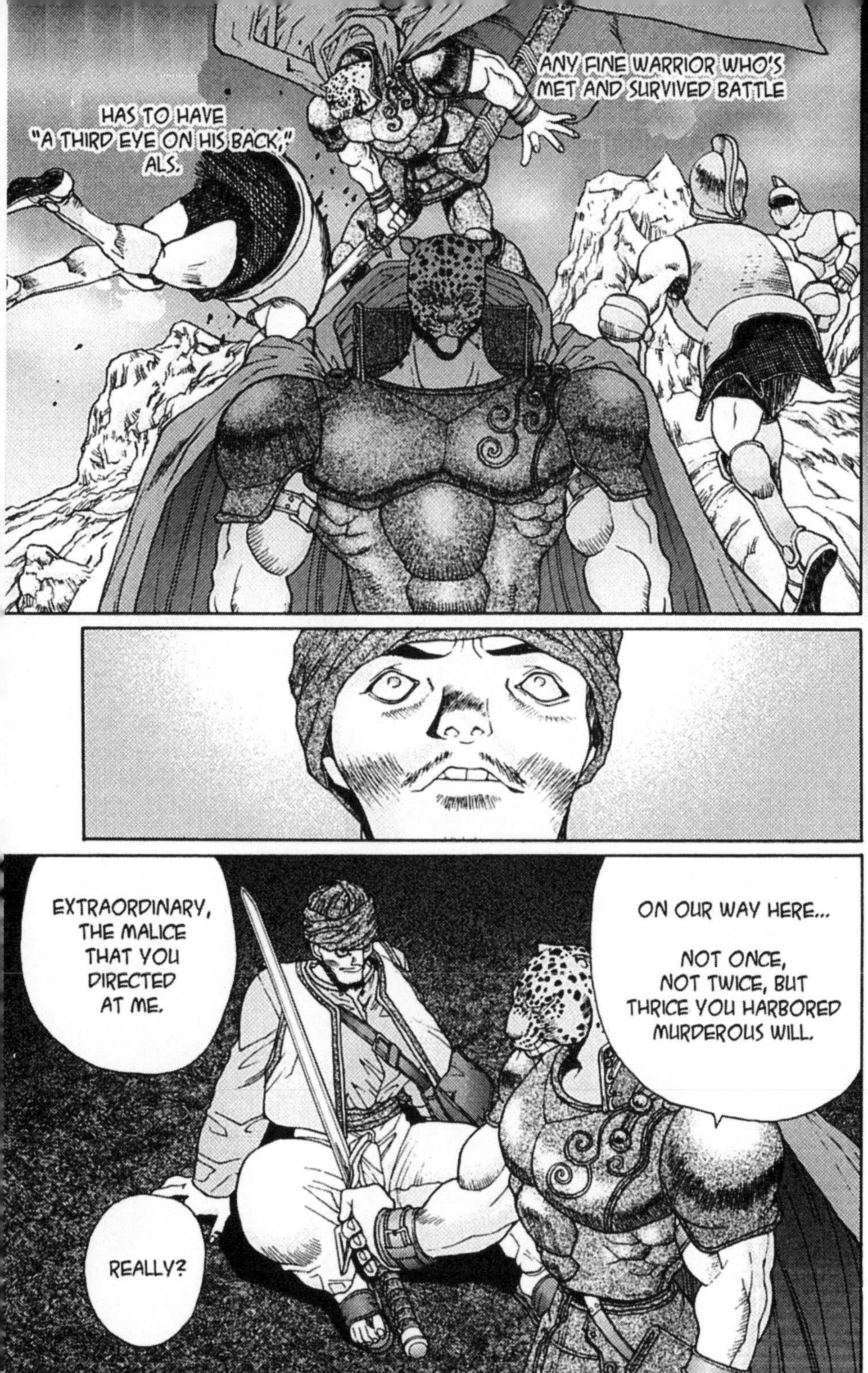
ANY FINE WARRIOR WHO'S MET AND SURVIVED BATTLE
HAS TO HAVE "A THIRD EYE ON HIS BACK," ALS.
ON OUR WAY HERE...
NOT ONCE, NOT TWICE, BUT THRICE YOU HARBORED MURDEROUS WILL.
EXTRAORDINARY, THE MALICE THAT YOU DIRECTED AT ME.
REALLY?

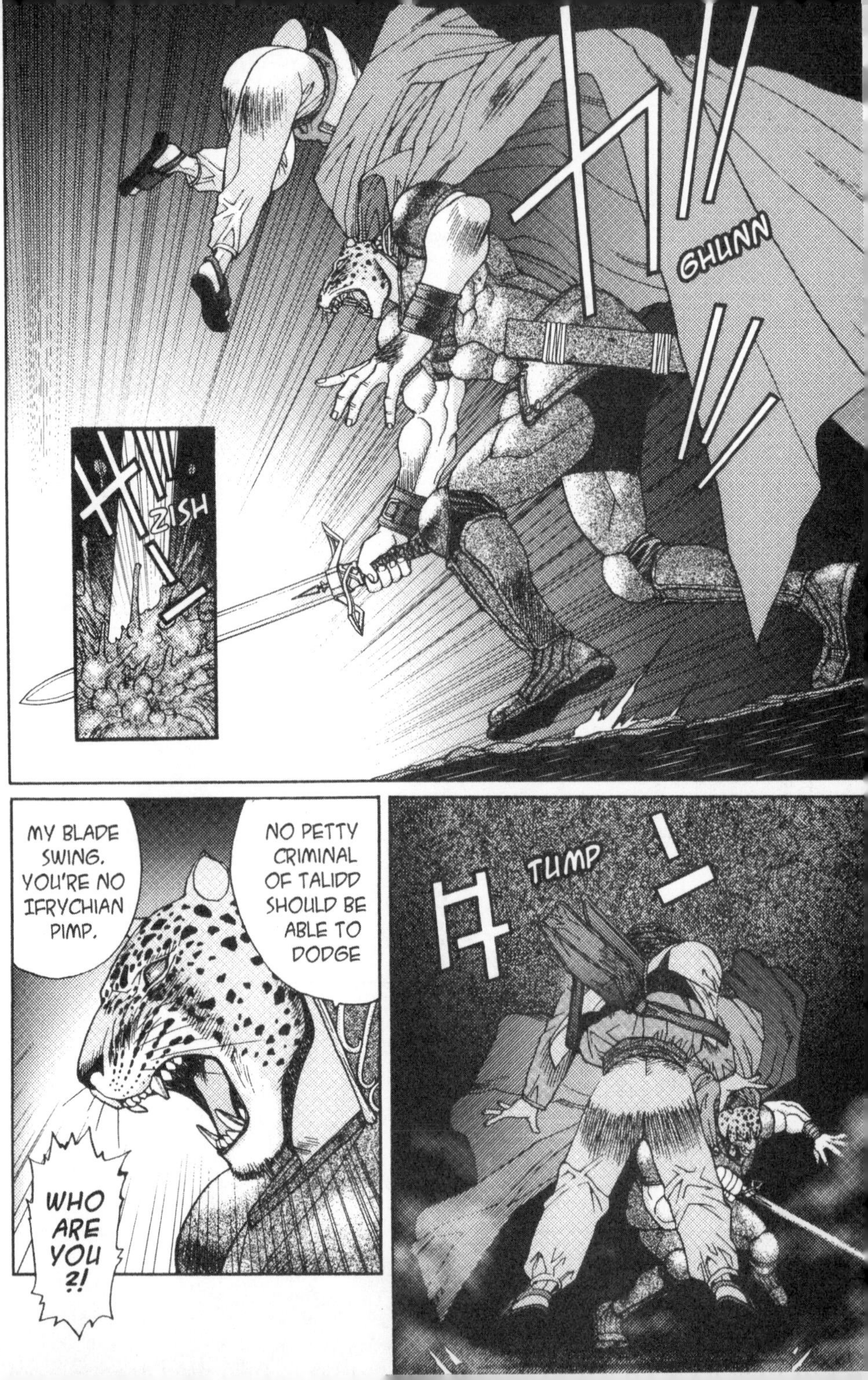
GHUNN
ZISH
TUMP
NO PETTY CRIMINAL OF TALIDD SHOULD BE ABLE TO DODGE
MY BLADE SWING. YOU'RE NO IFRYCHIAN PIMP.
WHO ARE YOU?!

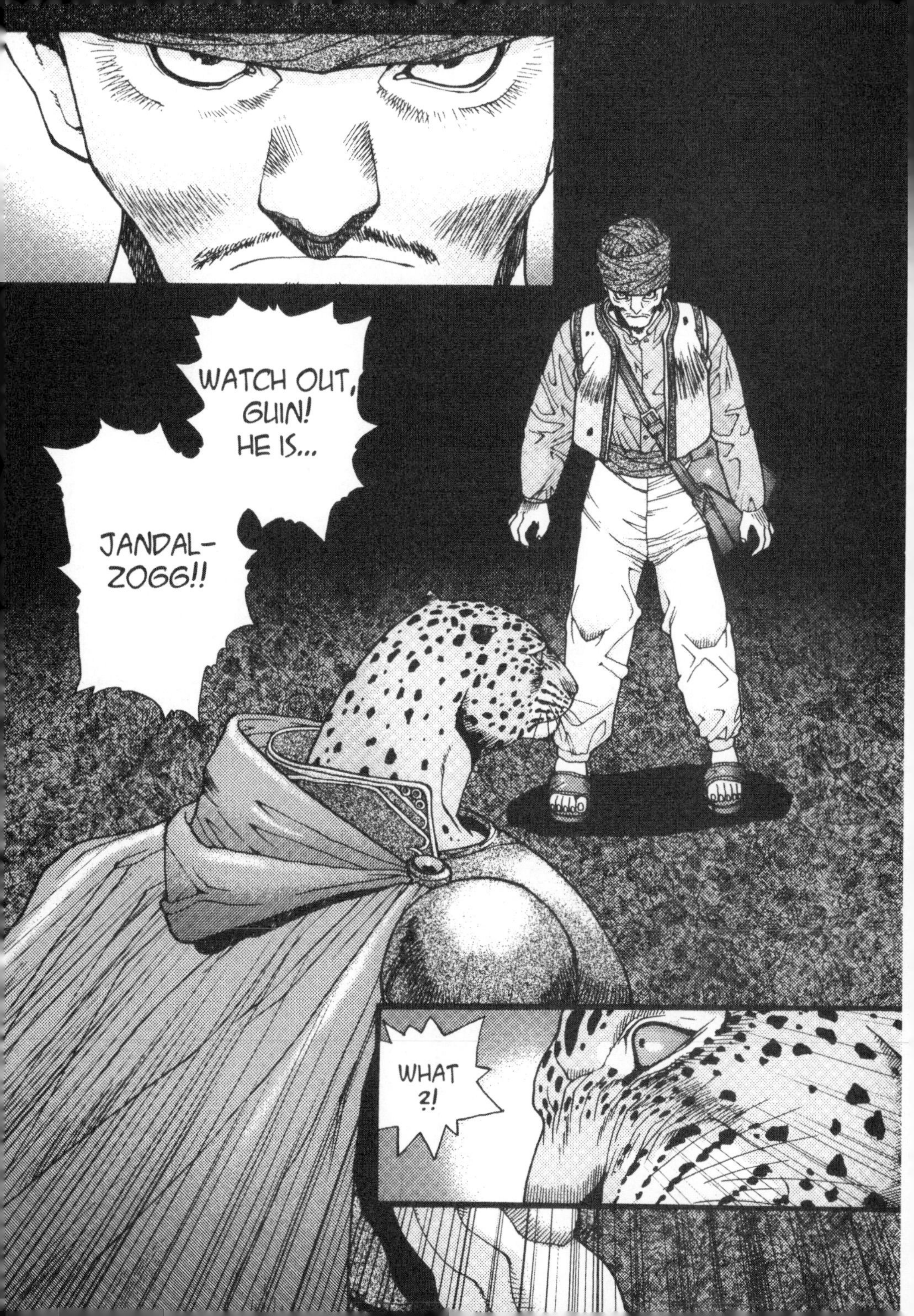
WATCH OUT, GUIN! HE IS...
JANDAL-ZOGG!!
WHAT ?!

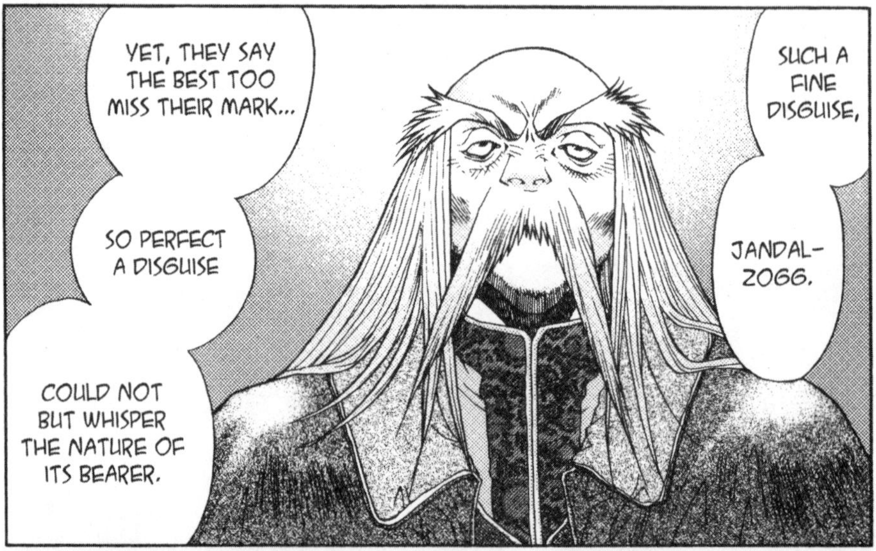
SUCH A FINE DISGUISE,
JANDAL-ZOGG.
YET, THEY SAY THE BEST TOO MISS THEIR MARK...
SO PERFECT A DISGUISE
COULD NOT BUT WHISPER THE NATURE OF ITS BEARER.
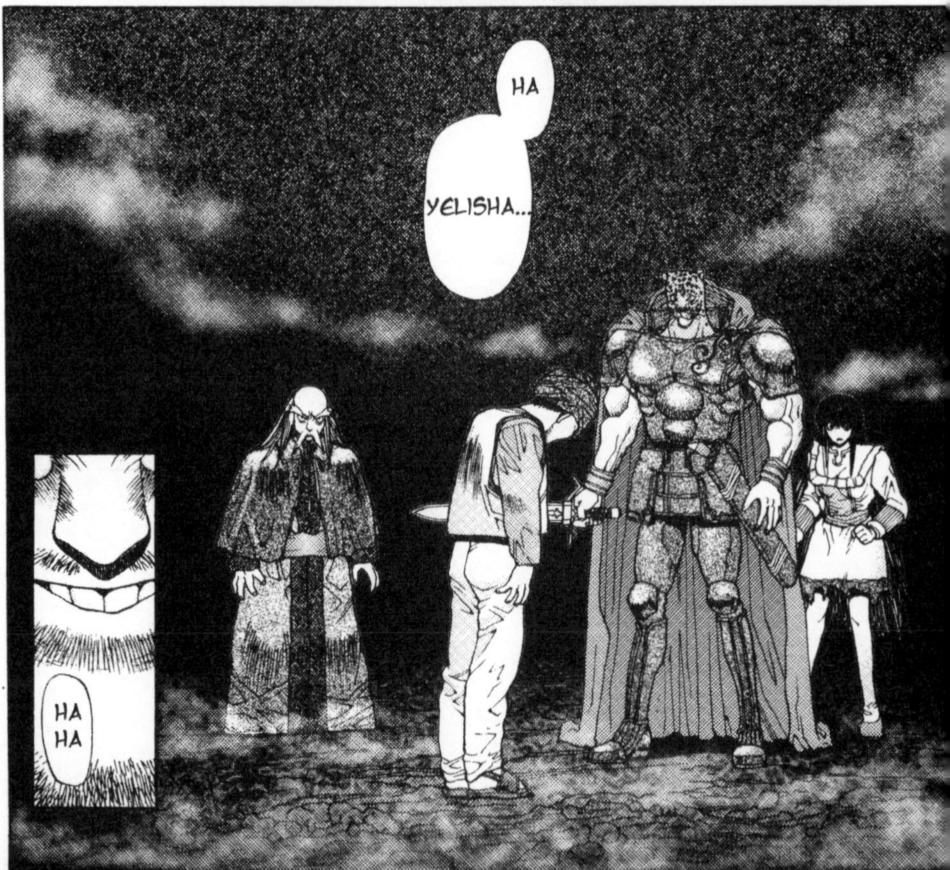
HA
YELISHA...
HA HA

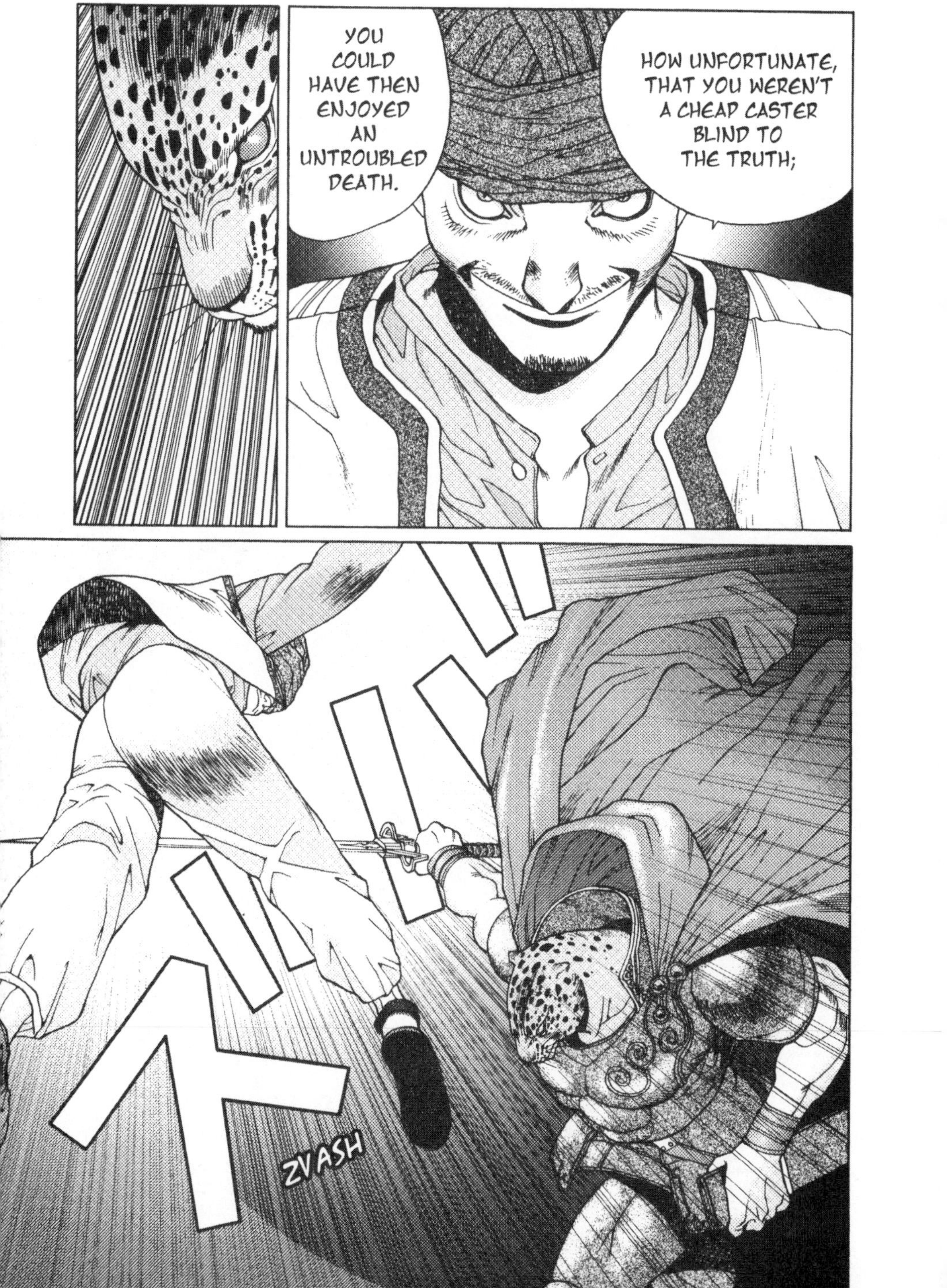
HOW UNFORTUNATE, THAT YOU WEREN'T A CHEAP CASTER BLIND TO THE TRUTH;
YOU COULD HAVE THEN ENJOYED AN UNTROUBLED DEATH.
ZVASH

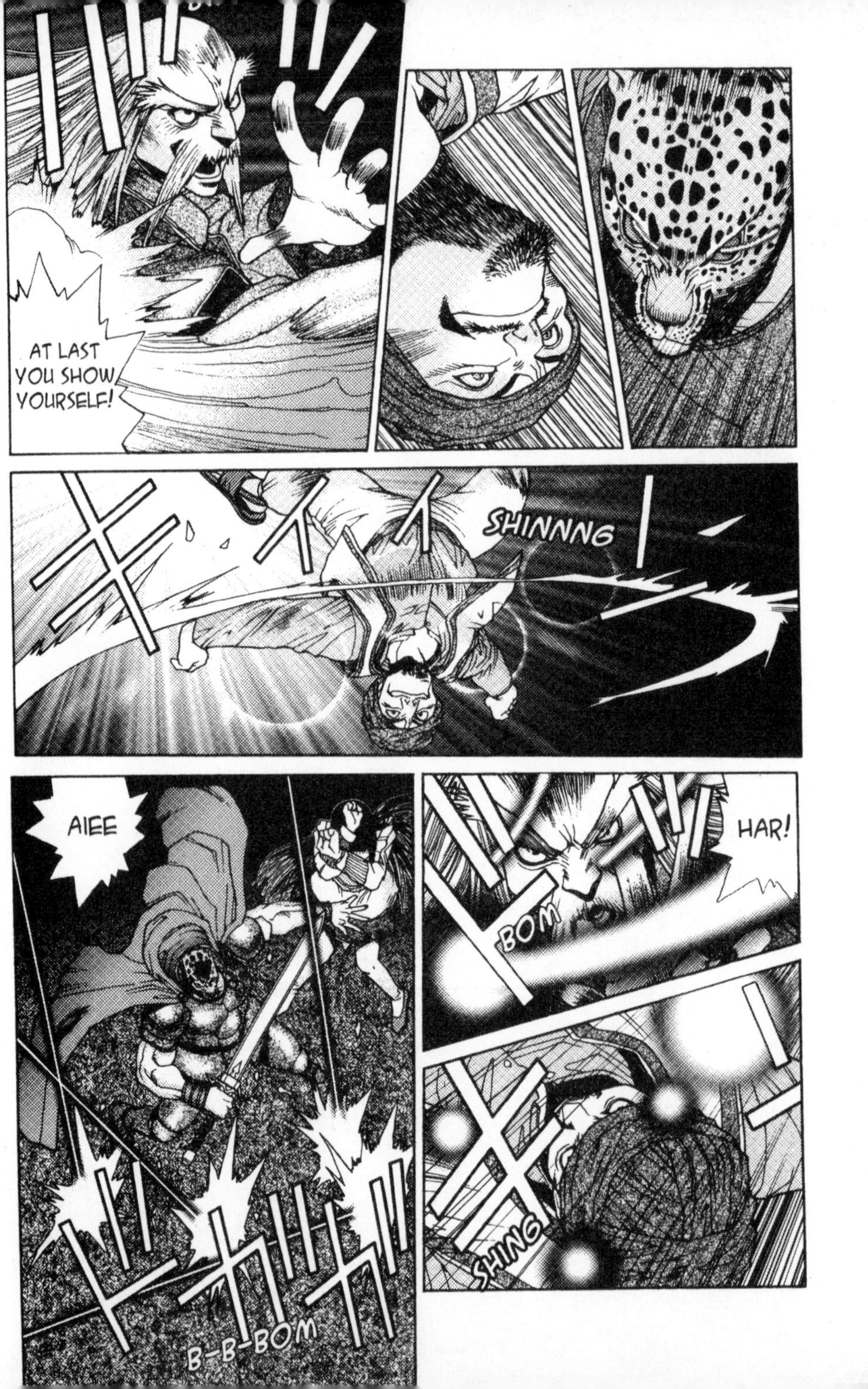
AT LAST YOU SHOW YOURSELF!
SHINNNG
HAR!
BOM
SHING
AIEE
B-B-BOM

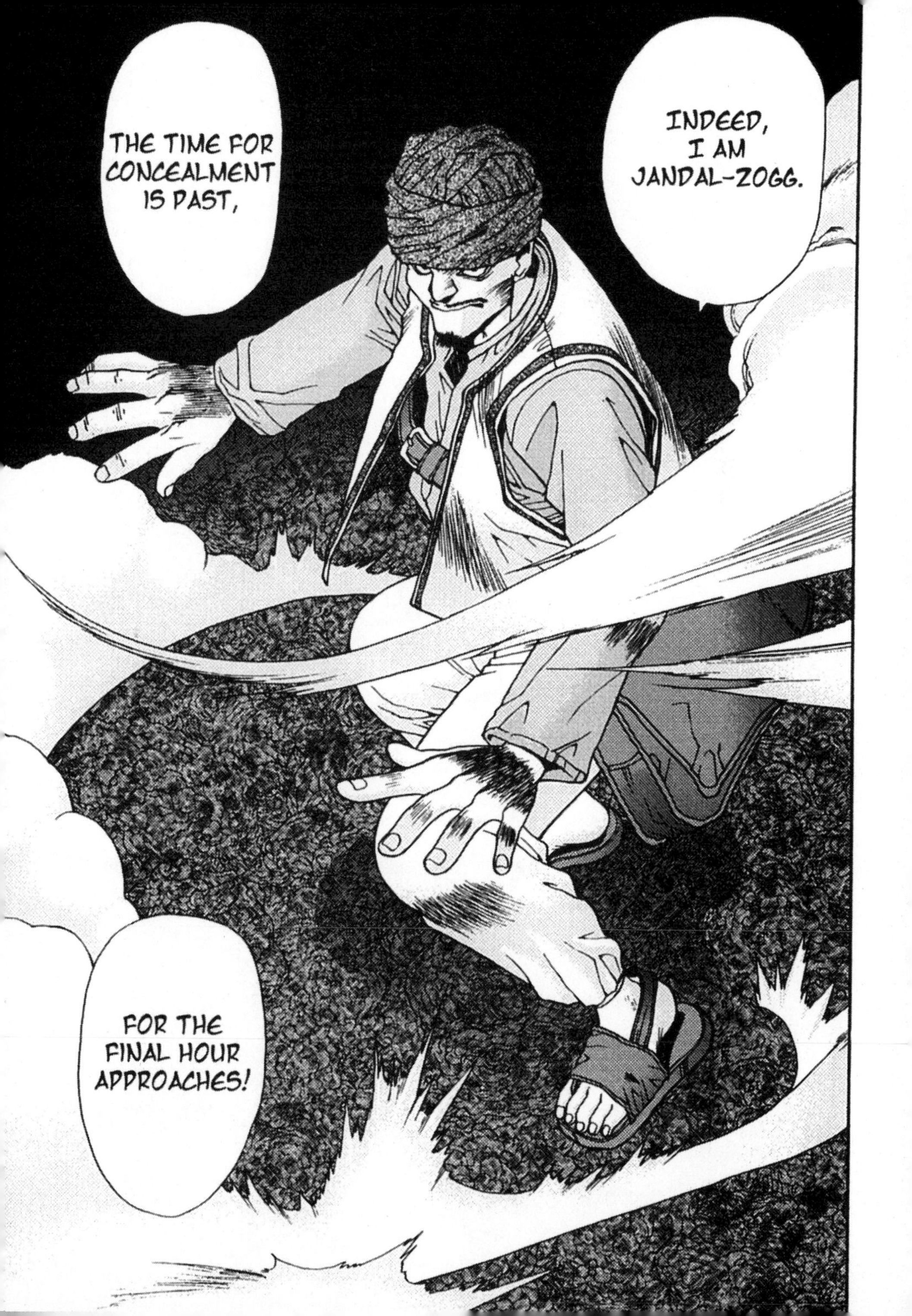
INDEED, I AM JANDAL-ZOGG.
THE TIME FOR CONCEALMENT IS PAST,
FOR THE FINAL HOUR APPROACHES!

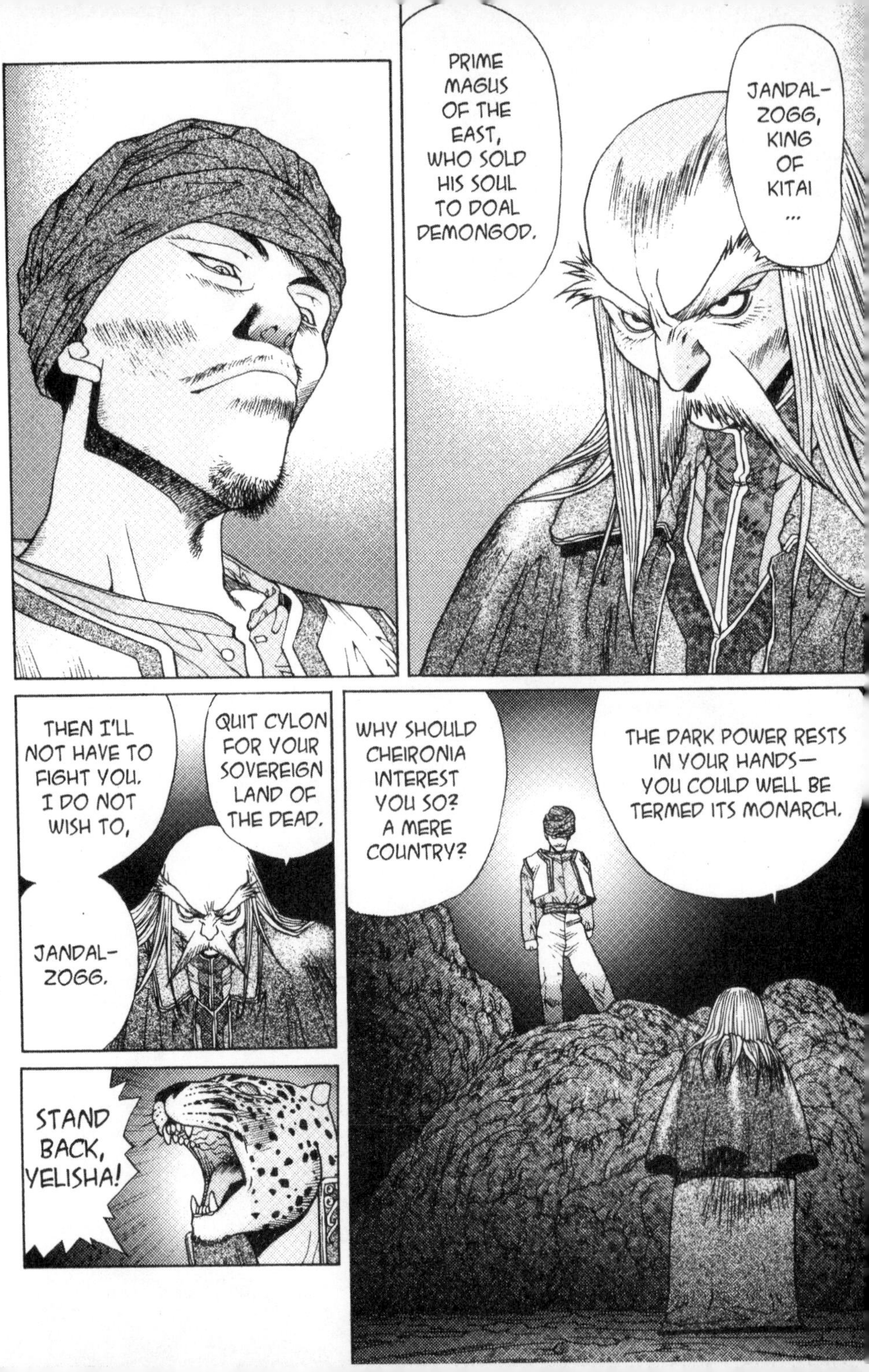
JANDAL-ZOGG, KING OF KITAI ...
PRIME MAGUS OF THE EAST, WHO SOLD HIS SOUL TO DOAL DEMONGOD.
THE DARK POWER RESTS IN YOUR HANDS— YOU COULD WELL BE TERMED ITS MONARCH.
WHY SHOULD CHEIRONIA INTEREST YOU SO? A MERE COUNTRY?
QUIT CYLON FOR YOUR SOVEREIGN LAND OF THE DEAD.
THEN I'LL NOT HAVE TO FIGHT YOU. I DO NOT WISH TO,
JANDAL-ZOGG.
STAND BACK, YELISHA!

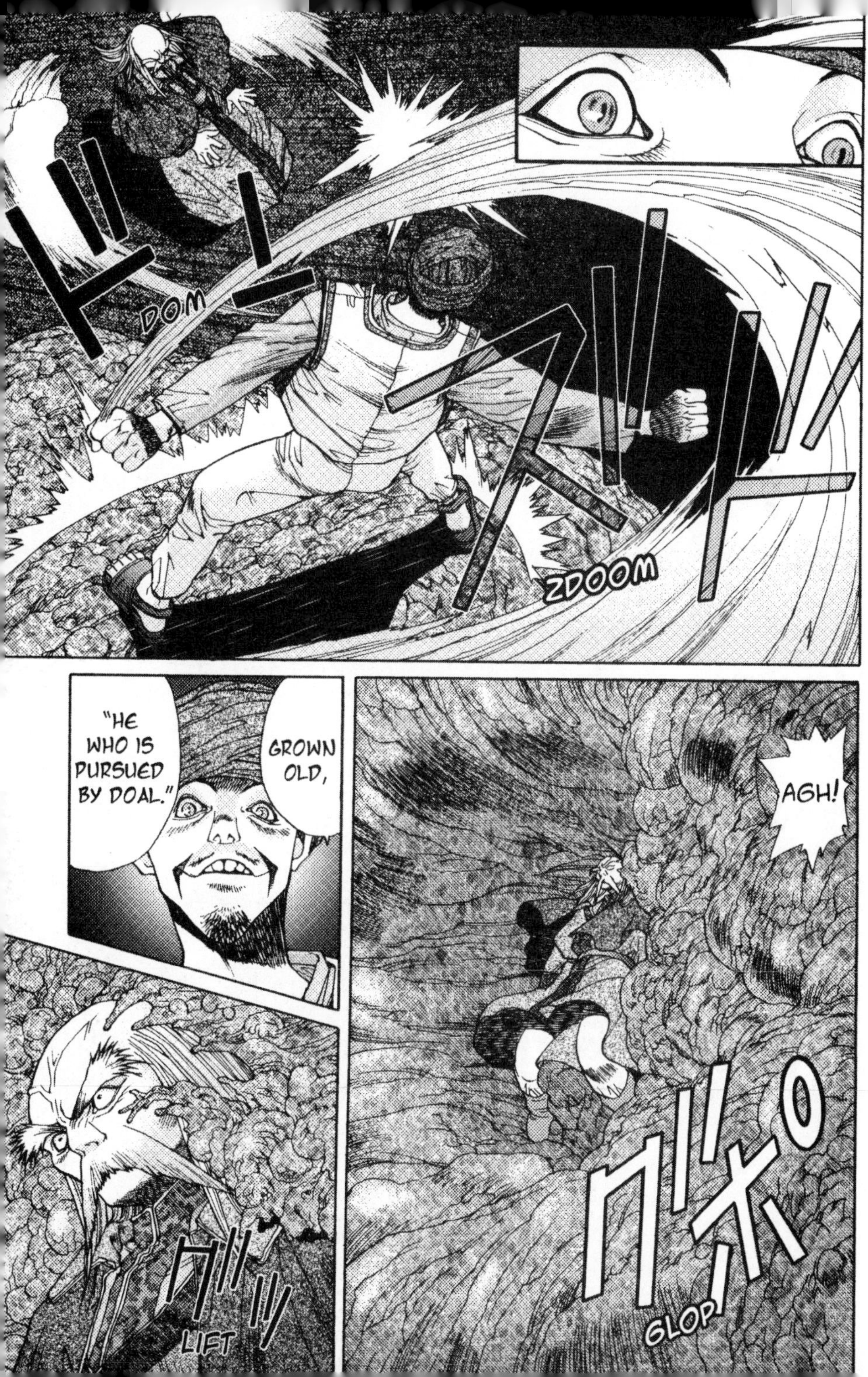
DOM
ZDOOM
AGH!
GLOP
GROWN OLD,
"HE WHO IS PURSUED BY DOAL."
LIFT

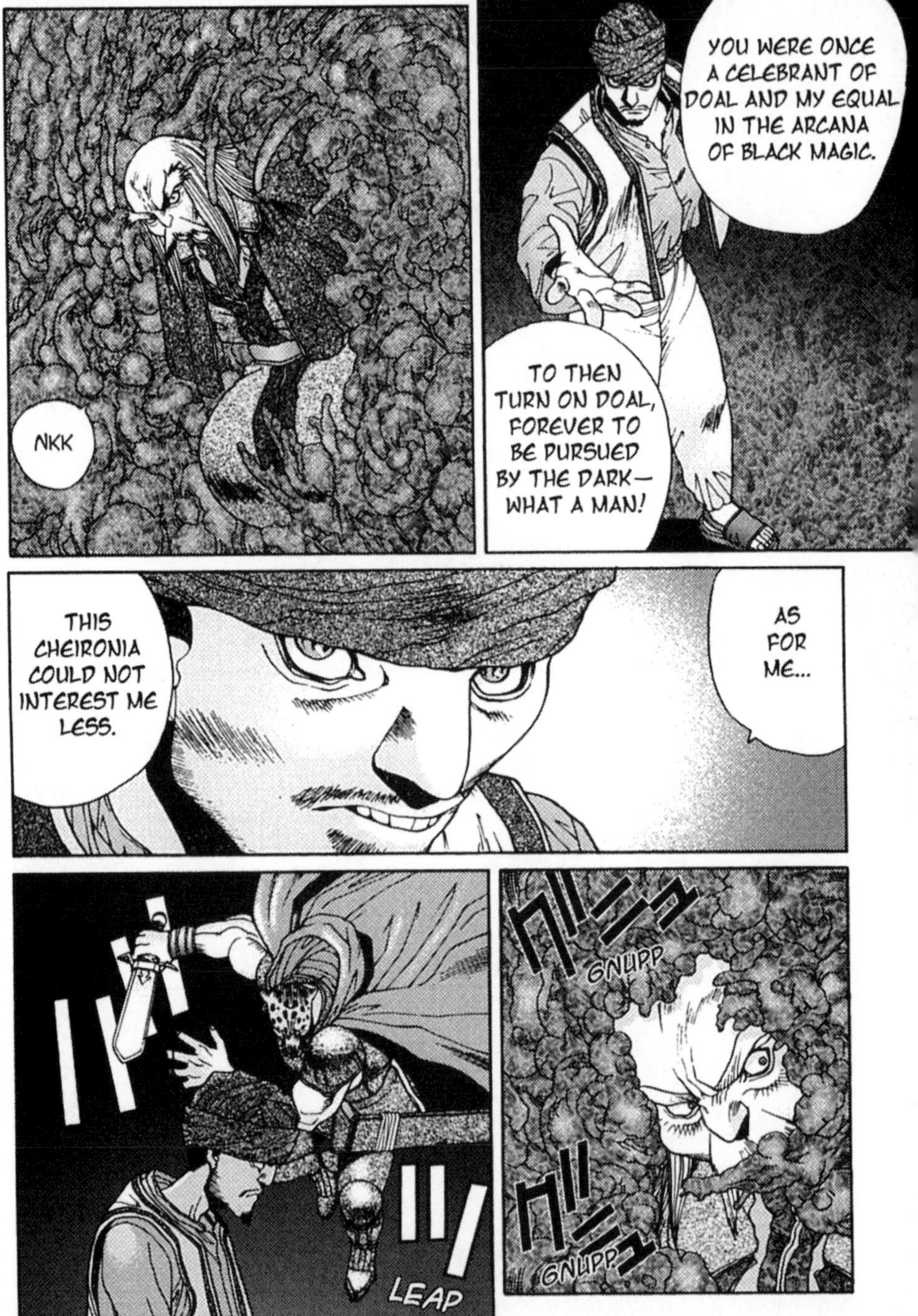
YOU WERE ONCE A CELEBRANT OF DOAL AND MY EQUAL IN THE ARCANA OF BLACK MAGIC.
TO THEN TURN ON DOAL, FOREVER TO BE PURSUED BY THE DARK— WHAT A MAN!
NKK
AS FOR ME...
THIS CHEIRONIA COULD NOT INTEREST ME LESS.
GNUPP
GNUPP
LEAP

SHINNNG

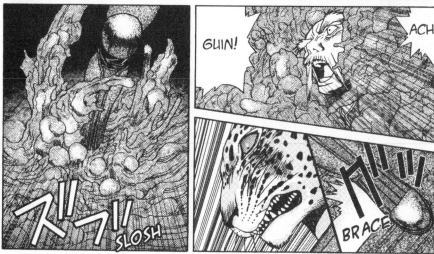

SLOSH

GUIN!

ACH

BRACE

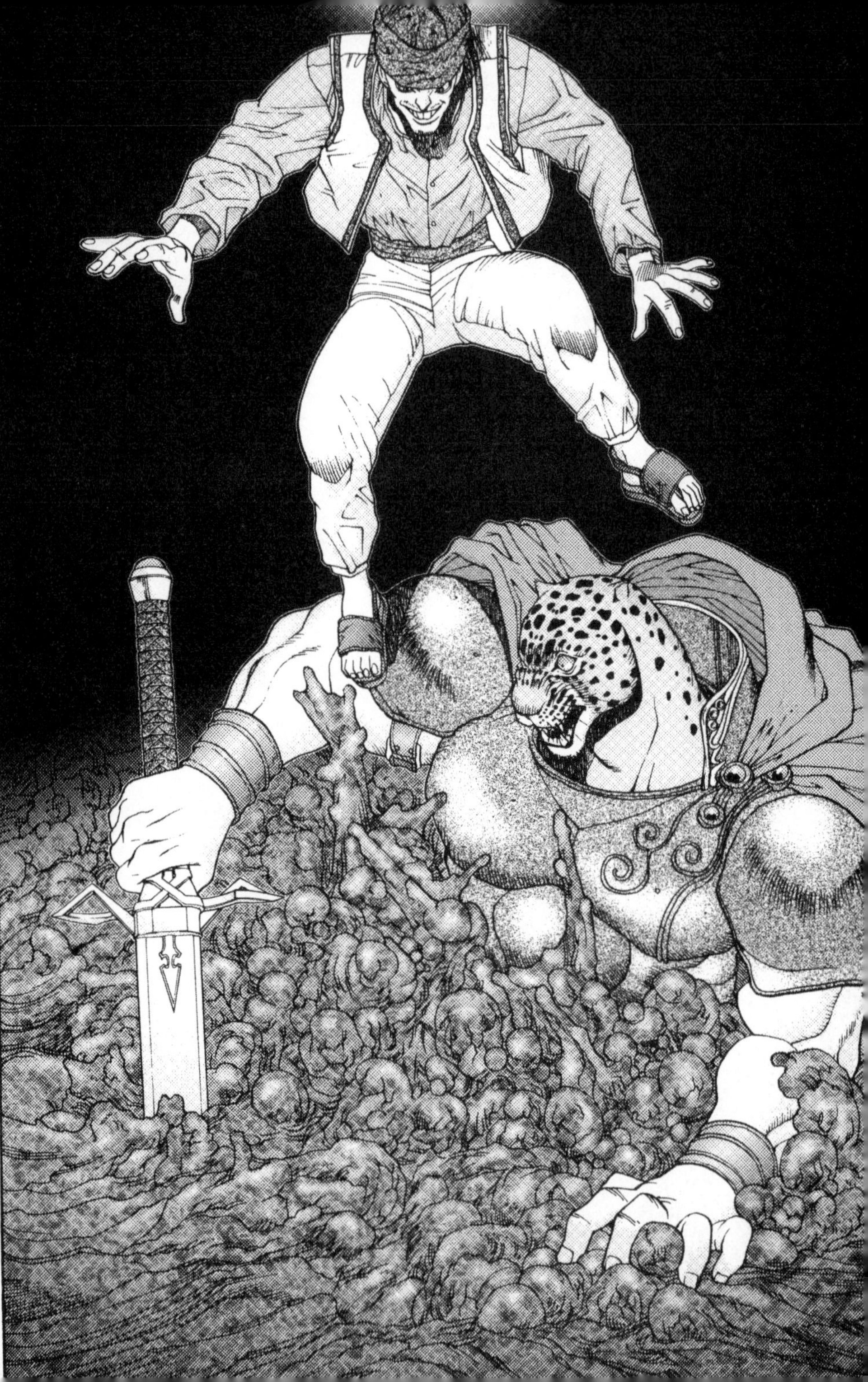

CHAPTER 24

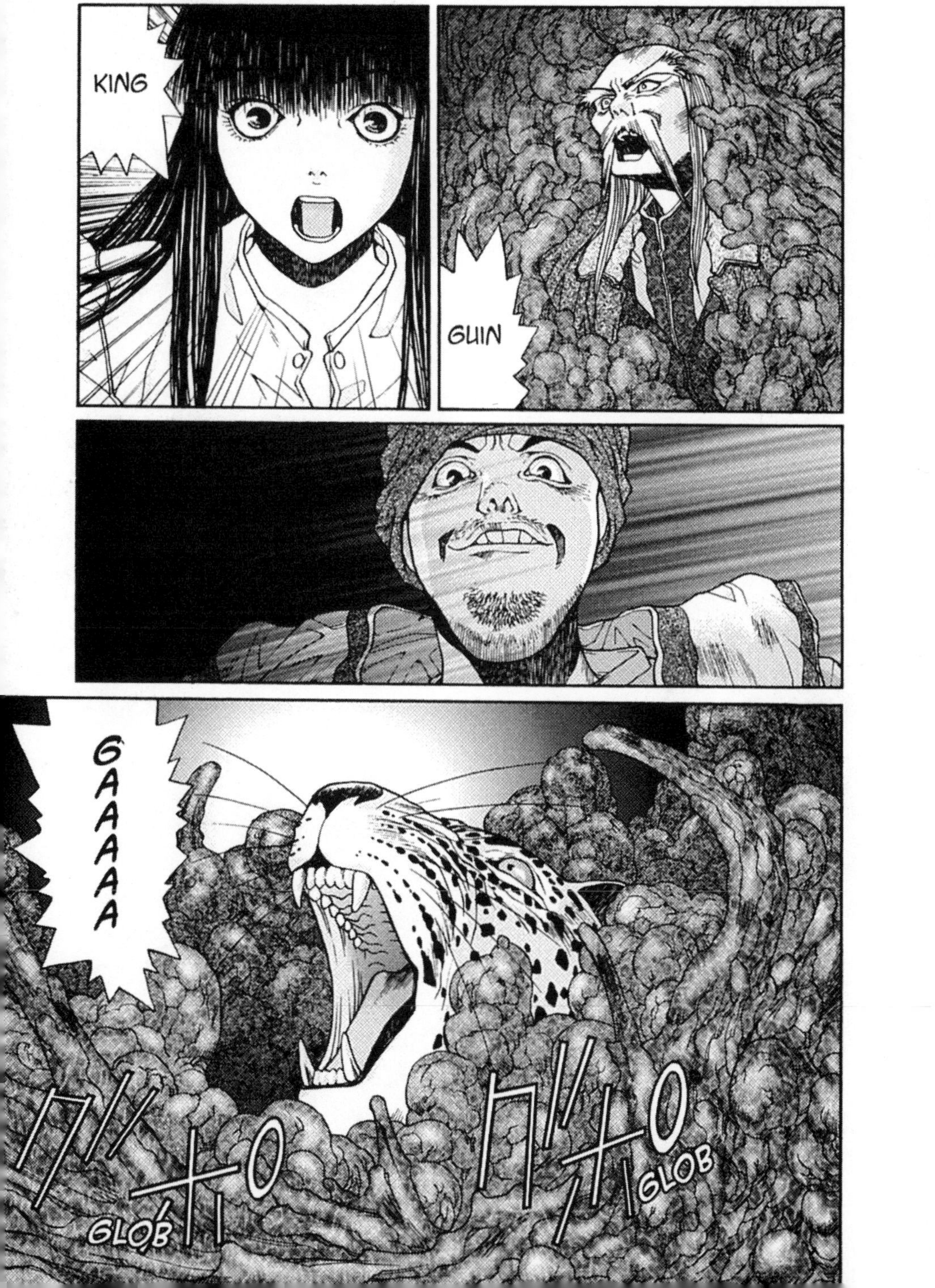
KING
GUIN
GAAAAAA
GLOB
GLOB

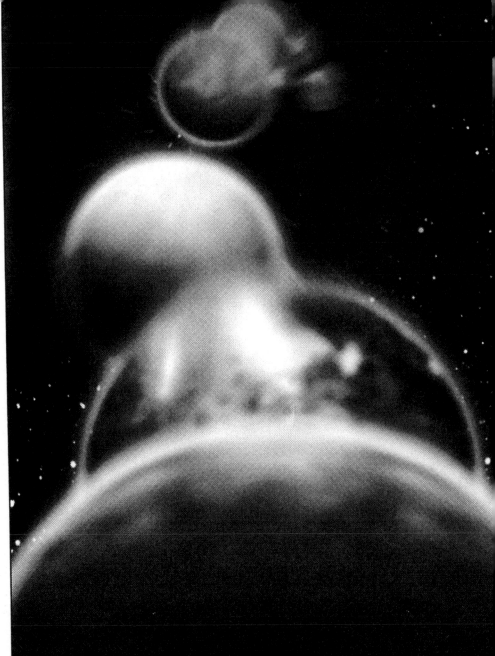

Chapter24

YOU'LL BREAK ME!

EASY...

OW

HERE!

SLICH

SLICH

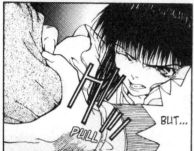

PULL

BUT...

THUD

QUICK, TO THE KING!

PHEW

OUCH.

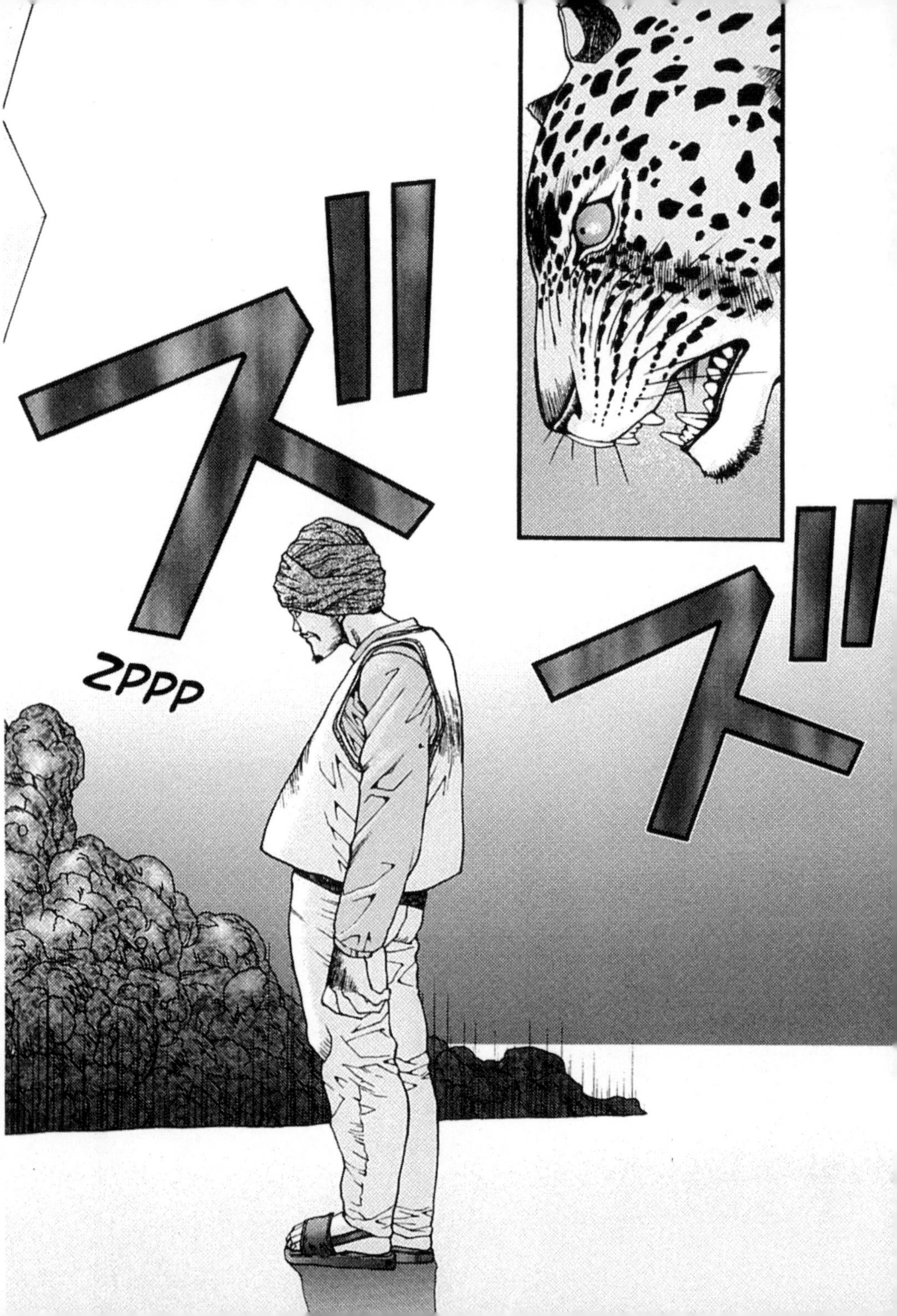
ズ
ズ
ZPPP

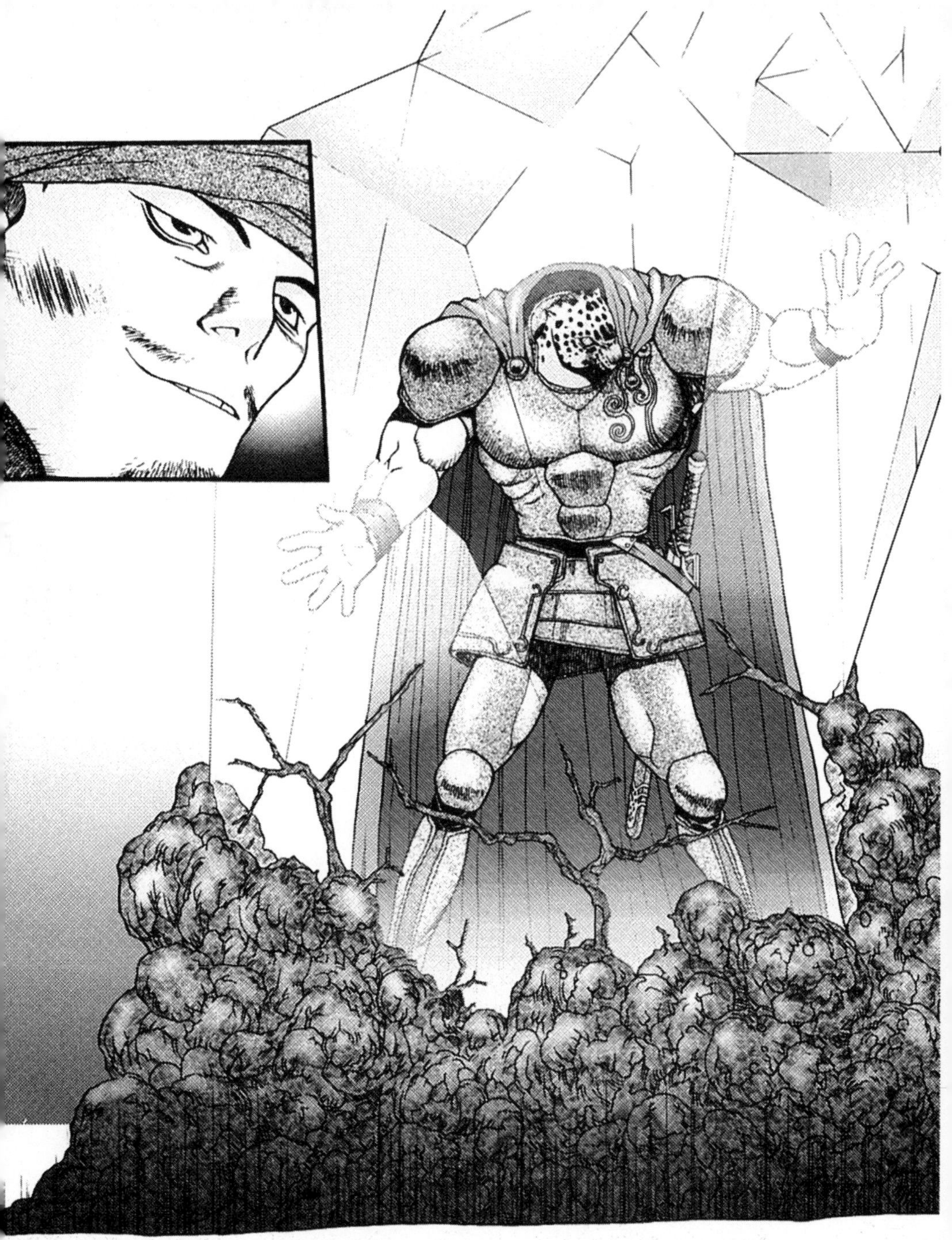

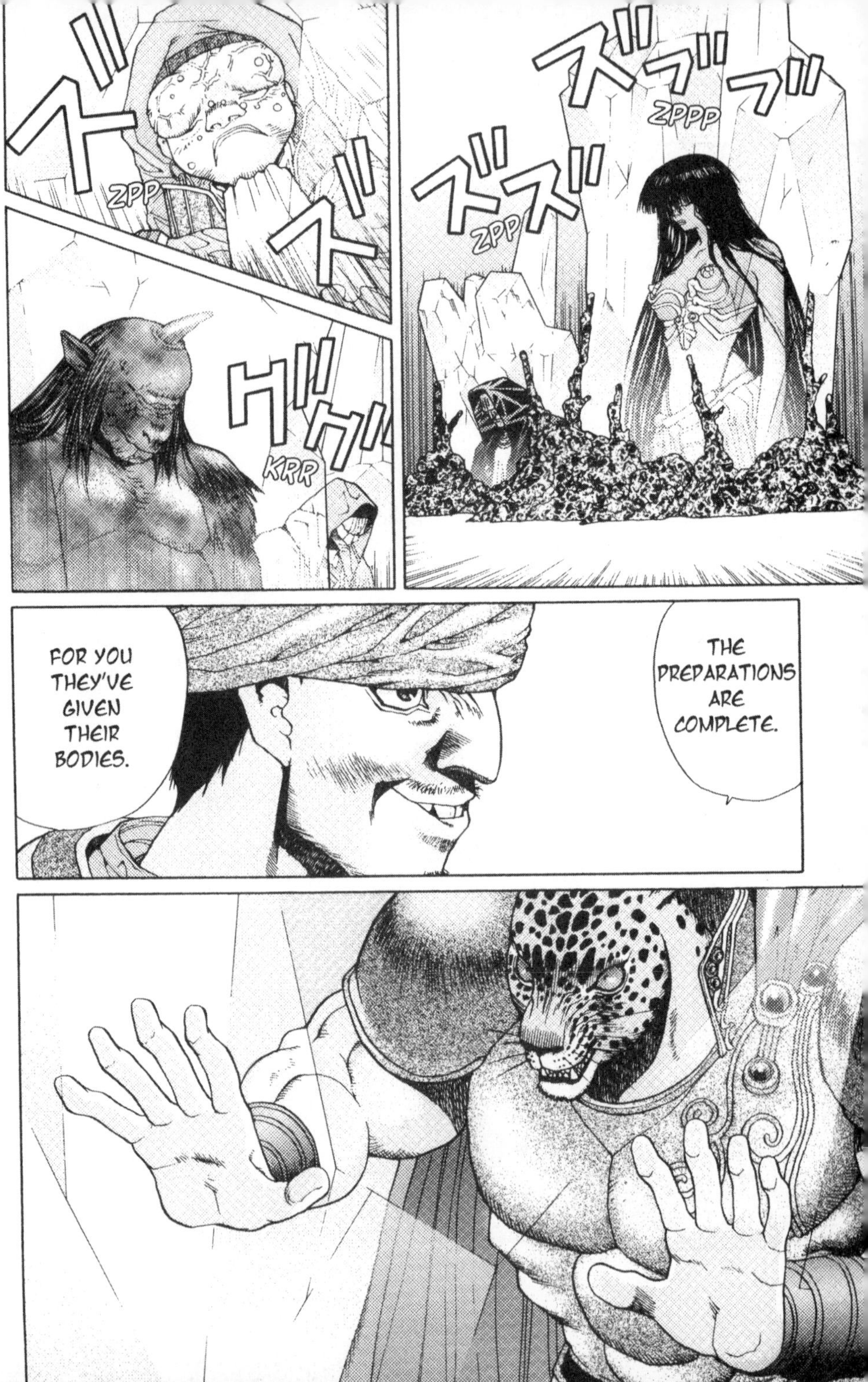
ZPPP
ZPP
ZPP
KRR
THE PREPARATIONS ARE COMPLETE.
FOR YOU THEY'VE GIVEN THEIR BODIES.

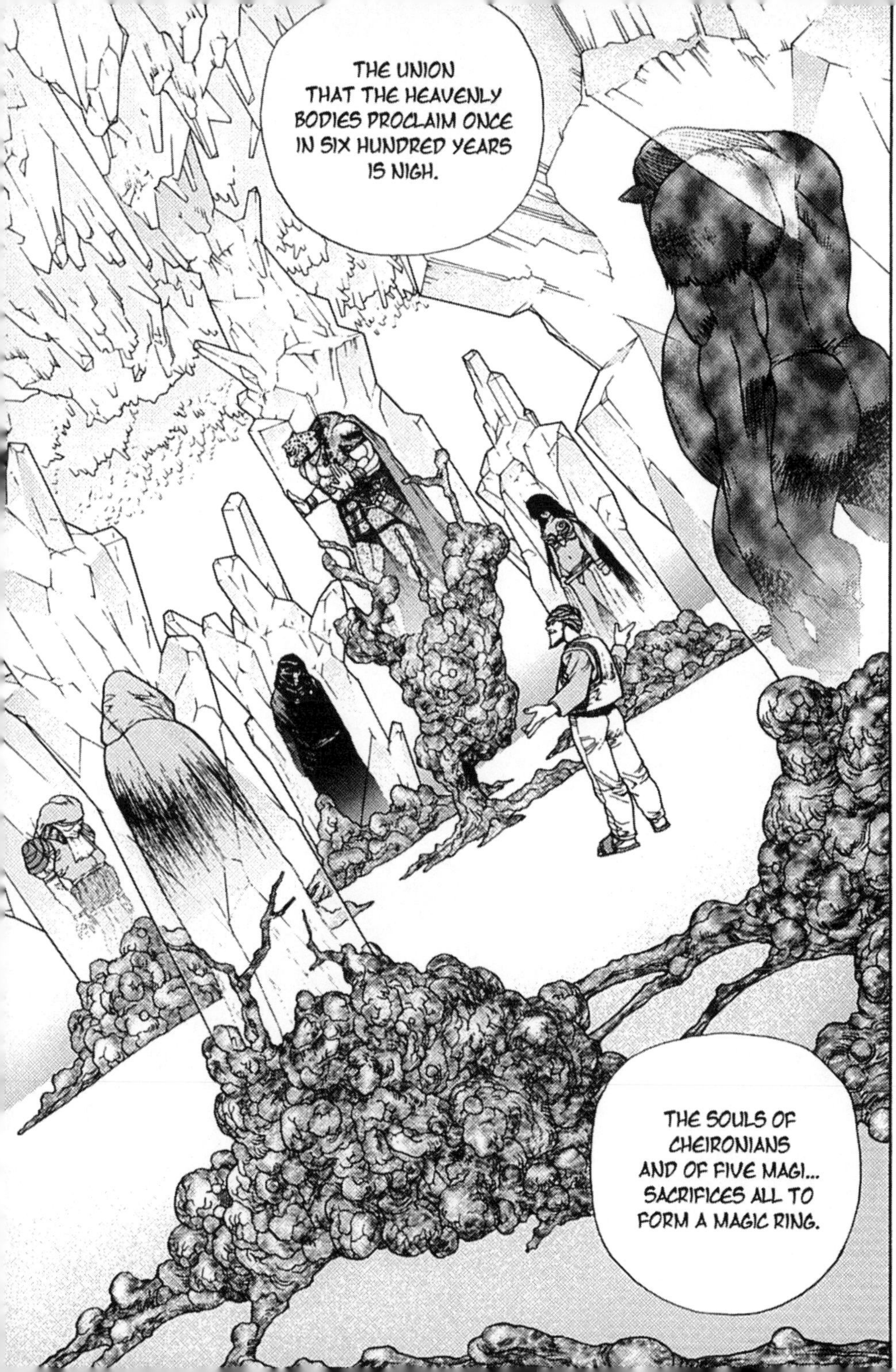
THE UNION THAT THE HEAVENLY BODIES PROCLAIM ONCE IN SIX HUNDRED YEARS IS NIGH.
THE SOULS OF CHEIRONIANS AND OF FIVE MAGI... SACRIFICES ALL TO FORM A MAGIC RING.

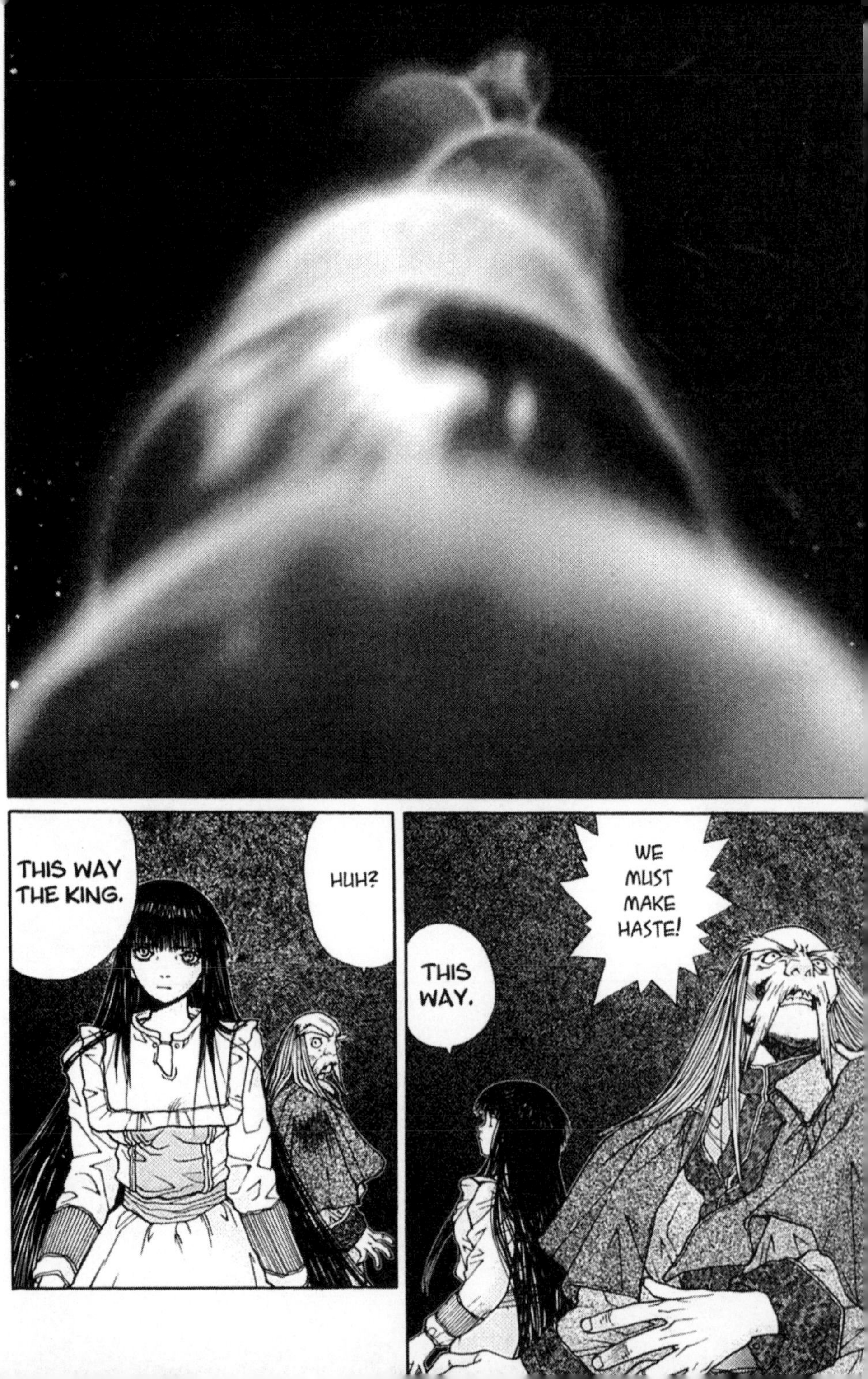
WE MUST MAKE HASTE!
THIS WAY.
HUH?
THIS WAY THE KING.

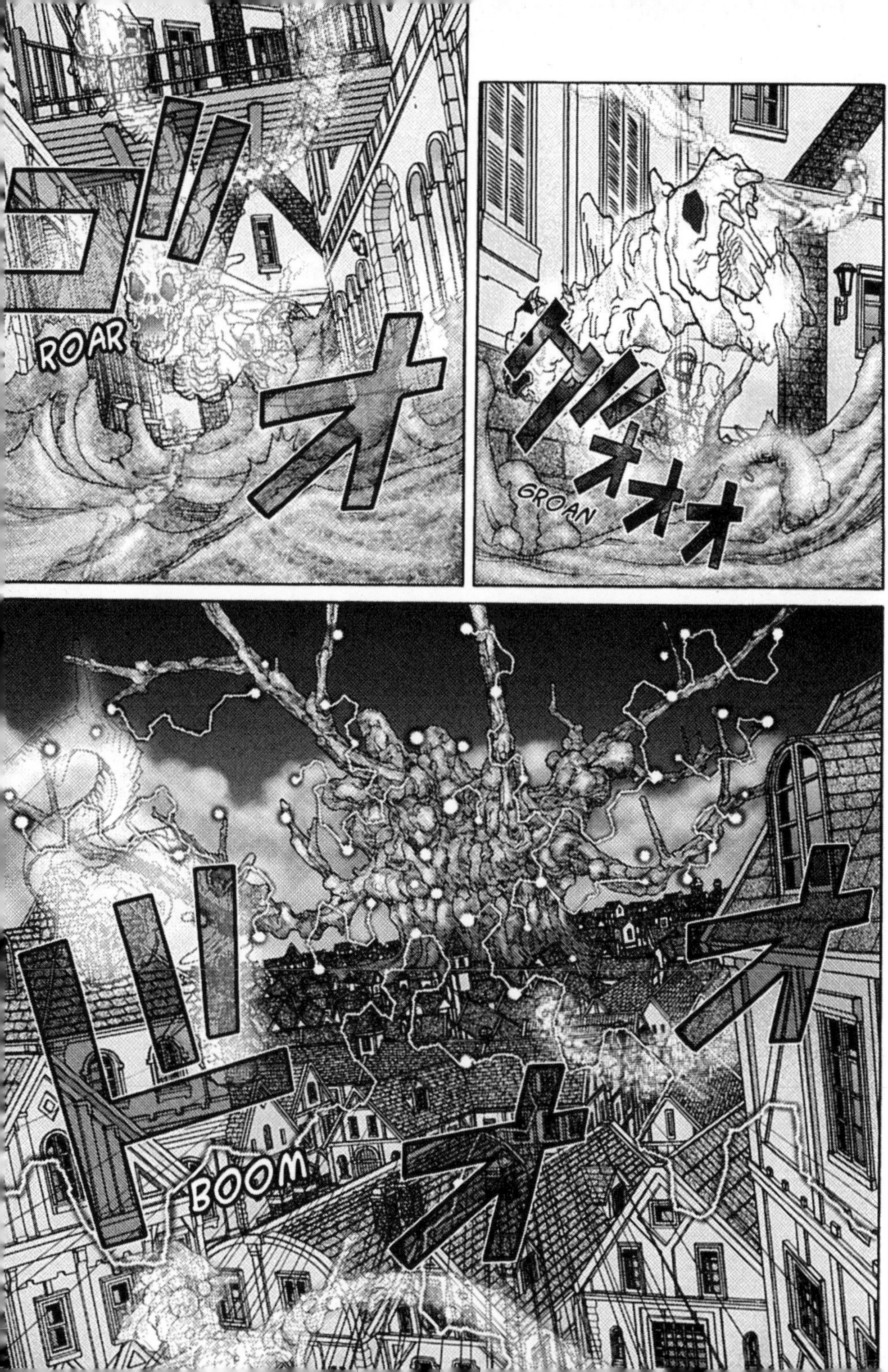
GROAN
ROAR
BOOM

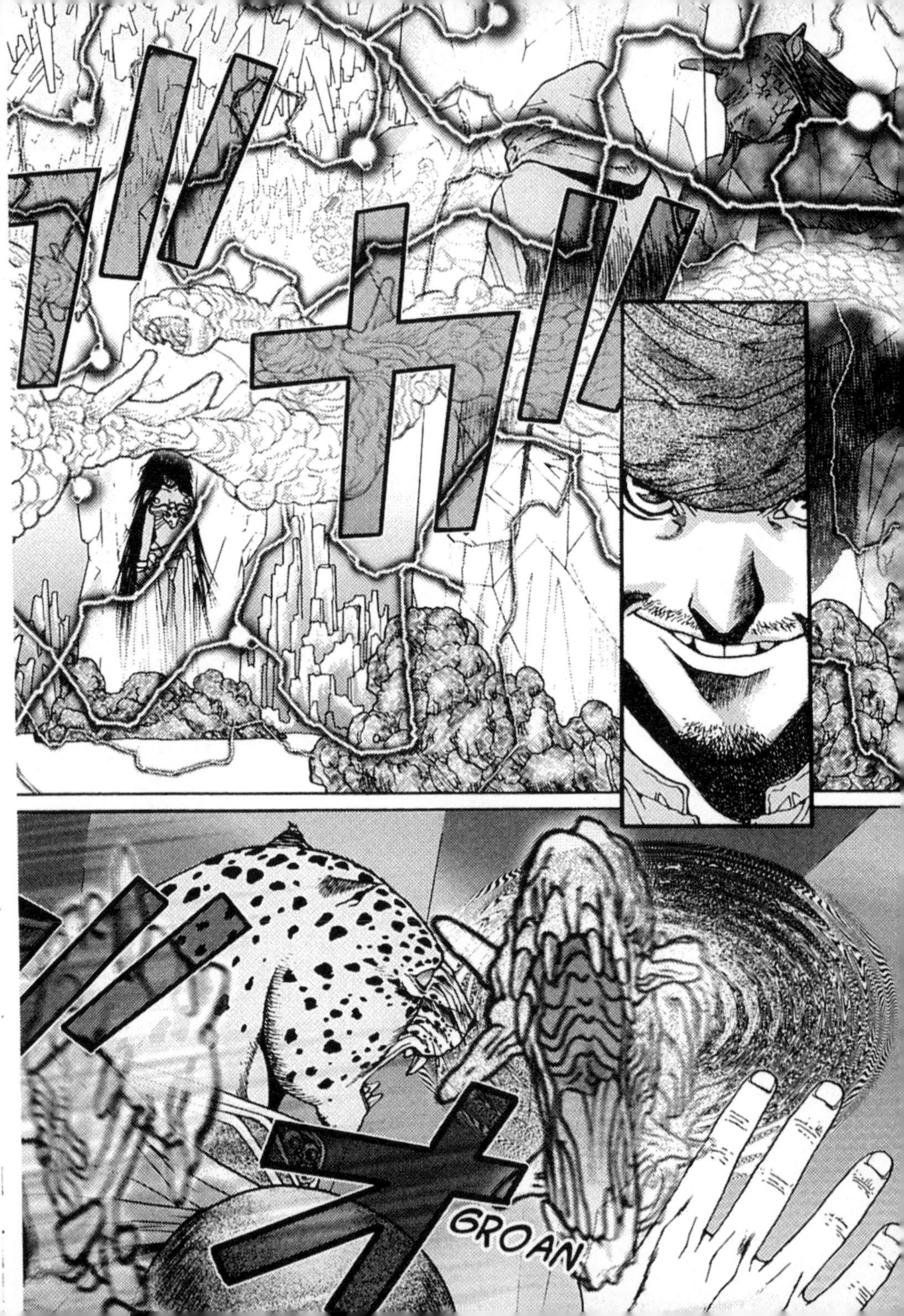
GROAN

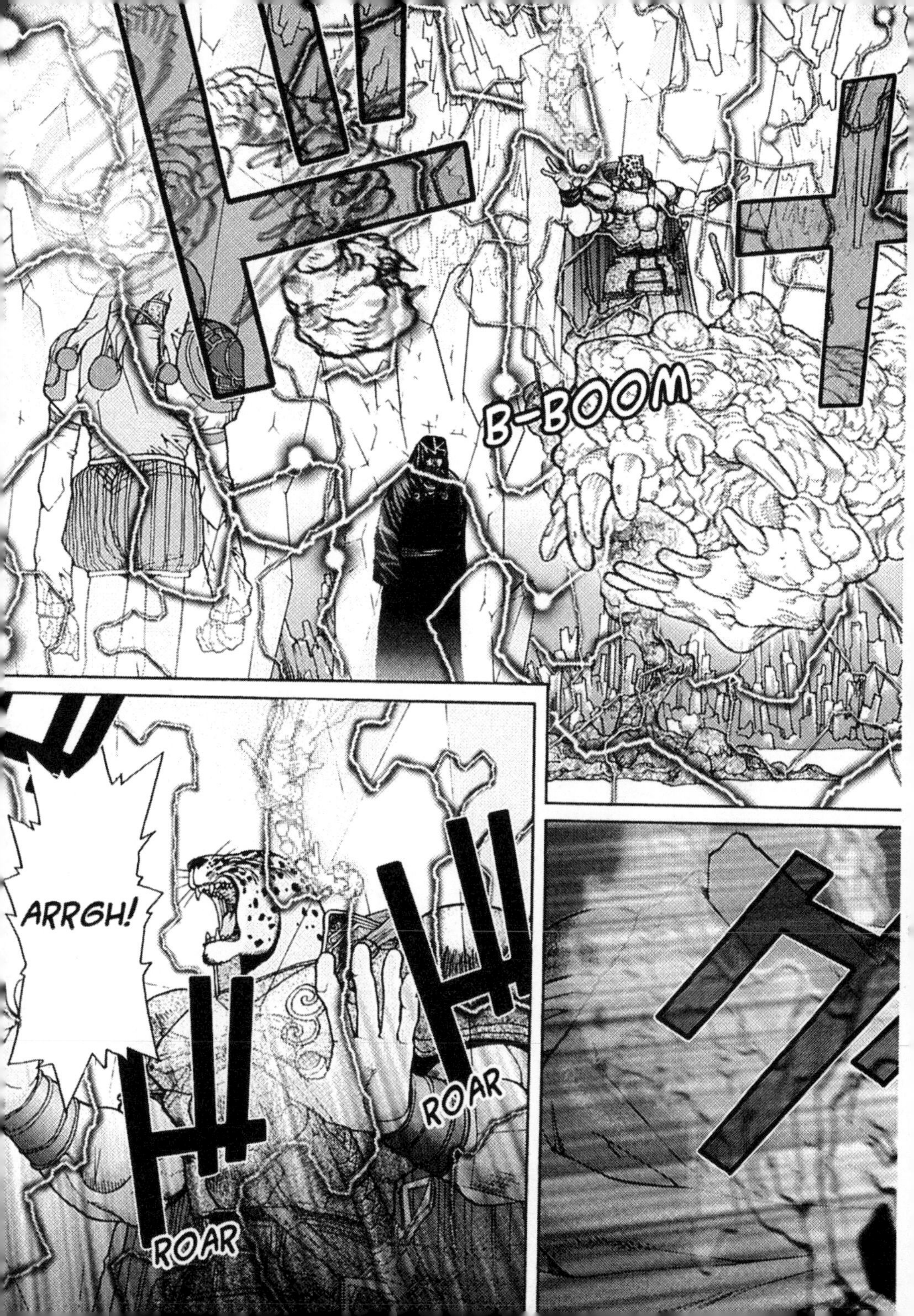
B-BOOM
ARRGH!
ROAR
ROAR

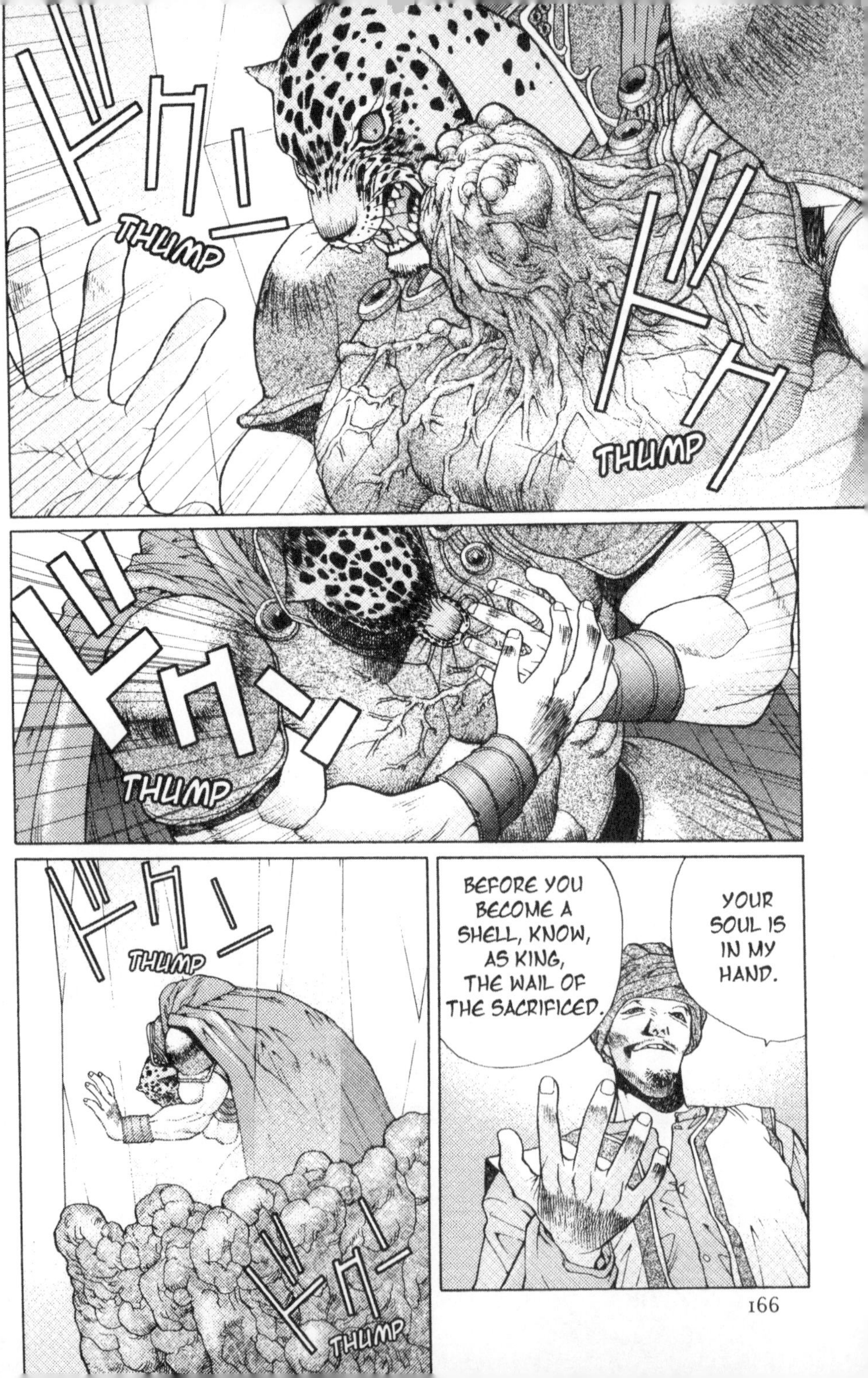
THUMP
THUMP
THUMP
YOUR SOUL IS IN MY HAND.
BEFORE YOU BECOME A SHELL, KNOW, AS KING, THE WAIL OF THE SACRIFICED.
THUMP
THUMP

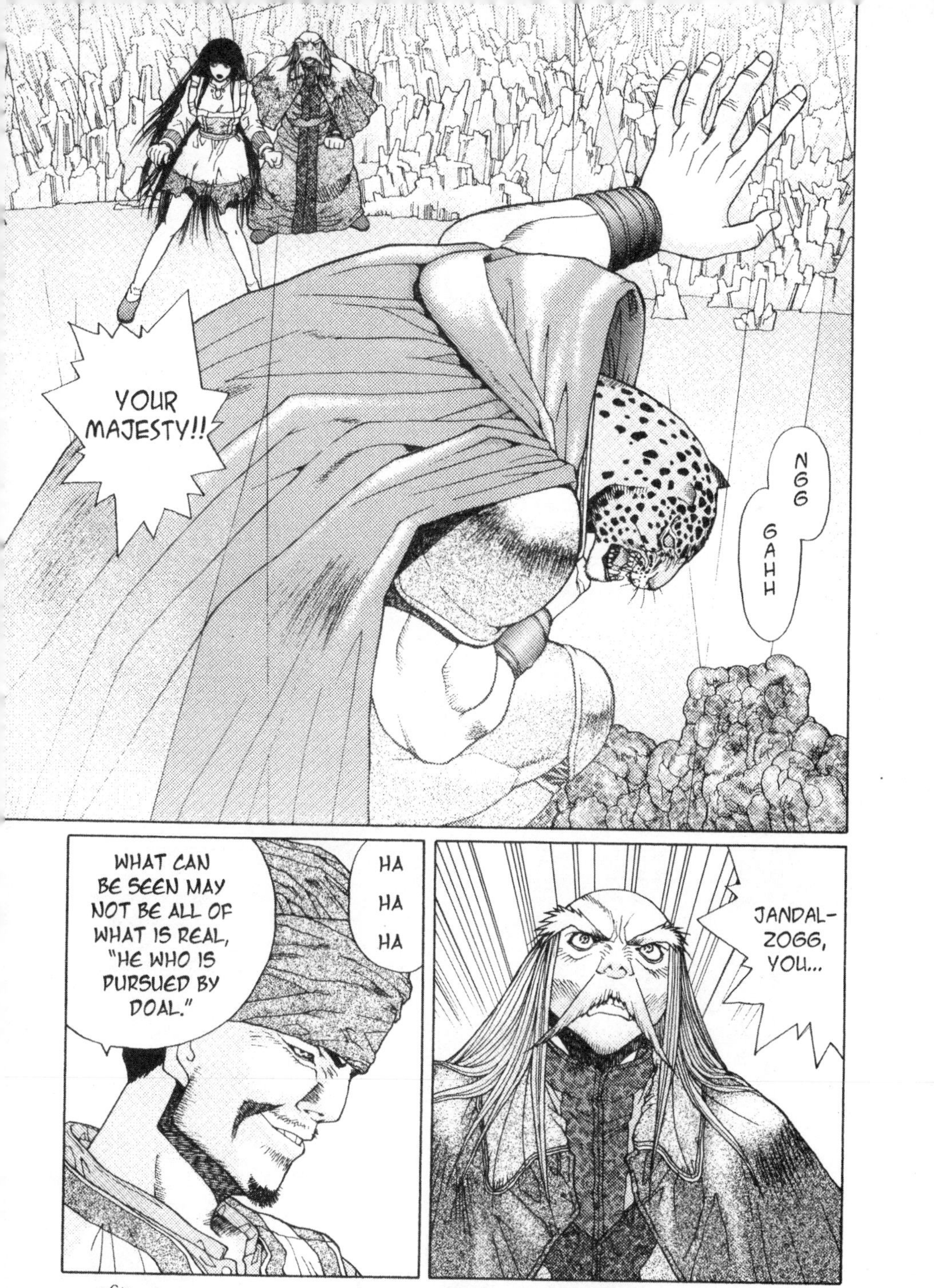
NGG GAHH
YOUR MAJESTY!!
JANDAL-ZOGG, YOU...
HA HA HA
WHAT CAN BE SEEN MAY NOT BE ALL OF WHAT IS REAL, "HE WHO IS PURSUED BY DOAL."

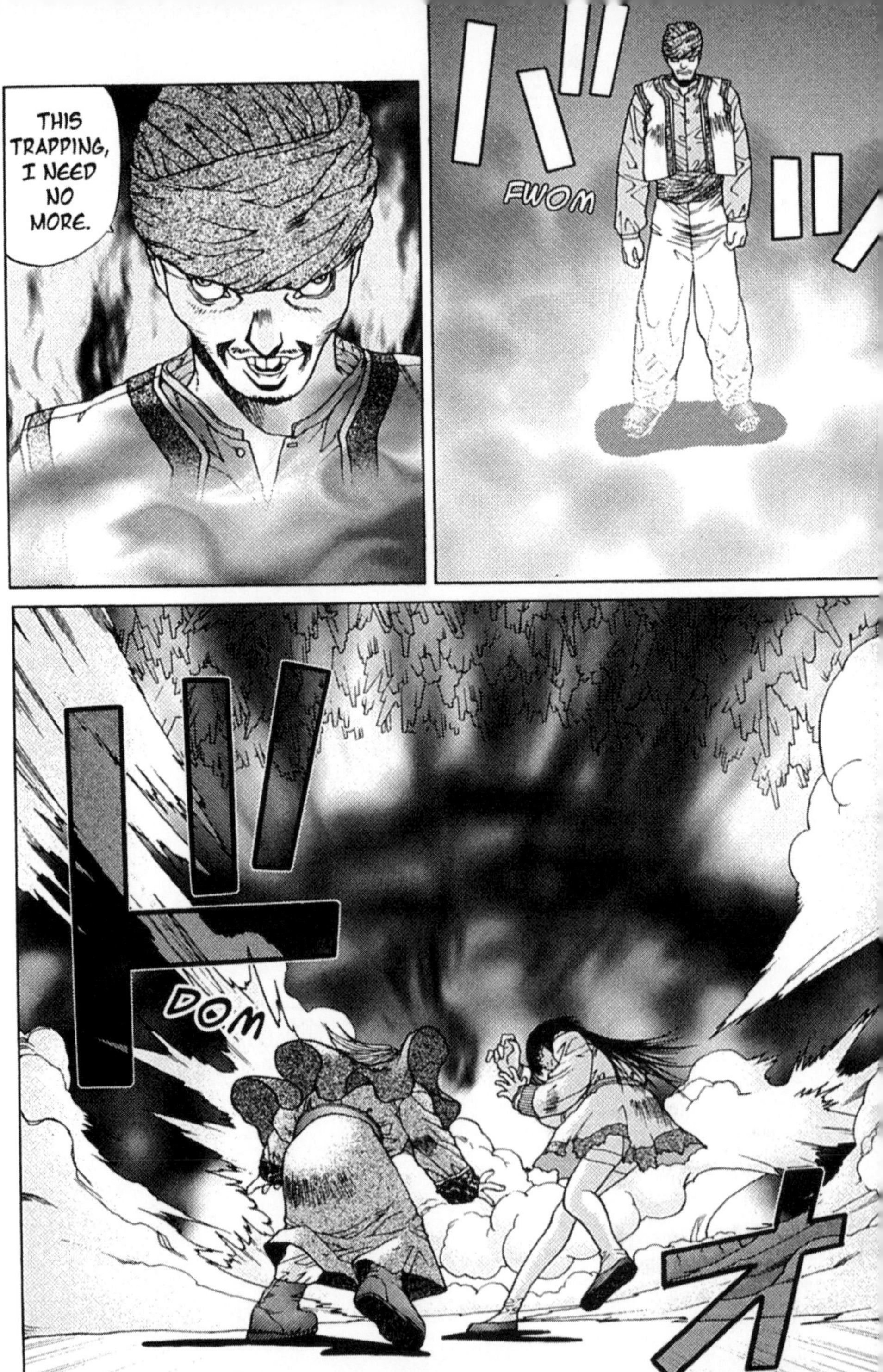
FWOM
THIS TRAPPING, I NEED NO MORE.
DOM

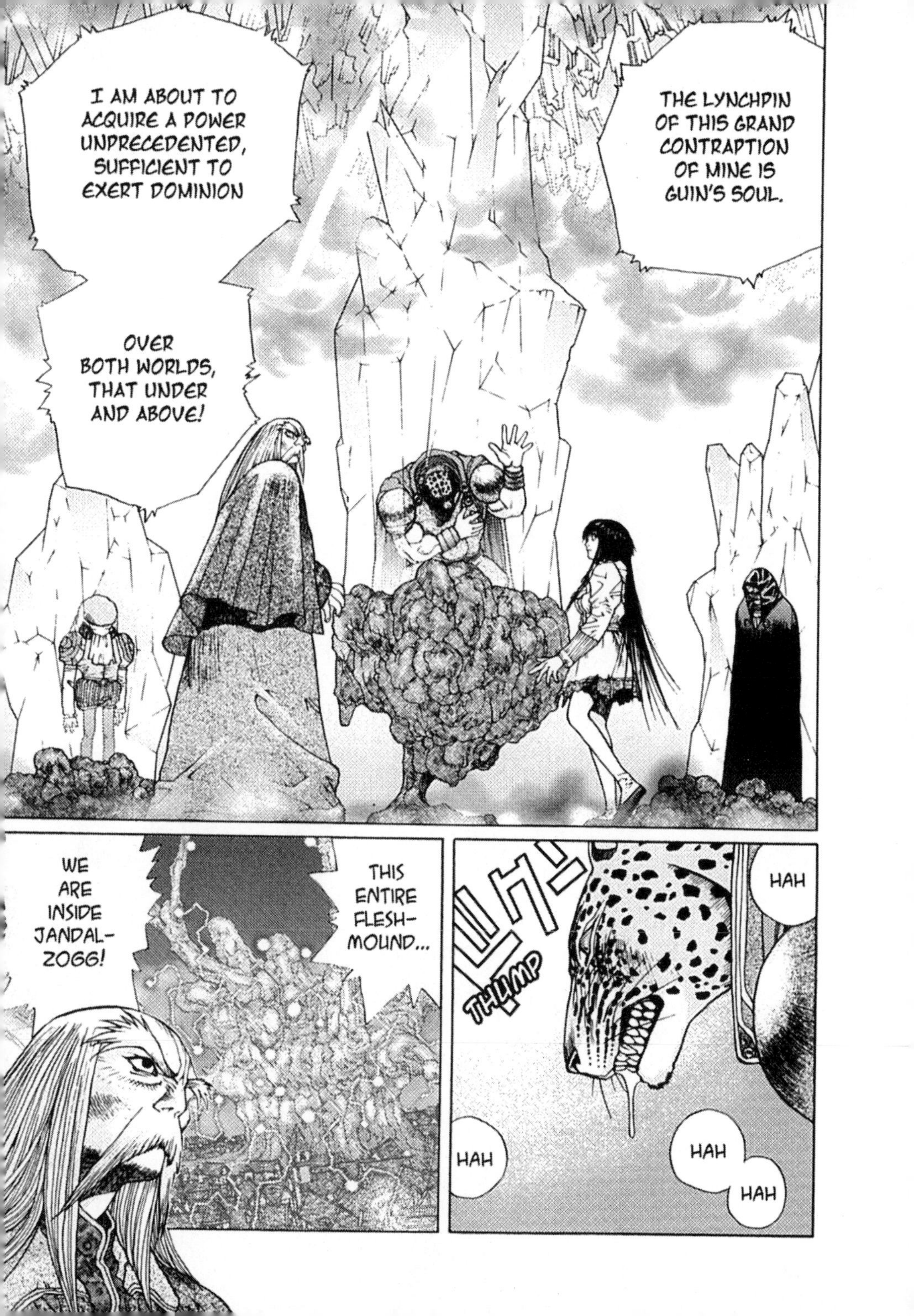
THE LYNCHPIN OF THIS GRAND CONTRAPTION OF MINE IS GUIN'S SOUL.
I AM ABOUT TO ACQUIRE A POWER UNPRECEDENTED, SUFFICIENT TO EXERT DOMINION
OVER BOTH WORLDS, THAT UNDER AND ABOVE!
HAH
THUMP
HAH
HAH
HAH
THIS ENTIRE FLESH-MOUND...
WE ARE INSIDE JANDAL-ZOGG!

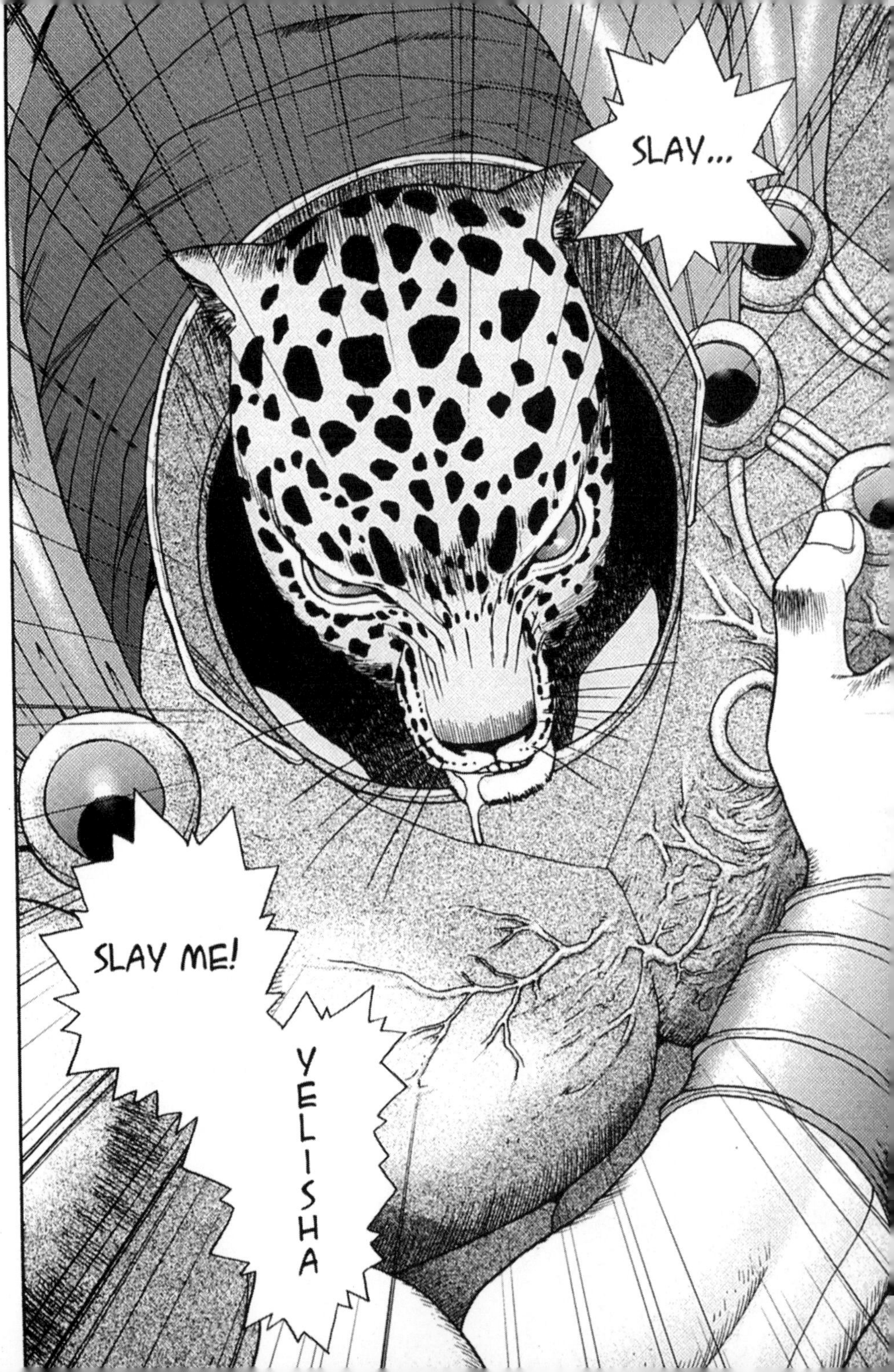
SLAY...
SLAY ME!
YELISHA

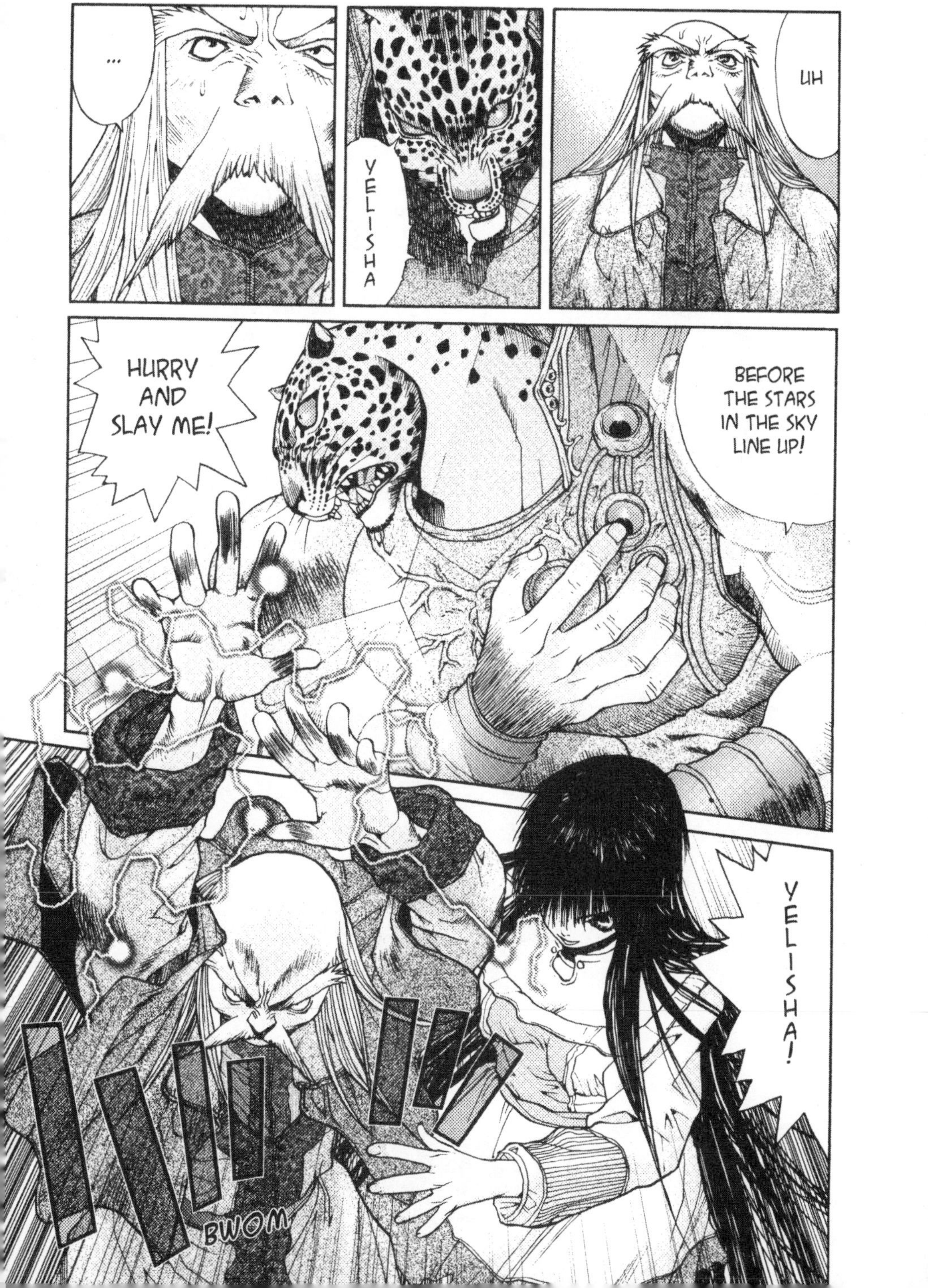
UH
YELISHA
...
BEFORE THE STARS IN THE SKY LINE UP!
HURRY AND SLAY ME!
YELISHA!
BWOM

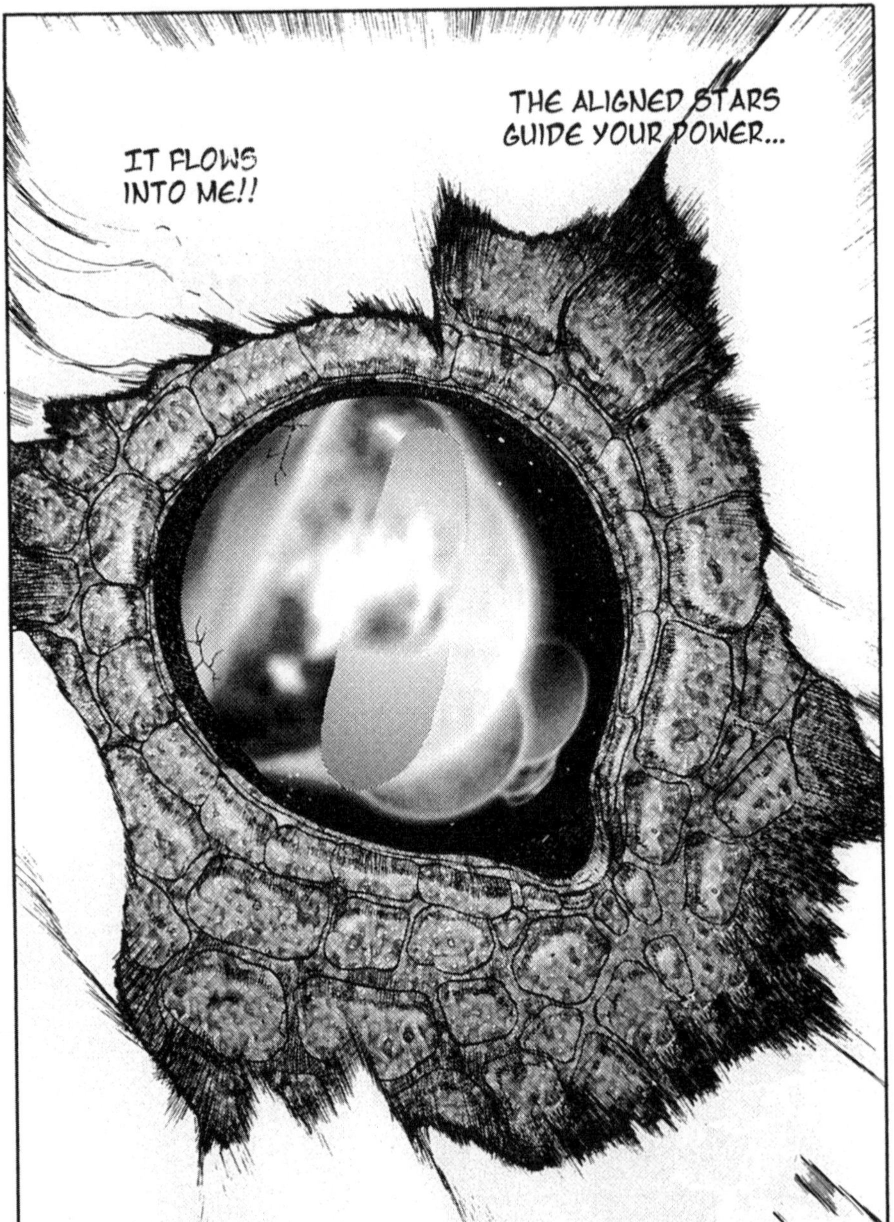

Final Chapter

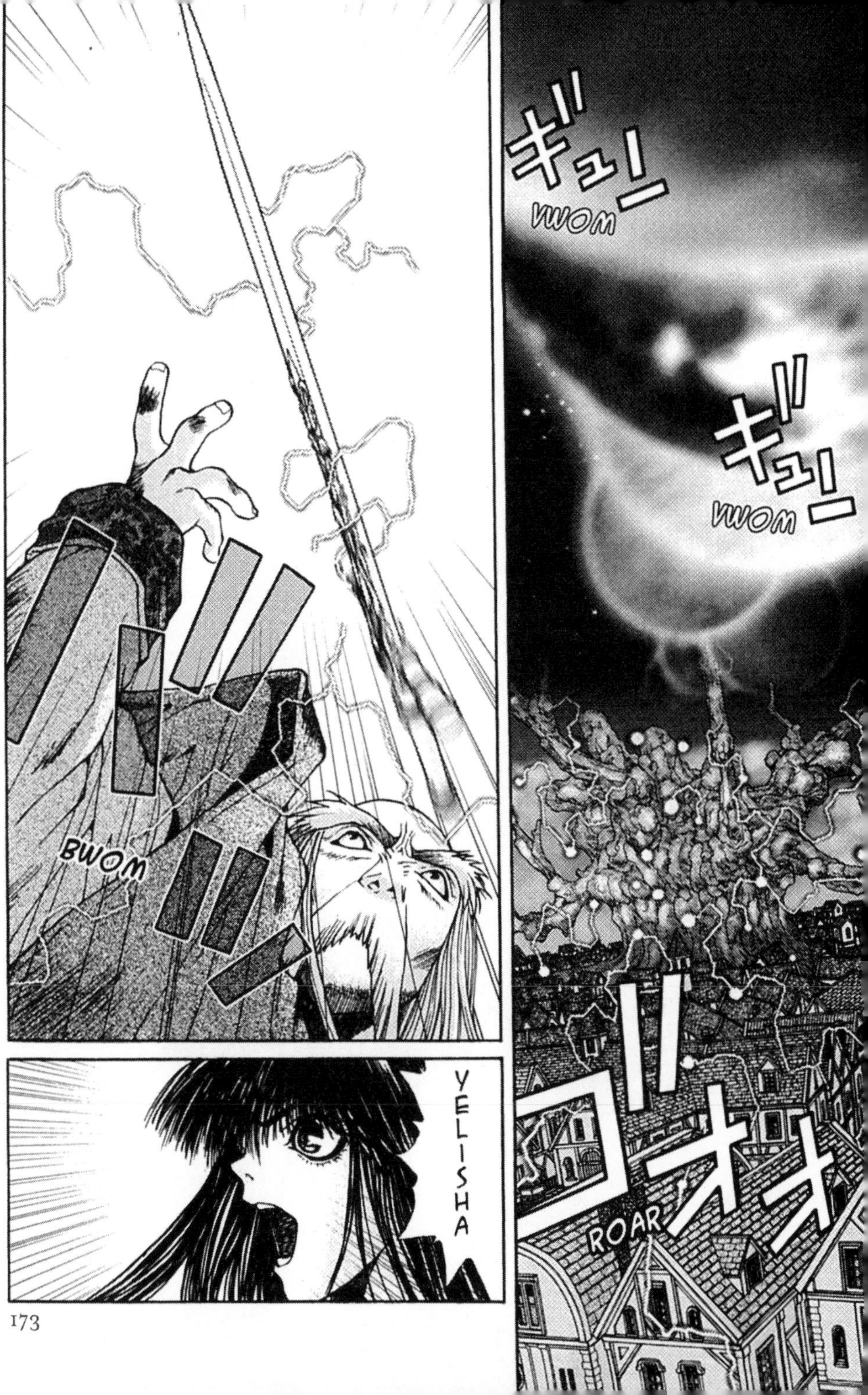
ギュー
VWOM
ギュー
VWOM
ゴオオ
ROAR
BWOM
YELISHA

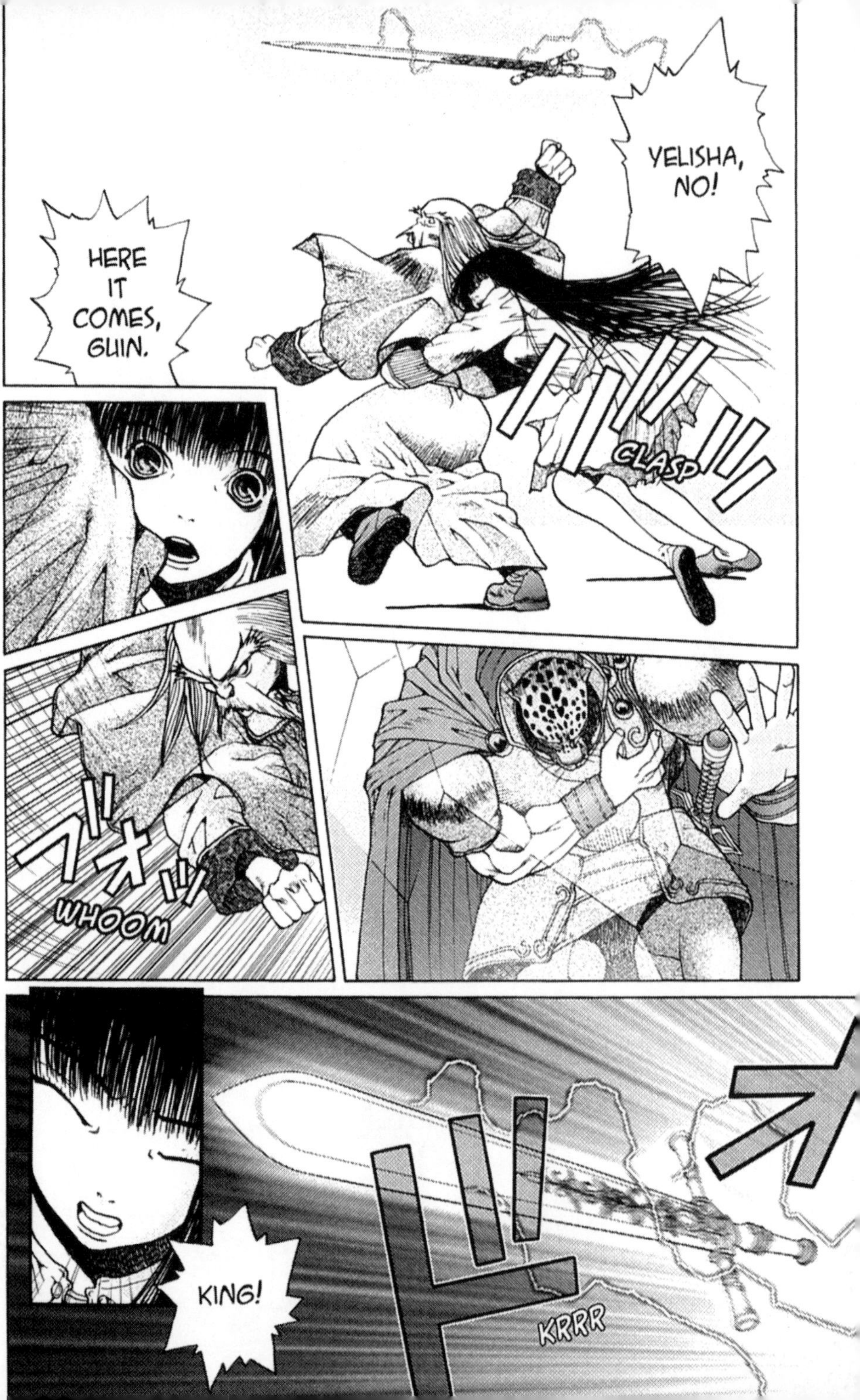
YELISHA, NO!
HERE IT COMES, GUIN.
CLASP
WHOOM
KING!
KRRR

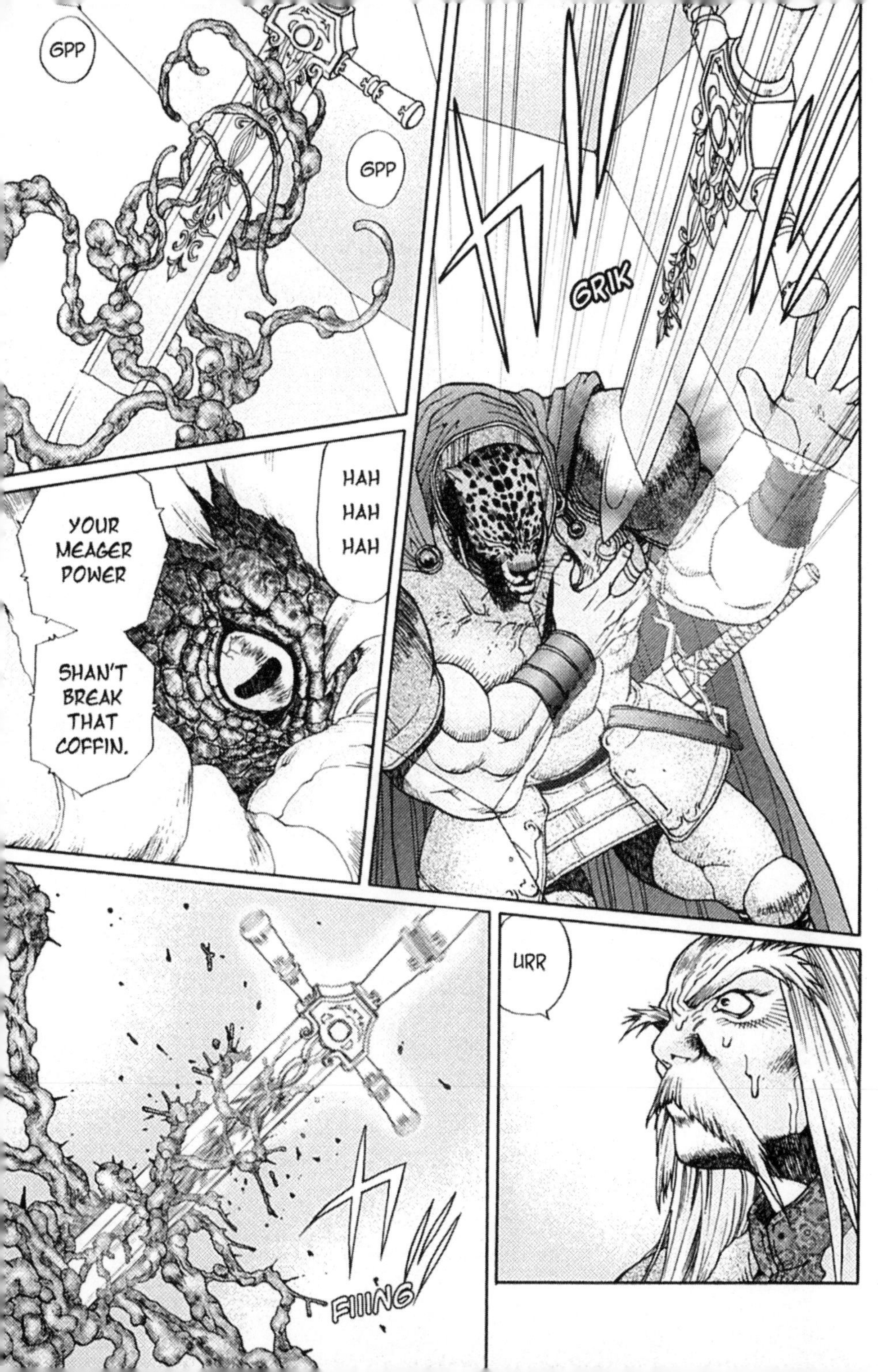
GRIK
GPP
GPP
HAH HAH HAH
YOUR MEAGER POWER
SHAN'T BREAK THAT COFFIN.
URR
FIIING

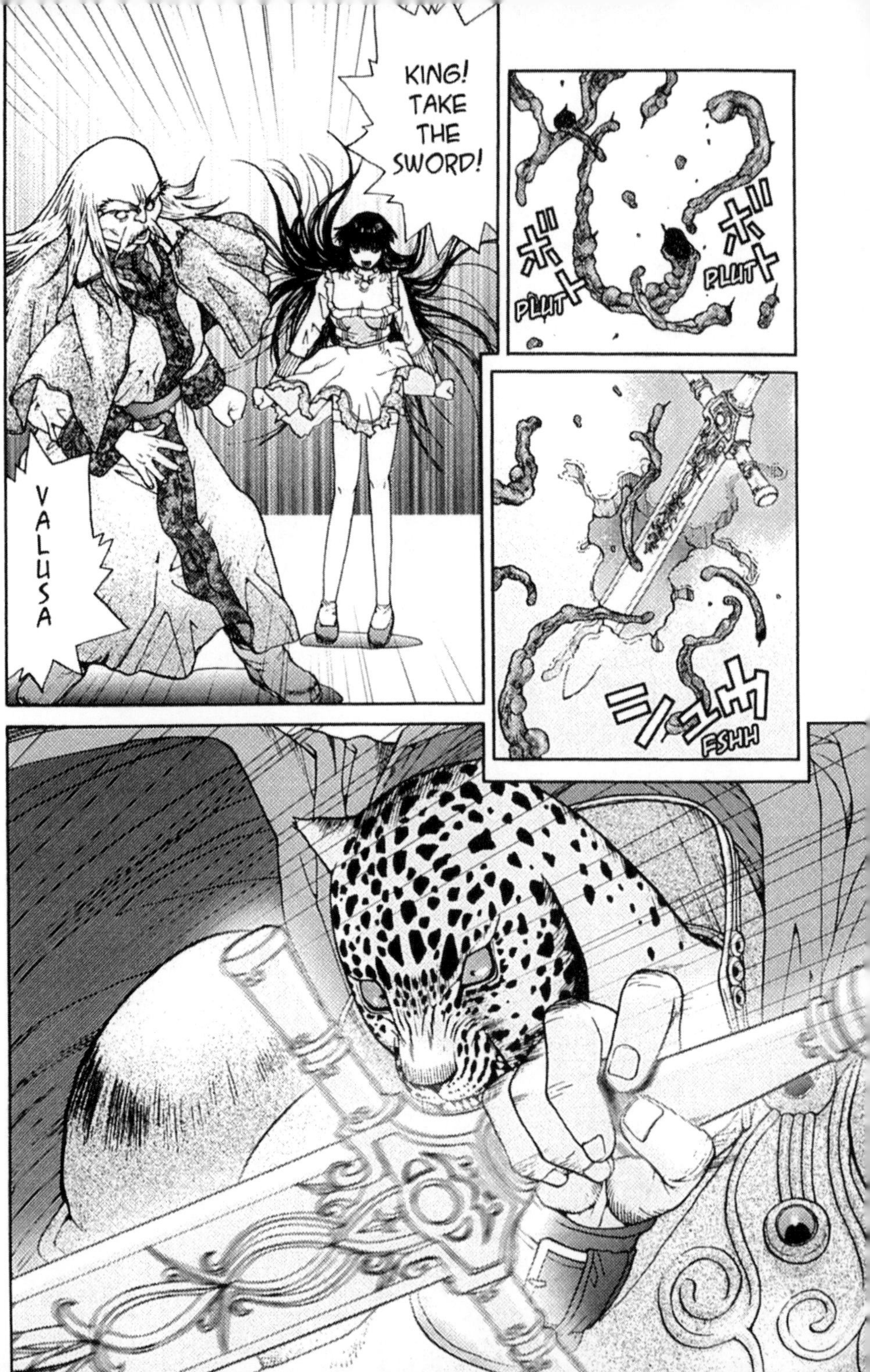
ボト
PLUT
ボト
PLUT
FSHH
KING! TAKE THE SWORD!
VALUSA

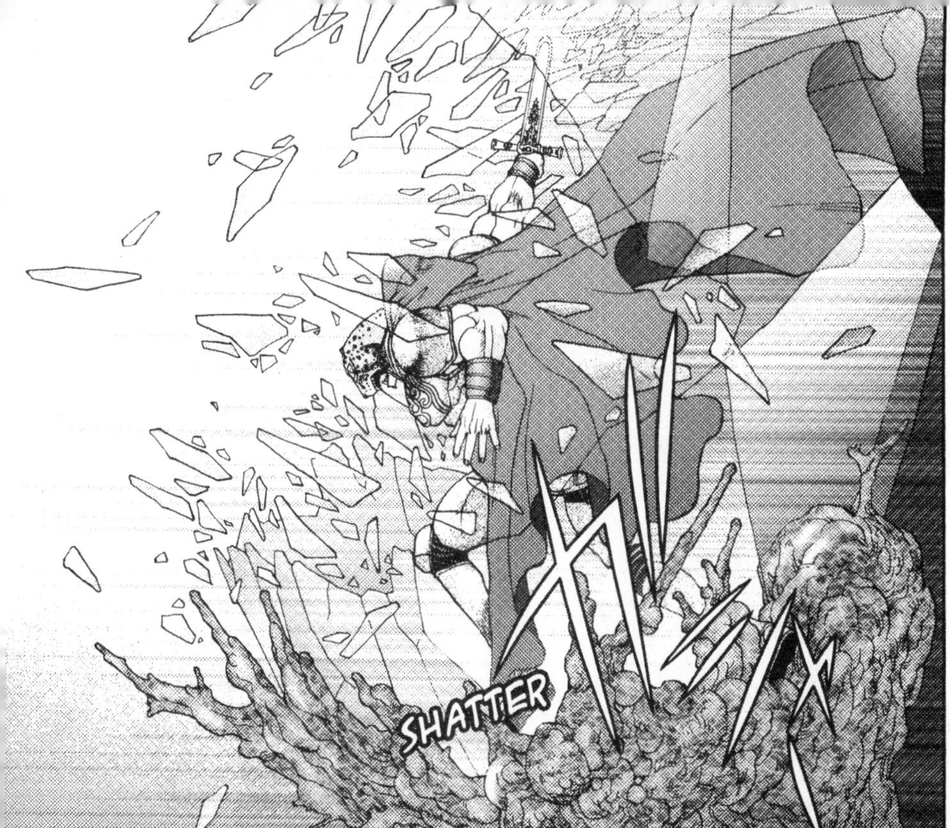
SHATTER

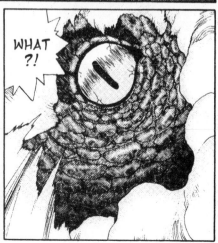

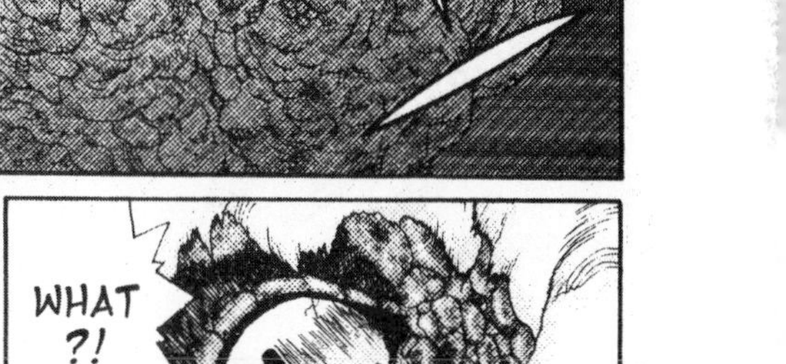
WHAT ?!

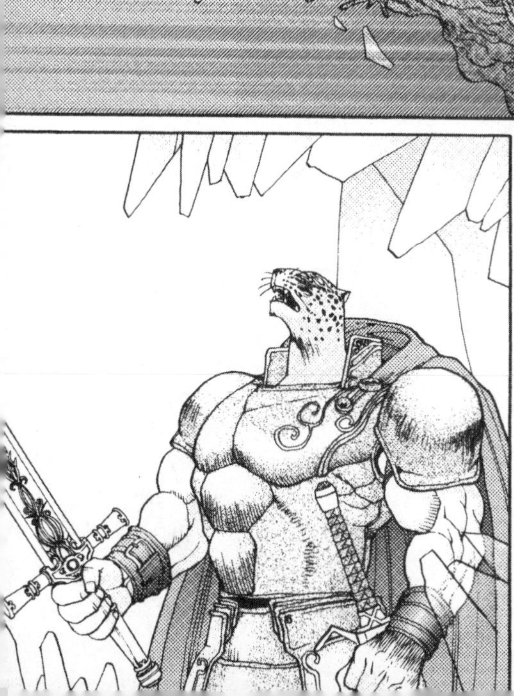

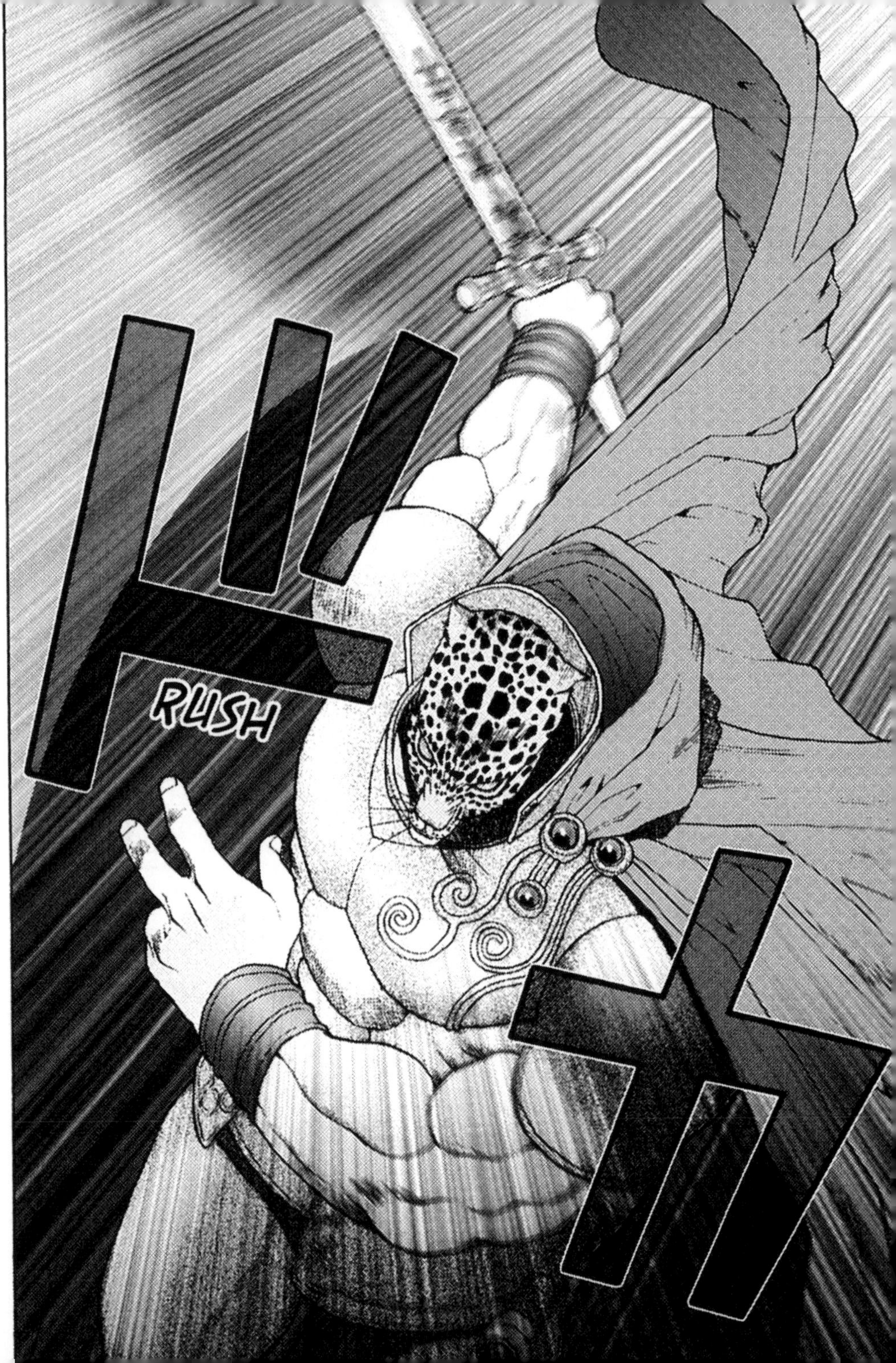
ドッ
RUSH

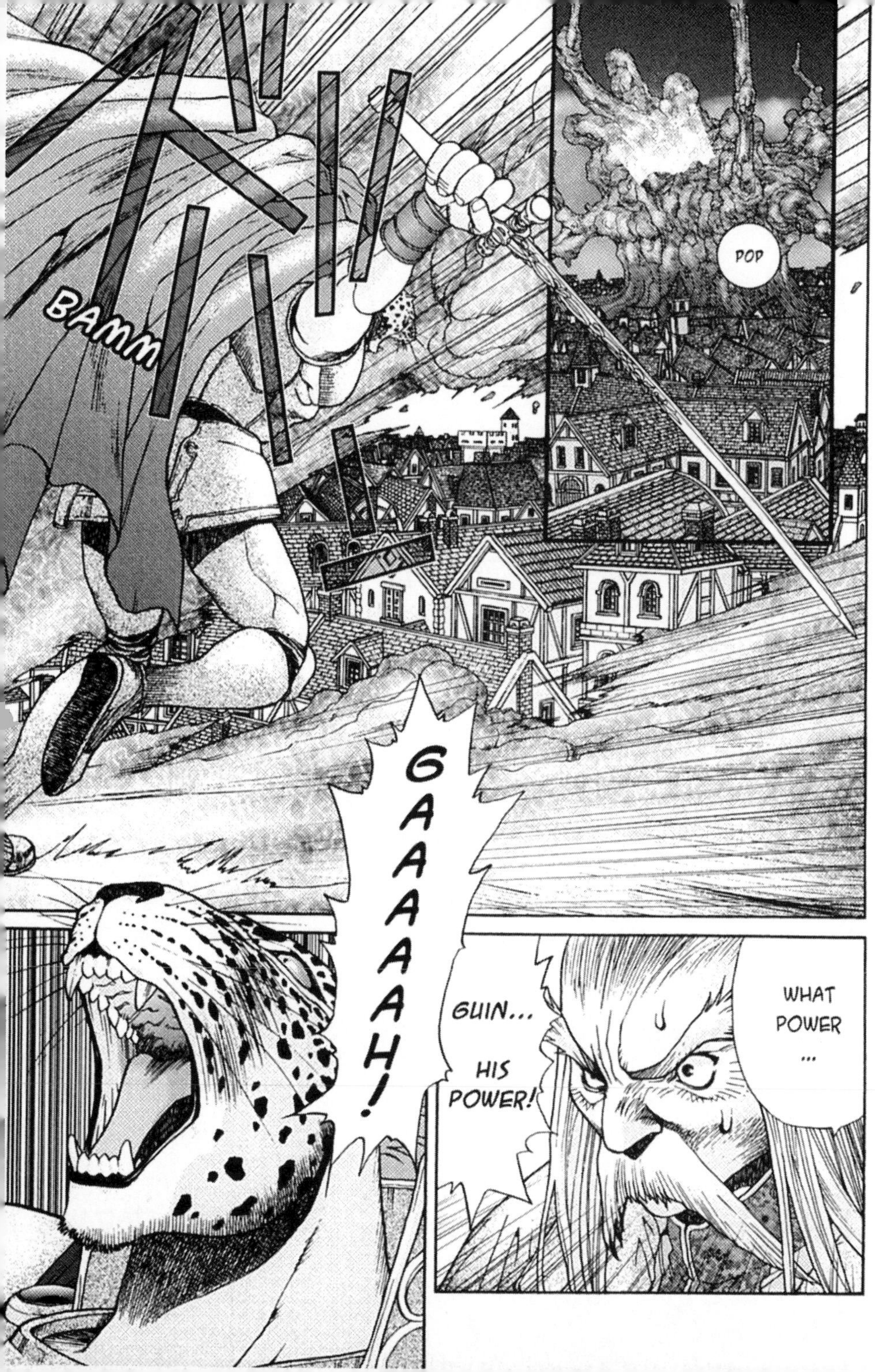
POP
BAMM
GAAAAAH!
WHAT POWER ...
GUIN... HIS POWER!

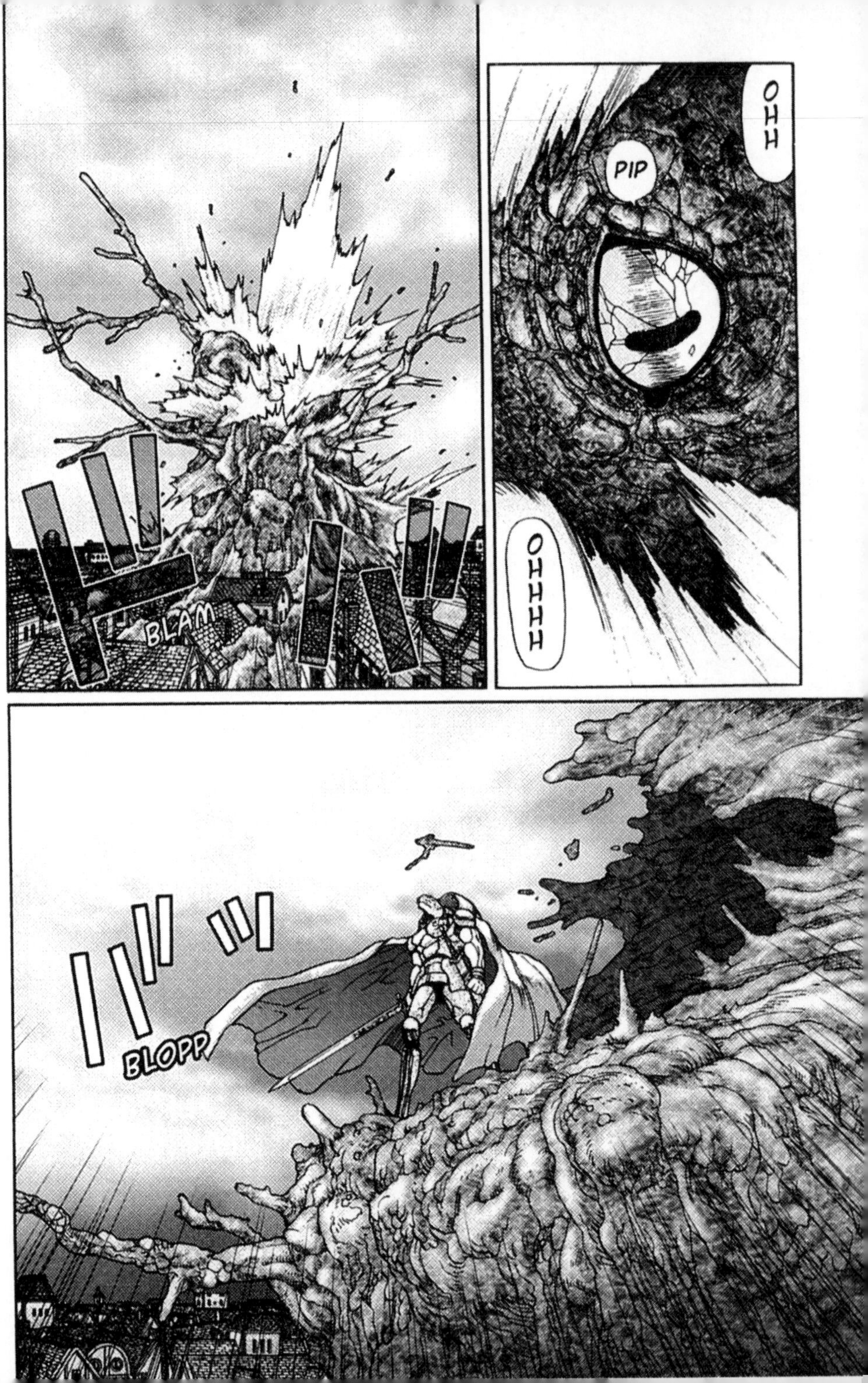
OHH
PIP
OHHHH
BLAM
BLOPP

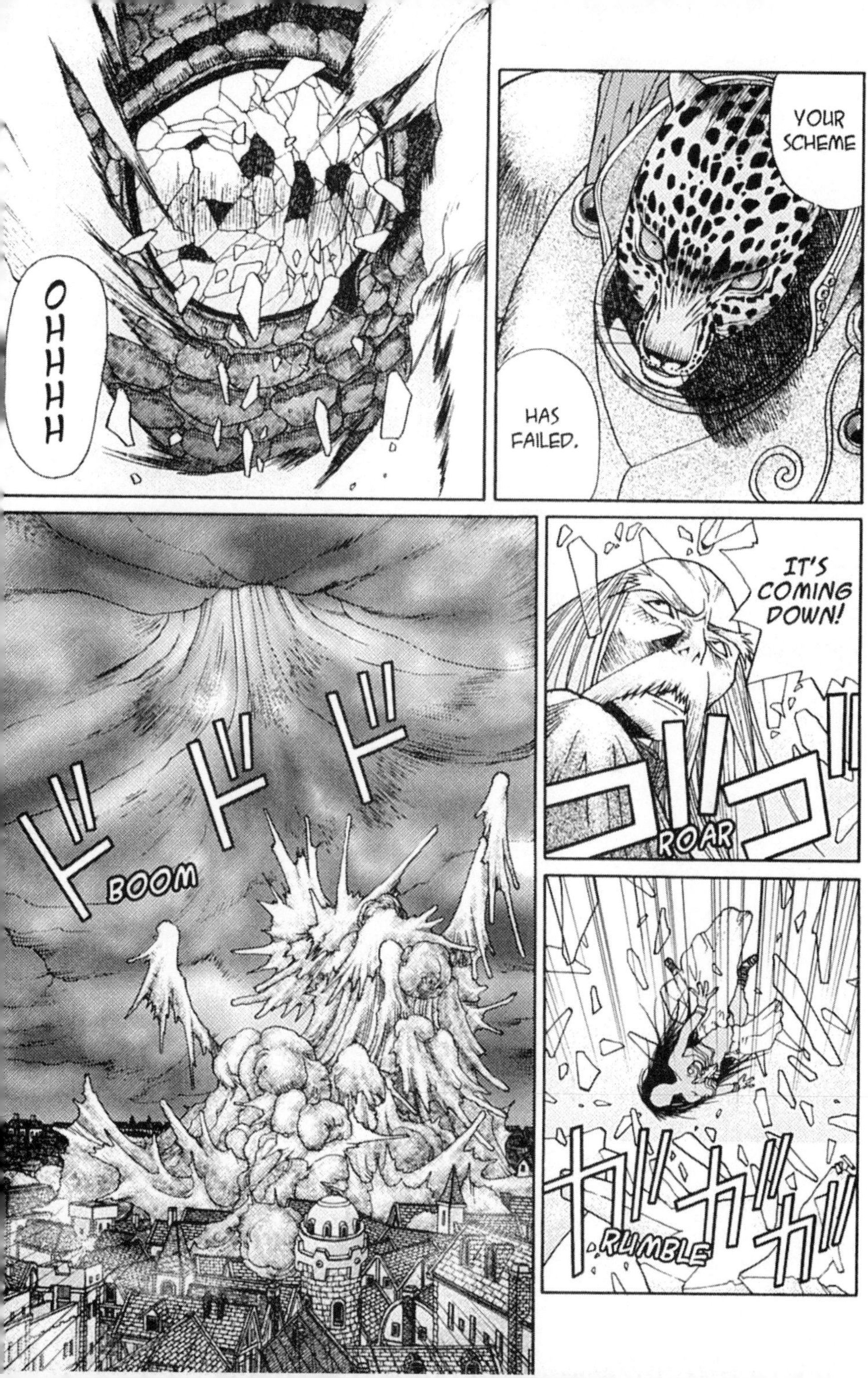
YOUR SCHEME
HAS FAILED.
OHHHHH
IT'S COMING DOWN!
ゴゴゴ
ROAR
ガガガガ
RUMBLE
ドドド
BOOM

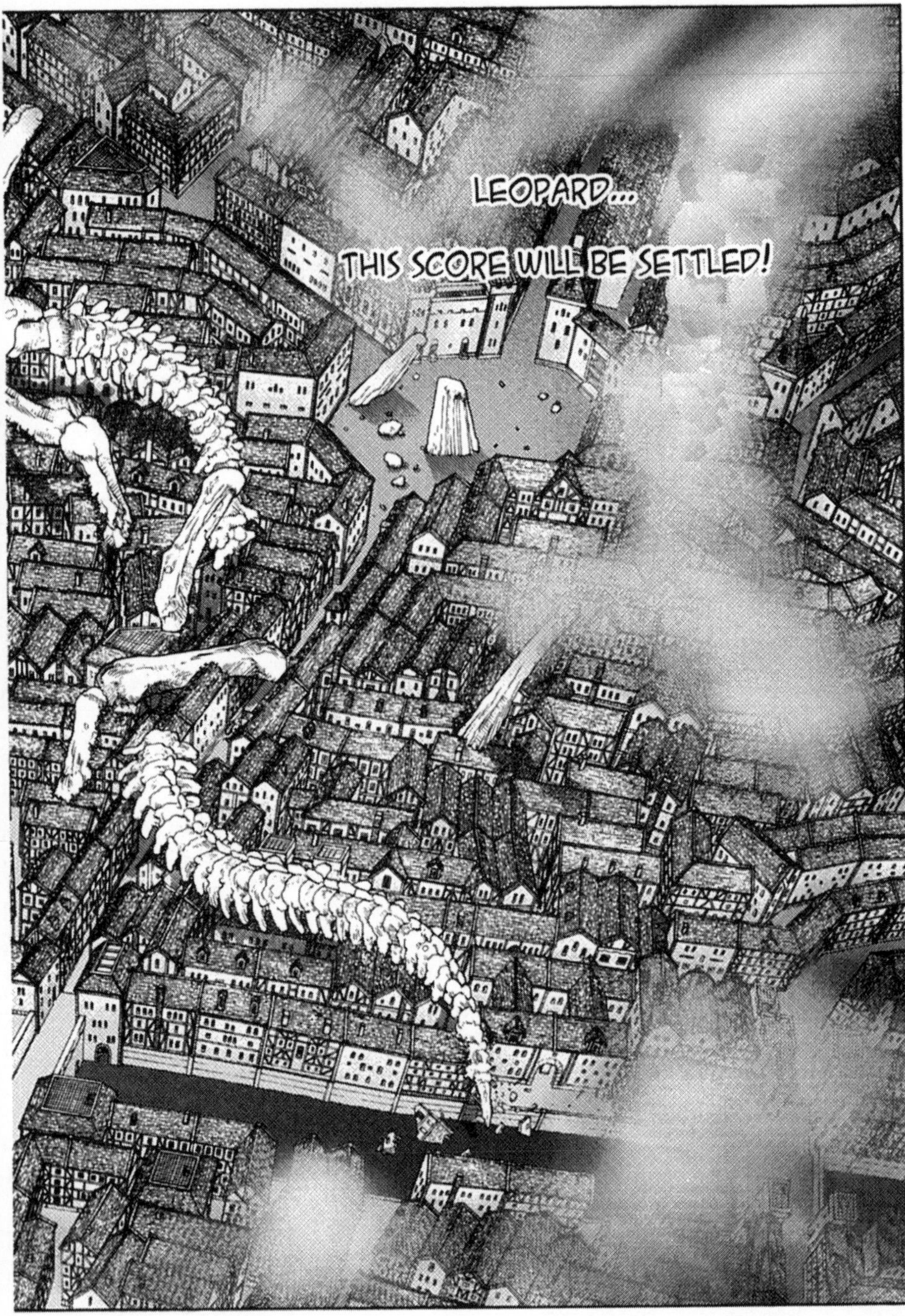
LEOPARD...
THIS SCORE WILL BE SETTLED!

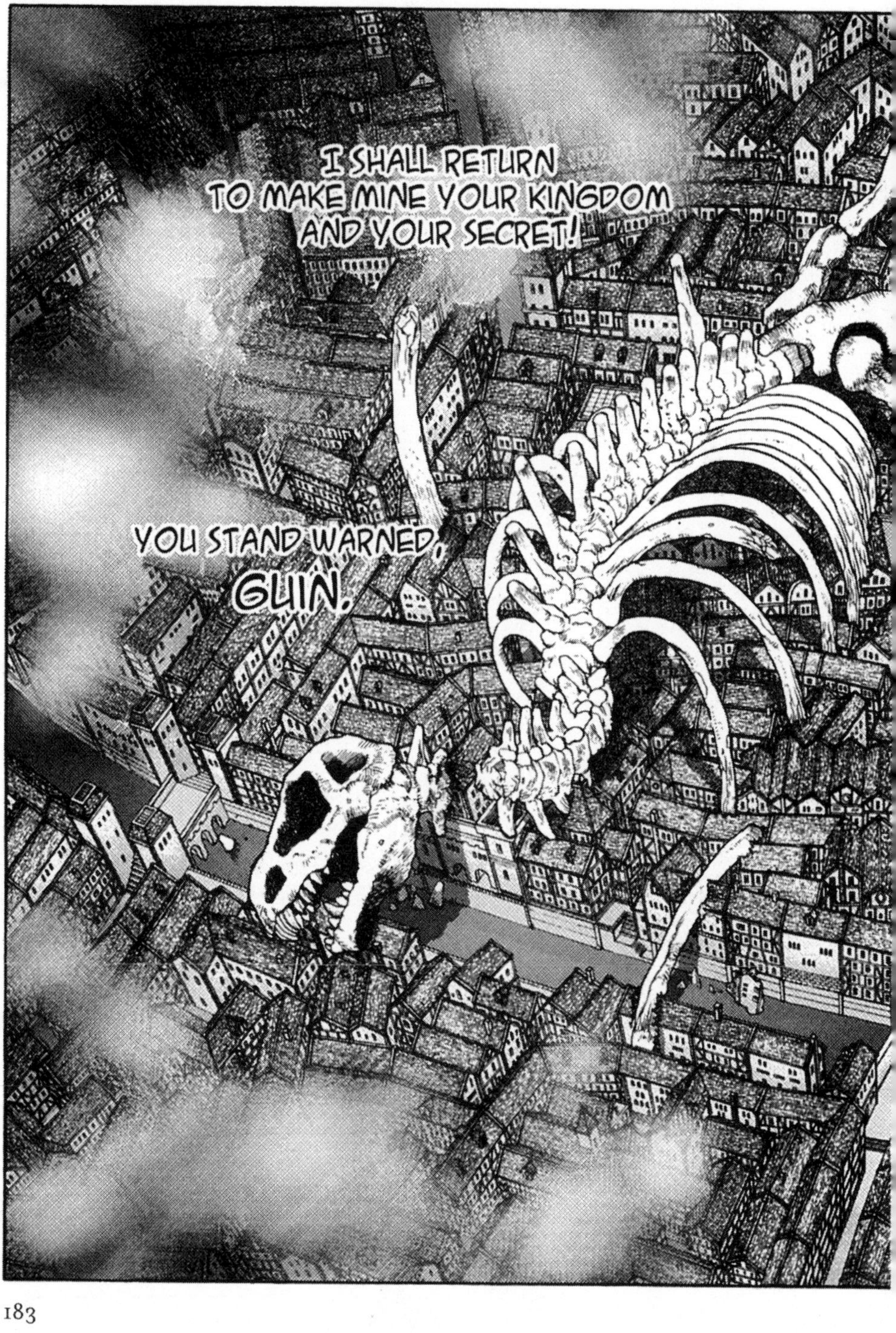
I SHALL RETURN
TO MAKE MINE YOUR KINGDOM
AND YOUR SECRET!
YOU STAND WARNED,
GUIN.

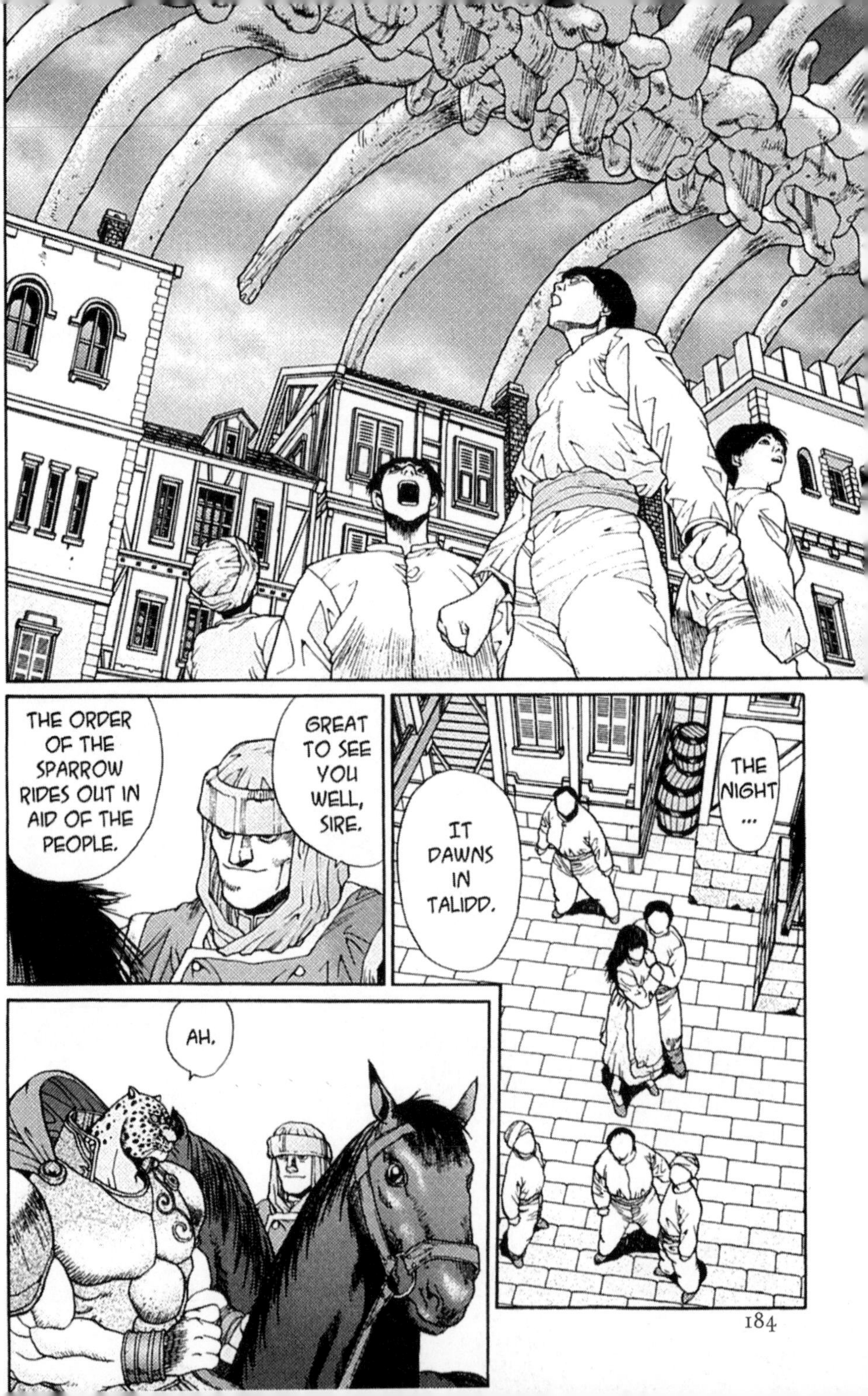
THE NIGHT...
IT DAWNS IN TALIDD.
GREAT TO SEE YOU WELL, SIRE.
THE ORDER OF THE SPARROW RIDES OUT IN AID OF THE PEOPLE.
AH.

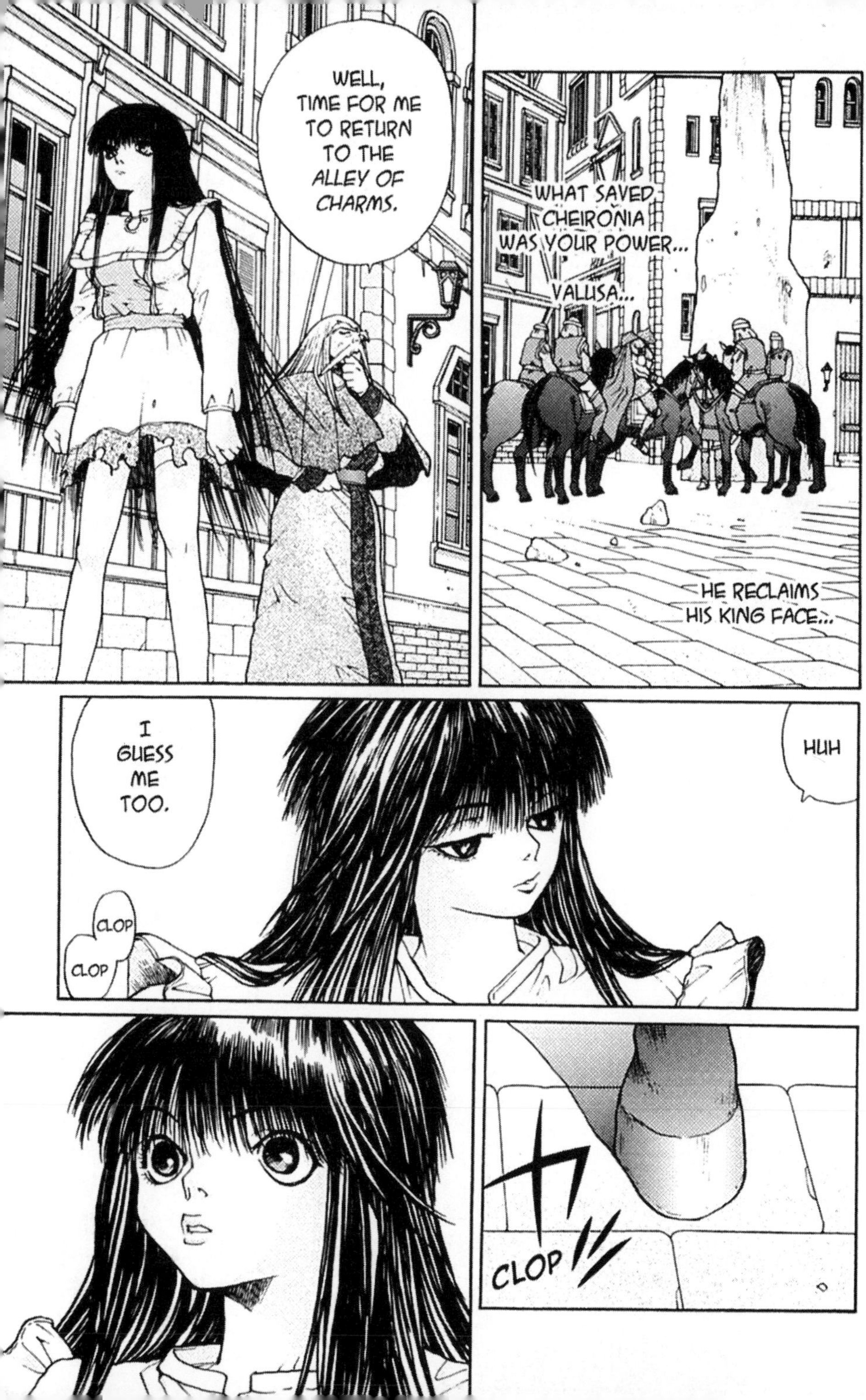
WHAT SAVED CHEIRONIA WAS YOUR POWER...
VALUSA...
HE RECLAIMS HIS KING FACE...
WELL, TIME FOR ME TO RETURN TO THE ALLEY OF CHARMS.
HUH
I GUESS ME TOO.
CLOP
CLOP
CLOP

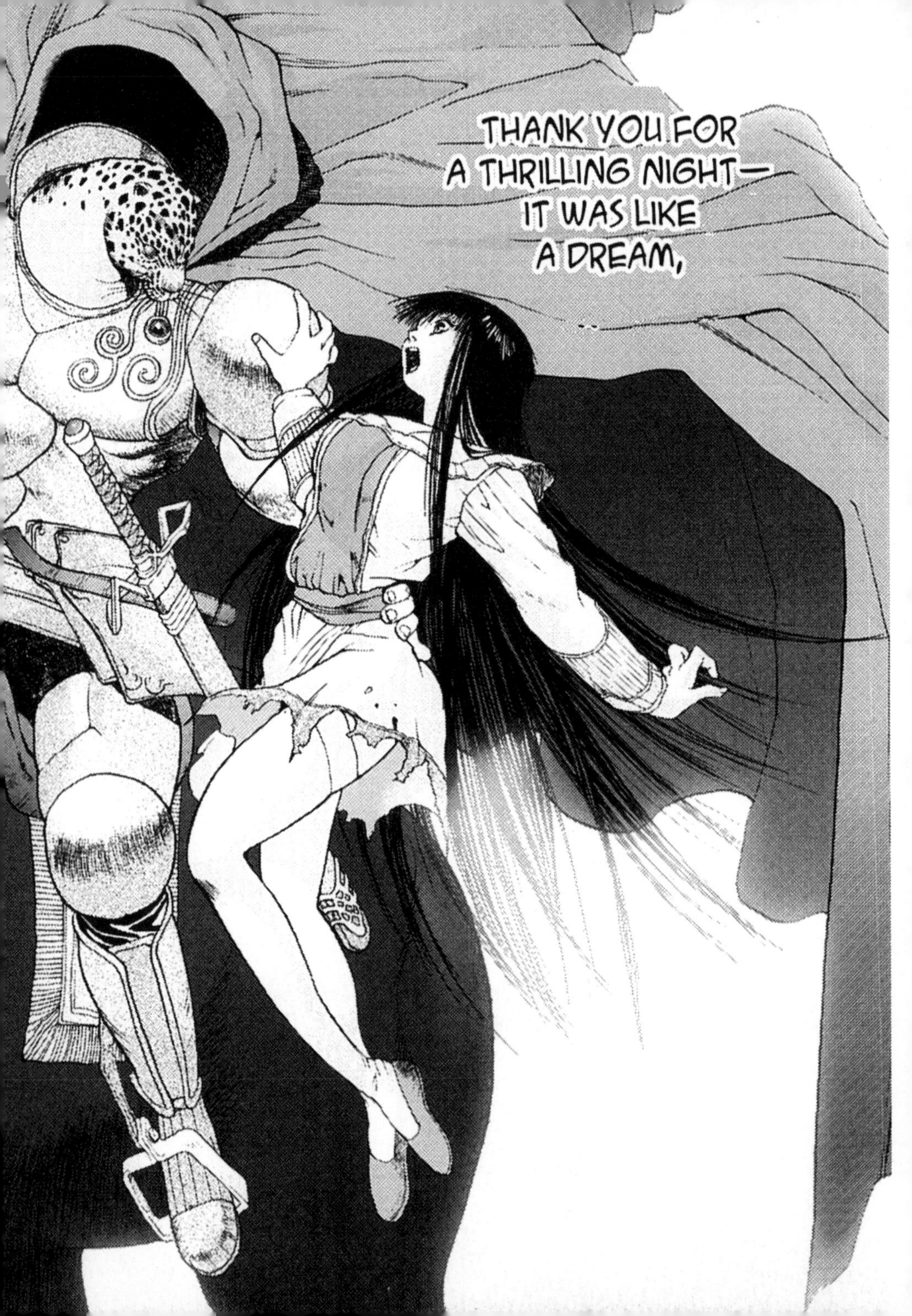
THANK YOU FOR A THRILLING NIGHT— IT WAS LIKE A DREAM,

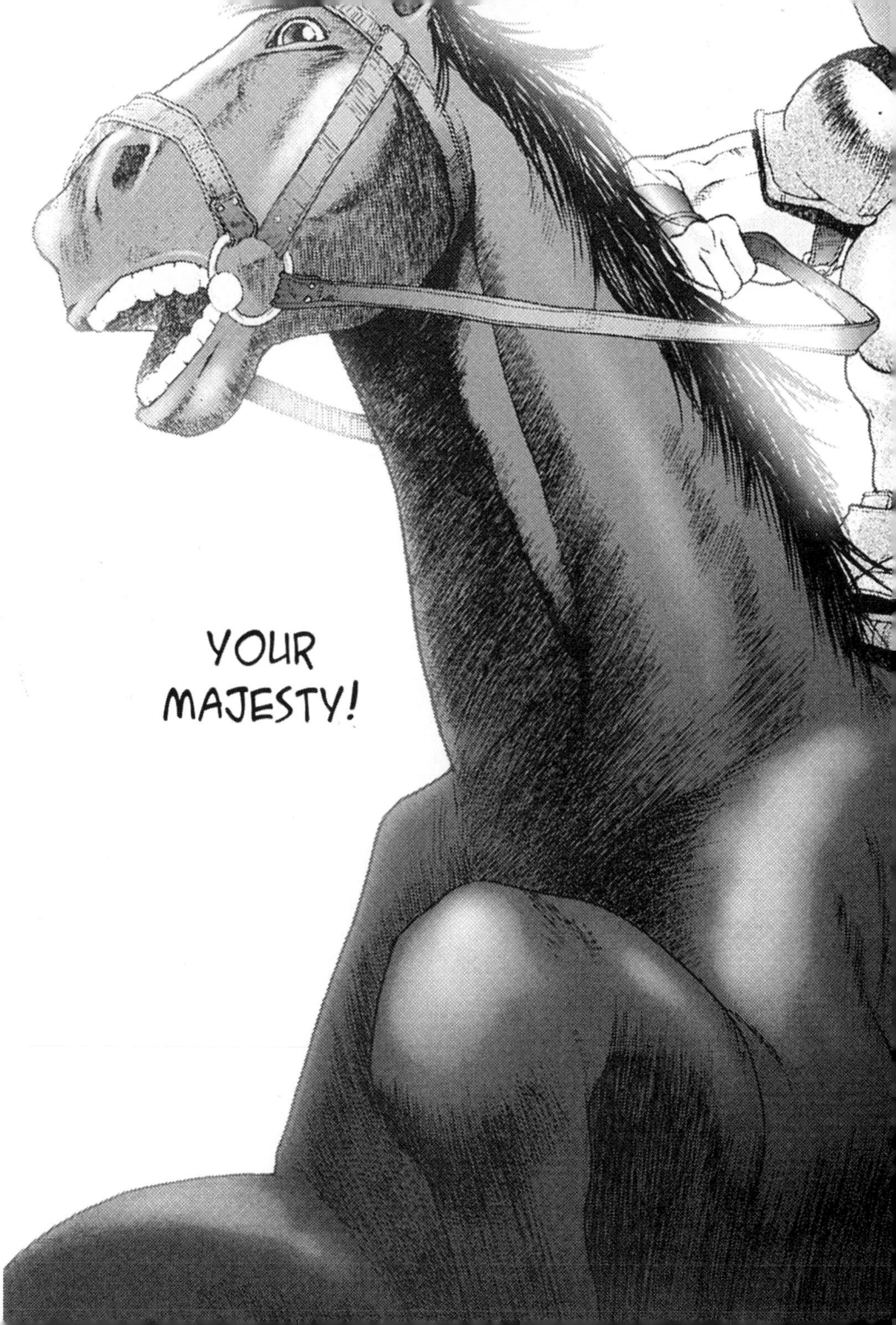
YOUR MAJESTY!

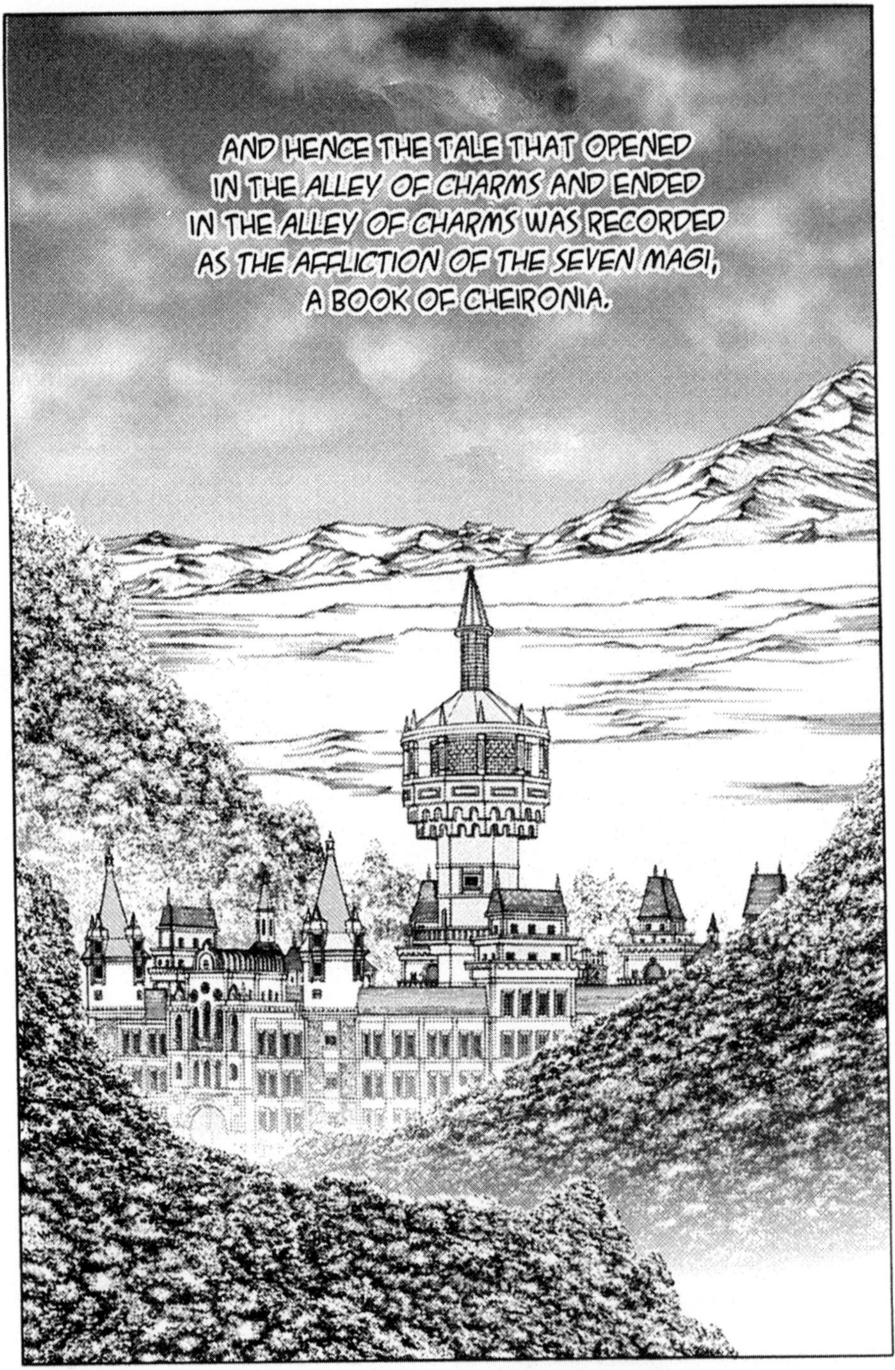
AND HENCE THE TALE THAT OPENED IN THE ALLEY OF CHARMS AND ENDED IN THE ALLEY OF CHARMS WAS RECORDED AS THE AFFLICTION OF THE SEVEN MAGI, A BOOK OF CHEIRONIA.

The End

About the Authors

Comics artist **Kazuaki Yanagisawa** is renowned for his fine pen-touch and excellence at adapting sophisticated source material. Other works by Yanagisawa include *Paparazzi* (story by *Lone Wolf and Cub*'s Kazuo Koike), a *Megami Tensei* comic based on the hit videogame cycle, and *The Summer of the Ocelot*, adapted from the novel by former *Golgo 13* storywriter Yoichi Funado.

The Guin Saga is the lifework of multi-talented **Kaoru Kurimoto**, who has written musicals based on her creation in addition to the bestselling novels. *The Seven Magi* first appeared in novel form in 1979 to great acclaim. The five-book opening episode of the saga proper is also being published by Vertical.

WRONG WAY!

Japanese books, including manga like this one,
are meant to be read from right to left.

So the front cover is actually the back cover, and vice-versa.

To read this book, please flip it over and start in the top right-hand corner.
Read the panels, and the bubbles in the panels, from right to left,
then drop down to the next row and repeat.

It may make you dizzy at first,
but forcing your brain to do things backwards makes you smarter in the long run.
We swear.